# NEW CHRIST:
# DIVINE FILIATION

CHARLES ANANG

Cover art: *The Baptism of Jesus*

Bartolomé Esteban Murillo (1618-1682)

Gemaeldegalerie, Staatliche Museen, Berlin

@ Art Resource, New York

Cover design by Deepthi Krovi

To the Blessed Trinity,
Mary Immaculate, St. Joseph, and
St. Paul & St. Charles Borromeo (two patrons)

*Nihil Obstat*        Rev. Fausto Bailo

                              *Censor Deputatus*

                              16 October 2019


*Imprimatur*        Thomas Cardinal Collins

                              Archbishop of Toronto

                              16 October 2019

# CONTENTS

The Church, as we know, continually needs to be reformed (*Ecclesia semper reformanda est*). The Second Vatican Council calls us to "read the signs of the times," and our times clearly manifest tremendous need for renewal, to address issues such as common-law unions without marriage, marriage breakdowns and broken families, the leaving behind of the practice of the faith, the loss of the sense of the sacred and of sin, etc. With an inspired insight, Pope John Paul II called for a "New Evangelization" in the Church at the beginning of this third millennium.

For renewal in the Church, the greatest need is to rediscover the ineffable identity of each baptized— essentially to experience the tender love of God the Father for each one. Jesus' identity is not one of His several roles, such as Creator, Redeemer, Son of Man, but as Son of the Father, which the Father revealed twice from heaven, "You are my Son, the Beloved." It is this paternal love that ravishes Jesus' heart, and spurs Him to a total devotion and obedience to, and love of, the Father. All His actions flow from this filial love for the Father. By His sacrifice at Calvary, He has won for us a share in His sonship. At Baptism, we are not just legally adopted, but we have been born spiritually from the womb of God, and are truly "sons in the Son." Everything we have received flows from our Father's love for His new children: a home (universe was created for his children), a personal guardian angel at birth, made children of God at Baptism after birth, fed with His Son's Body and healed from the wounds of sin at the age of reason (First Communion and Confession), strengthened by the Holy Spirit to give witness (Confirmation), given Christ within the sacrament of Marriage, and given Christ when sick or dying (Sacrament of the Sick). All the sacraments are given through Mother Church, but it is Mary (the Mother in the order of grace) and the angels and saints (as older brothers and sisters) who assist us to make them fruitful.

Thus the deepest need within the Church today is to understand and grow in this baptismal identity. Many Christians do not realize that they have been ontologically divinized to become sons and daughters of the Father in their second birth at Baptism. Even more, they do not realize that holiness is simply incorporation to Christ, begun objectively in Baptism, which requires a continual subjective growth in configuration. In sum, the baptized's trajectory is directed to becoming a "new Christ" (or, as Augustine teaches, the Church is to become the "Whole Christ"). In heaven, we will be in awe of the majesty of this union in Christ, becoming mystically one being in Christ, a fulfillment of the marriage union in which "two become one flesh." But all this finds its heart in our filiation, for each baptized to personally hear the words, "You are my Son, the Beloved." Union with Christ is for the sake of filiation (sonship or daughtership) of the Father.

In writing this manuscript, the author's initial sense was that this book should be addressed to everyone (laity, religious, and priests), especially since many chapter themes were originally given as talks or conferences to laity and religious sisters. Then a wise mentor counselled that each book should have a specific readership, and an initial Ignatian discernment indicated that the book's primary audience was priests, given their important role within the Church. Then a further Ignatian discernment led to a key insight: that the first half of this book actually addresses every baptized as a child of God, which itself can serve as a foundation for the second half, which applies most specifically and intensively to seminarians and priests. Thus, there are two volumes to this work. *New Christ: Divine Filiation* is the foundation for the second volume, *New Christ: Priestly Configuration*. The first volume addresses how one can grow as children of God through Baptism to become progressively more and more like Christ, to become a new Christ. It serves as a foundation for priestly configuration to Christ the High Priest.

Most books do not address divine filiation or the need to progressively grow in this filiation to become new Christs. Rediscovering this Christ-identity is a restoration of the Church's tradition of mystical life. Thus this book on forming new sons and daughters of the Father, to form new Christs, diverges from most books of its kind, addressing the themes not commonly covered in books on baptismal or priestly holiness: The Fatherhood of God, the Substitution of Christ, the Holy Spirit's Indwelling that leads to spiritual marriage with Christ, the two levels of human and spiritual life, the three loves, and four key depositions of Christ: human virtues, peace of heart and sacrament of the present moment, joy, and the spirituality of communion.

*Sources*

Three notes should be made regarding the sources to which this book has recourse. First, this book in certain sections has relied on a few sources (e.g., Jacques Philippe, Raniero Cantalamessa, Brian Kolodiejchuk, Pope John Paul II, St. Faustina, Jean-Pierre de Caussade, St. Francis de Sales, etc.) and *I wish to emphasize strongly that, where indicated, these are their insights and not mine, to give them their due credit.* Second, as Hans Urs von Balthasar teaches, it is important to address the contemporary divorce between theology and spirituality-mysticism. Thus, while this book does include some theological scholarship, it seeks to interpret it through the lens of our living mystical tradition, especially the saints, whose lives Pope Benedict XVI calls "theology in action." Third, while this book seeks to discern the Holy Spirit in the voice of contemporary authors or sources (e.g., Pope Benedict XVI, Hans Urs von Balthasar, Vatican II documents and the International Theological Commission), it would be gravely remiss to neglect the perennial legacy of Augustine, Aquinas, Teresa of Jesus, Newman, or Jordan Aumann, simply because they are of earlier eras.

*Acknowledgments*

I am indebted above all to my spiritual directors, as well as to friends, especially Maria and Therese De Manche, Joan Tardif, Dr. Patricia Murphy, and Yvonne Kam, all of whom have followed this process with their loving prayers and support. Within this group, Linda Beairsto has opened my eyes to a vast new readership audience I had not considered and was instrumental in self-publishing, above all introducing me to Karla Congson, who undertook to introduce me to key people and supervise the whole publishing process. I would like to draw attention in particular to four persons or groups. First, Fr. Timothy Gallagher who provided the Foreword for the original manuscript before it was divided and gave his invaluable direction to do this along with suggestions for key changes to the manuscript. Second, I am also indebted to the archdiocese of Toronto for its imprimatur (Thomas Cardinal Collins and Fr. Ivan Camilleri) and its theological censor, Fr. Fausto Bailo, for his kind work. Third, I also owe a debt of gratitude to a number of authors who have kindly reviewed sections summarizing aspects of their works or thought (Marc Cardinal Ouellet, Fr. Timothy Gallagher, Fr. Raniero Cantalamessa) and authorities on St. John of the Cross and the Eucharist. Finally, I wish to thank Katheryn Trainor for the immense labour of reviewing the manuscript twice, along with her many excellent suggestions and her competent editing.

The impulse to write this book came first from my spiritual director, but subsequently also from my seminary rector. I pray that this be simply the work of the Holy Spirit, attempted "because of the confidence I have in the Lord, confidence that he will help me to say *something*, on account of the great need of many people..."[1] I am simply sharing what has been passed on to me from spiritual directors and learned from retreat conferences, books read, and experience gained from guiding others, and from many mistakes made.

---

[1] St. John of the Cross, Prologue to *The Ascent of Mount Carmel* 3, quoted in Iain Matthew, *The Impact of God: Soundings from St. John of the Cross*, London: Hodder and Staughton, 1995.

This book is directed towards the spiritual birth, "mystical incarnation," and formation of the child of God through Baptism as a "new Christ," who is called to live anew the model of Christ. We find three main aspects of the formation of the new child of God, the new Christ: Trinitarian origin and background, incarnational form, and the formation of the new Christ by the Holy Spirit. The three main parts are: (I) "**Trinity: Filiation in Christ**" ("You are my Son, the Beloved"), involving relations with the Trinitarian Persons; (II) "**Incarnation: Model of Christ**" ("And the Word became flesh"), with two levels of Christ and three loves; (III) "**New Christ: Formed by the Holy Spirit**" ("He has done all things well"), with four dispositions of Christ.

Part I. **Trinity: Filiation in Christ ("You are my Son, the Beloved")**. The Trinitarian background focuses directly on the work of the economic Trinity creating new "Christs," the ultimate goal being their incorporation into inner-Trinitarian relations between Father, Son, and Holy Spirit. In Chapter 1, we begin with the origin of all, the heavenly Father, and imitating Pope John Paul II's *Dives in Misericordia*, look specifically at His attributes of love and mercy, as symbolized in the Divine Mercy image, a mercy that is expressed in the gift of sharing in Christ's sonship (Chapter 1: Father: Father of Mercy Generates New Christs). Then, in the second chapter, we proceed to the goal of human life: to undergo a transformation into, and friendship with, Christ (Chapter 2: Son: Substitution of Christ). All of this is accomplished through the Holy Spirit, described in two chapters: the overshadowing and indwelling of the Holy Spirit, who accomplishes the spiritual marriage with, and substitution of, Christ mentioned earlier (Chapter 3: Holy Spirit: Divine Indwelling & Spiritual Marriage); and looking at the work of the Holy Spirit in the life of Christ as a paradigm for ourselves (Chapter 4: New Christ: Incarnated by the Holy Spirit).

Part II. **Incarnation: Model of Christ ("And the Word became flesh")**. Part II is comprised of the two levels of "new Christ" that reflect the Incarnate Christ, human and divine, and the three loves that help to incarnate Christ in us. The two levels finds an analogy to a building: we first establish a strong foundation (Chapter 5: Level 1: Christ's Human Life) that supports the main element of the structure, the building itself (Chapter 6: Level 2: Christ's Divine Life). In this analogy, the foundation represents strengthening our human virtues and sanctifying the duties of one's state of life (as Jesus, for example, fulfilled His ministry in obedience to the Father) and the building can represent the more important aspect of love of, and obedience to, the Father through being led by the Holy Spirit. Without first fulfilling His mission (foundation), Jesus would not be pleasing to the Father; but the heart of Christ's life is His Sonship that is lived primarily in the moment-to-moment obedience to the Father through be led by the inspirations of the Holy Spirit (building).

What truly makes the entire structure (foundation and building, human and divine) incarnate for the baptized as a new Christ are three loves. To accomplish this generation of new Christs, there are two "mothers." There is the corporate mother, the Church, which is also the extension of the presence of Christ in space and time, and the individual mother, Mary, who is the "Mother of the Church" and of each individual person, and given a mandate by Christ at the cross to "mother" each of His children (Chapter 7: Loves 1 & 2: Church & Mary). As Vatican II has affirmed, the "source and summit" of Christ's presence and that which transforms us into other Christs is the Eucharist (Chapter 8: Love 3: Holy Eucharist).

Part III. **New Christ: Formed by the Holy Spirit ("He has done all things well")**. These four "dispositions"(human virtues, peace of heart and the sacrament of the present moment, joy, and the spirituality of communion) were chosen from trying to discern what constituted fundamental dispositions of Christ, formed by the Holy Spirit. "Human virtues" represent the foundation, our human virtues (Chapter 9: Human Virtues), for "grace builds on nature." In order to live the upper level (building) of being led by the Holy Spirit, the absolute prerequisite is peace of heart and living the present moment (Chapter 10: Peace of Heart & Sacrament of Present Moment). If we live these two dispositions just mentioned, then joy should follow, especially when we seek to conform to the will of God through the Holy Spirit (Chapter 11: Joy). And the Holy Spirit leads us to the crown of love, the "Spirituality of Communion" called for by Pope John Paul II (Chapter 12: Spirituality of Communion).

As mentioned, this first volume, *New Christ: Divine Filiation,* serves a foundation for the next volume, *New Christ: Priestly Configuration,* which describes a deeper configuration to Christ the High Priest and Shepherd (for the priest as an *Alter Christus*). Nevertheless, we might add here that most chapters in this book apply to all baptized and religious. For example, Part I deals with tools to grow to become the new Christ (e.g., order and living the Eucharist; a more comprehensive prayer program; spiritual direction and Confession; the Ignatian discernment of spirits; the Carmelite interior journey into God); and Part III describes our horizon of eternity (restoring our horizon of eternity; a treatment of the Last Things; and an elaboration of the work of the good angels and the attacks of the fallen angels). These themes relate to all the children of God, the new Christs. Two chapters in Part II are more specifically directed to priests: seminary years, priestly years.

# PART I: TRINITY

## *FILIATION IN CHRIST*

"You Are My Son, The Beloved"

# CHAPTER 1

## *FATHER OF MERCY GENERATES NEW CHRISTS*

> Jesus Christ is the face of the Father's mercy. These words might well sum up the mystery of the Christian faith. Mercy has become living and visible in Jesus of Nazareth, reaching its culmination in him…. he sent his only Son into the world, born of the Virgin Mary, to reveal his love for us in a definitive way. Whoever sees Jesus sees the Father (cf. Jn 14:9). Jesus of Nazareth, by his words, his actions, and his entire person reveals the mercy of God.
>
> We need constantly to contemplate the mystery of mercy. It is a wellspring of joy, serenity, and peace. Our salvation depends on it. Mercy: the word reveals the very mystery of the Most Holy Trinity. Mercy: the ultimate and supreme act by which God comes to meet us. Mercy: the fundamental law that dwells in the heart of every person who looks sincerely into the eyes of his brothers and sisters on the path of life. Mercy: the bridge that connects God and man, opening our hearts to the hope of being loved forever despite our sinfulness. (*Misericordiae Vultus*)[1]

God the Father is often identified as the Father of Mercy, such as in the revised formula of Absolution for the Sacrament of Reconciliation ("God, the Father of Mercies…), in Pope John Paul II's encyclical on the Father, *Dives in misericordia* ("Rich in mercy"), and in Pope Francis' quote above.

*Preface: God is Love*

The primordial and vital need for awareness of God's love is illustrated through an account given by a retreat master. He related the story of a Missionary Sister of Charity addressing young delinquents in a prison that went something like this. She asked the question, "How many of you believe that God loves you?" Of the fifteen or so young men present, not a single one put up his hand. She then went on to say, "The devil is a liar; and

---

[1] Pope Francis, *Misericordiae Vultus* (Bull of Indiction of Extraordinary Year of Mercy), accessed May 27, 2019,
http://w2.vatican.va/content/francesco/en/apost_letters/documents/papa-francesco_bolla_20150411_misericordiae-vultus.html.

his greatest lie is to try to convince you that God does not love you." It is, perhaps, not surprising that not one of these young men believed that God loved him, given the abandonment, abuse, and difficulties they must have faced in their lives. This example points to the truth that without the experience of being loved, especially of being loved by God, human life can become difficult, even unbearable. We need to experience that God in His essence is love.

> "*God is Love*"! And if we wish to depict Jesus Christ, God and Man, in a single word;… we can say: Jesus Christ is His Heart, is His Sacred Heart….
>
> *God is explained completely and entirely by this word: Charity*, for love explains everything although itself inexplicable. Jesus is completely explained by this name: The Sacred Heart! His sublime devotedness, His goodness, His mercy, all His divine virtues, His sacrifice, His death; His love explains all these. The Sacred Heart is divine Charity incarnate, Infinite Love humanized.[2] (Mother de la Touche, emphasis added)

The need to experience God's love finds its roots in a profound truth: man is created for love. This truth is derived from Scripture's affirmation in the Book of *Genesis* that man is made in the image and likeness of God. But God in His essence is love, and so man is made in the image and likeness of Divine Love. It is important to understand that, while God has many attributes like justice, truth, and beauty, His very essence is love. This truth has profound implications for man's nature, life, and destiny. Man, made in the image of "Love," is created out of love and for love. David Perrin identifies this truth in the teaching of John of the Cross. John, in describing the stages of the journey to God, who dwells in the center of one's being, points to love, of loving and being loved, as the heart of the human journey:

> Therefore the key to John's [of the Cross] anthropology is not primarily scholastic metaphysics, but rather that dynamic exchange of loving and being loved. As John says, "It is noteworthy, then, that love is the soul's inclination, strength, and power in making its way to God, for love unites it with God" (F 2, 13: Kav 645).

---

[2] Louise Margaret Claret de la Touche, *The Sacred Heart and the Priesthood*, 183-184.

John knows that "love is never idle, but in continual motion, it is always emitting flames everywhere like a blazing fire" (F 1, 8: Kav 643). John uses the elements of scholastic theology to amplify his intuitions and insights concerning the transformation of love in the human person. Each element which John accepts serves to trace the spiritual journey according to the needs and mode of the soul. The soul desires to rest in a deep love with God and it is this desire which moves the soul to search for more in life.[3]

John of the Cross sees anthropology as the "dynamic exchange of loving and being loved." Man is made for this relationship, and this love is that which drives man in his journey of life: "The soul desires to rest in a deep love with God and it is this desire which moves the soul to search for more in life."

Scripture attests to the centrality of God's love and mercy. Even in the economy of the Old Testament, an economy of justice, we find striking anticipations of God's mercy that will culminate in the sending of His Son. In general, when Scripture speaks of God, the Church attributes this reference to the Father. We could look to Exodus 34:6 as Yahweh's definition of Himself, and by extension, referring to the Father: "Yahweh, the Lord, a God compassionate and gracious, long-suffering, ever constant and true...." ("*Yahweh, Adonis, El Arum Wehannun, Erek Afayim, Werab-Hesed Weemeth...*" [Hebrew original Romanized]). These terms that define God have profound denotations. Yahweh is "mercy that is bent over misery" (*Hen*); has "generous fidelity to His own" (*Hesed*); and "unshakable solidity in His engagements" (*Emeth*); with "attachment of heart and of His own being to those whom He loves" (*Rahamim*); and "inexhaustible justice" (*Sedeq*), "capable of assuring all His creatures the plenitude of their rights, and of fulfilling all their aspirations."[4] Yahweh's definition of Himself is like that of a doting Father, so close to His people.

In the New Testament, we can illustrate its heart by selecting just one from among the many texts that emphasize God's mercy:

---

[3] David B. Perrin, *For Love of the World: The* Old *and* New Self *of John of the Cross* (San Francisco: Catholic Scholars Press, 1997), 22.

[4] Attila Miklósházy, "Old Testament Understanding of Grace" (lecture, *Creation, Anthropology, Sin,* Toronto School of Theology at the University of Toronto, 1981).

For the gifts and the call of God are irrevocable. Just as you were once disobedient to God but now have received mercy because of their disobedience, so they have now been disobedient in order that by the mercy shown to you they also may receive mercy. For God has consigned all men to disobedience, that he may have mercy upon all. (Rom 11: 29-32)

Two truths are noteworthy here. First, God never takes back His gifts: "For the gifts and the call of God are irrevocable." Second, God somehow makes use of our disobedience to give us His mercy: "For God has consigned all men to disobedience, that he may have mercy upon all." All of this implies that God's love is unconditional: He loves us before we fall, while we fall, and after we fall, and always with the same unconditional love.

Now, the Father is invisible and remains invisible to our unaided vision. But the Father can be known *ad extra* by special revelation, and above all, by the sending of His Son and the Holy Spirit— for His essence is known by His action, for God as "pure act" is one in essence and action. Within Tradition, there is an attribution of "mercy" to the Father, which, as mentioned, we find in the Absolution formula of Confession, "God, the Father of mercies…."

To view the Father's mercy and plan, it is helpful to view three elements: first, special revelations of the Father's mercy in the Divine Mercy charism of Faustina; second, the contemplation of the Passion of Christ through a theology of the Sacred Heart by Pope Benedict XVI; third, the gift of the Holy Spirit to cause divine filiation. While we associate these actions with the Son or the Holy Spirit, they ultimately reflect the Father's mercy, as it was He who sent them— the Son and the Spirit are His "hands" (Irenaeus). Thus, these divine actions give us, as it were, a peek, a way of indirectly penetrating the heart of the Father Himself. For example, Jesus Himself confirms that the Father's being and love are visible in the Son and the mysteries of the Son:

Philip said to him, "Lord, show us the Father, and we shall be satisfied." Jesus said to him, "Have I been with you so long, and yet you do not know me, Philip? He who has seen me has seen the Father; how can you say, "Show us the Father"? Do you not believe that I am in the Father and the Father in me? The words that I say to you I do not speak on my own

4

authority; but the Father who dwells in me does his works. Believe me that I am in the Father and the Father in me; or else believe me for the sake of the works themselves." (Jn 14: 8-11)

While the Father is invisible, His love is manifested in the implementation of His plan: in the universe of created reality, in the gift of the Holy Spirit, but especially in the gift of His "other self," His Son, who is a reflection of the Father: "He is the image of the invisible God, the first-born of all creation" (Col 1:15).

Joseph Ratzinger, in *The God of Jesus Christ: Meditations on the Triune God*, has identified the greatest danger facing mankind as the loss of fatherhood, and thereby filiation, by reducing fatherhood to a "biological phenomenon":

> God himself "willed to manifest and describe himself as Father." Human fatherhood gives us an anticipation of what He is. But when this fatherhood does not exist, when it is experienced only as a biological phenomenon, without its human and spiritual dimension, all statements about God the Father are empty. The crisis of fatherhood we are living today is an element, perhaps the most important, threatening man in his humanity. The dissolution of fatherhood and motherhood is linked to the dissolution of our being sons and daughters.[5]

He goes further. Man cannot look to human paradigms, as history teaches us in the failed example of the Greeks looking to Zeus, who was sometimes nice when he was in a good mood, but was "ultimately an egoist, a tyrant, unpredictable, unfathomable, and dangerous."[6] Ratzinger makes two critical points for our discussion: that only Jesus reveals the Father (as said above); and that, unlike Zeus, we look to a Father of love and mercy. We shall discuss the fallout of a loss of fatherhood later in this chapter.

---

[5] Joseph Ratzinger, *The God of Jesus Christ: Meditations on the Triune God*, on "Cardinal Ratzinger- Fatherhood and Apocalypse," studiobrien, accessed on May 30, 2015, http://www.studiobrien.com/cardinal-ratzinger-fatherhood-and-apocalypse/.
[6] Joseph Ratzinger, *The God of Jesus Christ: Meditations on the Triune God*, trans. Brian McNeil (San Francisco: Ignatius Press, 2008), 32.

## 1. Divine Mercy (St. Faustina's Revelations)

The Father's mercy finds a concrete expression in the Divine Mercy messages to the Polish religious Sister, St. Faustina Kowalska. It appears that God at times chooses to help us more deeply penetrate the love of His Heart by highlighting certain aspects, already revealed in public revelation, through private revelation in a concrete devotion, e.g., Sacred Heart devotion. The revelation of the heart of God in the "Sacred Heart" messages to St. Margaret Mary Alacoque may find a deepening in the revelation to St. Faustina of "Divine Mercy," moving beyond love to mercy. In selecting the "Divine Mercy" devotion to reveal the Father's mercy, we are simply following the encouragement of Pope John Paul II in his promotion of this devotion. In his *Dives in misericordia*, he explains mercy's origins in Scripture and Tradition, and as developed in theology, but the original stimulus for his attention to Divine Mercy goes back to his encounter with St. Faustina's revelations in Poland. Here the Father's mercy is highlighted in a vast panorama or vista where God is revealed, not just as love, but as gratuitous and undeserved mercy. Many elements are highlighted. The goal is to lead us to see the Father's mercy and thus to trust in His love for us.

St. Faustina came to know that at the heart of the Lord was not justice but mercy. She understood God's love theologically, through the great mysteries of the Incarnation and Redemption, especially in the fact that Christ did not need to go to the cross to save us.[7]

> God, You could have saved thousands of worlds with one word; a single sigh from Jesus would have satisfied Your justice. But You Yourself, Jesus, purely out of love for us, underwent such a terrible Passion. Your Father's justice would have been propitiated with a single sigh from You, and all Your self-abasement is solely the work of Your mercy and Your inconceivable love. On leaving the earth, O Lord, You wanted to stay with us, and so You left us Yourself in the Sacrament of the Altar, and You opened wide Your mercy to us. There is no misery that could

---

[7] "Sister Faustina came to know the immense love and abyss of Divine Mercy in the mystery of the Incarnation and Redemption: *Mercy has moved You to deign to descend among us and lift us up from our misery (Diary* 1745). She saw the infinite mercy of God in the fact that Jesus underwent His Passion on the cross, a passion that was not required, in order to satisfy Divine Justice; His love, however, poured forth with superabundance..." (*In Saint Faustina's School of Trust* (Cracow: The Congregation of the Sisters of Our Lady of Mercy, 2002), 21).

exhaust You; You have called us all to this fountain of love, to this spring
of God's compassion. Here is the tabernacle of Your mercy, here is the
remedy for all our ills. To You, O living spring of mercy, all souls are
drawn; some like deer, thirsting for Your love, others to wash the wound
of their sins, and still others, exhausted by life, to draw strength. At the
moment of Your death on the Cross, You bestowed upon us eternal life;
allowing Your most holy side to be opened, You opened an inexhaustible
spring of mercy for us, giving us Your dearest possession, the Blood and
Water from Your Heart. Such is the omnipotence of Your mercy. From it
all grace flows to us.[8] (*Diary* 1747)

From His incarnation, to His sacrifice on the cross, to the further self-
abasement of giving Himself in the Mass and remaining with us in the
Blessed Sacrament, Love gives Himself in action. We note in passing that,
as with the Sacred Heart visions, we also find here in the teachings in the
*Diary* of St. Faustina Christ's death linked intimately with the Eucharist.

St. Faustina saw God in His very essence as love and mercy and "this
mystery filled her mind and heart, formed her outlook on life, both
temporal and eternal, and helped her to penetrate and fill everything with
the spirit of faith." To understand these profound truths of God as mercy,
she strove to attain the spirit of faith, "to look at everything in life through
the prism of divine action"[9]:

> I fervently beg the Lord, to strengthen my faith, so that in my drab,
> everyday life I will not be guided by human dispositions, but by those of
> the spirit. Oh, how everything drags man towards the earth! But lively
> faith maintains the soul in the higher regions and assigns self-love its
> proper place; that is to say, the lowest one. (*Diary* 210)

Rising above natural thinking and human calculations, she asked Jesus to
strengthen her faith so its spirit would guide her, a spirit of faith that
"values everything on a higher level, gives to each event a hidden salvific
sense, and keeps the soul in the higher spheres, on the level of the
supernatural life."[10]

---

[8] St. Maria Faustina Kowalska, *Diary: Divine Mercy in My Soul* (Stockbridge, MA: Marians of
the Immaculate Conception, 2003), n. 1747, 619-620.
[9] *In Saint Faustina's School of Trust*, 22-23.
[10] Ibid., 23.

To see the essence of God as an unfathomable and ineffable mercy allowed St. Faustina to make the ultimate interior abandonment: to trust deeply in God and to abandon herself totally to Him and His providence. For St. Faustina, that all-important trust that the Christian and the priest require for their apostolate and mission depends on faith in God's love and mercy. We see three steps in her development to abandonment: first, with a supernatural outlook of a spirit of faith, St. Faustina perceived in each moment the unique treasures of divine grace and here on earth the beginning of eternal life in the human soul; second, she wanted to evaluate all events in life, especially difficult moments, and neighbours, in the spirit of faith, to see them as God sees them; third, the ensuing surrender is described by a commentator in the following texts:

> By Faith we recognize that God is Love and Mercy; deep knowledge of this gives birth to trust; and trust is abandonment or complete surrender to God as Sister Faustina expressed in these simple words: *Let Him do with me as He wishes* (*Diary* 589). Between faith and trust there exists a proportional relationship: the greater the faith, the greater the trust.

> Knowledge of the mystery of Divine Mercy is the principal motive of trust. *I know the full power of Your mercy, and I trust that You will give me everything* (*Diary* 898). Without this knowledge of God in His mercy, trust would be deprived of its foundation and would hang in emptiness…. The mercy of God is our singular motive of trust, for it is not our perfection that moves God to show us His goodness but His self-communicating will manifested in His constant self-giving to people and in His infinite readiness to forgive. This is why Sister Faustina did not hesitate to state that, even if she had the sins of the whole world, she would not stop trusting in Divine Mercy, which drowns all misery and nothingness (cf. *Diary* 1552)…[11]

We note here that there is a proportional relationship between faith and trust. Specifically, "Knowledge of the mystery of Divine Mercy is the principal motive of trust. I know the full power of Your mercy, and I trust that You will give me everything." The result of this knowledge of Divine Mercy is that, if she had all the sins in the world— sin is not an obstacle— she would not stop trusting. This led her to great abandonment, to accept everything as from the hand of God.

---

[11] Ibid., 26-27.

The spirit of faith gradually led St. Faustina to a total surrender of her whole self to God. This total gift of self and of her autonomy arose from the conviction of the merciful love of the Heavenly Father, in whose protective arms we may peacefully place ourselves…

… Accepting everything from Him, she drew closer to Him through everything…. The desire to accept everything from the fatherly hand of God led Sister Faustina to complete abandonment in every circumstance in life.[12]

Thus, the inscription at the bottom of the image of Divine Mercy, "Jesus, I trust you," is a synthesis of the spiritual life.

I accept everything that comes my way as given me by the loving will of God, who sincerely desires my happiness. And so I will accept with submission and gratitude everything that God sends me. (*Diary* 1549)

Love casts out all fear. Since I came to love God with my whole being and with all the strength of my heart, fear has left me…. I have come to know Him well. God is love, and His Spirit is peace…. I have placed my trust in God and fear nothing. I have given myself over to His holy will; let Him do with me as He wishes. (*Diary* 589)

There is no room for fear, for "I have come to know Him well. God is love…" Various revelations highlight the importance of knowledge of this truth. The entire mission of St. Faustina is to transmit this knowledge so that people would draw to Him with filial confidence: "Your task is to write down everything that I make known to you about My mercy, for the benefit of those who by reading these things… will have the courage to approach me" (*Diary* 1693). It was to teach us to trust in Jesus' love for us: "I desire trust from my Creatures" (*Diary* 1059). That which wounds Jesus the most is the lack of trust in His mercy. The Lord Jesus points out as well that all disbelief or mistrust of souls springs from failure to recognize God as the Father of Mercy:

"Oh, how much I am hurt by a soul's distrust! Such a soul professes that I am Holy and Just, but does not believe that I am Mercy and does not trust in My Goodness." (*Diary* 300)

---

[12] Ibid., 24-25.

My Heart is sorrowful, Jesus said, because even chosen souls do not understand the greatness of My mercy. Their relationship [with me] is, in certain ways, imbued with mistrust. Oh, how much that wounds My Heart! (*Diary* 379)

## 2. The Sacred Heart in the Theology of Pope Benedict XVI

*God's One Word of Love*

We have argued that man's entire progress in life rests on the knowledge and awareness of God's love for us. This knowledge is especially important for all Christians, but also priests and religious, who are called to be friends and collaborators of Christ, called to share Christ's many burdens and trials. Everything begins from this point of departure. Moving from the overall panorama of the "Father of Mercies" in the Divine Mercy charism entrusted to St. Faustina, we now contemplate the Father of Mercies from the deepest vantage point: the love of the Father revealed in His Son's "Sacred Heart." Pope Benedict XVI offers a unique approach: looking into the heart of Christ by "looking upon the one they have pierced," that is, by silent adoration and contemplation of the heart of Christ through the wound, that is, through His Passion. Here is revealed the deepest vision, not only of the Son, but of the Father who sent and sacrificed His Son.

In an encyclical on social doctrine, *Caritas in veritate*, Pope Benedict XVI himself also enunciates the centrality of our discussion, that God is love:

> For the Church, instructed by the Gospel, charity is everything because, as Saint John teaches (cf. 1 Jn 4:8, 16) and as I recalled in my first Encyclical Letter, "God is love" (*Deus Caritas est*): *everything has its origin in God's love, everything is shaped by it, everything is directed towards it.* Love is God's greatest gift to humanity, it is his promise and our hope.[13]

All life comes down to this: "Charity is love received and given":

> Charity is love received and given. It is "grace" (*cháris*). Its source is the wellspring of the Father's love for the Son, in the Holy Spirit. Love comes down to us from the Son. It is creative love, through which we have our being; it is redemptive love, through which we are recreated. Love is revealed and made present by Christ (cf. Jn 13:1) and "poured into our

---

[13] Pope Benedict XVI, *Caritas in veritate* n. 2.

hearts through the Holy Spirit" (Rom 5:5). As the objects of God's love, men and women become subjects of charity, they are called to make themselves instruments of grace, so as to pour forth God's charity and to weave networks of charity.[14]

Without this knowledge, we may attempt to carry our burdens primarily out of duty, and get discouraged and perhaps even fall. But with personal experience of God's love, we can confront any obstacle, accomplish any task. As Pope Benedict XVI teaches, men and women imbued with God's love can fulfill the task to "make themselves instruments of grace, so as to pour forth God's charity and to weave networks of charity."

The pope has a very clear insight into the experience God's love in the context of the Sacred Heart of Jesus. He explicitly enunciated the need for it in his address on an anniversary of the publication of the document on the Sacred Heart, *Haurietis aquas*, in 2006, affirming that the contemplation of the Sacred Heart is not a passing devotion but is rather at the heart of our Christian life: "The response to the commandment of love is made possible only by the experience that this love was first given us by God."

> It was only the experience that God first gave us his love that has enabled us to respond to his commandment of love (cf. *Deus Caritas Est*, n. 17). So it is that the cult of love, which becomes visible in the mystery of the Cross presented anew in every celebration of the Eucharist, lays the foundations of our capacity to love and to make a gift of ourselves… becoming instruments in Christ's hands: only in this way can we be credible proclaimers of his love. However, this opening of ourselves to God's will must be renewed in every moment: "Love is never "finished" and complete" (cf. *Deus Caritas Est*, n. 17).
>
> Thus, looking at the "side pierced by the spear" from which shines forth God's boundless desire for our salvation cannot be considered a transitory form of worship or devotion: the adoration of God's love, whose historical and devotional expression is found in the symbol of the "pierced heart", remains indispensable for a living relationship with God (cf. *Haurietis Aquas*, n. 62).[15]

---

[14] Ibid., n. 5.
[15] Pope Benedict XVI, "Pope Benedict XVI in a Letter to Fr. Peter-Hans Kolvenbach S.J., Superior General of the Society of Jesus (Jesuits), for the 50th anniversary of Pope Pius

One sentence reveals three key concepts, linking the Eucharistic presence of the cross to our experience of God's love, so that we can give ourselves in our Christian life: "… the cult of love, which becomes visible in the mystery of the Cross presented anew in every celebration of the Eucharist, lays the foundations of our capacity to love and to make a gift of ourselves." First, we glimpse the mystery of God's love by contemplating the mystery of God's love in this sacrifice of His Son on the cross. Second, this self-same sacrifice is re-presented in the Eucharistic sacrifice. Through this contemplation of Christ's sacrificial love, especially in the Eucharist, the priest is more and more able to "receive" God's love for him. Third, Pope Benedict XVI thus concludes its indispensability for the spiritual life: "The adoration of God's love, which found historical-devotional expression in the symbol of the pierced heart, remains irreplaceable for a living relationship with God."[16]

Pope Benedict XVI's keen insight has been the object of study by Mark Kirby. He believes that he has found elements of a theology of the Sacred Heart in the theology of Pope Benedict XVI, principally in two books, *Behold the Pierced One* and *The Spirit of the Liturgy*.[17] The central insight that he has adduced from Pope Benedict XVI's theology of the Sacred Heart is that God the Father has spoken one word but without words, and that one word is a revelation of His love for us that is carved out in the side of His Son, Jesus Christ. All are called to contemplate "the One whom they have pierced," to contemplate the Sacred Heart, the love of God for us. He concludes with the absolute indispensability and centrality of spending time in silence and solitude to contemplate this love:

> Theology is, first of all, God's word addressed to us. Apply this immediately to the Sacred Heart of Jesus. The pierced Heart of the Crucified is God speaking a word to us, a word carved out in the flesh of Jesus' side by the soldier's lance. It is the love of God laid bare for all to see: "God stepping out of his hiddenness."

---

XII's Encyclical 'Haurietis aquas' on devotion to the Sacred Heart of Jesus," *L'Osservatore Romano*, Weekly Edition in English, 14 June 2006, 4.

[16] Ibid.

[17] Mark Kirby, "Sacred Heart: God's Word addressed to us," *L'Osservatore Romano*, Weekly Edition in English, 25 May 2005, 10.

When we speak of a theology of the Sacred Heart, we mean this first of all: not our discourse about love, but the love of God revealed first to us, the poem of love that issues forth from the Heart of God. This is exactly what St. John, whom the Eastern tradition calls, "The Theologian", says in his First Letter: "In this is love, not that we loved God but that he loved us and sent his Son to be the expiation for our sins" (1 Jn 4:10).

The difficulty here is that, in order to receive this word inscribed in the flesh of the Word (cf. Jn 1:14), we have first to stop in front of it, to linger there and to look long at the wound made by love. "They shall look on him whom they have pierced" (Jn 19:37). To contemplate is to look, not with a passing glance, but with the gaze of one utterly conquered by love. Jeremiah says, "You have seduced me, O Lord, and I was seduced; you are stronger than I, and you have prevailed" (Jer 20:7).[18]

Our principal point is once again underlined here: all that God has said and done for us is synthesized in one word: love. And that love is incarnated and made visible in this sacrifice of His Son on Calvary. Everything begins with this word of love: "In this is love, not that we loved God but that he loved us and sent his Son to be the expiation for our sins" (1 Jn 4:10).

But the difficulty lies in hearing this word: "We have first to stop in front of it, to linger there and to look long at the wound made by love. 'They shall look on him whom they have pierced' (Jn 19:37)." To linger and contemplate the one we have pierced is to be "utterly conquered by love," to be "seduced" by His love: "You have seduced me, O Lord, and I was seduced; you are stronger than I, and you have prevailed (Jer 20:7)." Through Pope Benedict XVI's intuition, we have a deeper insight into the love of the Father manifested by the sacrifice of His Son.

Pope Benedict XVI concludes that we are called to be adorers of the Sacred Heart of Jesus. He emphasizes the vital and unbreakable link between adoration and apostleship: "It is in adoration that the apostle receives the word of the pierced Heart that, in turn, becomes his life's message."

The call to be an adorer and an apostle of the Sacred Heart is addressed to every Christian. The apostle is, in essence, the bearer of a word, one sent forth and entrusted with a message. The message that the apostle carries into the world is the one he has learned by looking long with the eyes of

---

[18] Ibid.

adoration at the pierced Heart of the Crucified. The word of Crucified Love is hard to pronounce — not with our lips but with our lives. Adoration is the school wherein one learns how to say the Sacred Heart. It is in adoration that the apostle receives the word of the pierced Heart that, in turn, becomes his life's message.

Adoration and apostleship together model a spirituality accessible to all Christians: the word received in adoration is communicated in the dynamism of one sent forth with something to say.[19]

The saints too have found their core in the contemplation of God's Love in Christ's Passion. Mother Teresa of Calcutta and Chiara Lubich have at the heart of their powerful spiritualities, the love of Jesus Crucified, in "I thirst" and "Jesus abandoned" respectively. Likewise, St. Thérèse of Lisieux is called by the title, "St. Therese of the Child Jesus and of the Holy Face," the one who offered her life as a victim to Christ's love. And St. Edith Stein is called "St. Teresa Benedicta a Cruce," "St. Teresa Blessed by the Cross," having the cross as her center in offering her martyrdom for her Jewish people and for Germany.

In a particular way, the priest of Christ, His "other self," as well as religious, must be imbued with the same mercy and love of the Sacred Heart of Jesus, or the heart of Divine Mercy. But they must learn to do so by first contemplating the love of the Father in the Son's sacrifice to see into the Sacred Heart.

### 3. Divine Filiation

*The Love of the Father*

To understand what it means to be a child of God, we must ask what is Christ's fundamental identity. Though Christ has many tasks (e.g., Creator, Redeemer, Son of Man, etc.), His fundamental identity is "Son of the Father." While Jesus did many things in His ministry, He did not identify Himself with His work, but with His identity, as loved infinitely by His Father, who twice from heaven said: "This is my beloved Son." From this identity and love proceeded everything from Jesus; every act and every word flowed from His Father. Where the Jews could not pronounce

---

[19] Ibid.

Yahweh's name and recited very formal prayers, Jesus introduced a whole new dynamic, calling God, "*Abba*." And everything about Jesus was the love of *Abba* for Him. When He taught us how to pray, the first two words are the most important, "Our Father" (Our *Abba*); when He was in great distress, "*Abba*, take this cup away from me"; when He abandoned Himself in His darkness on Calvary, "*Abba*, into your hands I commit my spirit."

*Search for the Father*

I would like to suggest that, since we are made in God's image and for Him, and more specifically in the image of Christ (Col 1, Eph 1), all human life is not merely a longing and search for the Transcendent or for God in general, but specifically for *God the Father*. Cardinal Robert Sarah mentions this briefly in *God or Nothing*: "The Father made us for himself... This is why, consciously or not, we are constantly in search of the Father" (p. 211). This need for fatherhood is especially critical in our times. Within the period of only one year at a regional diocesan seminary, three retreat directors all spoke about the need for fatherhood in our times (Abbot John Braganza of Mission, BC, Fr. Chris Hellstrom, and Fr. Peter Cameron). Fr. Cameron highlighted this deep need the most. He quotes the words of a World War II orphan, Kathleen Eaton, in *Lost in the Victory: Reflections of American War Orphans of World War II*:

> Sometimes before I fall asleep, or on his birthday, Father's Day, or a holiday, I ache for him. I want to hear his voice, smell his aftershave, watch him eat, write a letter, shave, comb his hair, and to hold me. Growing up, I could feel him close to me, like a guardian angel. I would talk to him in my head... I think about him every day, and still I feel he guards me.

He also notes the example of Albert Camus, one of modernity's foremost proponents of the theory of absurdism (that life is senseless). After his death in an automobile accident at 47, they found 147 manuscript pages that Camus had written— all of them about his search for his father (who was mortally wounded as a soldier in World War I when Camus was but a year old). Apparently, Camus' search for his father was a stronger force in him than the conscious awareness of the senselessness of everything around him (absurdism). (*Why Preach*, 147).

Peter Cameron also mentioned the power of spiritual fatherhood in the life of Augustine, who himself was drawn to the faith through Ambrose as a father and his kindness:

> That man of God, Ambrose, received me like a father, and as bishop, told me how glad he was that I had come. My heart warmed to him, not at first as a teacher of the truth, which I had quite despaired of finding in your Church, but simply as a man who showed me kindness... (*Confessions* 5.13.107).

The author himself, formed in a high school run by Irish Spiritans, was deeply influenced by the paternal attention of one priest, whose anniversary of death he faithfully remembers each year. The importance of the love of a father recalls the words of St. John Bosco to his boys: "You have many teachers but only one who loves you as much as Don Bosco"; "For you I study, for you I work, for you I live, for you I am ready even to give my life."

We find this fatherhood in other saintly figures. St. Josemaría Escrivá suggested an epitaph for himself on the tombstone, something about his sinfulness, but the governing councils in an act of inspiration chose an inscription that they felt synthesized what they felt from him— simply *"El Padre"* ("The Father"). This is because of the fatherly disposition he showed towards all his spiritual children. In one instance, with a spiritual son in a crisis, he said that he would show the young man that he had a father in Fr. Josemaría Escrivá. The members of Communion and Liberation have experienced a similar paternal affection and devotion from their founder, Msgr. Luigi Giussani. It was reported that Chiara Lubich once addressed ten thousand Buddhist leaders and remarkably they called her "mother"; they may have recognized something of the face of God in her. One might say that God the Father encompasses a "feminine" dimension as well.

In sum, we need above all God our Father, for Christ came to lead us to His Father. Thus, in human life, there are two great loves: spousal love and filial love. The prototype for both is found in the Trinity in the relationship between the Father and the Son, that is extended to us. First, the baptized have a *spousal love* with Christ, a union that is not well known outside of mystical doctrine. This spousal love with Christ is highlighted by Fergus Kerr in his work, *Twentieth-Century Catholic Theologians*, in which he notes the rise of nuptial theology in the Twentieth century, especially in the writings of figures like John Paul II and Henri de Lubac. And, in the second step, it is Christ who incorporates us and leads us to the *filial love* of the Father, which filiation is our greatest treasure. To this end, the world needs spiritual fathers.

## Fatherhood of Priests

At the spiritual level, the world needs priests, who are configured to Christ, who has essentially re-presented the Father to us, to become an icon of the Father for the parish family, which is what it means to be an "another Christ" (*alter Christus*). If every thought of Christ was turned towards the Father, and if He re-presents the Father to us ("He who sees me, sees the Father"), then Christ, though Son, re-presents the figure of "father" to us (for Christ generated us at the cross). The priest, who is configured to Christ as shepherd at Ordination, is by extension also a spiritual father. Jacques Philippe in a retreat to seminarians explained that this means that the priest is "an icon of the God the Father," participates in God's fatherhood, and that the parishioners should be able to experience the tender love of the Father in the priest. What this argues for is that the priest, as *alter Christus*, is fundamentally a father to his flock. While Christ is also the Good Shepherd, the more fundamental identity of Christ is re-presenting the Father, and the more fundamental identity of the priest is as spiritual father. Thus, the task of the priest is to be an icon of the Father's love, and to do that, the priest must first be deeply united to Christ. The people need above all to see God's "Fatherhood" in the priest.

## Divine Filiation

If man is created "out of love," here we see more clearly that he is also created "for love." While the heart of our faith is the Son's sacrifice, the Paschal mystery, the sacrifice had a goal, to obtain a great fruit. Christ died to obtain for us the greatest fruit of the Father's love, not just justification from sin, but divine filiation through the gift of the Holy Spirit. The one word that the Father has spoken that we contemplate in Christ's side, has given the fruit of the waters of Baptism, through which we have been born again and become children of God the Father. "For you did not receive the spirit of slavery to fall back into fear, but you have received the spirit of sonship. When we cry, 'Abba! Father!' it is the Spirit himself bearing witness with our spirit that we are children of God" (Rom 8:15-16). This is our greatest joy and consolation: sharing in the one Sonship of Christ, to become sons and daughters in the one Son. The Church teaches us that we have become "adopted children" of God the Father. But "adopted" here has a quite different sense from the human parallel of adopted children. A child adopted by a couple is legally adopted by a process that entails signing of paperwork, becoming legal guardians, having custody of and seeking to raise the child as their own. However, the child was not born from that couple and does not have the biological configuration derived from that couple, like genes and chromosomes. That is not to say that the adopted child does not enjoy the same rights and love as the children born from that couple would.

The understanding that by Baptism we become "adopted children" of God can be perceived more clearly if we begin with Jesus' own words to Nicodemus:

> Jesus answered him, "Truly, truly, I say to you, unless one is born anew, he cannot see the kingdom of God." Nicodemus said to him, "How can a man be born when he is old? Can he enter a second time into his mother's womb and be born?" Jesus answered, "Truly, truly, I say to you, unless one is born of water and the Spirit, he cannot enter the kingdom of God. That which is born of the flesh is flesh, and that which is born of the Spirit is spirit. Do not marvel that I said to you, 'You must be born anew.'" (Jn 3:3-7)

Jesus is not speaking of a legal adoption, but being "born anew," of a second but divine birth, being "born of the Spirit," the Spirit being the Holy Spirit. Sacramentally and mystically, each baptized, to use a human image, enters into and is born anew from the "womb" of God. There is therefore an ontological transformation, and the result is a "man-god," as it were, a man who now participates in the divinity of God, sharing in His divine life. It is analogous to the Incarnation of the Son of God, who became the "God-man," but accomplished this dual aspect in reverse, from God to God-man. While we do not become "God" in the absolute and full sense, we do participate in His divine life, and are now "divinized," as the Eastern Church Fathers emphasize. We participate in the Sonship of God's Son we can truly call God "*Abba*," "Father." Paul develops this adoption at some length in his Epistles.

18

The greatness of the gift of divine filiation finds signs of what the Heavenly Father provides for His newly "adopted" children. Our conception in our mothers' wombs is first a creation by God, a sending of His children into the world, analogous to the Father sending His own Son forth at the Incarnation. But, before the creation of Adam and Eve, He had first created and adorned a "cradle," a home, for His children, the universe. He gives a guardian angel to watch over His children and to bring the children back home safely. He gives "foster-parents," our biological parents, and other family and friends and teachers to raise and form us. He gives us two spiritual mothers, Mary and the Church.

Through the seven sacraments in the Church, He accompanies us from birth to death: Baptism after birth, Confession and First Communion at the age of reason, Confirmation as we approach adulthood, Marriage so that Christ may accompany the couple in their love and mission, the Sacrament of the Sick for our sickness and as we approach death, not to mention the "daily" sacraments of Confession for healing and, above all, the Eucharist in which God gives us the Body and Blood of His only Son— we feed on God! All of these sacraments are made possible by the Sacrament of Holy Orders. The Church also teaches us through the two sources of divine revelation, Scripture and Tradition, and we are safely led by the charism of the Magisterium that interprets these two fonts of divine revelation. To make all of this possible, He gives us the hierarchy, "spiritual fathers" (the Pope who is the "Holy Father," each bishop who is a "spiritual father" of his flock, and each priest who is called "father"). God also gives His children a powerful family, the communion of saints, the angels and saints in heaven, to assist and intercede for us. These are but a sample of what the Heavenly Father provides in "fathering" his "children in the one Son" (*filii in Filio*).

### The Profound Experiences of St. Josemaría Escrivá and St. Marguerite D'Youville

How tremendous is this gift of filiation? Let us look to two examples in which the discovery of their "divine filiation" transformed their lives: Josemaría Escrivá de Balaguer, the founder of the personal prelature of Opus Dei, and St. Marguerite d'Youville, the foundress of the Congregation of the Sisters of Charity (Grey Nuns) of Montréal.

Josemaría Escrivá de Balaguer describes an experience, when travelling by streetcar, in which he was given a deep experience of God as "Abba" and we as his children.[20] Biographer Andrés Vásquez de Prada sets this experience in context: "As confirmation that the project was His own, God made His presence felt time and again to lay a solid foundation both for the spiritual structure and the people who would work within it. In mid-October, 1931, while in a streetcar, he received the gift of an exalted form of prayer." Here are St. Escrivá's own words in a fuller text quoted from John Coverdale:

> In mid-October, 1931, while in a streetcar he received the gift of an exalted form of prayer. "I felt the action of God, bringing forth in my heart and on my lips, with the force of something imperatively necessary, this tender invocation: Abba! Pater! ("Abba! Father!"). Probably I made that prayer out loud. And I walked the streets of Madrid for maybe an hour, maybe two, I can't say; time passed without my being aware of it. People must have thought I was crazy. I was contemplating, with lights that were not mine, that amazing truth. It was like a lighted coal burning in my soul, never to be extinguished."
>
> When God sent me those blows back in 1931, I didn't understand them… Then all at once, in the midst of such great bitterness, came the words: "You are my son (Ps 2:7), you are Christ." And I could only stammer: "Abba, Pater! Abba, Pater! Abba! Abba! Abba!" Now I see it with new light, like a new discovery, just as one sees, after years have passed, the hand of God, of divine Wisdom, of the All-Powerful. You've led me, Lord, to understand that to find the Cross is to find happiness, joy. And I see the reason with greater clarity than ever: to find the Cross is to identify oneself with Christ, to be Christ, and therefore to be a son of God." [21]

Andrés Vásquez de Prada describes the ecstasy that captured his heart in its very depths and would forever change him. Michele Dolz writes that a

---

[20] For a succinct summary, one might look to Scott Hahn, *Ordinary Work, Extraordinary Grace: My Spiritual Journey in Opus Dei* (Toronto: Doubleday, 2006). For a fuller treatment, see the recent 3-volume publication: Andrés Vásquez de Prada, *The Founder of Opus Dei: The Life of Josemaría Escrivá*, vol. I: *The Early Years* (Princeton, NJ: Scepter Publ., 2001); *The Life of Josemaría Escrivá*, vol. II: *God and Daring* (Princeton, NJ: Scepter, 2003); *The Life of Josemaría Escrivá*, vol. III: *The Divine Ways on Earth*, (Princeton, NJ: Scepter, 2005).

[21] St. Josemaría Escrivá, *Apuntes no. 60*, quoted in John F. Coverdale, *Uncommon Faith: The Early Years of Opus Dei, 1928-1943* (Princeton, NJ: Scepter, 2002), 93-94. See also Andrés Vásquez de Prada, *The Founder of Opus Dei: The Life of Josemaría Escrivá*, vol. I: *The Early Years*, 295.

childlike trust was engendered by this gift and revelation: "His spiritual life already characterized by a childlike trust, now saw the mystery of his adoptive sonship in Jesus Christ with extraordinary depth."[22]

So overwhelmed was St. Escrivá by this experience that he made divine filiation the heart of the Opus Dei spirituality.

> I understood that divine filiation had to be a basic characteristic of our spirituality: Abba, Father! And that by living from within their divine filiation, my children would find themselves filled with joy and peace, protected by an impregnable wall; and would know how to be apostles of this joy, and how to communicate their peace, even in the face of their own or another's suffering. Just because of that: because we are convinced that God is our Father....[23]

Alvaro del Portillo, his collaborator and confessor for forty years, as well as his successor as Prelate of the Opus Dei prelature, points to the tremendous gift of filiation that flows from Baptism. In the 1992 testimony on the holiness, and therefore the identification with Christ, of Josemaría Escrivá, del Portillo wrote:

> What constitutes the nucleus of Monsignor José Maria Escrivà de Balaguer's message is the consciousness of the radical transformation that occurs in man through the working of baptismal grace: made a participant in the divine nature, man becomes a son of God and because of this he is called to sanctity. This boldness appears admirably synthesized in the point of Furrow: "Look – we have to love God not only with our heart but with his" (n. 809).[24]

No less striking is the experience of St. Marguerite d'Youville, the foundress of the Grey Nuns in Montréal, Québec. Her life was marked by tremendous sufferings: the early death of her father, the rejection by the family of her first love and fiancé when the family's finances took a downturn, the death of a few children at childbirth, the illegal selling of alcohol to the aboriginals by her husband and his neglect of the family, the harshness of her mother-in-law.

---

[22] Michele Dolz, *St. Josemaría Escrivá* (Princeton, NJ: Scepter, 2002), 25.
[23] Josemaría Escrivá, *Letter 8 Dec 1949,* quoted in Andrés Vásquez de Prada, vol. 1, 296.
[24] http://robertaconnor.blogspot.ca/2005/06/june-26-benedict-xvi-communio-opus-dei.html.

During one of the lowest ebbs of her life, reeling under the crushing weight of many troubles in 1727, she received a profound interior illumination of God as Eternal Father, who holds everyone in His providence and that we are all brothers and sisters. From that moment on, Marguerite was transformed forever. When she realized that her married life was not to be a happy one, she prepared herself and prayed: "'Our Father... confirm in my heart and mind the attitude of being truly Your child. Show me how to approach You with filial reverence, love and trust, the way a child should approach her father.'"[25] As the sense of God as loving Father increased and became part of her everyday life, she gained strength to accept rejection in her marriage.

She would face even greater troubles and yet continued to march forward with great courage and trust: the death of her husband, the death of four children, the death of one of the first members of her foundation, the capture of one of her sons by the British forces, opposition from the bishop and those in authority. She was also held in contempt from being associated with the downtrodden, and the derogatory appellation of *Soeurs grises*, "tipsy Sisters," she chose to keep as the name of her Congregation, *Grey Sisters*. Her great trust in God the Eternal Father was made manifest in the disaster when the hospital that housed her beloved sick and poor burnt down, and she asked those around her to kneel down and pray the great hymn of praise and thanksgiving, the *Te Deum*. Later on, she would commission a painting of God the Eternal Father by Challe in France. This painting, one of two items that miraculously survived a fire at the Mother House, and hung on a wall in the former Mother House in Montréal.

---

[25] Rita McGuire, *Marguerite d'Youville: A Pioneer for our Times* (Ottawa: Novalis, 1982), 63. There are fewer English biographies of St. Marguerite d'Youville than French ones: one well known biography is Estelle Mitchell's *Marguerite d'Youville: Foundress of the Grey Nuns* (Montréal: Palm Publishers, 1965); a recent biography is Antoine Sattin's *Life of Mother d'Youville, foundress and first superior of the Sisters of Charity or Grey Nuns* (Montréal: Méridien, 1999); and a succinct introduction to this saint is Marie Cecilia Lefevre & Rose Alma Lemire's *A Journey of Love: The Life Story of Marguerite d'Youville* (Lexington, MS: Sisters of Charity of Montréal).

## Conclusion

The great secret of Christianity is divine filiation. Jesus did not just come to save us from our sins, nor just die to give us the Holy Spirit, nor send the Holy Spirit to make each a new Christ. He did all these things so He could share with us His greatest gift: His filial relation to the Father and His Father's love for us as "sons in the one Son" (*filii in Filio*). Each of us at our Baptism should hear the tender words of the Father to Jesus at His Baptism, "You are my Son, the Beloved," throughout our lives. A Spanish laywoman wrote that the Holy Spirit Himself taught her that on the cross, Jesus "renegotiated" with the Father to prolong His agony till He could obtain for us the gift of the Holy Spirit to give us a share in His Sonship.[26] Thus the remission of sins (justification) is the lesser gift from Calvary; divine filiation, being "sons in the one Son" and having a participation in the Trinitarian communion, is the higher and ineffable divine gift.

Many in the Church, in everyday moments, have come to experience the Father's love, such as Raïssa Maritain.

> At the first invocation, *Kyrie eleison*, obliged to absorb myself, my mind arrested on the Person of the Father. Impossible to change the object. Sweetness, attraction, *eternal youth* of the heavenly Father. Suddenly, keen sense of his nearness, of his tenderness, of his incomprehensible love which impels him to demand our love, our thought. Greatly moved, I wept very sweet tears... Joy of being able to call him Father with a great tenderness, to feel him so kind and so close to me. (Raïssa Maritain, on praying the Litany to Sacred Heart)[27]

The heart of God is love, or most deeply, pure mercy, and this is precisely the heart of the heavenly Father to whom Tradition attaches the attribute of mercy. In St. Faustina, we find a confirmation of this deep truth and the life of one who has experienced this truth and lives with sheer abandon in being loved by "Mercy." Pope Benedict XVI teaches us that we too must discover this truth of the Father as Mercy by gazing upon the One we have pierced, by silent adoration of the wound that permits us to "see" into, or experience, His heart, and, by extension, the Father's heart. And it is above all in the unheard-of and wholly unmerited gift of divine filiation, won for

---

[26] Francisca Javiera del Valle, *About the Holy Spirit* (New York: Scepter, 1998), 40-41.
[27] Jacques Maritain, ed., *Raïssa Journal* (Albany, NY: Magi, 1974), 35.

us by that same sacrifice, of being given a share of Christ's very sonship within the Trinity that should lead us into ecstasy, as it did St. Josemaría Escrivá and St. Marguerite d'Youville, "Abba, Father." We truly have been created out of love and for love; for divine filiation.

The difficulty is that many have not experienced the Father's love. It is the role of the priest, as spiritual father, to remind the children of God of this reality, especially in his homilies, and to enable the gift to become a reality. "When God created us, He created us out of love. There is no other explanation because God is love. And He has created us to love and to be loved."[28] The experience of the Father's love will enable us to live with the great confidence of children who have been loved and can now go out to face the world. It may help to try to see ourselves the way God sees us. In a very fine work, *I Believe in Love*, Fr. Jean d'Elbée, presents a wonderful insight, "How does Jesus see me?":

> Ask yourself, "How does Jesus see me?" He sees me as His child since my baptism. He sees me, since my confirmation, filled with the superabundance of the gifts of His Spirit, marked with the indelible character of a soldier of His kingdom. He sees married people bathed in the grace of the sacrament of marriage. And, looking at husband and wife, He thinks of His union with the Church. He sees me as His lamb which has so often let itself be led back to the fold in His arms, purified by absolution. He sees my soul transformed into Himself by Mass and Communion - my soul, where His Father and He have made their dwelling place because, "If anyone loves me he will keep my word, and my Father will love him, and we will come to him and will make our abode with him" (John 14:23). These are the actual realities of sacramental graces![29]

The child of God must have personal experience of the Father's love in order to share this love with others, especially when he has his own family. The following words are what a consecrated laywoman heard in her heart when she asked God the Father who she was to Him after Baptism. May each child of God through Baptism hear his version of the Father's words:

---

[28] "Centenary of Mother Teresa's Birth: Created for Greater Things, To Love and be Loved," August 30-October 3, accessed May 26, 2019, http://www.motherteresa.org/Centenary/English/August.html, main page, week 1.
[29] Jean C. J. d'Elbée, *I Believe in Love: A Personal Retreat Based on the Teaching of St. Thérèse of Lisieux* (Manchester, NH: Sophia Institute Press, 2001), 96.

My little one how much I love you. I chose you from all eternity.
You are Mine, My beloved.
I wrapped you in the silence of My deep, abiding love.
I held you O so tenderly within My heart, My beloved child.
I nestled you close in My heart.
Pure, holy, radiant, a heart fit for a King to love, cherish, abide in,
        to be one with for all eternity.
My love for you is boundless, infinite, everlasting.
I placed My stamp on you, My beloved child, Mine for all eternity,
My bond of love for all eternity, My seal, My mark, My kiss of
        love. This kiss lasts for all eternity.
A heart simple, true, open to receive My love, My life, My gift.

This entire book's task is now to unveil the generation of the child of God: divine filiation.

# CHAPTER 2

## *SUBSTITUTION OF CHRIST*

### *("Another Christ, Christ Himself")*

> The Spirit has completed the divine circle of his flight. The Father and the Son, uniting in their eternal kiss of love, join the soul in their embrace.... His [Holy Spirit's] ideal is to produce Jesus in us, and through Jesus and with Jesus, to take us to the bosom of the Trinity and glorify the Father with the supreme glorification of Jesus.... souls are purified, illuminated, and enkindled until they are transformed into Jesus, who is the ultimate ideal of God's love and of the aspirations of the soul, the glorious summit of the mystical ascent... where we find God.[1] (Luis Martinez)

The new child of God through Baptism has a life-long task to become fully configured to Christ (a new Christ, to be fully a child of the Father as Christ was the beloved Son). Blessed Dina Bélanger calls it a "Substitution of Christ" and Venerable de Armida calls it a "mystical incarnation." It is captured succinctly by St. Josemaría Escrivá's goal for the baptized, to become "another Christ, Christ himself" (*alter Christus, ipse Christus*).[2]

*The Love of the Father Begins with an Experience of the Love of Christ*

At the most fundamental level, man is created for love and needs to experience love. Let us look to the wisdom of the author of *Theology of the Body*. In *Redemptor hominis* 10, "The Human Dimension of the Mystery of Redemption," John Paul II affirms that "man cannot live without love" and that that love is found and fulfilled by drawing close to Christ and appropriating His mysteries:

> *Man cannot live without love. He remains a being that is incomprehensible for himself, his life is senseless, if love is not revealed to him, if he does not encounter love, if he does not experience it and make it his own, if he does not participate intimately in it.* This, as has already been said, is why Christ the Redeemer "fully reveals man to himself". If we may use the expression, this is the human dimension of the mystery of the Redemption. (emphasis added)

---

[1] Luis Martinez, *The Sanctifier* (Boston: Pauline Books and Media, 2003), 50-52.
[2] St. Josemaría Escrivá de Balaguer, *Christ is passing by*, n. 183.

Robert Cardinal Sarah sets us within a Trinitarian basis of love. He teaches, for example, that Vatican II completed the task of Vatican I and gave a new dimension to mission. Mission flows from the Trinity: it has its source in the mission of the Son and of the Holy Spirit, both by decree of the Father. There are many elements that can take place within mission (e.g., education, freedom from oppression, social activities, agriculture), but these are not the essence of mission:

> To be a missionary is not about giving things but communicating the foundation of Trinitarian life: the love of the Father, of the Son, and of the Holy Spirit. To be a missionary is to lead people toward a personal experience of the immeasurable love that unites the Father, the Son, and the Holy Spirit so as to allow oneself to be seized at the same time by the ardent furnace of love that manifested itself so sublimely on the Cross. To be a missionary is to help others to become disciples of Jesus, to experience a profound friendship with Jesus, and to become one and the same being with Jesus (*God or Nothing*, 234).

Cardinal Sarah writes that Christianity is about the encounter with love of Christ, that the relationship with the Trinity, and specifically the Father, begins with the encounter with Christ's love:

> Yes, in *Deus caritas est*, Pope Benedict XVI writes that at the origin of being Christian there is not an ethical decision, a philosophical or moral idea, but *an encounter with an event, a Person.* (p. 154, emphasis added);

> Yes, Christianity is summed up in a person who comes to reveal and offer his love: "God so loved the world that he gave his only-begotten Son, that whoever believes in him should not perish but have eternal life" (Jn 3:16). This is certainly not about "moralism" but about "morality." The first moral precept is love of God and of neighbour, is it not? The fulfillment of the Law, St. Paul says, is love (Rom 13:10). (p. 155)

> Although Christian communities exist that are still vital and missionary, most Western populations now regard Jesus as a sort of idea but not as an event, much less as a person whom the apostles and many witnesses of the Gospel met and loved and to whom they consecrated their whole life. (p. 167).

The New Testament is full of encounters with Christ that transformed hearts. These were encounters where they experienced the love of the heart of Christ. We point out a few. For example, Paul knew that he was a great sinner but became aware that God loved him despite his sins ("He loved me and gave himself up for me," Gal 2:20). With this experience, Paul became an indefatigable preacher of Christ's love. Consider also the transformation of the Samaritan woman at the well; it was not primarily Christ's words but the love that emanated from His Sacred Heart, the love of the Good Shepherd, that reached her heart. Consider the tender love of Mary Magdalene for the person of Jesus (how she searched for Him at the tomb and embraced His feet when she recognized Him), a love that must have risen from the profound experience of Jesus' love for her. We find perhaps an even more tender showing of love from the sinful woman at Simon's house, who wept at his feet and wiped his feet with her hair, and whom Jesus held up as an example to Simon and the guests.

In the lives of the saints, we meet special souls who were essentially overwhelmed by encountering the love of Christ. Here are some examples. St. Thérèse of Lisieux was wooed by the love of the divine Eagle (Jesus) and her response was to make an oblation of her life to make up for the love that He was not receiving from the human family. After her private letters were opened up for the canonization process, it was revealed that Mother Teresa of Calcutta had visitations from Jesus, who asked her to go to the streets of Calcutta to look after the poorest of the poor. When she hesitated out of fear, He appealed to her love for Him: "Did you not say you love me? Did you not say that you would do anything for me?" St. Ignatius of Loyola encountered the love of Jesus during his conversion and at Manresa, and he called his new order the *Company of Jesus*, and the Jesuit Mother Church in Rome is called the *Gesù* (Jesus). St. Teresa Benedicta a Cruce (Edith Stein) was converted after spending the night reading the life of St. Teresa of Jesus, after which she exclaimed, "This is truth," for her St. Teresa of Jesus' life spoke of Christ.

In the previous chapter on our Trinitarian origin, we have glimpsed the Father's heart of Mercy, an overflowing and overwhelming Mercy. In the overarching panorama, the Father's heart of Mercy is active in two utterly ineffable actions of munificent mercy: the sending of the Son to be sacrificed, and granting us the unheard of sharing of the Son's very divine filiation. This divine filiation, becoming sons and daughters of God, actually comprises two elements in the context of the Pauline terminology:

29

becoming the "Body of Christ" and the "Bride of Christ." Chapter 2 now examines the "Body of Christ" as the Pauline incorporation in Christ, or mystically, as "substitution of Christ." The Pauline incorporation in Christ itself has two aspects: a substitution of Christ and a friendship with Christ. That is, the incorporation in Christ involves a union with Christ that includes both an ontological union of substitution or "transubstantiation" as well as a union of friendship (we shall examine the "Bride of Christ" dimension in Chapter 3 on the Holy Spirit, with the espousals or marriage with Christ that combines the aforementioned two elements).

The goal of this substitution of and friendship with Christ presupposes a prior foundation, which is expressed superbly in the two pillars Jesus revealed to St. Catherine of Siena as the foundation of all Christian life: knowledge of self and knowledge of God (His love). This chapter, consequently, begins by examining the two pillars in the doctrine of St. Catherine of Siena to establish the foundation that permits a transformation into Christ to take place. Second, we shall look at the intimate identification with Christ in the Pauline incorporation to Christ through the teachings of Blessed Dina Bélanger (substitution) and Venerable Concepción Cabrera de Armida. And finally, we will develop more fully how this substitution of Christ is lived out in friendship with Christ through Robert Hugh Benson.

## 1. The Foundation of the Two Pillars of St. Catherine of Siena's Doctrine

### St. Catherine of Siena

The doctrine of St. Catherine of Siena was chosen for this doctrinal elaboration because of her significant impact on the Church, both ecclesially and spiritually, and because of her insights as a doctor of the Church. St. Catherine is probably best known as the one who helped restore the papacy from Avignon to Rome in the 14th century. But, along with St. Teresa of Avila, St. Thérèse of Lisieux, and St. Hildegard of Bingen, she stands out as one of only four female doctors of the Church, despite her having written only one work, *The Dialogue of Providence* (which consists mainly of God speaking to her in a dialogue), though there are also some extant letters. So powerful was her example, her personality, and her teaching that many sought her guidance and some became her spiritual children or disciples, in person or by correspondence. Spiritual writers generally acknowledge that self-knowledge, the first pillar, in particular is the foundation of the entire spiritual life. St. Catherine of Siena's entire spirituality is well-known for placing self-knowledge as its first foundation. The teaching originally comprised three pillars, which can be reduced to two pillars that constitute the foundation of the entire spiritual life for everyone: (A) knowledge of my poverty or nothingness before God; and (B) the knowledge or awareness of God's love for me.

## A. "You are she who is not; whereas I am He who is"

St. Catherine reveals that it was Christ Himself who taught her this by private revelation and the first teaching concerned knowledge of self, "self-knowledge." During the three years of her formation by our Lord, Catherine's experience of God evolved based upon what Christ taught her about the foundational relation between creatures and Creator, or, more specifically, knowledge of herself and knowledge of God. It was presented in the following profound statement:

> Do you know, daughter, who you are, and who I am? If you know these two things, you will be blessed. You are she who is not; whereas I am He who is. Have this knowledge in your soul and the Enemy will never deceive you and you will escape all his wiles; you will never disobey my commandments and will acquire all grace, truth and light.[3]

"You are she who is not; whereas I am He who is." Here we see a reiteration and perhaps even a deepening of the great revelation to Moses, when he asked, "Who should I say is sending me?" And Yahweh revealed who He was in that lofty and dense statement, a statement full of awe, "I am who I am" (Ex 3:14). God is being or existence itself, possessing all the attributes of being, including beauty, truth, and justice.

A biographer of St. Catherine of Siena elaborates upon the depth of this revelation to her: "Catherine's ascent to God is all in this truth: all her enlightenment came from this discovery; her teaching and the secret of her power in dealing with souls proceeded from this idea...."[4]

---

[3] Blessed Raymond of Capua, *The Life of St. Catherine of Siena* (Rockford, Illinois: Tan, repr. 2003), 79. A fine narrative-style biography is Louis de Wohl's *Lay Siege to Heaven* (San Francisco: Ignatius Press, 1991).
[4] Igino Giordani, *St. Catherine of Siena* (Boston, MA: Daughters of St. Paul, 1980), 35.

With that lesson Catherine became fundamentally learned: she was founded upon a rock; there were no more shadows. *I, nothing; God All. I, nonbeing; God, Being....*

For Catherine this was a discovery so memorable that from then on she explained it to everyone who would listen... The discovery enabled the girl from Fontebranda to remove the barricade of egoism which always impedes progress....

This humiliating of herself, this weeping, this annihilation of herself in the conviction of her nothingness, all served to purify Catherine's soul of every shadow, to make it a limpid crystal, an absolute void through which the light of God passed unhindered.

.... The answer [to her greatness despite her simplicity] is evident: she succeeded in being no longer herself, so that Christ might live in her; because becoming completely humble, she was, like Mary, a handmaid of the Lord, a void which the spirit of God made full of grace. And this divine grace made her godlike.[5]

Several foundational elements are presented here. First, all her enlightenment and power and secret proceeded from this truth, and with it, she was now "founded upon a rock," she could not be misled. Second, this truth could be synthesized thus: "*I, nothing; God All. I, nonbeing; God, Being.*" This knowledge enabled her to detach herself from the world of nonbeing, realizing its transience and contingency, establishing her nothingness before and her dependence on God. Third, in this knowledge of her nothingness, she sought annihilation of self, to open herself to be filled with God's being, which made her "godlike." These three dimensions reveal the tremendous power of this truth of self-knowledge that God revealed to her. This first foundation stone constitutes the absolute foundation of all Christian life, establishing at the outset the primordial relationship between God the Creator and his creatures. Once this objective relationship is correctly established, the subjective relationship with the Creator can properly develop.

Now we must make a critical distinction, to avoid an erroneous sense of self-knowledge. This knowledge of our poverty is not a certain offhand putting myself down, "Oh, I am such a miserable sinner." It is not about

---

[5] Ibid., 36-37.

myself existing at a very low grade in the chart of reality, being nothing special. What is being spoken of here is an ontological poverty in relation to God. There is an utterly infinite chasm that separates the creature from the Creator, who is existence itself, who has brought all into existence by His Word. The Scholastic philosophy of St. Thomas Aquinas, drawing from the teachings of Aristotle, captures this reality by teaching that God is "*esse subsistens*," "subsistent being," being itself, and all creatures receive and participate in the being of God.

We must draw a fuller picture to see the depth of this dependence on God for our existence, action, and redemption. First, beyond creating us, God has to preserve us in existence each and every moment (*conservatio*), otherwise we would disappear into nothingness. Then He collaborates with us in each and every activity, including intellectual activity, in order that we can move or act or think (*concursus divinus*). Perhaps most moving of all is that God in His providence guides and directs all things for the good of His children (*providentia*). Thus, there are four activities of God in our existence: creation, preservation, concursus, and providence. If we are to assume, as scientists suggest, that evolution is taking place, we might include evolution as yet another activity guided by God. Greater yet are two realities that increase the depth of this chasm that separates us from God. First, the tragedy of sin moves us beyond that original state of nothingness, as it were, from this state of being "nothing," to the negative portion of the scale— we have now become enemies of God. Second, remembering that God does not need us, as Scripture attests, while yet enemies of God, He proceeds to redeem us by sacrificing His own Son.

The importance of this overarching self-knowledge, of this first pillar, cannot be overemphasized. This first truth of self-knowledge, of knowledge of nothingness before— and dependence on— God is reflected strongly in the very self-abasement in Christ and His Mother in Scripture. Though He is God, as Philippians 2 reveals, the Son descends in self-abasement at the incarnation and even more deeply in going to the cross. God seeks to descend in order to identify Himself with us and to save us— as the Church Fathers teach, "God has become man so that man can become God."

In contrast, man in his pride seeks to "ascend." For example, Adam, made from dust but for a destiny of communion with God, is tempted by the sin of pride, "you will become like God," and by his sin returned to dust. Many texts from the Gospels confirm this true path of Christ: "He must increase, I must decrease" (St. John the Baptist); "unless you become like little children you will never enter the kingdom of heaven."

This truth in our Lady is revealed in the foundation of her greatness, as inspired by the Holy Spirit in the *Magnificat*, "for he has regarded the low estate of his handmaiden" (Lk 1:48. It is found also in the tone of the *Magnificat*, "and has lifted up the lowly"; and in the whole orientation of the Beatitudes, "Blessed are the poor in heart… blessed are the meek." The entire mystical tradition follows this path, as exemplified by St. Thérèse of Lisieux's teaching that holiness is not about growing bigger but rather about becoming smaller. It is possible that many do not make great progress in the spiritual life because they lack this indispensable knowledge of self before God's love, perhaps in this way fulfilling our Lord's words, "For many are called but few are chosen" (Mt 22:14).

## B. "My daughter, think of Me; if you will do this, I shall immediately think of you"

The first foundation stone of self-knowledge sets the stage for the second foundation stone. St. Catherine's instruction was completed by our Lord when He told her later:

> "My daughter, think of Me; if you will do this, I shall immediately think of you." Catherine understood: she thought only of Him; and she came to realize how He always thought of her: and in this exchange by which the divine love in a certain sense elevated the creature to the level of the Creator (called forth non-being into being), she saw that love which, if it made God human, made man godlike. Thenceforward, Catherine took no thought at all of what she ate or what she drank or of what happened to her; she left it all to Him. And this conduct of hers became also the norm of her followers.[6]

This is quite a striking promise: "My daughter, think of Me; if you will do this, I shall immediately think of you." To "think" of God is not to avert to Him impersonally, indifferently, platonically. To think of God is to think of

---

[6] Ibid., 37.

Him with affection and attention, to give one's heart to Him and to depend on Him at all times. And in this trust and love of God, "Thenceforward, Catherine took no thought at all of what she ate or what she drank or of what happened to her; she left it all to Him." She is now able to live in abandonment, which allows God to form and lead her, which we have seen in St. Faustina.

We note that it is the first foundation stone that enables us to live the second. The first enables us to see our total nothingness and helplessness, that is, our total dependence on God. Knowing our nothingness then, knowing that there is no point in looking at ourselves, we now turn our entire attention to the One who is Being itself and who loves us. Hence, God begins with the endearing words, "my daughter," and ends with the assuring words of a Father, "think of Me; if you will do this, I shall immediately think of you." We no longer have to think about ourselves, no longer have to give so much attention to our spiritual progress, no longer have to be troubled by crises or difficulties. Once we have learned the all-important first lesson of not relying on ourselves, we can now trust in the only one who can help us in each and every situation. St. Josemaría Escrivá identifies himself as the donkey who carried Jesus to Jerusalem (*Christ is Passing By* , n. 181). If the donkey thought that the crowd was giving him adulation, that donkey is a real "ass."

This self-knowledge leads to an identification with the will of God and bearing all that He sends, as found in St. Catherine of Siena's book, *The Dialogue*:

> Thus, the vision of the book [St. Catherine's *Dialogue*] is rounded out: it begins with sin, with hell, and culminates in the enjoyment of God: the fate of the soul that seeing, recognizes, and recognizing, loves… and loving, tastes of God, the Supreme Good, and tasting God, denies its own will, to make it God's will: and God's will is our sanctification on earth that will merit us the beatific vision in heaven. When our own will becomes the will of God, the soul bears with reverence and perseverance every trial sent by Him, or permitted by Him, accepting it and using it as a means of grace: it comports itself as Jesus upon the cross, blessed and suffering; suffering in body, blessed in soul. United in her will with God she is made one with Him and He one with her. The passage from the human to the divine is made across a bridge, which is Jesus Christ

Himself: a bridge thrown across a river which, flowing through the valley, continually assumes new forms, a figure of the changeable and transitory nature of all things. Upon the bridge there is dispensed the blood of Christ, food for wayfarers and pilgrims: this is the Church, governed by the Vicar of Christ and his ministers.[7]

In the second foundation stone, everything changes as we begin to identify with God's will. The result is that "the soul bears with reverence and perseverance every trial sent by Him, or permitted by Him, accepting it and using it as a means of grace: it comports itself as Jesus upon the cross, blessed and suffering; suffering in body, blessed in soul." It is a passage from "the human to the divine," through a bridge, that is Jesus Christ Himself: *"My daughter, think of Me; if you will do this, I shall immediately think of you."*

There are thus two wrong turns. First, St. Catherine teaches that, if we focus on one or the other of the two foundation stones, we encounter difficulties: if we focus only on our nothingness and on our sinfulness, we might become discouraged and give up hope of any progress; if we focus exclusively on God's love for us, then that "love" tends to become sentimental, and we can end up treating God as a grandfather. Second, we discern a dynamic concerning the two elements: the second element, the awareness of God's love for us, is always the dominant focus we hold; but the first element, the awareness of our nothingness, is where we always begin. An illustration of this dynamic is found in the progression at Mass: we begin with the *Confiteor*, "I confess to Almighty God," and before receiving Communion, we say, "Lord, I am not worthy that you should enter under my roof…"; but our primary focus will end up with the sacramental "communion" of love, the dialogue of love with God.

Let us look at two other common traps that undermine these two pillars. The trap that contravenes the second pillar of keeping our eyes on Jesus is to be caught up with "perfection," with our spiritual development, instead of focusing on the goal of the spiritual life, the two commandments of love. A young man entering the seminary can sincerely desire to be holy, an indispensable disposition. However, he can easily become caught up with discernment and progress in the spiritual life or with a poor self-image, with

---

[7] Ibid., 220-221.

the result that he can easily become centered on self. The reliance on our talents and on our progress and to be obsessed with taking our spiritual barometer can be aspects of self-absorption or self-love. Instead, holiness is essentially and predominantly love, the spiritual life is all about forgetting self and opening ourselves to the two loves (two great commandments), love of God and love of neighbour. St. Augustine identifies the two divergent paths in his vision of the "two cities" in *City of God*: the love of self and the love of God. St. Augustine also sees the problem of all spiritual life as deriving from self-love:

> Two loves thus establish two cities: love of self unto contempt of God built the earthly city, and love of God unto contempt of self built the heavenly city….
>
> The one city glories in itself, the other in God…. The one… is controlled by lust of power; the other inspires human beings to mutual service, leaders by commanding, subjects by obeying. The one, in its lords, loves his own strength; the other says to its God: "I will love you, Lord, who are my strength."[8]

Thus, the opposite of love is not hate, but selfishness, a disordered love of self. St. Catherine of Siena teaches that all sin derives from an improper "self-love." Self-knowledge, on the other hand, reveals our great misery before God (first foundation stone), which enables us to rely on God's love (second foundation stone).

The trap that contravenes the first pillar of self-knowledge is a hidden Pelagianism. Pelagius, of course, was a British monk in the early Church who moved to Rome and was scandalized by the decadence he found there. Opposing Manichaeism, which saw human and material reality as sinful, and coming from his austere Celtic monastic background, he preached a rigorous program of conversion. Unfortunately, in his zeal for our self-initiative, he overemphasized human effort and preached an erroneous doctrine, whereby man never contracted original sin from Adam and Eve, and thus retained original justice, thereby obviating the need for Christ's grace, which, for him, only serves as an external help (e.g., example,

---

[8] Augustine, *City of God* XIV, 28, quoted in Agostino Trapè, *Saint Augustine: Man, Pastor, Mystic* (New York: Catholic Book Publ. Co., 1986), 241. Fr. Trapè's translation is preferred here for its succinctness.

assisting grace and not a transforming grace). A hidden Pelagianism, therefore, ends up involving a secret reliance upon ourselves and our gifts to win God's favour and our salvation: "If I say many Rosaries, go to daily Mass, and spend much time in adoration of the Blessed Sacrament, I will win heaven." Peter Kreeft, in a conference given to seminary spiritual directors in Boston, explained how he begins a certain course each year by asking two questions: "How many of you believe that you are going to heaven?"; and "Why do you think so?" The responses almost referred to their "good works" before God. We are each blessed with differing gifts, such as organizational skills, popularity, knowledge, eloquence, art. These gifts are gifts from God, "charisms," lower graces, but they can easily make us forget the Giver and make us self-sufficient. We can end up seeking the gifts of the Giver and not the Giver Himself, the "Uncreated Grace."

*The First Pillar in St. Faustina's Life and Teaching: Supreme Foundation of Humility*

Concrete examples in the life and teachings of St. Faustina can again come to our assistance, strongly reinforcing the importance of self-knowledge: the awareness of our poverty before and absolute dependence on God. We find a striking example of this self-reliance or Pelagianism in a correction Jesus gave St. Faustina. She had made a resolution to work on something, which usually resulted in progress in her spiritual life. On one occasion, however, it seemed to have the opposite effect: "In the evening, I was reflecting on why, today, I had lapsed so extraordinarily, and I heard the words: 'You were counting too much on yourself and too little on Me.' And I understood the cause of my lapses" (*Diary* 1087).

She discovered the key to the spiritual life: dependence on God. This fits with Christ's teaching about the requirement for those seeking entry into heaven: "Unless you become like little children, you will never enter the kingdom of heaven." It is easy for us to fall into a trap of thinking that we are "good" because we pray, do a little penance, and do good things. St. Paul reveals that it is not our good works but our misery that draws down God's mercy. The secret is to come before God in total helplessness and lack of fervour:

> My Jesus, You know that there are times when I have neither lofty thoughts nor a soaring spirit. I bear with myself patiently and admit that that is just what I am, because all that is beautiful is a grace from God.

38

And so I humble myself profoundly and cry out for Your help; and the grace of visitation is not slow in coming to the humble heart. (*Diary* 1734)

The value of humility is priceless, Sister Faustina called it the most precious virtue, primarily because without it we cannot be united with God: "My bride, you always please Me by your humility. The greatest misery does not stop Me from uniting Myself to a soul, but where there is pride, I am not there" (*Diary* 1563).[9]

We find in St. Faustina's teaching the depths of this truth. "A lowly soul captivates God, so to speak, by her humility, inducing Him to bestow on her His mercy and graciousness. 'Although You are great, Lord, You allow yourself to be overcome by a lowly and deeply humble soul (*Diary* 1436),' we read in the Diary."[10] For St. Faustina, humility, similar to the greatest among the virtues, love, testifies to the greatness of the soul. There is also no love without humility, only a love that is humble can be called true love, and God reigns fully only in a pure, humble heart, empty of self (*Diary* 573). In such a heart God finds His greatest delight; such souls enjoy His special favours (cf. *Diary* 778). They can always count on God's aid (cf. *Diary* 1211), since they are prepared to receive it. As waters flow into the valleys, so does God's grace flow into humble souls. Humility renders a soul happy (cf. *Diary* 450); it is the source of her equanimity and interior peace (cf. *Diary* 450); and it assists in penetrating more deeply into the mysteries of God's life, which are hidden from the wise and the learned, but revealed to the simple. Recognition and acknowledgement of her sins and failures cause her to be raised to the throne of God:

> Once the Lord said to me, "My Heart was moved by great mercy towards you, My dearest child, when I saw you torn to shreds because of the great pain you suffered in repenting your sins. I see your love, so pure and true that I give you first place among the virgins. You are the honour and glory of My Passion. I see every abasement of your soul, and nothing escapes my attention. I lift up the humble even to my very throne, because I want it so." (*Diary* 282)

There is a striking text that links awareness of our sinfulness and peace of heart by St. Dorotheus, Abbot in the Early Church, *Why are We Troubled?*,

---

[9] *In St. Faustina's School of Trust*, 72.
[10] Ibid., 73.

reflecting on the book of Job 29:1-10 and 30:1, 9-23. He here explains why we get so ruffled by the criticism of others. He illustrates the value of fraternal correction and self-accusation in the spiritual life. "The reason for all disturbance is that no one finds fault with himself."

## 2. The Substitution of Christ & the Mystical Incarnation

### A. The Great Secret

The first step of self-knowledge or knowledge of one's utter poverty before God enables the goal of Christian life, a substitution of Christ with a total annihilation of one's ego. A visiting scholar who taught at the Patristic Institute Augustinianum in Rome, in a lecture, pointed to the heart of St. Augustine's teaching as drawn from St. Paul and St. John: deification and assimilation to Christ. He decried that this truth has been shunted aside since the eighth century. Paul expresses this profound truth in different forms: incorporation into Christ, the new man, the new creation, and so on. One can argue that Gal 2:20, "It is no longer I who live, but Christ who lives in me," encapsulates the heart of Paul's teaching. That is, the heart of Christian life, consequently, is not merely keeping moral norms, nor about being or doing good; it is to become incorporated into Christ to the point of "becoming" Christ.

Historical and contemporary scholarship on Paul's theology in large part tends to focus on the doctrine of justification. From a Biblical analysis, James Dunn, an Evangelical scholar, in *The Theology of Paul the Apostle*, gives a contemporary presentation of this incorporation under the aspect, "Participation in Christ." This participation in Christ for him involves a *Christ mysticism*. More than a juridical verdict pronouncing our innocence or remission of sins through Jesus' sacrificial death, "Paul's 'in Christ' language is much more pervasive in his writings than this talk of 'God's righteousness.'"[11] Martin Luther was concerned about his salvation and judgment before the judgment seat of God, and thereby focused primarily on justification as the remission of sins. But as Dunn correctly points out, a language of participation or incorporation in Christ is far more dominant in Paul's epistles. Dunn quotes a key statement from Albert Schweitzer as support: "The doctrine of righteousness by faith is therefore a subsidiary

---

[11] James Dunn, *The Theology of Paul the Apostle* (Edinburgh: T & T Clark, 1998), 391.

crater, which is formed within the rim of the main crater— the mystical doctrine of redemption through being-in-Christ."[12]

James Dunn supports this insight above all in an analysis of the prepositions used by Paul and the frequency with which they are employed. Predominant is the phrase "in Christ" ("*en Christo*"), which occurs 83 times in the Pauline corpus, not including the equivalent phrases, like "in Him." They usually take the form of "in Christ" or "in Christ Jesus."[13] He adds that "An equally striking feature of Paul's theology is his 'with Christ' motif." Though this phrase occurs infrequently, it is significant:

> For the real force of the "with Christ" motif is carried by the remarkable sequence of about forty "with" compounds which constitute yet another distinctive feature of Paul's writing. He uses them both to describe the common privilege, experience, and task of believers and to describe the sharing in Christ's death and life....
>
> Paul's language indicates rather a quite profound sense of participation with others in a great and cosmic movement of God centered on Christ and effective through his spirit. Here again the term like "mysticism" is only an attempt to indicate that profundity and to signal that there are depths and resonances here which we may not be able fully to explore, but for which we need to keep our ears attuned.[14]

He notes other complementary formulations which carry the same idea: "*Into Christ*," "*The body of Christ*," "*Through Christ*," "*of Christ*," as well as an overlapping between Christ and Spirit.[15] These various inclusions in Christ comprises different aspects, including union, participation, identification, and incorporation, but we shall refer to it simply as "incorporation in Christ." This vision of, and the consequences deriving from, participation in Christ had already been drawn out more fully with the Church Fathers, as, for example, we find clearly in the corpus of St. Augustine.

Similarly, from a dogmatic theology perspective, the German theologian, Michael Schmaus, views incorporation to Christ as the global action of what

---

[12] Albert Schweitzer, *Mysticism*, 225, quoted in James Dunn, *The Theology of Paul the Apostle*, 392.
[13] Ibid., 396.
[14] Ibid., 402-404.
[15] Ibid., 404-408.

Christ's Paschal mystery has accomplished for us and includes the individual aspects of redemption: Participation in God's Covenant; New Order; Indwelling of Trinity; Interior Renewal and Sanctification of the Sinner (New Life, Filiation, Forgiveness of Sins, plus Infused Virtues and Gifts of Holy Spirit).[16]

## B. The "Substitution of Christ" in Blessed Dina Bélanger

The theology of incorporation to Christ must lead to its full term or completion, "Christ who lives in me" (Gal 2:20). Some mystics have pointed to this completion. Among them, Blessed Dina Bélanger of Québec City, from her mystical experiences, calls this reality, "Substitution of Christ." Blessed Dina Bélanger died at the age of 32 at Québec City in 1929, and was beatified in 1993 by Pope John Paul II. There is a little side note that suggests her importance for mystical spirituality. A French Carmelite scholar teaching at the renowned Teresianum in Rome, well versed in the teaching of the great discalced Carmelites, who incidentally gave the Pope Benedict XVI and the papal household the Lenten spiritual exercises in 2011, raves about her.[17]

It can be argued that this "substitution of Christ" forms the heart of her spirituality. Blessed Dina reveals that Christ formed her in stages, one that led to the culmination in a vision of being taken up into the sanctuary of a temple, where her fallen "ego" or "self" was annihilated, and all that was left was Christ. In this substitution, Jesus takes over:

> If I left everything in the care of Jesus, what would happen? Jesus, in return, undertook to do everything : to think, speak, act etc. not only with me, but in my place. **He substituted himself for me** and **I let him have his way**. Oh! What a choice gift it is to understand how to let the Saviour live within one's self! I wish I could obtain this grace for every soul : the earth would be a valley no longer of bitter tears, but of tears of joy.

---

[16] Michael Schmaus, *Dogma 6: Justification and the Last Things* (London: Sheed and Ward, 1977), Chs. 4-7, 45-110.
[17] François Marie Léthel, Discalced Carmelite Professor at the Teresianum in Rome ("Pontificia Facoltà Teologica — Pontificio Istituto di Spiritualità"), wrote the Introduction to the *Autobiography of Blessed Dina Bélanger*.

Jesus took over everything : was my life going to be one of inactivity? — Oh! Certainly not! My share in this work was love![18]

As with St. Faustina and St. Catherine of Siena, this substitution entailed abandonment. If she left everything to Jesus, it would allow Jesus to act in her, to the point that He substituted Himself for her. She realized as she grew in the spiritual life that that was the goal. What was the fruit of this substitution of Christ? Deeper and deeper as she went, our Lord embedded this truth in her mind and inner heart. She marvelled at the profundity of this union, for she witnessed the miracle of Jesus taking over her person and, as it were, mystically acting in her. Blessed Dina's ego is annihilated, only Christ remains!

> On 2 November, the monthly retreat day, I united in spirit with the community, in my solitude, and this is what I wrote: My ideal: **The substitution of Jesus for myself.** We are no longer two people, Jesus and I; we are just one: Jesus alone. He uses my faculties, my body. It is he who thinks, wills, prays, looks, walks, writes, teaches, in a word : who lives. And I am very small in the middle of his glowing Heart, so small that only he can see me there. I have abandoned everything to him, now nothing concerns me. My sole task is to contemplate him and to say to him continually : Jesus, I love you, I love you, I love you! It is the heavenly canticle, my eternity has begun! How happy I am![19]

"Jesus and I; we are just one: Jesus alone. He uses my faculties, my body. It is he... in a word: who lives." Since only Christ remains, it leads to the practice of abandonment of past, present, and future; of all to Jesus:

> Until 2 November, Jesus increased his inspirations so as to teach me the perfect practice of genuine self-abandonment; I thought I had understood this sublime word ; no, I had not fathomed its delightful depths. Abandonment of the past, of the present and of the future, of joy, pain, desire, thought, word and action, abandonment of everything to his mercy and his good will : that is what Our Lord wanted from me. Complete abandonment which, as a result, brought freedom from sensitivity and all anxiety.[20]

---

[18] Bl. Dina Bélanger, *Autobiography of Blessed Dina Bélanger* (Québec City: Les Religieuses de Jésus-Marie, 1997), 156.
[19] Ibid.
[20] Ibid.

Blessed Dina Bélanger tells us how this abandonment is lived in relation to the past, future, and present. This is a valuable teaching for most of us, as what troubles us is often the past and the future, and sometimes the present as well. Regarding the past, she would let Jesus' merits cover up the past failings; as to the future, she would allow Jesus' merits in His providence to provide and prepare for the future; and even as to the present, she would allow Jesus' merits to complete and repair what was lacking in her actions in the present. Her only concern was to keep her eyes on Jesus.[21] As long as her eyes were fixed on Jesus, Jesus could act in her. This was her secret: "Obedience was my rule of total perfection."

> I tried to offer Jesus the entire day, that is, not refusing him and working only for him. I wanted my life to be an unbroken prayer, by remaining continually united to him in my prayer, my work and my rest. In the month of November, this life of union with my perfect Model became the subject of my particular examen. What joy I felt when I realized that the divine Hand was leading me in this direction! It responded to all my aspirations.[22]

We gain a second precious learning from a temptation that constituted the principal obstacle to this substitution, and therefore to all spiritual life. On this occasion, the thought came to her, "You are not generous or mortified enough." Being the saintly and generous person she was, she immediately began to examine herself in this regard and acknowledged her fault and began to make resolutions to remedy this. But then, as if by divine intuition, she stopped and asked herself where this thought came from. She realized immediately that, even though the thought itself was a good thought, it came from the devil.

What was the devil's strategy? Scripture tells us that the devil acts as an angel of light, and here, employing a good thought, his strategy was to make her reflect back upon herself, to focus on herself. In focusing on herself, she would no longer be able to keep her eyes on Jesus and be united to Him, the consequence of which is that she was not allowing Jesus to act in her. There would be no substitution of Christ— this is how vital and central self-forgetfulness is to a Christian. Perhaps the greatest weakness of Christians is they magnify their daily happenings and troubles, instead of

---

[21] Ibid., 222.
[22] Ibid., 120-121.

entrusting them to the Lord and "minimizing" them, not making them mountains, but restoring them to their proper size as mole hills.

Blessed Dina Bélanger wanted to tell the whole world about the joy of abandonment.[23] For her, it was a waste of time to look at herself.[24] Allowing Jesus to act in her through the substitution of Christ enabled Christ to do great things in her: "One single act of love offered by Him to the Father could save millions of worlds."[25] Herein we see the secret of the power of the saints.

An example from Scripture involving St. Peter illustrates this point further. We recall the example of Jesus, after praying by Himself, walked on water towards the apostles, who were in a boat. After they overcame the initial fright with the comforting words of Jesus, Peter asked, "Lord, if it is you, bid me come to you on the water?" (Mt 14:28). Jesus said, "Come." Lo and behold, a mere man walked on water! We all know what followed next, Peter began to sink into the water. Why did this happen? Peter began to fail because he took his eyes off Jesus. As long as his eyes were on Jesus, Peter could "walk on water," and Peter could guide Christ's Church. Instead, "when he saw the wind, he was afraid" (Mt 14:30). When he took his eyes off Jesus, like most do, he focused on the storm, and implicitly, on his weakness as man, that is, on himself. When we run into conflicts, we tend to focus on the enormity of the crisis and also look at our past failures and become discouraged at the thought that "it's happening again." We end up focusing on ourselves again, instead of setting our eyes on the Lord.

Blessed Dina Bélanger teaches us, among other things, two great truths. First, that the goal of the spiritual life is the "the substitution of Christ." Through Baptism, we have been incorporated to Christ objectively, but the subjective configuration must continue throughout our lives, primarily through the Eucharist, till we become fully Christ. Second, congruent with St. Catherine of Siena's teaching of the second foundation stone, her subjective living of this objective grace of substitution by Christ entails her taking her eyes off herself and keeping her eyes on Jesus her Spouse in great abandonment.

---

[23] Ibid., 188.
[24] Ibid., 214.
[25] Ibid., 161.

45

## C. The "Mystical Incarnation" of Venerable Concepción Cabrera de Armida

Blessed Dina Bélanger's autobiography has introduced us to a transforming union that leads to a "Substitution of Christ." We find in the doctrine of another mystic a more explicit development of this substitution of Christ. The French Dominican theologian, Fr. Marie-Michel Philipon, elaborates upon this transformation in the thought of Venerable Concepción Cabrera de Armida, familiarly known as "Conchita." Conchita was unique, a lay woman and mother, living through the troubled times of persecution against the Church in Mexico and much personal suffering (early death of her husband and children, as well as illness), who was personally led to the heights of spiritual life. Instructed by Jesus, her writings have been a fount of mystical insights and have given rise to new religious communities.[26]

Her own saintly spiritual director and sometimes retreat master, Luis Martinez, then Archbishop of Mexico City, offers insight into this transformation. In his noted work, *The Sanctifier*, he writes of this transforming union as a "mystical incarnation," distantly analogous to Christ's Incarnation. It is "like a mystical prolongation" of Christ's life:

> This life of Jesus in souls is like a mystical prolongation of his mortal life. It is like a mystical incarnation in souls by which he renews, mystically also, the mysteries of his life— now those of his infancy, sometimes those of his public life, at times those of his passion and again, those of his Eucharistic life— according to the profound and loving designs of God in his saints.[27]

This mystical incarnation, analogous to the Incarnation of Christ in His mother's womb, is a spiritual incarnation in each of Christ's disciples:

> This mystical incarnation in souls is produced in the image and likeness of the divine Incarnation of the Word in the immaculate bosom of Mary. The transforming union is the work of the Holy Spirit, who brings to souls the divine fecundity of the Father. But in this mystic work, as in the divine Incarnation, the Holy Spirit requires the cooperation of the

---

[26] Pope John Paul II declared her venerable on December 20, 1999. A Mexican mystic, writer, and foundress, her writings were widely distributed and inspired the establishment of the five apostolates of the "Works of the Cross" in Mexico that continue today.

[27] Luis M. Martinez, 40.

creature; the soul overshadowed by the Holy Spirit, guided and moved and made fruitful, so to say, by him, *forms Jesus in itself*.... that soul can be called mystically mother of Jesus, as the Divine Master himself taught us with these words: Whoever does the will of my Father in heaven, he is my brother and sister and mother (Mt 12:50).... In the spiritual life, in the generation of the Word in us, we are mothers...[28] (emphasis mine)

Let us look at the "mystical incarnation" in three steps: uniqueness of this transforming union, the stages of spiritual development of Venerable de Armida, and finally the elements constitutive of this union. It is a mystical Incarnation, in which the soul is conformed in love to the crucified Christ, and with Him offers the crucified Christ to the Father for the redemption of the world.

First, Philipon identifies the unique aspect of Conchita's spirituality that begins with God as love. He notes that "Our spiritual life is linked to our concept of God. If metaphysics is the moral foundation, dogma governs the mystical. The mystery of the Trinity and the Incarnation of the Word animate Christian spirituality."[29] He notes that different saints have different "concepts of God": "St. Augustine's God is the 'Supreme Good' drawing all things to Himself. St. Thomas Aquinas's God is the God of Sinai: 'I am who I am.' St. Thérèse of Lisieux's God is 'Merciful Love.' Conchita's God is 'Crucified Love' which brings us to 'Infinite Love.'"[30] Conchita received an intuition and mysteriously understood the essence of God. She received a supernatural movement, like "a light which, like a flash of lightning, that illumined the hiddenmost and innermost depths of her spirit.... I saw how God is Love. Not only does He possess love, but He is Love itself, eternal Love, uncreated Love, infinite Love..."[31]

Second, Philipon notes the stages of her spiritual development. He notes first the three classical stages of ascent to God in love according to St. Thomas Aquinas: purgation, virtues, Trinitarian communion. The primary concern of beginners is "to avoid sin and imperfections, to purge away sins of the past and to be free of them in the future," thus the first effect of love

---

[28] Ibid., 41.
[29] Marie-Michel Philipon, *Conchita: A Mother's Spiritual Diary* (Society of St. Paul, trans. 1978, repr. 2014), 137.
[30] Ibid.
[31] Ibid.

is to remove obstacles. In the second stage, for those making progress, the indispensable means of union is love applied above all to the practice of virtues. And finally, "For the perfect, love is based on the end, enjoyment of the Three Divine Persons, and consummation in the unity of the Trinity."[32]

Then, he makes a distinction in the variety of forms of transforming union, of which Venerable de Armida's is a new type: "There is not one sole form of transforming union, but a thousand varieties, or rather an infinity of possible realizations, according to the creative freedom of the Spirit of God and various needs, according to the epochs of the Mystical Body of Christ."[33] Finally, in Conchita's own spiritual life, we find the following steps: "As an adolescent, she rapidly took the first steps of the spiritual life. At the age of nineteen, after her brother Manuel's death, she resolutely lived first as a young girl, then as a married woman, firmly without sin and in an ever and ever more heroic ascent toward God."[34]

Then the advanced stages were attained: at the age of 32, there were the spiritual betrothals (Jan. 23, 1894), three years later, the spiritual marriage (Feb. 9, 1897), that was surpassed by the mystical incarnation (March 25, 1906). He describes this spiritual marriage as a higher form of transforming union, of which there are an infinite number of possible union stages, as well as, despite its supreme rarity, "a grace of transformation in Christ received in germ from baptism and on."[35]

Let us analyze this mystical incarnation in more detail. The description comes from the very words of Venerable de Armida in her *Diary*. This particular form of transforming union is an assimilation specifically to the crucified Christ. The Incarnate Word takes possession most intimately of the heart of the creature, communicating life that assimilates by way of immolation:

> Jesus becomes flesh, grows and lives in the soul, not in a material sense but through sanctifying grace, which is unitive and transformative.... The soul which receives it feels, more or less periodically, the stages of the life

---

[32] St. Thomas Aquinas, III *Sent.* 29. 8. 1.
[33] Marie-Michel Philipon, *Conchita: A Mother's Spiritual Diary*, 156.
[34] Ibid., 156-157.
[35] Ibid., 157.

of Jesus in it. These stages are ever marked by sufferings, calumnies and humiliations, in sacrifice and in expiation as it was the life of your Jesus on earth.[36]

We note that this is a real, though mystical, re-living of Jesus' life, and especially "ever marked by suffering, calumnies and humiliations." It is the work of the Holy Spirit, who takes over in the soul to give the "physiognomy of Jesus." This configuration to Jesus leads to the identification of her will to Jesus' will and a simplifying of itself to allow the most perfect likeness possible. The mystical incarnation is "nothing other than a most powerful grace of transformation which simplifies and unites to Jesus by purity and by immolation...." It is this likeness to Jesus and nothing else that makes her powerful before the Father:

> Because of this likeness of the soul to the Incarnate Word, the eternal Father finds pleasure in it, and the role of Priest and Victim which Jesus had on earth is communicated to it, in order that it obtains graces from heaven for the whole world. That is why, the more a soul is like Me [Jesus], the more the Eternal Father hears it, not due to its worth but due to its likeness and its union with Me and in virtue of My merits which constitute what counts for obtaining graces. (*Diary*, Dec. 11, 1913).[37]

We note here especially that "the role of Priest and Victim which Jesus had on earth is communicated to it." This dual role applies to all baptized being conformed to Christ, but it is especially so for the ministerial priest, who as *alter Christus*, is called to be "priest and victim."

What then is the principal act of such a new "priest and victim?" It is an offering made up, "not in two acts but in one and the same indivisible initiative, the oblation of Christ to His Father, and, in union with Him, through Him and in Him, the total oblation of our own life for the salvation of the world and for the greatest glory of the Trinity."[38] The principal movement consists of the offering of the Son to the Father, united with our personal unreserved oblation that is constantly renewed. Christ alone was on the cross on Calvary, but now He offers Himself with the whole Church.

---

[36] Ibid., 157.
[37] Ibid., 158.
[38] Ibid., 158-159.

The world needs this "spiritual shock" for its conversion: "In fact, the Father wishes that I Myself [Jesus], united to your soul as victim, have you sacrifice Me and immolate Me with the same love of the Father on behalf of a world which has need of this spiritual shock and of a grace of this nature in order to be converted." It is only Christ's sacrifice in the creature that allows the vast horizon of Redemption to take place, as it did in the "obscure and silent existence of the Mother of God, in the evening of her life, by application of the merits of Christ, for the benefit of the nascent Church...."[39] This is the greatest secret that our Lord also taught Blessed Dina Bélanger.

> The soul thus crucified is called to live, not in the narrow outlooks of its daily routine, but in union with Christ and under the vast horizons of the Redemption of the world.... Although, of itself it is so insignificant, it acquires an infinite value for the glorification of God and the salvation of men due to its union with the very Person of the Incarnate Word, Priest and Host... It is the secret of the boundless fecundity of the communion of saints.[40]

### 3. Friendship with Christ

The path to the Father is through Jesus Christ. Joseph Ratzinger teaches that this is possible because Jesus is in constant absorption and union with the Father in prayer:

> A Jesus who was not continuously absorbed in the Father and was not in continuous intimate communication with him would be a completely different being from the Jesus of the Bible, the real Jesus of history. Prayer was the center out of which he lived, and it was prayer that showed him how to understand God, the world, and men. To follow Jesus means looking at the world with the eyes of God and living accordingly.[41]

Consequently, to know the Father, we must have friendship (union) with Christ. The substitution of Christ is now completed with its interior heart: the "think of me" of St. Catherine of Siena's friendship with Christ. The substitution of Christ takes place, both by the objective transformation through the sacraments, especially of Baptism and the Eucharist, and by the

---

[39] Ibid., 159-160.
[40] Concepción Cabrera de Armida, quoted in Marie-Michel Philipon, *Conchita*, 137.
[41] Joseph Ratzinger, *The God of Jesus Christ*, 33-34.

subjective union or friendship with Christ; it is not merely an ontological linking, but also the union of hearts, so to speak. Most books on spirituality presuppose friendship with Christ, few actually discuss it explicitly, though the lives of saints exemplify this friendship with Christ.

## A. Robert Hugh Benson's *Friendship with Christ*

Robert Hugh Benson's *Friendship with Christ* depicts the fundamental Christian failing. He describes Christians who are so faithful in many ways but never find the core of Christianity, "friendship with Christ."

> They pray, they frequent the sacraments, they do their utmost to fulfill the Christian precepts; and when all is done, they find themselves solitary…. They adore Christ as God, they feed on him in Communion, cleanse themselves in his precious blood, look to the time when they shall see him as their judge; yet of that intimate knowledge of and companionship with him in which the divine friendship consists, they have experienced little or nothing.[42]

Clearly, fidelity to the moral norms and to one's duties in one's state of life is the indispensable first step in Christian life. But that foundation is for the sake of fostering the goal of friendship and union with Christ. Christ created us in order to give Himself to us and for us to give ourselves to Him— that is, for a mystical marriage. The longing of the Sacred Heart is that "he should be admitted, not merely to the throne of the heart or to the tribunal of conscience, but to that inner secret chamber of the soul where a man is most himself, and therefore most utterly alone."[43] Benson identifies the secret of the saints: companionship of Christ.

> Now, the consciousness of this friendship of Jesus Christ is the very secret of the saints…. We keep the commandments that we may enter into life; we avoid the sin that we may escape hell; we fight against worldliness that we may keep the respect of the world. But no man can advance three paces on the road of perfection unless Jesus Christ walks beside him.[44]

---

[42] Robert Hugh Benson, *Friendship with Christ: Exploring the Humanity of Jesus Christ* (Princeton, NJ: Scepter, 2001), 17-18.
[43] Ibid., 18.
[44] Ibid., 20.

Benson highlights the great chasm between ordinary religious dutifulness or common sense and this friendship with Christ that scales mountains and produces lovers as well as giants of history:

> Common sense never yet drove a man mad; it is common sense that is thought to characterize sanity; and common sense, therefore, has never scaled mountains, much less has it cast them into the sea. But it is the maddening joy of the conscious companionship of Jesus Christ that has produced the lovers, and therefore, the giants, of history. It is the developing friendship of Jesus Christ and the passion that has inspired those lives, which the world in its duller moods calls unnatural, and the Church, in all her moods, supernatural.[45]

The background to all of this is Jesus' great desire for friendship with us: more than anything else, Jesus delights to be among men.

> Catholics, then, above all others, are prone— through their very knowledge of the mysteries of faith, through their very apprehension of Jesus Christ as their God, their high priest, their victim, their prophet and their King— to forget that his delights are to be with the sons of men more than to rule the Seraphim, that, while his majesty held him on the throne of his Father, his love brought him down on pilgrimage that he might transform his servants into his friends.[46]

The gift that God gives is His very Self. This is the truth that the British medieval mystic Juliana of Norwich reveals. In a remarkable insight, she teaches that God makes no distinction in His love for the soul of Christ and for us.

> I saw no difference between God and our substance, but saw it as if it were all God. And yet my understanding accepted the fact that our substance is in God; that is to say, that God is God and our substance is a creature in God. For the almighty truth of the Trinity is our Father, for he made us and preserves us in himself; the deep wisdom of the Trinity is our mother, in whom we are enclosed; the lofty goodness of the Trinity is our Lord, and in him we are enclosed and he in us.[47]

---

[45] Ibid.
[46] Ibid., 17.
[47] Juliana of Norwich, *Revelations of Divine Love* (New York: Image Books, 1977), chapter 54, 179-180.

In this gift, she emphasizes the incorporation into Christ mentioned above: God dwells in us and we in God.

> And because of the great, endless love that God has for all mankind, he makes no distinction in love between the blessed soul of Christ and the least of the souls that will be saved.... We ought to rejoice greatly that God dwells in our soul, and much more greatly, that our soul dwells in God. Our soul is made to be God's dwelling place, and the dwelling place of our souls is God, who is uncreated. It is a lofty understanding inwardly to see and to know that God, who is our maker, dwells in our soul, and it is still loftier and greater understanding inwardly to see and to know that our soul, which is created, dwells in God's substance. From this substance, we are what we are, by God. [48]

For our part, under the glow of that unconditional love of God, there can only be one response: love of God, *love-in-response* (von Balthasar). Archbishop Fulton Sheen in one of his talks spoke of three levels of motivation in our lives: coercion, duty, and love. Applied to the example of defending one's country, one can be drafted into the army against one's will, that is, coercion; or one can feel the bonds of duty, which drive one to defend one's country or the country's interest, which is a very admirable trait; but by far the best is love, which includes duty, but goes to the point of even dying for one's beloved country and loved ones. We can survey all that God has done for us. He has held nothing back and could justifiably ask, "Is there anything that I could have done that I have not done for you?"

It is clear that God wants our love, our friendship. Scripture everywhere reveals this desire of Christ, as in Jesus' words about standing and knocking at the doors of our hearts to gain entrance ("I stand at your doors and knock," Rev 3:20), or His words to His apostles at the Last Supper, "but I have called you friends" (Jn 15:15), or His promise of continual presence, "where two or three are gathered in my name, there am I in the midst of them" (Mt 18:20); "Behold, I am with you all days" (Mt 28:20).

And most especially Christ's reproach to the world, not that the lost creature ran away from Him, but that the friend "came into his own home,

---

[48] Ibid., 179.

and that his own people received him not" (Jn 1:11).[49] St. Peter Chrysologus teaches that God wishes to be loved, not feared: "I appeal to you by the mercy of God. This appeal is made by Paul, or rather, it is made by God through Paul, because of God's desire to be loved rather than feared, to be a father rather than a Lord. God appeals to us in his mercy to avoid having to punish us in his severity."[50]

## B. Francisca Javiera del Valle's Teaching

In sum, how should we approach the spiritual life? Francisca Javiera del Valle, a laywoman and mystic in Spain, wrote in her book, *About the Holy Spirit*, that there are many good things one can ask of God. But given the overwhelming and unconditional love of God, we should turn from focusing on the gifts we receive to focus on the Giver. Most Christians, when they pray, are likely to be absorbed in asking God for favours. Del Valle teaches that the only thing we should ask for is for the grace to love Him in return:

> For to seek God for what he gives us, or for the sweetness we feel when we are with him, is a sure way of never tasting or feeling those very sweetnesses and consolations that we are seeking. Besides, it is a great obstacle and impediment to achieving union with God....
>
> We must seek, serve, and love God unselfishly, not in order to be virtuous nor to acquire holiness or grace or even heaven itself nor for the happiness of possessing him, but solely for the sake of loving him. And when he offers us graces and gifts, we should tell him that the only gift we want is the gift of love, in order to love him. If he says to us: "Ask me for anything you like," we should ask for nothing except love and more love, in order to love him and to love him more. This is the greatest thing we can ask for or desire, because he is the only thing worth loving or desiring.[51]

She teaches that Jesus is not loved, the greatest tragedy that is unrequited love— God is not loved! Against this background, the only thing we ought

---

[49] Robert Hugh Benson, *Friendship with Christ*, 20.
[50] St. Peter Chrysologus, *Sermo 108*: PL 52, 499-500; *Liturgy of the Hours*, vol. 2 (New York: Catholic Book Publ., 1976), Tuesday of Fourth Week of Easter, OOR, 770-771.
[51] Francisca Javiera del Valle, *About the Holy Spirit* (New York: Scepter Press, 1998; Spanish orig. *Decenario del Espiritu Santo*, 1932), 62.

to ask for is the grace to love Him in return. Nothing else really matters, for He in His unfailing love for us, will always look after our needs: *"My daughter, think of Me; if you will do this, I shall immediately think of you."*

## C. Mother Teresa's Key Message to Her Sisters

Mother Teresa of Calcutta, in what is perhaps her most important letter to her Sisters, when she revealed her secret about Jesus' personal call for her to go to the streets of Calcutta, points to the all-important personal meeting with Jesus, which is likely the greatest need of our people today:

> Jesus wants me to tell you again how much love He has for each one of you – beyond all you can imagine. I worry some of you still have not really met Jesus – one to one – you and Jesus alone. We may spend time in chapel – but have you seen with the eyes of your soul how He looks at you with love? Do you really know the living Jesus – not from books but from being with Him in your heart? Have you heard the loving words He speaks to you?

> Ask for the grace, He is longing to give it. Never give up this daily intimate contact with Jesus as the real living person – not just the idea.

> How can we last even one day without hearing Jesus say, "I love you" – impossible. Our soul needs that as much as the body needs to breathe the air. If not, prayer is dead – meditation only thinking. Jesus wants you each to hear Him – speaking in the silence of your heart.[52]

Mother Teresa points to this one to one meeting of Jesus in the hearts of the Sisters, to hear His "I love you," so that they can persevere and love the poor. She counsels them never to lose this intimate contact through the giving up of prayer.

## D. St. Teresa of Jesus' Friendship

Let us leave the last word to St. Teresa of Jesus, famous for her personal love for Jesus. Of her works, though *Interior Castle* treats of the famous interior journey within, it is *The Way of Perfection* that is regarded by her spiritual children as the "Teresian Gospel." This work is not viewed so

---

[52] Mother Teresa, A letter to the Missionaries of Charity, Easter 1993, quoted in Joseph Langford, *Mother Teresa's Secret Fire: The Encounter that Changed her Life and How it can Transform your own* (Huntington, IN: Our Sunday Visitor, 2008), 54-55.

much as the greatest and most intimate work but, for various reasons, as the work that "gives us not only a message but a living person, Our Holy Mother."[53] But the entire message of the work is that Teresa, this "Holy Mother," is all about Christ.

> This is the very heart and soul of the book. Christ is the centre: He is the All. This is the message Our Holy Mother is giving us. It is the message of the 42 chapters: Christ is our Friend, our only Friend…. *"The chief point is that we should resolutely give Him our heart for His own and should empty it of everything else, that He may take out or put in whatever He pleases as if it were His own property. This is the condition He makes, and He is right in doing so: do not let us refuse it Him"* (W 28:12).[54]

St. Teresa of Jesus has many titles for Jesus, but the one that predominated is Jesus under the aspect of the "only friend." She felt the presence of Jesus within her throughout her life. Perhaps, what captures something deep and personal of St. Teresa of Jesus for Jesus, and Jesus for her, is this famous incident. On one occasion, she met a man climbing a stairway in her convent and who asked her who she was, to which she replied, "I am Teresa of Jesus." When St. Teresa asked Him who He was, His reply was "I am Jesus of Teresa." This is the love we are called to imitate. A Carmelite commentator makes a fine definition: "Friendship is a very Teresian approach to prayer."[55] After her so-called conversion, she changed from her religious name to Teresa of Jesus, dedicating her all to Him.

---

[53] Otilio Rodríguez, *The Teresian Gospel* (printed in Darlington Carmel, 1993), 35.
[54] Ibid.
[55] Ibid., 38.

# CHAPTER 3

## *DIVINE INDWELLING & SPIRITUAL MARRIAGE*

*(The Personal Divine Love that Unites)*

O most holy humanity, who but God alone can know how much you suffered during those three hours you were hanging on the Cross! Forgetting the most painful state to which men reduced you, taking no account of your great sufferings, and never ceasing to pray and implore your heavenly Father to grant you the favour you were asking for the whole human race, you wanted to unite them all and make of them one body and soul.... You excused them, saying: "Father, forgive them, for they know not what they do," and you continued discussing and negotiating their eternal happiness! You prayed that your torments might be prolonged. You arranged that the holy and divine Spirit be sent to us, to teach, direct, and govern us, because without the Holy Spirit man cannot be raised to the dignity to which you wish to raise him.... What he wants to obtain for us was that gift above all other gifts; but before being granted it, he has to go through suffering above all other sufferings. Consider, then, the price Christ had to pay to obtain the Holy Spirit for us from God! He wanted to gather us all together in him, which means the establishment of his holy Church, and this could not subsist without the Holy Spirit. So He prolonged his life, which as God he could do, until he obtained the Holy Spirit for us from the Father.[1] (Francisca J. del Valle)

Having examined the gift of the Father's Mercy in the sending of His Son, we now proceed to the sending of the Holy Spirit that accomplishes all— He is the Gift from which all other gifts (graces) flow. By virtue of the Son's sacrifice, the Holy Spirit, who is the Love that unites the Father and the Son, is released from Christ's heart and sent to dwell within hearts, fulfilling the Old Testament prophecies. It is the *Holy Spirit's indwelling*, analogous to His overshadowing of Mary to bring about the Incarnation, that causes the substitution of Christ and the friendship with Christ. Thus, analogous to marriage in which "two become one flesh," the union of Christ and the soul produces both one being (substitution of Christ, becoming the Christ's Body) and one heart (friendship, spiritual marriage, becoming Christ's Bride).

---

[1] Francisca Javiera del Valle, *About the Holy Spirit*, 39-41.

## 1. The Great Discovery of St. Augustine

Let us allow the marvelous discovery of St. Augustine of Hippo to introduce the divine indwelling of the Holy Spirit and His role of union within us. St. Augustine recounted in his autobiography, *Confessions*, that his conversion was accomplished through a great discovery, that of interiority: the presence of the indwelling of the Blessed Trinity within his soul. This discovery explains why St. Augustine is known not only as "Doctor of Grace," but also as "Doctor of Love" and "Doctor of Interiority." Augustine's theology is foundational for the entire Western Church. Not only is he one of the four Western doctors of the Latin Church, she also mainly follows the theological track of this great doctor of the Church. His prodigious output, accomplished primarily while he was burdened with the tremendous responsibilities as bishop of Hippo and the concerns of the African Church, surpasses the theological output of all the other Church Fathers of the West combined.

The title of "Doctor of Interiority" has to do, following years of turmoil, with a discovery during his conversion. St. Augustine's difficult journey began with a year of inactivity at the age of sixteen when his parents could not afford to send him to school. This led to a state of attachments to created pleasures, as he relates: "The briars of lust grew over my head and there was no one to root them out."[2] This began a long period of estrangement from God and family, escaping from his family in his native Tagaste to go to Carthage, to Rome, and then to Milan, and finally back to Tagaste from Rome's port, *Ostia Antica*. In that early period, in 373 A.D., after reading Cicero's *Hortensius*, a strong yearning for true wisdom was awakened in him, a search that led him to the Manicheans and later, a second sect, living with two different women, and many years of agonizing search and inner turmoil. While it appears that it was primarily the prayers and tears of his mother, St. Monica, that obtained the grace for his conversion, the figure and example of the great St. Ambrose in Milan also played a key role. After his conversion, Augustine synthesized in his famous *Confessions* this experience of discovering that God had been calling out to him all those years. The key to his discovery is what he described a few

---

[2] Augustine of Hippo, *Confessions* II.3.6, quoted in Agostino Trapè, *St. Augustine: Man, Pastor, Mystic* (New York: Catholic Book Publishing Co., 1986), 38.

paragraphs before his famous text, where he tells his readers that he entered the depth of his soul, "Urged to reflect upon myself, I entered under your guidance into the inmost depth of my soul. I was able to do so because you were my helper. On entering into myself I saw, as it were with the eye of the soul, what was beyond the eye of the soul, beyond my spirit: your immutable light...."[3]

Here is the text of Augustine's discovery that many are familiar with:

> Late have I loved you, O Beauty ever ancient, ever new, late have I loved you! You were within me, but I was outside, and it was there that I searched for you. In my unloveliness I plunged into the lovely things which you created. You were with me, but I was not with you. Created things kept me from you; yet if they had not been in you they would not have been at all. You called, you shouted, and you broke through my deafness. You flashed, you shone, and you dispelled my blindness. You breathed your fragrance on me; I drew in breath and now I pant for you. I have tasted you, now I hunger and thirst for more. You touched me, and I burned for your peace.[4]

Once he made the critical step of entering the depths of his heart, of interiority, Augustine made the great discovery of the presence and indwelling of God the Blessed Trinity within him. It took him so long to find Him because he was caught up with the activity and things of life and not attentive to this indwelling presence, whose presence in his soul surpassed the dignity and value and beauty of all the universe with its myriad of galaxies.

The first aspect of the great discovery of Augustine was that God was not far away in heaven, nor that he had to look for Him outside himself, but that, to find and encounter Him, he had only to enter the depths of his heart. Augustine then synthesized this discovery of the path to finding God thus: *"ad interior, ad superior"*— "God within, and above." To find God, I first turn to find the immanent God in my innermost being, then humble

---

[3] Augustine, *Confessions*, Bk. 10, Ch. 27. A contemporary and critical translation can be found in *The Confessions*, from the series, *The Works of St. Augustine: A Translation for the 21st Century* (New York: New City Press, 1997), vol. I, 262. An outstanding critical edition in French-Latin is *Les Confessions*, in the series *Oeuvres de Saint Augustin* (France: Études Augustiniennes, 1980).
[4] Ibid.

myself to find the God who is so transcendent to me, who infinitely surpasses me. God is "more inward than my innermost and higher than my uppermost" ("*interior intimo meo et superior summo meo*").[5] *Interior intimo meo* can be more freely rendered as God being "closer to me than I am to myself." This points to another discovery.

The second aspect of Augustine's great discovery was that God was a Lover and a Spouse and that he lived in a love story. It was not just an ontological discovery— it was, above all, a deeply personal discovery of love: not "Late have I met you" but "Late have I loved you." This discovery leaves Augustine breathless and overwhelmed, like a beloved wounded by the love of the Lover: "You breathed your fragrance on me; I drew in breath and now I pant for you. I have tasted you, now I hunger and thirst for more. You touched me, and I burned for your peace." Augustine has been wounded by divine love. He also discovers the "height and depth" of God in this discovery made possible through entering the depths of his soul.

With this introduction of Augustine's great discovery, let us proceed to these two aspects in the following two sections: the profundity of the indwelling of the Holy Spirit; and the Holy Spirit, as personal love within the Trinity, accomplishing divine espousals with the

## 2. Theological Foundation and Mystical Illustrations of the Divine Indwelling

Man was not just created in God's image and likeness through having an intellect and free will, nor simply to go to heaven. He was created to become the temple or dwelling place of the Holy Trinity Itself, to attain therein an ineffable and glorious union.

### A. Divine Indwelling as Fulfillment of Creation and the Old Testament

Charles Cardinal Journet, in his Thomistic cosmic vision, described three ascending levels of creation: nature, man, and grace. This vision enables us to see the infinite distance between creation and the grace, both uncreated and created. First, nature— creation at the natural level— is already

---

[5] *Confessions* 3.6.11.

wonderful, mirroring something of God's beauty and order. Second, as great as nature is, it is nothing compared to man, who is made in the image of God Himself; in fact, all creation is made for man.[6] The book of Genesis describes this priority in the seven days of creation. The first three days describe the creation of the universe as a dwelling place, the second three days describe the ornamenting and populating of the cosmos. Inscribed by the author of Genesis (Gen 1) in this creation narrative is a pyramid structure, an ascending order in which the earlier elements are created for the sake of later elements. Man was created at the end of the sixth day, and thus all creation is made for his sake. And man, created on the sixth day, was created for the seventh day, for God.

## Fulfillment of First Creation in Grace

Third, beyond the first two levels of nature and man, there is the level of grace. According to Paul, renewal by grace constitutes a "new creation." That is, there are two "creations," the first creation of man at the level of nature was for the sake of the second creation of grace, a supernatural creation. Until Christ's coming, the first creation awaited its fulfillment in the second, for man was made for God and had a capacity for God— he is a "God-bearer." So, in the Thomistic vision, while man, made in the image and likeness of God, towers above creation, the level of nature, the new creation through Baptism makes man God-like (divinization, *theosis*). We could loosely apply Scripture's words, "For as the heavens are higher than the earth, so are my ways higher than your ways" (Isa 55:9), to indicate how the new creation infinitely surpasses natural creation.

## Fulfillment of Marriage

We also find a nuptial analogue on the cross in this second creation by grace. As the Church Fathers explained, the second creation was

---

[6] Charles Journet, *The Meaning of Grace* (Princeton, NJ: Scepter Publs., 1960), Ch. 1, 15-28. Cardinal Journet opens up to us something of the tremendous legacy of St. Thomas Aquinas, whose *Summa Theologiae* is built upon a creation structure in three "Parts": Creator, Creation, and Redeemer (for English translation, see *Summa Theologica of St. Thomas Aquinas*, the English Dominican Province (Westminster, MD: Christian Classics, 1946 & 1947). Those wishing to access St. Thomas Aquinas without having recourse to his primary texts might be well served in going to some of his well-known modern interpreters, such as Charles Journet and Reginald Garrigou-Lagrange, whose works are still general enough to be accessible to the average believer. There are several contemporary Thomistic schools today.

accomplished through the sacrifice on Calvary, when water and blood, representing the waters of Baptism and the blood of the Eucharist or all the Sacraments, flowed from the side of Christ, giving birth to the Church and its individual members, the new creation described by Paul.[7] There is a nuptial parallel here. As Eve, the spouse of Adam, was taken from Adam's side when he was asleep, the Church, the bride of Christ, was born from the side of Christ, the second Adam, as He was asleep in death. What takes place in each newly baptized in this new creation is a mutual embrace: the more important of the two is that Christ "embraces" us, what Paul refers to as the incorporation to Christ into His Mystical Body (Church); and Christ, as it were, is "embraced" by each baptized, or what we normally refer to as the indwelling of the Blessed Trinity within us, the divine indwelling.

A helpful image might be to see this as analogous to a mutual embrace between husband and wife: Christ holding us and we holding Christ, we in Christ and Christ in us. In this way, creation has finally attained its ultimate fulfillment. Thus we say theologically that creation was made for the sake of Redemption, and more globally, the universe was made for man, and man was made for union with God.

## Fulfillment of Jerusalem Temple and Ark of Covenant

Besides the fulfillment of creation (in a second creation) and of marriage between Adam and Eve (in the Church), we see another fulfillment taking place in Baptism. The Church Fathers understood that the entire Old Testament prefigured the coming of Christ in the New Testament; but Christ came to die in order to give the Holy Spirit to dwell within man. Thus, not only is the divine indwelling the fulfillment of creation as described earlier by Journet, it is also the fulfillment of the entire Old Testament. Examining this fulfillment of the Old Testament is worthwhile as it opens up deeper insights. The heart of the Old Testament faith was the Temple in Jerusalem, their entire Jewish religious life revolved around the Temple. But what made the Temple sacred was the presence of the Ark of the Covenant in the "Holy of holies" accompanied by the *Shekinah* cloud of glory, indicating some form of God's presence or dwelling. The Ark of the

---

[7] 2 Cor 5:17: "Therefore, if any one is in Christ, he is a new creation; the old has passed away, behold, the new has come"; Gal 6:15: "For neither circumcision counts for anything, nor uncircumcision, but a new creation."

Covenant itself contained the tablets of the Ten Commandments, as well as a piece of the manna from the Israelites' sojourn through the desert to the promised land, and the staff of Aaron.

Then Jesus Himself would state that He was the fulfillment of that Temple. When asked for a sign that confirmed the authenticity of His mission, Jesus said the fateful words pregnant with divine meaning: "Destroy this temple, and in three days I will raise it up." When the Jews objected that it took forty-six years to build the temple, Jesus corrected them, indicating that He Himself is the true temple: "But he spoke of the temple of his body" (Jn 2:18-22). The old Temple only prepared for and prefigured this new Temple. For the Ark of the Covenant only contained the word of God in stone and the manna from heaven for bodily nourishment. Christ instead is the Word of God in flesh, and He is the Bread of Life in sacrament (Jn 6:35), substantially present.

But Christ, the true Temple shares the Holy Spirit with us, so that, each baptized person, incorporated in Christ, has become a temple of the Holy Spirit: "Do you not know that you are God's temple and that God's Spirit dwells in you? If anyone destroys God's temple, God will destroy him. For God's temple is holy, and that temple you are" (1 Cor 3:16-17). By extension, each of us who are baptized have become the fulfillment of the Old Testament Temple, but unlike the provisional presence in Jerusalem, God truly dwells in us in a personal presence. For we have been created for this purpose, to be God's heaven on earth, and this privilege has been won for us through Christ's Paschal mystery.

It is important to understand how exalted is this second creation. The first creation participated in God's being in power, the level of nature; the second creation participates in the being of God Himself, being made "divine" by participation, that which the Eastern Church Fathers call "divinization" (*theosis*). In the Old Testament Temple, God dwelt in some preliminary way in the *Shekinah* cloud of glory; in Christ and in His people by Baptism, God comes to dwell in an "uncreated" or personal presence, causing as well the created effects of His indwelling, what theology calls sanctifying or habitual grace. Scripture alludes to this divinization and divine indwelling in a number of texts:

... that through these you ... become partakers of the divine nature (2 Pet 1:4);

If a man loves me, he will keep my word, and my Father will love him, and we will come to him and make our home with him (Jn 14:23);

Behold, I stand at the door and knock; if anyone hears my voice and opens the door, I will come in to him and eat with him, and he with me. (Rev 3:20)

The transcendence and profundity of this transformation in the Catholic understanding stands out even more clearly in contrast to the vision of Martin Luther. Luther's understanding of justification is described in theology as "forensic" or "alien" or "imputed" (*"iustitia imputata Christi"* or *"iustitia aliena"*) that is, as extrinsic to man.[8] According to the Catholic understanding, Luther, in his deep sense of his own continued sinfulness, confused his interior "sense of sinfulness" with sin itself (Catholic theology teaches this sense is an interior disorder that inclines us to sin, namely, concupiscence), and concluded that sin was not actually remitted by Baptism but "covered over" by Christ, as if by a cloak. Being covered with this "cloak" that is Christ, God the Father, looking upon His children, is pleased because He sees Christ or sees them through the lens of Christ. In this vision, Christ is, in effect, reduced to an external presence as a cloak or covering. This forensic or extrinsic justification does not capture the depth and richness of Paul's vision, which St. Augustine himself had perceived. It is the fulfillment of the Old Testament prophecies, where God Himself will give us a new heart.

---

[8] Some today argue that it was not Luther but Melanchton who taught a forensic or alien (extrinsic) justification: "Luther himself did not teach a doctrine of forensic justification in the strict sense. The concept of a forensic justification necessitates a deliberate and systematic distinction between justification and regeneration, a distinction which is not found in Luther's earlier works," in Alister E. McGrath, "Forerunners of the Reformation? A Critical Examination of the Evidence for Precursors of the Reformation Doctrines of Justification," Harvard Theological Review 75 (1982): 225. Whether or not this fits the facts, the reality is that the Sacred Congregation for the Doctrine of the Faith, under Cardinal Ratzinger, pointed out that "clarifications" are needed in the theology in the Joint Declaration on the Doctrine of Justification document (by the Lutheran World Federation and the Catholic Church), and prominent among them was the question of forensic justification, that is intrinsically linked to Luther's anthropology, the *simul justus et peccator* ("at once just and sinner") principle.

## B. Three Important Aspects of this Divine Indwelling

Francis Fernandez, in his book *In Conversation with God*, describes the importance of this divine indwelling. He further highlights three important aspects regarding living this divine indwelling. First, it is intended for everyone, it is the vocation of all baptized:

> The good fortune of having the presence of the Blessed Trinity in the soul is not meant only for extra-ordinary individuals, endowed with exceptional charisma or qualities, but for the ordinary Christian, who is called to sanctity in the midst of his or her professional activities and who wants to love God with all his being...[9]

This was highlighted in a dominant way during the Second Vatican Council, where one of the primary emphases in its most important document, *Lumen gentium,* was a chapter entitled, "The Universal Call to Holiness." Everyone is called to holiness, and all, whether priests, religious, or laity, are called to ascend the stages to union with God.

The second aspect points to the sublime grace of what we already possess in Baptism, which includes the divine indwelling, as mentioned. The grace we possess now through Baptism is no different in nature from that of heaven, for heaven has already begun with sanctifying grace: "This presence that theologians call *indwelling* differs only in quality from the blessedness of those who have already attained the state of eternal happiness in Heaven. Although it belongs to the three divine Persons, it is attributed to the Holy Spirit, for the work of sanctification is proper to love."[10] St. Thomas Aquinas presents this truth in the famous phrase, "Grace is the seed of glory." The present state derived from Baptism is already the beginning of the heavenly state, a difference not of essence, but of degree.[11]

The third aspect is the consequence of the first two aspects: we are called to converse intimately with each Person of the Trinity.

---

[9] Francis Fernandez, *In Conversation with God*, vol. 6, Feast days Jan-June, n. 40, "The Indwelling of the Holy Trinity in our Souls" (New York: Scepter, 1992), 256.
[10] Ibid.
[11] See Reginald Garrigou-Lagrange, *The Three Stages of the Interior Life: Prelude of Eternal Life*, vol. I (Rockford, IL: Tan, 2009 repr.), 33-37.

The whole of a Christian's supernatural life is directed towards this knowledge of and intimate conversation with the Trinity, who become eventually the *fruit and the end of our whole life*. It is for this end that we have been created and raised to the supernatural order: to know, to talk to and to love God the Father, God the Son and God the Holy Spirit, who dwell in the soul in grace. In this life the Christian comes to have an *experiential knowledge* of these three Divine Persons, a knowledge that, far from being something extraordinary, is appreciable within the normal paths of sanctity...[12]

This intimate interior dialogue is found in the lives of saints, which Trinitarian dynamic increases as they progress in union with Him. This reality is evident in the lives and teachings of saints like St. Thomas Aquinas, St. Teresa of Avila, St. John of the Cross, St. Elizabeth of the Trinity, and Blessed Dina Bélanger.

## C. Divine Indwelling as Explained by Saints

Many Catholic spiritual writers have described the exalted grandeur of this divine indwelling. We shall draw extensively from a Carmelite commentator, Iain Matthew. He quotes a sublime text from John of the Cross, that the Beloved "tells you now that you yourself are the abode wherein He dwells, and the closet and hiding place where He is hidden," for we are the "temple of the Living God."

> Oh, then, soul, most beautiful among all creatures, so anxious to know the dwelling place of your Beloved that you may go in quest of Him and be united to Him, now we are telling you that you yourself are His dwelling and His secret chamber and hiding place.... *Behold,* exclaims the Bridegroom, *the kingdom of God is within you.* [Luke 17:21] And His servant the apostle St. Paul declares: *You are the temple of the living God.* [2 Cor 6:16][13]

A saint tremendously influenced by St. John of the Cross, St. John Paul II, also always appeared to be "in God," no matter what he was doing. There was that deep interior quality or recollection to his person. One priest during his studies in Rome, after watching Pope John Paul II doing the

---

[12] Francis Fernandez, *In Conversation with God*, vol. 6, 258.
[13] St. John of the Cross, *Spiritual Canticle* 1.7. In *The Collected Works of St. John of the Cross*, eds. Kieran Kavanaugh & Otilio Rodriguez (Washington, DC: ICS Publications, 1979), 418.

ablutions during the Offertory at a Holy Mass celebrated at St. Peter's Basilica, commented, "He is a mystic even when he washes his hands at Mass." John Paul II, as is well known, was deeply influenced by the Carmelite spirituality of St. John of the Cross through an early friend, a tailor, Jan Tyranowski, and has himself written a doctoral thesis on "Faith according to St. John of the Cross." This thesis was directed by the famous Dominican, Reginald Garrigou-Lagrange, who himself understood the vital importance of this divine indwelling.[14] As a young man, Karol Wojtyla was enamoured with the contemplative spirituality of the Carmelite Order and wanted to become a contemplative Discalced friar. But, happily, his archbishop, Adam Cardinal Sapieha, would hear nothing of it and convinced him after three refusals to become a diocesan priest.[15] The future Pope John Paul II nevertheless retained that deeply contemplative spirit. The teaching of the divine indwelling or of God's presence within us through Baptism is very prominent in the teachings of St. John of the Cross.

> It should be known that the Word, the Son of God, together with the Father and the Holy Spirit, is hidden by His essence and presence in the innermost being of the soul. A person who wants to find Him should leave all things through affection and will, and enter within himself in deepest recollection. The kingdom of God is within you (Lk 17:21). You are the temple of God (2 Cor 6:16).
>
> God, then, is hidden in the soul, and there the good contemplative must seek Him with love, exclaiming: "Where have you hidden…?" … There is just one thing: even though He does abide within you, He is hidden.[16]

For mystics, this truth is close to their hearts and foundational.

The turning inward to find God within is a secret that God seems to have taught his saints. This teaching was dominant is a figure introduced earlier, St. Faustina Kowalska. In her *Diary*, St. Faustina relates that one of the first

---

[14] See Reginald Garrigou-Lagrange, "The Blessed Trinity Present in Us, Uncreated Source of Our Interior Life," *The Three Stages of the Interior Life*, Ch. 4, 97-108.

[15] John Elson, "Pope John Paul II: Lives of the Pope," *TIME Magazine*, Monday, Dec. 26, 1994.

[16] St. John of the Cross, *Spiritual Canticle* 1.6-8, in Kieran Kavanaugh & Otilio Rodriguez (trans.), *The Collected Works of St. John of the Cross* (Washington, DC: ICS Publications, 1979), 418-419.

and most insistent teachings of both Jesus and our Blessed Mother to her was this teaching that she called, "contemplation." Jesus revealed to her the presence of the Blessed Trinity within her through Baptism, and that the primary "work" in her life was union or dialogue with the Blessed Trinity within her. She found she was able to keep God company in her soul, without it taking away from her exterior work. What she calls "contemplation" is sometimes referred to as the practice of the "Presence of God" or of interior "Recollection."

Concepción Cabrera de Armida, the foundress and mystic discussed in the last chapter, tells us that our Lord also taught her this practice, "essential for the sanctification of the soul wishing to be all mine," and thus "You must never leave this inner sanctuary, even in the midst of your obligations."

> The "inner cloister" is essential for the sanctification of the soul wishing to be all mine. You must never leave this inner sanctuary, even in the midst of your obligations. This constant interior recollection will facilitate these activities in the very measure you practice them in God's presence…. Seek perfection to come closer to Me. You have there a practical path to reach it. The pure and recollected soul lives in me and I in it, not in confusion and pride, but in interior solitude and in the sacrifice of contempt of self… There, in this sanctuary, which no one sees, is found true virtue and consequently the contemplation of God and the dwelling of the Holy Spirit.[17]

She points out that not only is this interior recollection or "inner cloister" necessary for sanctification, and not only does it not hinder our daily obligations, it in fact facilitates these activities, while enabling the soul to live solely for God. But it requires being "in interior solitude and in the sacrifice of contempt of self" to practice presence to God's presence.

---

[17] Concepción Cabrera de Armida, *Account of Conscience*, Vol. 9, 389-390: August 15, 1897, quoted in Gustavo Garcia-Siller, *Transforming Prayer for Pilgrims* (Modesto, CA: Ediciones Cimiento, 2006), 17.

## 3. Spiritual Marriage with Christ through the Holy Spirit

### A. The Twentieth-Century Turn to Nuptial Theology

Fergus Kerr, editor of *New Blackfriars Journal*, in his survey of *Twentieth-Century Catholic Theologians*, notes that a newly current nuptial theology, drawn in Tradition from Origen, has been taken up by some of the key theological figures of the twentieth century (Henri de Lubac, Hans Urs von Balthasar, Pope John Paul II) and in important documents from the Sacred Congregation for the Doctrine of the Faith presided over by Cardinal Ratzinger. It has also been a dominant theme in recent papally endorsed or inspired theology.[18]

Iain Matthew too notes that this nuptial relationship between God and man has a long tradition, including in Scripture: that "The interpretation of the creature's relationship with God on the analogy of marriage is, of course, biblically grounded," from Hosea, through the Song of Songs, to Jesus referring to himself as a bridegroom and the new Jerusalem described as a bride.[19] The nuptials are to Christ, the Bridegroom of the Church and each soul, but it is the Holy Spirit who accomplishes this union. For the Holy Spirit is the personal love with the Trinity who unites Father to Son, and by extension, who unites each baptized to Christ, and in Christ, to the Father.

Pope John Paul II, in a homily, spoke the well-known words, "our God in his deepest mystery is not a solitude, but a family, since he has in himself fatherhood, sonship and the essence of the family, which is love."[20] Perhaps, conversely, we can go one step further to say that the deepest part of the Trinity is that they are one (love unites). For the most profound aspect of the Trinity is that it is one, a unity that is founded on its essence of love and total self-expropriation. It is the unity that gives rise to its infinite perfections, such as life, beauty, and truth. It is its unity that expresses itself in an eternity, that God acts in one eternal act, that expresses itself in many acts. All perfection leads to unity and finds its

---

[18] Fergus Kerr, *Twentieth-Century Catholic Theologians: From Neoscholasticism to Nuptial Mysticism* (Malden, MA.: Blackwell Publ., 2007).
[19] Iain Matthew, *The Impact of God: Soundings from St. John of the Cross* (London: Hodder & Stoughton, 1995), 81-82.
[20] Pope John Paul II (homily given at Palafox Major Seminary, Puebla de Los Angeles, Mexico, on January 28, 1979).

source from unity. As the three Persons are one, so all creation is called to participate in that unity and union.

Holiness therefore entails removing all obstacles and distractions so as to direct and to supernaturalize all human action towards the goal of union with the Trinity. Practically, it calls for renunciation of our wills to align with God's will and even more, to allow the Principle of unity, the Holy Spirit, to possess our hearts, such that it is He who acts and loves in us. In doing this, the Spirit accomplishes a spousal union with, and transformation into, Christ. We can also say that it is union with the Holy Spirit that accomplishes union with Christ, as we say within our Tradition that Mary is the "spouse of the Holy Spirit." And within Christ, we then become, in the Holy Spirit, sons and daughters of the Father.

Even within the Church, few are aware that not only corporately are we Bride of Christ but that each soul is a spouse of Christ. In the deepest core of each person there is a deep longing for union, not only for lay people, but also within the hearts of priests and religious and all consecrated souls. Human marriage is a preparation for this divine marriage, where God will be the soul's "all in all." Nothing in this finite life, not even marriage, as beautiful as it can be, can fill the "infinite" void within each heart and its desire for eternal, infinite, and unconditional love. St. Francis de Sales understood this truth well:

> Here, in this frail life, the soul is truly Spouse and fiancée of the *Immaculate Lamb* but not yet married to him. Fidelity and promises are given, but the execution of the marriage is deferred; that is why there is always room for us to retract it, although we may never have any reason for it since our faithful Spouse never abandons us unless we compel him to do so by our disloyalty and perfidy. But, being in heaven, the nuptials of this divine union being celebrated, the bond of our hearts to their sovereign Principle will be eternally indissoluble.[21]

The higher the soul scales "Mount Carmel" of St. John of the Cross or the deeper it proceeds through the "Mansions" that St. Teresa of Jesus describes, the more nuptial the journey becomes. We find a hint of this at the end of St. Thomas Aquinas' life, when, after being asked by the Lord in

---

[21] St. Francis de Sales, quoted in André Ravier, "The 'Treatise on the Love of God,'" *Francis de Sales: Sage & Saint* (San Francisco: Ignatius, 1988), 211.

a vision what he wished as reward for his work, he replied, "Only You, Lord" (*non nisi te, Domine*).[22] Similarly, Paul, torn between staying to look after the Church or being with Christ, agonized, "I am hard pressed between the two. My desire is to depart and be with Christ, for that is far better" (Phil 1:23). The language used by mystics is reminiscent of the *Song of Songs* (a favourite book of St. Francis de Sales). Its author uses language of the lover and beloved, such as "the loving languor of the heart wounded by love"; "These kisses of the present life... relate all to the eternal kiss of the future life, like attempts, preparations and pledges from him..."[23]

## B. St. John of the Cross' Nuptial Vision

Let us turn to St. John of the Cross to enter more deeply into the depths of this nuptial vision. Iain Matthew offers some profound insights into St. John of the Cross' vision. First, for St. John, the nuptials have their origin in and template with the Blessed Trinity. It is the Blessed Trinity that forms the background of our faith: it is a vision of the Father emptying Himself and giving Himself in love to the Son, and the Son in turn emptying Himself and giving Himself completely to the Father, all of this in and through the Holy Spirit. What is striking here is that John uses the language of "lover" and "beloved," the language of marriage also being applied to the Father and the Son.

> They are "lover and beloved" who "live" in each other, and whose shared vitality is the Holy Spirit. The Trinity appears here as act, event, where the Father is always conceiving the Son, the Son is always reinvesting love in the Father. Theirs is not a stale or level love; it escalates up and out the more intensive it is: "love, the more it is one, / the greater the love it bestows." Already we have a lesson here. Poverty and bestowal are the co-ordinates of John's system.... Things are that way because that is how God is: Father, Son and Spirit are each absolutely poor because they each give themselves completely— so each is utterly rich with the other's generosity. "So the Son's glory / is the glory he has in the Father; / and all the Father's glory / he possesses in the Son."[24]

---

[22] "An Undivided Heart," accessed May 13, 2015, http://vocationblog.com/tag/st-thomas-aquinas.

[23] Iain Matthew, *The Impact of God*, 81-82.

[24] Ibid., 120.

Thus, we find the archetype of marriage or of lover and beloved within the relationship between Father and Son (von Balthasar explains that this is a "supra-sexual" spousality), and this union is accomplished by the Holy Spirit. The total giving or expropriation (emptying) of self is found in all three Persons of the Trinity, and becomes the form or paradigm for human love. To understand human loves and friendships, we must keep in mind that all loves on earth (spousal, filial, friendship, etc.) find their archetype within God, and specifically between the "Father" and the "Son" (created human relations are an extension of the Trinitarian relations).

Second, Iain Matthew, from his deep knowledge of John of the Cross, describes the extension of this bridal relationship within the Trinity now to humanity, an extension of the love between the Father and the Son outside the Trinity, seen in their discussion on the project of creation of finding a bride for the Son:

> "A bride who might love you,/my Son..." The Father wants to share his appreciation of his Son. The Son thinks that is a wonderful idea— "thank you very much, Father...."— because the bride can then relish the beauty of the Father. Father wants bride to enjoy Son; Son wants bride to relish the Father. It is as if creation were the fruit of an excess of unselfishness.[25]

We note in passing as well that, like von Balthasar, St. John of the Cross also sees Mary in the role of representing humanity and the Church as bride. She was the first bride, begins the Son's marriage with humanity. "There will be a wonderful exchange, if Mary will allow it... She will: She surrenders to the Word, and the Wedding of the Bridegroom-Son and the Bride-humankind takes place."[26]

Third, for John of the Cross, all reality is Jesus Christ Himself— the human compass points specifically to Christ. Christ will be our eternal Spouse in heaven. However, this will not be manifest from John's writings unless one knows how to interpret them and also knows how to find designations of Christ in words like "lover" and "beloved," as well as to know how to find hinge paragraphs or chapters.[27]

---

[25] Ibid.
[26] Ibid., 122.
[27] Ibid., 116-118.

For St. John, the spiritual journey is about making space within ourselves ("caverns"), and we do so specifically to possess Jesus Christ Himself. John teaches us to seek "faith, faith, faith"— but "What is this faith for which we sacrifice everything else?" "The answer: Jesus Christ. In giving us, as he did, his Son, who is the only Word— he has no other— he has spoken it all to us, once and for all, in this only Word; he has no more to say."[28]

We are told, "Set your eyes on him alone," and that Jesus is everything: "my total locution and vision, my total revelation and the whole of my reply.... Brother, Companion, Master, Ransom and Reward":

> If I have already said all things to you in my Word, my Son, and if I have no other, what kind of answer could I give you now, or what could I leave you that would surpass this? Set your eyes on him alone, because in him I have said all to you [...] and you will find in him even more than you are asking, more even than you desire. [...] He is my total locution and vision, my total revelation and the whole of my reply. This I have already spoken to you, [...] *giving* him to you as Brother, Companion, Master, Ransom and Reward.[29]

Fourth, for St. John then, the spiritual journey takes one deeper into Christ. That is, the path begins with the bride's (each soul's) search first through meditation on the mysteries of Christ, then by practicing these mysteries, until the bride is no longer satisfied with messages or insights but only with the Messenger Himself.

> What began, then, as a wholesome piety (*1A* 13), develops into a raging sore (*CB* 7)— Give me no more messages: "You be the messenger and the message!"... The layers keep unfolding, until finally the Healer becomes her home, his mysteries the living space in which both can be alive (*CB* 37). She, and he, enter the caverns, *las cavernas*, which are himself.... "Oh my dove, in the clefts of the rock..." (Song of Songs 2:14). Using Solomon's language, John's stanza reflects within the union for which he has been striving, and anticipates the fullness of heaven.[30]

John describes the longing this way: the bride longs to be "absorbed, transformed, drunk with the love... hiding herself in the heart of her

---

[28] Ibid., 124.
[29] St. John of the Cross, *Ascent of Mount Carmel*, Bk 2, 22:5; quoted in Iain Matthew, 125.
[30] Iain Matthew, *The Impact of God*, 126.

Beloved"; "The soul longs really to enter these caverns, Christ's caverns, so that she might indeed be absorbed, transformed, drunk with the love their wisdom contains, hiding herself in the heart of her Beloved."[31]

## C. Pure Love as only Response to Divine Love

This infinite gift Christ's gift of Himself calls for pure (single-hearted) love on our part. Let us turn briefly to St. Francis de Sales' spirituality, as it highlights the centrality of pure love, what he also calls "true love" in this path of nuptial love. His path involves a "heart to heart," a "game of Love"; the game takes place within one's heart. He employed the analogy between the human person and the temple of Jerusalem that has three different courts. In this analogy, it is in the innermost court that is the Holy of Holies where Yahweh resides, corresponding to our "heart," the core of our beings— this is where God dwells, acts, and launches his appeal of love. The human heart, though lulled to sleep because of the first sin, can be quickly reawakened, like a partridge chick that had been stolen as an egg, but immediately recognizes its true mother's cry when it hears it for the first time and flies to her.

All of human history is about God launching His appeals, working with the rejections and openings within the heart— hence, what St. Francis de Sales describes in his *The Treatise on Divine Love* (his *opus magnum*) as a "game of love." It converges with von Balthasar's insight of a "Theodrama," where the whole world is a stage where God calls each soul in love. Therefore, the world and all of history is a "game of love" in which God calls from His heart to each heart, so that it would be ravished by a taste of God, like Augustine was, and incrementally give itself to God in "pure love."[32] Where Journet describes the ontological order of nature, man, and grace, St. Francis de Sales goes one step further to the heart of reality: man, spirit, and *love*. His anthropology can be summed up in these words: "Man is the perfection of the universe; spirit is the perfection of man; love the perfection of the spirit; charity the perfection of love."[33] This means that all creation and reality lead to the love of God.

---

[31] St. John of the Cross, *Spiritual Canticle* 37.5, quoted in Iain Matthew, *The Impact of God*, 126-127.
[32] André Ravier, *Francis de Sales*, 199-212.
[33] St. Francis de Sales, *Treatise on the Love of God*, trans. John K. Ryan (Rockford, IL: Tan, 1975), vol. II, Book X, chap. 1, 141.

Such a gift of Self on the part of God in Christ calls in return for pure or *disinterested* love on our part. Spiritual writers, over and over, teach us this power of pure love of God. Again, John of the Cross comes to our aid: "Blessed be the soul who loves! God is a captive, submitting to her every wish. That is God's way: if you approach him with love and treat him well, you shall have him do whatever you want; but if you did try some other way, you may as well keep quiet!"[34] One might say that God is defenceless before pure love and is "forced" to acquiesce to every request of such a beloved. The power of pure love has to do with the fact that we will be loving God with his own love: "Love greatly those who speak against you and do not love you, because in this way love will come to birth in a heart that has none. That is what God does with us: he loves us, that we might love him, through the love he has for us."[35] Iain Matthew explains this idea further, especially seeing the Holy Spirit as personal Love within the Trinity:

> Love is God's activity: "our" love like a kite, hanging in the wind of God's love for us. The activity of God is called the Holy Spirit. He is the "flame," the "principal agent," the "principal lover." Love is first his gift of himself, disembarking into the soul. "Hope does not disappoint us, because God's love has been poured into our hearts through the Holy Spirit who has been given to us" (Rom. 5:5).[36]

St. John of the Cross understood the obstacles to pure love. He explains by distinguishing two levels, the level of the sense and the level of the spirit. To follow the level of the sense, that is, to be a "sensual" man, is to be a hostage to one's likes and dislikes, which make one's self at the center of one's life and feeds one's ego. In these disordered desires and gratifications, as happened to Augustine, one loses joy, with much "fatigue, anxiety, confusion, a sense of guilt," and because the horizon is less than God, "the world becomes suffocating." But when my being is "in God," there is freedom and joy.[37] It is a call to move beyond sense to spirit, to love.

A consequence of this vision is the need to experience God's love to live a deeply Christian life. The difficulty in life is that I may not be able to respond— it is one thing to know the truth, it is another to be able to do it.

---

[34] St. John of the Cross, *Spiritual Canticle* 32.1, quoted in Iain Matthew, 110.
[35] St. John of the Cross, letter 33, to a Carmelite nun, late 1591, quoted in Iain Matthew, 110.
[36] Iain Matthew, *The Impact of God*, 110-111.
[37] Ibid., 39-45.

This is what the young Augustine faced— despite his great ability to brilliantly analyze situations— the inability to break free from "hard bondage," especially to lust. Even after his conversion, following years of companionship, he cried to the Lord, "Grant me chastity and continence, but not yet."[38]

The answer lies in having a greater love push out the lesser love. It involves two aspects: one must remember that God is the Protagonist, and that the *Canticle* reveals "the bride 'went out' because she was 'wounded' by Another." Unless one is wounded by the love of Jesus, the Protagonist, one remains in bondage and is unable to break free. But how does one accomplish this, to become "wounded" by Him? John tells us that we do so by getting to know the figure of Christ through the Gospels, by making Him the center of one's life, by having the "image of Christ around" and experiencing his gaze, and by asking him to give us this love.[39]

> Practically, John advises, have the image of Christ around; acquire a "passion" for him by "getting to know his life." Let a new light into the situation by reading or thinking of the gospel of Jesus. The gospel eyes shine through the gospel pages and can bring clarity in what seem impossible situations.
>
> More practically still, let a new love into the equation. Have the person of Christ around, the risen Christ whose gaze is his love and whose love "is never idle." Where other loves enslave us or our mediocrity imprisons us, there is a way forward: asking *him* to *give* us the love that we are looking for elsewhere. "Give me the love I am looking for in them." That is the ultimate "kind of remedy" to find a place where we can be with him and, for all of our limp confusion, ask him, allow him, the "principal lover," to love.[40]

We must "let a new love into the equation." The answer is not for us to push out the lower love, but to allow a greater love to do this: "to find a place where we can be with him and... ask him, allow him, the 'principal lover,' to love." It is like two who met and fall in love wanting to spend all their time with each other.

---

[38] Augustine, *Conf.* 8.7.17 ("*Da mihi castitatem et continentiam, sed noli modo*").
[39] Iain Matthew, *The Impact of God*, 47-50.
[40] Ibid., 50.

We have come full circle with Augustine's discovery. Each person is the fulfillment of the Temple of Jerusalem as a personal dwelling place of the Holy Spirit as well as a spouse of Christ (and a child of God in Chapter 2). Thus, through Baptism, we have the deepest intimacy with God, and, even more, a share with the Trinitarian relations within their Infinite Communion of love.

We can also look more schematically at different levels of "grace" in Pauline theology. Many Catholics view grace a "thing" (reifying grace) they receive principally through the sacraments, but they are focusing on the lowest gifts. Let us look at the levels of grace, beginning at the bottom. First, charisms (e.g., the charismatic gifts) are gifts given to build up the Church, but they are the lowest of graces and do not make the possessor holy. Second, sanctifying grace is the created grace of union that makes us holy, comprising remission of sins, divine filiation, and the inflow of divine life. Third, what causes the created effect of sanctifying grace is the indwelling of the Holy Spirit (or Trinity), the Uncreated Grace. But, for Paul, grace (*charis*) is above all the ineffable love of God in sending the unfathomable gift of His Son, especially to the cross. This greatest gift is expressed in Paul by Gal 2:20, the heart of his theology: "He loved me and gave himself up for me." So for Paul, *charis* has the following hierarchy of value of "grace" or gifts:

> Christ's love in His sacrifice for us (spousal dimension)
> Indwelling of the Holy Spirit (Uncreated Grace)
> Sanctifying grace (created grace)
> Charisms

As with Augustine, it is the indwelling of the Holy Spirit that makes one a child of God (sanctifying grace) at Baptism and more and more fully a spouse of Christ (completed in the Seventh Mansion).

# CHAPTER 4

## *MYSTICALLY INCARNATED BY THE HOLY SPIRIT*

*(The Father's Divine Gift through the Pierced Heart of Christ)*

> Jesus Christ is the first-born, and the apostles were moved more by the guidance of his spirit [Holy Spirit] than by imitating his works.... His most holy soul was always inspired by the Holy Spirit and always responsive to its slightest breath.... His soul received its orders constantly and carried them out in his daily life.... it is this same Jesus Christ, always alive and active, who continues to live and work fresh wonders in the souls of those who love him. If we wish to live according to the Gospel, we must abandon ourselves simply and completely to the action of God. Jesus Christ is its source.... What he has done is finished, what remains to be done is being carried on every moment. Every saint shares in this divine life, and Jesus Christ, though always the same, is different in each one. The life of each saint is the life of Jesus Christ. It is a new gospel.... To let God act and obey his demands on us: that is the gospel and the whole scripture and the law.[1] (Jean-Pierre de Caussade)

*Preface*

In Chapter 3, we looked at the general theology of the Holy Spirit (Indwelling and Spiritual Marriage) to provide the necessary foundation for the next step, the "incarnating" of the "new Christ" by the Holy Spirit at Baptism. It became evident to the Council Fathers at Vatican II that the Latin Church, in contrast to the Eastern Churches, had neglected the role and place of the Holy Spirit, as was evident from her theology and liturgical preaching. Even more, the concept of being led by the Holy Spirit in daily life appears to be foreign to many Christians. We begin by looking at the Holy Spirit in the life of Christ, for which we shall depend heavily on the exegetical analysis of Fr. Raniero Cantalamessa, the Preacher to the Papal Household and past member of the International Theological Commission. Second, for the recovery of the place of the Holy Spirit, we turn to the teachings of Concepción Cabrera de Armida, mystic and foundress, as presented by French Dominican theologian, Marie-Michel Philipon.

---

[1] Jean-Pierre de Caussade, *Abandonment to Divine Providence* (Toronto: Image, 1975), 84.

## 1. Holy Spirit in the Life of Christ: Conception and Baptism

"For the law of the Spirit of life in Christ Jesus has set me free from the law of sin and death." (Rom 8:2)

*The "New Law" that is within us is the Holy Spirit*

We turn to sacred Scripture to deepen our understanding of the role of the Holy Spirit in Christ's life. To understand the role of the Holy Spirit in the life of children of God through Baptism as "new Christs," it is necessary to further develop the role of the Holy Spirit in Christ. We look to Fr. Raniero Cantalamessa's exegetical analysis, which is enriched by patristic insights, offering a patristic meditation as well.[2] In his *Life in Christ: A Spiritual Commentary on the Letter to the Romans*, he focuses on Chapter 8 of the Letter to the Romans, a chapter on the Holy Spirit.[3] The selections of Fr. Raniero Cantalamessa's analysis offer helpful insights in three aspects: A. The Holy Spirit as the Fulfillment of the Law and Prophecies of a New Heart; B. Jesus' Foundation is Intimate Prayer with the Father in the Holy Spirit; C. Jesus Receives the Holy Spirit at Baptism to Pour Him into the World.

## A. The Holy Spirit as the Fulfillment of the Law and Prophecies of a New Heart

Pentecost is a feast that began in the Old Testament, first commemorating the first fruits of the harvest (Num 28:26 ff.), and then later, commemorating the Law given on Mount Sinai fifty days after the Passover, transforming a feast of nature into one of salvation history. It thus celebrates three things: the Law given on Mount Sinai; the making of the Covenant; and the making of them "a kingdom of priests and a holy nation" (cf. Ex 19:4-6).

---

[2] First, *Fr. Cantalamessa's works accept all of Paul's Letters.* This section will treat the entire corpus simply as "Pauline," in origin or in influence. Second, *it presupposes the Old Testament and the Gospels.* The theology of Paul, a trained Pharisee, presupposes the Jewish Scripture, that is, the Old Testament, and also presupposes the Life of Christ that Paul preaches, which comes to us through the Gospels especially. So the theology of Paul presupposes all this background and the Bible as a whole, as *Dei Verbum* teaches us

[3] Rom 8: 1-17; 26-27. The word "Spirit" appears thirty times in the letter, nineteen of which occur in this chapter. Romans 8 can serve both to summarize some of the material covered in this chapter and as a good introduction to Paul's understanding of the work of the Holy Spirit

For when the people left Egypt, they walked for fifty days in the desert, at the end of which God gave Moses the Law and made a covenant with the people making them "a kingdom of priests and a holy nation" (cf. Ex 19:4-6). It would seem that in Acts Luke deliberately describes the descent of the Holy Spirit so as to evoke the theophany of Sinai.[4]

The Church Fathers, like Augustine, see this Old Testament feast now fulfilled in the descent of the Holy Spirit at Pentecost. Finally, the prophecies of Jeremiah and Ezekiel on the new covenant become clear: "This is the covenant which I will make with the house of Israel after those days, says the Lord: I will put my law within them and I will write it upon their hearts" (Jer 31:33).[5] He will no longer write the Law on tablets of stone but upon their hearts: "A new heart I will give you, and a new spirit I will put within you; and I will take out of your flesh the heart of stone and give you a heart of flesh. And I will put my Spirit within you, and cause you to walk in my statutes and be careful to observe my ordinances" (Ezek 36: 26-27).[6] The Holy Spirit fulfills the Old Testament feast: now giving the new Law, the Holy Spirit; making a new and eternal Covenant; and making the baptized a "kingdom of priests and a holy nation," and even more, children of the Father.

What St. Paul says about the gift of the Spirit can only be understood in light of the Pentecost and the New Covenant: "The whole discourse on the Spirit in the *Letter to the Romans* is a counterpoint to the discourse on the Law. The Spirit Himself is defined as being the ultimate Law; the 'law of the Spirit' means, in fact, 'the law,' which is the Spirit.'"[7] That the apostle has in mind all the prophecies linked to the theme of the New Covenant is clear from the passage, a "letter from Christ, written not with ink but with the Spirit of the living God, not on tablets of stone but on tablets of human hearts" (2 Cor 3:3), where he calls the apostles "ministers of a new covenant, a covenant which is not of written letters, but of the Spirit; for the written letters kill, but the Spirit gives life" (2 Cor 3:6).[8] There is a transition already within the Old Testament to an interior view in two

---

[4] Raniero Cantalamessa, *Life in Christ: A Spiritual Commentary on the Letter to the Romans* (Collegeville: Liturgical Press, 1990), 116.
[5] Ibid., 117.
[6] Ibid.
[7] Ibid.
[8] Ibid., 117-118.

prophets: "It is only in the prophets, in Jeremiah and Ezekiel, in particular, that we pass from the outward and public view of the action of the Spirit to an *interior* and personal view."[9] St. Paul affirms that the ancient and written law gives only "knowledge of sin" (Rom 3:20) but does not take away sin.

Without this interior transformation of a "new heart," that is the Holy Spirit Himself, there is no change of heart. Because of the "old man," we are accustomed at times to feel a certain opposition and even hostility to God and others. It was Jesus on the cross that removed the hostility and obtained for us a new heart, the Holy Spirit:

> On the cross Jesus took the heart of stone from the whole of mankind; he took away all the ill feeling, enmity and resentment against God that mankind had accumulated under the law. Jesus "crucified the old self" and "destroyed the sinful body" (Rom 6:6). He took on our death and gave us his life in exchange, that is, his love for the Father, his obedience, his new relationship with God, his "spirit of sonship".... The Holy Spirit, which at Pentecost is poured into the Church, comes, therefore, from Christ's death and resurrection; it is a paschal Spirit.[10]

But this new Law cannot be simply proclaimed and received by the ear without an inner healing. It was not sufficient that Jesus proclaimed a new Law of the Spirit on the Mount of the Beatitudes, but that Law had to be engraved in man's heart at Pentecost, giving us "his love for the Father, his obedience, his new relationship with God, his 'spirit of sonship.'" That is why the apostles, even after they received the new rule of Christ in His words, were still weak:

> They [apostles] had heard everything, for example, that we should turn the other cheek to those that strike us, and yet at the moment of the Passion they were not strong enough to carry out anything of what Jesus had commanded....
>
> Therefore, without the inner grace of the Spirit, the Gospel and the new commandment too would have remained an old law, a written word.[11]

---

[9] Ibid., 118.
[10] Ibid., 120.
[11] Ibid., 121.

A noted Orthodox theologian, Nicholas Cabasilas, indicates the convergence of Byzantine theology with Catholic Tradition. It was only at Pentecost that "they were renewed and embraced a new life." The fruit was that "They became guides for others and made the flame of love for Christ burn within themselves and in others."

> The apostles and fathers of our faith had the advantage of being instructed in every doctrine and furthermore, they were instructed by the Savior himself... They witnessed his death, resurrection and ascension into heaven; yet, having seen all this, they showed nothing new or noble or spiritual that was better than the old state until they were baptized with the Spirit at Pentecost. But when they were baptized and the Paraclete had been poured into their souls they were renewed and embraced a new life. They became guides for others and made the flame of love for Christ burn within themselves and in others...[12]

We have finally received the fulfillment of the tremendous promises made in the Old Testament in the Holy Spirit: "God's love has been poured into our hearts through the Holy Spirit who has been given to us" (Rom 5:5). This love is the love God loves us with and through which, at the same time, enables us to love Him and our neighbor. It is a new capacity to love. Love is the sign that reveals the new life given by the Spirit.[13]

## B. Jesus' Foundation is Intimate Prayer with the Father in the Holy Spirit

Examining how the Holy Spirit moves Jesus in His prayer in the Spirit gives us a sense of the depth by which He was led by the Spirit. In a second work, *The Holy Spirit in the Life of Jesus*, Fr. Cantalamessa assembles various texts about Jesus at prayer from the four Gospels and gives us a penetrating insight into Jesus' prayer life, one that serves as a paradigm for us. Luke gives us a glimpse of the prayer life of Jesus here and there: "After Jesus too had been baptized and was praying... heaven was opened and the Holy Spirit descended upon Him" (Lk 3:21-22). In this text, "Luke appears to hold the view that it was Jesus' prayer that rent the heavens apart and

---

[12] Nicholas Cabasilas, *Life in Christ* II, 8; *PG* 150, 553, quoted in Raniero Cantalamessa, *Life in Christ*, 122. Cabasilas is a 14th century mystic and theologian and held as a saint by the Orthodox Church.
[13] Raniero Cantalamessa, *Life in Christ*, 122.

caused the Holy Spirit to come down."[14] A further insight is revealed by another text: "Yet the news about him spread all the more, so that crowds of people came to hear him and to be healed of their sicknesses. But Jesus often withdrew to lonely places and prayed" (Lk 5:15-16). He notes that the adversative "but" in this second text is significant: "It creates a contrast between the crowds thronging around and Jesus' determination not to let himself be overwhelmed by them and so have to give up his dialogue with the Father."[15] This is a remarkable insight: Jesus' dialogue with His Father holds first place.

## *Jesus' Foundation is Ceaseless Prayer*

Now turning to another Lucan text, he finds this insight reinforced: "Jesus departed to the mountain to pray and He spent the night in prayer to God. When day came, He called His disciples to Himself and from them He chose twelve" (Lk 6:12-13). In this third text, this habit of prayer apart and the succession of work that follows indicate that "by day Jesus just carried out what he had seen at night in prayer."[16] Other scenes reinforce the centrality of prayer and discerning the Father's will. This was the case at the Transfiguration. Fr. Cantalamessa discerns that Jesus did not go up to be transfigured, rather this was a surprise from the Spirit; Jesus went up the mountain only "to pray." Likewise, it was Jesus' intention to go into the desert to pray and to fast, as it were, to acquire a deeper understanding of the Father's revelation and to prepare for His mission; the tempting was the intention of the Holy Spirit.[17]

Fr. Cantalamessa draws upon a beautiful poetic meditation by Péguy on night, since we can associate night and the prayer of Jesus: "Night is the place, night is the being in which he bathes, in which he feeds, in which he creates, re-creates, builds himself up, is refreshed. Night is the place, night is the being where he rests, retreats, meditates; to which he keeps running..."[18]

---

[14] Raniero Cantalamessa, *The Holy Spirit in the Life of Jesus* (Collegeville: Liturgical Press, 1994), 51.
[15] Ibid.
[16] Ibid., 52.
[17] Ibid.
[18] Anton Péguy, *Le porche du mystère de la deuxième vertu*, in *Oeuvres Poétiques Complètes* (Paris: 1975), quoted in Cantalamessa, *The Holy Spirit in the Life of Jesus*, 53.

When Jesus prayed, "something happened to His face and His entire being, much like with Moses."[19] There is a short revelatory phrase in a scene in Gethsemane that recalls Moses: "Kneeling down, He prayed" (Lk 22:41).[20] We add another scene in Gethsemane that is not included in Fr. Cantalamessa's analysis, about Jesus' response when in agony: "And being in an agony he prayed more earnestly" (Lk 22:44). This text reveals Jesus' filial confidence in the Father and reliance on prayer. In sum, we find a profound revelation into Jesus: Jesus proceeds from prayer to mission, it is where we can find the deepest opening into His profound relationship with His Father.

*Jesus Transformed Prayer into an Intimate Filial Dialogue with the Father*

Turning next to Fr. Cantalamessa's analysis of Paul, three insights into Jesus' prayer in the Spirit are revealing. First, he examines how Jesus transformed the formal Jewish prayer into a spontaneous, unheard-of filial approach, "Abbà."[21] Above all, Jesus restored a free, familiar, spontaneous character to a system of prayer often only half-understood, formal, and very nearly fossilized; He brought prayer back within popular reach. The official prayer was formulated in Aramaic, a bit like Latin in our time. Jesus was not content with the official prayer at three fixed times, but sometimes prayed right through the night. In other words, He did not confine himself to repeating prayers already composed and well-known, but created a prayer of His own through the Holy Spirit that is contemplative.

> The secret of renewing prayer is thus the Holy Spirit; He is the powerful breath that can put life back into our dried-up prayers, as He did into the dry bones of Israel (cf. Ezek 37:1 f.). Spiritualizing prayer means making it possible for the Spirit to pray more and more within us, so that our prayer will be ever less active and ever more passive, ever less discursive and ever more contemplative, until we reach— if God so wills— that "prayer of quiet" in which our heart is borne beside the heart of Christ and with him, cries, 'Abba, Father!'[22]

---

[19] Raniero Cantalamessa, *The Holy Spirit in the Life of Jesus*, 53.
[20] Ibid.
[21] Ibid., 59-60.
[22] Ibid.

Another dimension that must have marked Jesus' prayer in the Spirit is praying ceaselessly: "With all prayer and supplication, pray at every opportunity in the Spirit" (Eph 6:18). These two things— praying in the Holy Spirit and praying ceaselessly— are interdependent, in the sense that the Holy Spirit makes continuous prayer possible. Isaac of Nineveh, a great spiritual master of the seventh century, writes:

> Once the Spirit comes to dwell in someone, the latter will not be able to stop praying, for the Spirit will never stop praying inside him. Thus, whether he sleeps or wakes, prayer will never be absent from that person's soul. Whether he is eating or drinking, or sleeping or working, the sweet fragrance of prayer will effortlessly breathe in his heart. Henceforth he no longer prays at fixed times, but continuously.[23]

Jesus' profound and unceasing relationship to the Father in prayer is prayer in the Spirit. It offers a profound example for the baptized new Christ.

*The Power of Prayer*

Third, the power of prayer in the Spirit can be seen in the symbolism of the battle of the Israelites against the Amalekites. While the entire Israelite army was struggling vigorously on the battle field, Moses was up the mountain with his arms raised in prayer. While the Israelites strove with Amalek, Moses strove with God, and it was Moses who assured the victory of his people (cf. Exod 17:8-16). Amalek, Origen explains, symbolizes the hostile forces barring the way for God's people: the devil, the world, and sin. When the people of God and their pastors pray, they are stronger and repulse Amalek; when they do not pray (when Moses got tired and lowered his arms), Amalek is stronger.[24]

Fr. Cantalamessa uses the imagery of the Karst river that is subterranean and that comes to the surface every so often. When we are embroiled with our tasks, the living water of the Holy Spirit is subterranean; when we are aware of His presence, He gushes above ground and makes his power felt[25]: "For all who are led by the Spirit of God are sons of God. For you did not

---

[23] Isaac of Nineveh, *Mystic Treatises* 35, trans. J. Wensinck (Amsterdam: 1923), quoted in Cantalamessa, *The Holy Spirit in the Life of Jesus*, 59-60.
[24] Ibid., 56.
[25] Ibid., 58.

receive the spirit of slavery to fall back into fear, but you have received the spirit of sonship. When we cry, 'Abba! Father!' it is the Spirit himself bearing witness with our spirit that we are children of God…" (Rom 8: 15-16). Here we see the power for the Church of prayer in the Spirit, the power that was Jesus' foundation.

Synthesizing these insights, we have found that Christ's centre of gravity was His prayer at night with the Father. But more than that, it was an unceasing and filial prayer from which radiated His power, and this prayer was always to the Father in the Spirit.

## C. Jesus Receives the Holy Spirit at Baptism to Pour Him Out to the World

From Fr. Cantalamessa's *The Holy Spirit in the Life of Jesus*, we also discover the patristic understanding of how Christ receives the Holy Spirit at His Baptism in order to breathe the Holy Spirit into the world from the cross. St. Athanasius writes: "The descent of the Holy Spirit on Jesus in the Jordan was for our benefit… to make us holy, so that we might share in his anointing and of us it might be said, 'Do you not know that you are the temple of God and that the Spirit of God dwells in you' (1 Cor 3:16)."[26] Fr. Cantalamessa explains that the anointing of Christ was an anointing "for our benefit," a fact that St. Peter confirms: "God has raised this Jesus to life, and we are all witnesses of it. Exalted to the right hand of God, he has received from the Father the promised Holy Spirit and has poured out what you now see and hear" (Acts 2:32-33).[27]

The Second Vatican Council teaches that the Lord Jesus "has made His whole Mystical Body share in the anointing of the Spirit with which He Himself has been anointed."[28] When we invoke the Spirit, we do not look for Him in heaven but to the cross of Christ. This is the "spiritual rock" from which living water pours over the Church to quench the thirst of believers.

---

[26] St. Athanasius, *Oratio I contra Arianos* 47, PG 26, 108f., quoted in Cantalamessa, *The Holy Spirit in the Life of Jesus*, 12.
[27] Ibid., 13.
[28] *Presbyterorum ordinis* 12.

As the rain, in its season, falls abundantly from the sky, collecting in the rocky recesses of the mountains until it finds an outlet and becomes a spring gushing continuously day and night, summer and winter, so the Spirit that came down and collected entirely in Jesus during His earthly life, on the cross found an outlet, a wound, and became a fountain gushing to eternal life in the Church. The moment when Jesus on the cross "handed over the Spirit" (John 19:30) is, for the evangelist, also the moment when "he poured out the Spirit"; the same Greek expression should be understood, according to John's idiosyncratic usage, in either sense: literally as "breathing" and mystically as "giving the Spirit."[29]

## Jesus "Gave up His Spirit" at the Cross

It is the Spirit "collected entirely in Jesus during His earthly life" whom He releases through the outlet of His "wound" into the world at His death, "He gave up His Spirit." At the literal sense level, "giving up his spirit" denotes Christ's human death, but the deeper spiritual sense indicates a releasing of the Holy Spirit from His Heart into the world. This spiritual meaning is found in the Church Fathers, including St. Gregory the Great and St. Gregory Nazianzen. We distinguish the two purposes of the two descents of the Holy Spirit on Jesus. At the first descent of the Holy Spirit that caused the hypostatic union at the Incarnation, the Holy Spirit descended to confer personal holiness on Jesus. At the second descent of the Holy Spirit at the Baptism of Jesus, the Holy Spirit gave Jesus both power and authority (e.g., teaching, miracles, forgiveness of sins), but principally He became a vessel to hold the Holy Spirit, so that the Holy Spirit can be poured out to the world. Hans Urs von Balthasar teaches that Jesus' inversion and obedience to the Holy Spirit allows the former to acquire the power to give the Holy Spirit to the Church.

No human being, especially with sin, can acquire the Holy Spirit. Fr. Cantalamessa quotes a notable text of Cabasilas that explains how Jesus destroyed two separations so that the Holy Spirit could be given to us: "There is a double wall of separation between us and the Spirit of God: that of nature and that of the will corrupted by evil; the former was taken away by the Saviour with his incarnation and the latter with His crucifixion, since

---

[29] Raniero Cantalamessa, *The Holy Spirit in the Life of Jesus*, 13-14.

the cross destroyed sin."[30] Through the Incarnation, the human nature of Christ was like an alabaster jar that contained the fullness of the Spirit, and when the alabaster jar was shattered on the cross, as at the anointing by Mary at Bethany, the Spirit was poured out, filling "the whole house," that is to say, the entire Church, with perfume. The Holy Spirit is the trail of perfume Jesus left behind when He walked the earth.[31]

*The Holy Spirit is the Secret of Jesus' Preaching and Miracles*

There appears to be a two-fold parallel between the events in Christ's life and two sacraments in the Christian's life: a parallel between our Baptism to Jesus' Incarnation; and a parallel between our Confirmation to Jesus' Baptism at the Jordan. Our Baptism makes us children of God (analogous to the Son of God becoming man at the Incarnation), and our Confirmation makes us witnesses to Christ (analogous to Christ being sent forth into ministry after His Baptism).

| Jesus | Christian |
|---|---|
| Incarnation | Baptism |
| Baptism | Confirmation |

In this parallel, the grace we receive at Confirmation, which completes Baptism, is for others, as Jesus' Baptism is for the sake of His ministry to others. After His Baptism, we see Jesus immediately moving into His mission. As soon as He is anointed in the river Jordan by the Holy Spirit, He, as it were, becomes the Christ, the "Anointed," whereby the Father is the One who anoints and the Holy Spirit is the unction itself. As soon as this happens, Jesus is immediately driven by the (Holy) Spirit into the desert, where He conquers Satan with a three-fold "no." Immediately after this, He begins His ministry with the holiness of the Holy Spirit in His person, the power of the Holy Spirit in His miracles, and the authority of the Holy Spirit in His words. It is the Spirit, as the *Hebrews* tells us, who moves Him to die upon the cross. Thus, the secret of the power of Jesus as man is not His divine powers but the Holy Spirit; as the Christian's secret too is the Holy Spirit.

---

[30] Ibid.
[31] Ibid., 14.

*A Note: The Holy Spirit is also the Secret of Priests*

Turning to another book by Conchita, we are led to see how the Holy Spirit is "everything" for the priest. While she acknowledges the work of the Holy Spirit in each baptized, she affirms that there is a unique action of the Holy Spirit in the ministerial priest. The priest has to know that the Holy Spirit is the very "Divine Action" of his priestly life. We know that without the Holy Spirit in the hearts of the baptized, man is not capable of being moved in the supernatural order of grace. But this is also true of each and every priestly action.

> Even for my priests this is as subordinate in his memory, because He [Holy Spirit] is THE DIVINE ACTION of the priest, and ought to be the most intimate Person that exists in him, his heartbeat and his life. He ought to circulate through the soul of the priest like the blood in his veins. He ought to impregnate his thoughts, words and works. He ought to be his very same spirit as He was mine.[32] (Jesus' words to Conchita)

The Holy Spirit should be "his heartbeat and his life" and "ought to circulate through the soul of the priest like the blood in his veins." Priests are called to be transformed into other Christs. Every priestly power, especially sacramental power, is an action of the Holy Spirit.

> Who anointed them for the priesthood? Who gave them the power in their words in the congregation? Who led them to the altar and made them worthy for ordination, of being transformed into Me [Jesus], of making me lower myself into their hands, of effecting the transubstantiation?...
>
> It is possible to say with certainty that in the spiritual life— in that of the priest most specially— there is not a single act in which the Holy Spirit does not assist him, accompany him, and penetrate him.[33]

---

[32] Concepción Cabrera de Armida, "The Holy Spirit and Priests," *To My Priests*, 217.
[33] Ibid., 218.

## 2. Recovery of the Role and Place of the Holy Spirit

"But you shall receive power when the Holy Spirit has come upon you." (cf. Mt 28:18-20; Mk 16:15-20)

Against the background provided by Fr. Cantalamessa, the mystical doctrine of Concepción Cabrera de Armida (familiarly known as "Conchita") provides a general overview of the Holy Spirit's role in Christ and in the Church. While her writings contain private revelations with Jesus, we can confidently employ her teachings as they coincide with the Catholic faith and because they have been theologically analysed and formulated by a competent theologian, Fr. Marie-Michel Philipon.[34] We are presented with a vast vision of the Holy Spirit in the life of Christ, in the universal Church (including the Early Church and the contemporary Church), and in each new Christ (Baptism).

### A. Jesus Acted through the Holy Spirit, Not through His Divinity

First, Philipon highlights in Conchita's writings a relatively unfamiliar fact on the vital role of the Holy Spirit in the life of Jesus. As man, Jesus did not employ His divine powers, but acted through the power of the Holy Spirit. For within the Trinity, it is God the Father who eternally generates the Son; on earth, as man, it is the Holy Spirit who overshadowed Mary, and is the sole direct cause of His Incarnation. Thus, the great secret of the action of Jesus Christ as man is not His divine nature, for, in order to live His humanity fully, He did not employ His divine powers, but allowed the Holy Spirit to work in Him. This dynamic also fulfills the Father's plan for Jesus to be the pattern for us in all things (as man, He is one with us in all things, except for sin). Within the divine plan, the relationship between Jesus and the Holy Spirit is to be transplanted to the Church and to each soul.

Conchita reveals the intimate depths of the relationship between the Holy Spirit and Jesus. It is the Holy Spirit who adorns Jesus with all His virtues and gifts, like a mother, tenderly forming Him and leading Him. It is the Holy Spirit who is the source of all His inspirations, including that of going

---

[34] Marie-Michel Philipon, ed., *Conchita: A Mother's Spiritual Diary* (New York: Alba House, 1978; French orig. *Journal spirituel d'une mère de famille*, 1975). See also Concepción Cabrera de Armida, "The Holy Spirit and Jesus," *To My Priests* (Cleveland: St. Andrew Abbey, translation of *A mis sacerdotes*, Modesto, CA: Ediciones Cimiento, 1929), 214-215.

to the cross for us, and who offers His Sacrifice to the Father. It is the Holy Spirit who sustains and consoles Him in His difficult moments, especially His interior sufferings which He endured throughout His life, and especially His martyrdom on Calvary. The foundation of Jesus is His love of and obedience to the Father, but all this took place through the mediation of the Holy Spirit, who is also the bond between the Father and the Son in heaven. How greatly did the Holy Spirit love and care for Jesus, and how greatly did Jesus love and obey the Holy Spirit in return.[35]

Second, having looked at the Holy Spirit in Jesus' life, we examine the massive work of the Holy Spirit in the Church. Before doing so, it is helpful to have the overall historical context. There are three ages of salvation: the age of the Father, the age before Adam and Eve sinned; the age of Christ, since the Fall the world awaited the Messiah until His Paschal mystery and Ascension; and the age of the Holy Spirit, since Christ has left to return to the Father and has now given us the "Advocate," who is the "Paraclete" and the "Counsellor." We are now living in the third age of salvation history, the age of the Holy Spirit.

## B. The Holy Spirit is the Divine Gift from which all Gifts in the Church Derive

Going back to the overarching economy, we see that the Holy Spirit within the Trinity is the Gift between the Father and the Son. Now, principally through Christ's sacrifice, this "secret" of heaven, dwelling within the Incarnate Son on earth, has been released from the Son, becoming the Gift from which all gifts derive. We can see clearly the role and leadership in this age in the *Acts of the Apostles*, which can be said to be the Gospel of the Holy Spirit. There we find a revelation of how the Holy Spirit constitutes the very heart of the Church. The very existence of the Church, and all that she is, comes from the Holy Spirit. To her has been given both the hierarchical and charismatic gifts. It is the Holy Spirit that makes Christ present through the sacraments, it is He who gives Priestly Orders that make the sacraments possible, He who inspires the sacred writers to write the Books of Scripture, He who interprets Scripture, and guides us through the Magisterium Church's Teaching and Tradition, including the liturgy. It is He who inspired the Desert Fathers, taught the Church Fathers and

---

[35] Ibid., 134-135.

Doctors of the Church, who strengthened the martyrs and confessors. It is He who prays within each one of us, who unites us through the Eucharist to the Son, and within the Body of Christ, to the Father.[36]

## C. All the Problems in the Church Ultimately Derive from not Turning to the Holy Spirit

Third, we are given a revelation of the source of the problems of contemporary life. According to Conchita, Jesus revealed the lack of recourse to His great Gift, the Holy Spirit, as the cause of the problems of our times. All the problems of the world today stem from a lack of honouring and recourse to the Holy Spirit: weakness, errors (relativism, atheism, and secularism), temptation, sensuality, and self-worship. The Holy Spirit would teach us its antithesis, the path of humility, adoration, and the cross. If Jesus were to come back today, His main complaint or lament would be that we do not turn to the Gift that He has given us that is the answer to all of our problems.[37] There is a revealing and touching text that Conchita says is an appeal from Christ, an appeal that turns into a lament:

> There exists a hidden treasure, a wealth remaining unexploited and in no way appreciated at its true worth, which is nevertheless that which is the greatest in heaven and on earth: the Holy Spirit. The world of souls itself does not know Him as it should. He is the Light of intellects and the Fire which enkindles hearts.
>
> If there is indifference, coldness, weakness, and so many other evils which afflict the spiritual world and even My Church, it is because recourse is not had to the Holy Spirit....
>
> It is time that the Holy Spirit reign. But it is necessary that He reigns, here, right close, in each soul and in each heart, in all the structures of My Church. The day on which there will flow in each pastor, in each priest, like an inner blood, the Holy Spirit, then will be renewed the theological virtues, now languishing, even in the ministers of My Church, due to the absence of the Holy Spirit. Then the world will change, for all the evils deplored today have their cause in the remoteness of the Holy Spirit, the sole remedy....

---

[36] Ibid., 128-130.
[37] Ibid., 130-132.

The decisive impulse for raising up My Church from the state of prostration in which she lies, consists in reviving the cult of the Holy Spirit.[38]

The whole Church can be renewed by due recourse to the Holy Spirit.

In sum, Conchita, through Philipon, reveals the critical role of the Holy Spirit in forming Christ to manhood and guiding Him in His ministry, including to the cross, as well as the revelation that it is the Holy Spirit who accomplishes all in the Church, and the neglect of whom leads to the Church's contemporary problems. As with Augustine, the great difficulty is to hear His voice. One American religious sister came to understand that the problems within the Church today are not due to disobedience so much as they arise from an inability to hear the Holy Spirit, a lack of contemplation.

How to live in the Holy Spirit will be described in Chapter 6, "Jesus' Divine Life," which depicts the upper level of the entire structure at which the new Christ listens to the Holy Spirit, being led, as Christ was, by the Holy Spirit through the Gifts of the Holy Spirit. The goal is to attain utter surrender or abandonment, such that the Holy Spirit possesses the heart of each new Christ, so that he becomes fully configured to Christ as a child of the Father.

---

[38] Ibid., 130-131.

# PART II: INCARNATION

## *MODEL OF CHRIST*

"And the Word became flesh"

# CHAPTER 5

## *CHRIST'S HUMAN LIFE*

### *(Sanctifying the Foundation)*

> Let the following conviction become deeply impressed upon your mind;
> namely, that a soul *cannot* lead an interior life without the *schedule* we have
> referred to, and the *firm resolution* to keep it all the time, especially where
> the rigorously fixed *hour of rising* is concerned.[1] (Jean-Baptiste Chautard,
> emphasis added)

Part I presents Christ, in His Trinitarian origin and Incarnation, as the
template and the goal of the baptismal transformation in Christ: "God
became man so that man can become god" (St. Athanasius, *De Incarnatione
Verbi Dei*); or, the Son of God became a God-man, so that man can
become a "man-god" in the template of Christ, to incarnate a "new Christ"
in Baptism, a new child of God the Father.

*Two Levels and Three Loves*

Part II develops the thesis that each person incarnated in this template of
Christ has two dimensions: "Two Levels" and "Three Loves." The "Two
Levels" correspond to the two levels of Christ, human and divine, namely,
sanctifying one's human foundation and being led by the Holy Spirit (Chs. 5
& 6 respectively). The "Three Loves" correspond to two "Mothers," the
Church and Mary, who give birth to us spiritually (Ch. 7), and the
Eucharist, which assimilates us progressively into Christ (Ch. 8). Where
Baptism incarnates us objectively into a child of God the Father, there has
to be continued subjective assimilation into Christ as Son— the old image
of Baptism as planting a seed that needs to be fertilized, watered, and given
sunshine to grow applies here. Thus, unlike Christ, who at the Incarnation
is naturally the Son of God and has one human mother, the baptized as a
new Christ has two mothers (Church and Mary) and also needs Christ in
the Eucharist to bring about a life-long assimilation to Christ— this is the
logic of "Three Loves." He takes on Christ's physiognomy as child of God,
with all its sentiments and loving affection.

---

[1] Jean-Baptiste Chautard, *The Soul of the Apostolate* (Rockford, IL: TAN, 1946), 195-196.

The "Two Levels" flows from the paradigm is the Incarnate Word, and it would appear that many Christians lack an explicit awareness that all human life, as well as interior life, has two levels, a "both… and…" ("both/and") structure. One of the best formulations of this is St. Thomas Aquinas' famous dictum, "Grace builds upon nature."[2] The consequence of not understanding the presence of a two-fold structure is that many fail to build the "nature" foundation for their "grace" edifice. This can frequently happen to young people who have had conversion experiences. They are often tempted, in their desire for holiness, to focus principally on the "grace" elements of prayer and devotion, and not first put effort into establishing the virtues of the "nature" foundation, such as human virtues like punctuality, responsibility, affability, concern for those around them. As with a building, without a strong foundation of "nature," the divine edifice of "grace" can collapse. Jesus, though fully divine, was fully human in His foundation: "Jesus increased in wisdom and in stature, and in favor with God and man" (Lk 2:52) and "He did all things well" (Mk 7:37). This chapter's theme of Jesus' strong human foundation points to the reason why many, even when they try hard, do not make much progress in their interior life.

Applying the analogy of a house to the "Two Levels" (foundation and building), we will now examine in Chapter 5 the path of strengthening the foundation of the house, namely, specifically through having a plan of life (structure, order, schedule). Before doing so, the first section seeks to establish the principle of two levels, the "both/and" principle

## 1. "Two Levels" of the Incarnate Word:

## Christ's Human Life (Ch. 5) and Christ's Divine Life (Ch. 6)

### A. The Incarnate Word's Two Levels are Found in Creation and in Grace

Besides the three-fold pattern based on the Trinity that we find in the universe, as in Augustine's triad of man's faculties of intellect, will, and

---

[2] St. Thomas Aquinas, *Summa Theologiae*, I, 1, 8, ad. 2: "*cum enim gratia non tollat naturam sed perficiat*," referred to in Pope John Paul II's Encyclical, *Fides et Ratio*, 43. One might consider the works of James Schall, S.J., especially his thoughts on faith and reason in Pope Benedict XVI (see also *Fides et Ratio*, n. 43).

memory (*vestigia Trinitatis*),[3] there appears to be a dominant recurring pattern of two levels, built upon the paradigm of the two natures of the Incarnate Word, God and man. Since "all things were created through him and for him" (Col 1:16; see also Eph 1, Jn 1), one would expect that all creation reflects the two dimensions of Christ's humanity and divinity. We find this pattern is abundantly evident both at the level of nature and of grace.

First, we find a dual pattern in *creation*: a spiritual universe (God, angels) and a material universe; and the material universe itself is composed of two materials, animate (organic) and inanimate (inorganic) creatures. Then, within this material universe itself, man himself has dual aspects of body and spirit, and has been created in two genders, male and female. We also see the recurring two-fold pattern in man's life as well. For example, parents and teachers are called to be both loving and firm (discipline); and a good citizen is called to love his own family but also be concerned about his neighbours and society in general.

The recurring pattern of two levels becomes more striking when we look at the level of *grace*. First, man has two creations: the first creation of Adam and Eve, and because of their sin, a second creation of grace from Christ's side on the cross; or our creation in our mothers' wombs, and our second creation of grace begun at Baptism (we even find a diptych for these two creations in the structure of Col 1).[4] Second, grace itself has two fulfillments, beginning with Baptism that finds its fulfillment in glory (heaven), or as St. Thomas Aquinas teaches, "Grace is the seed of glory."[5] Third, man has two eschatologies or "last things," his individual eschatology at death, and the general eschatology at the eschaton, beginning with Christ's second coming.[6] Fourth, the life of the Church itself manifests

---

[3] Augustine, *Confessions* 13.1; *Trinity* 9:2-8; 10-17-19. "The most central analogy [in the human person] is the triad of being, knowing, and willing. From the central triad emerges three elaborations: the mind, its knowledge of itself, and its love for itself; memory... intelligence... will..." (quoted in Stanley James Grenz, "The Triune God," in *Theology for the Community of God* (Vancouver, BC: Broadman and Holman Publishers, 1994), 62).

[4] Col 1:15-20 describes in two parallel sections the two creations in Christ, of the universe and of the Church: "He is the image of the invisible God, the first-born of all creation..." & "He is the head of the body, the Church...."

[5] Reginald Garrigou-Lagrange, *The Three Ages of the Interior Life: Prelude of Eternal Life*, 33-37.

[6] Joseph Cardinal Ratzinger divides his work on eschatology, *Eschatology: Death and Eternal Life*, Dogmatic Theology 9 (Washington, DC: CUA Press, 1988), in this twofold manner: "Death and Immortality: The Individual Dimensions of Immortality" (Part Two) and "The Future Life" (Part Three).

many examples of this two-fold form: *Lumen gentium* describes the Church as a "mystery," ("sacrament"), which has both historical and divine dimensions[7]; sacraments comprise material elements and invisible divine action; Christian life comprises both human aspects (work, raising a family, being a good citizen) and spiritual aspects (Sunday Eucharist, daily prayer), or alternatively, fulfilling the duties of one's state in life, while being led by the inspirations of the Holy Spirit. The list goes on and on.

Noted authors identify and point out special pairings that impact Christian life. St. Augustine notes two kinds of life that are necessary to the Christian life: the active life of sweat and labour symbolized by Peter, and the contemplative life symbolized by John. What is striking is that St. Augustine reveals that all in the Body of Christ, the Church, participate in the work of both Peter and John (St. Augustine makes no mention of a subordination of one to the other):

> Yet we should make no mental separation between these great apostles. Both lived the life symbolized by Peter; both were to attain the life symbolized by John. Symbolically, one followed, the other remained, but living by faith they both endured the sufferings of this present life of sorrow and they both longed for the joys of the future life of happiness.
>
> Nor were they alone in this. They were one with the whole Church, the bride of Christ, which will in time be delivered from the trials of this life and live for ever in the joy of the next. These two kinds of life were represented respectively by Peter and John, yet both apostles lived by faith in this present, passing life and in eternal life both have the joy of vision.[8]

Another example of these two levels can be found in Pope Benedict XVI's new Encyclical, *Caritas in veritate*. In Chapter Six, "The Development of Peoples and Technology," he writes of the distinction between the objective and subjective side to human action.

> Technology is the objective side of human action whose origin and *raison d'être* is found in the subjective element: the worker himself. For this reason, technology is never merely technology. It reveals man and his

---

[7] *Lumen gentium* n. 1.

[8] Augustine, *Tractatus in Iohannis Evangelium*, 124, 5,7, quoted in OOR of Saturday of Sixth Week of Easter, *The Liturgy of the Hours*, vol. II (New York: Catholic Book Publ., 1976), 948-949.

aspirations towards development, it expresses the inner tension that impels him gradually to overcome material limitations. *Technology, in this sense, is a response to God's command to till and to keep the land.*[9]

A more prominent pairing emphasized by Pope Benedict XVI is the link between charity and truth as enunciated in *Caritas in veritate*, and even more, between reason and truth.

## B. In the "both/and" Pattern, the Foundation is for the Sake of the Building

This two-fold pattern could be more clearly elaborated under the larger umbrella of the "both/and" principle. A professor in a lecture on dogmatic theology pointed out to his students the "both/and" principle, and noted that it represents the Catholic approach, while the "either/or" principle represents the Protestant approach. For example, he noted that Martin Luther would find the Catholic approach on grace in holding to both "grace" *and* "works" as one of "sitting on the fence," of being ambivalent, of not making a decisive choice of either "grace" *or* "works."

The Catholic position in this scheme of the "both/and" structure contains a double dynamic regarding the two elements. In the image of a house as a basic paradigm, there are the following two dynamics: the foundation is of secondary priority for us, but it is where we begin; the building, in which we live, is what we are interested in; it is more important, but it is only built after, and upon, the foundation. Jesus Himself employed the analogy of the house and the importance of a strong foundation, comparing those who build on the foundation of rock to those who build on the ground:

> Every one who comes to me and hears my words and does them, I will show you what he is like: he is like a man building a house, who dug deep, and laid the foundation upon rock; and when a flood arose, the stream broke against that house, and could not shake it, because it had been well built. But he who hears and does not do them is like a man who built a house on the ground without a foundation; against which the stream broke, and immediately it fell, and the ruin of that house was great (Lk 6:47-49; cf. Mt 7:24-29).

---

[9] *Caritas in veritate* n. 69.

Thus, the foundation comes first, upon which the building is erected. The purpose of the foundation, however, is the building itself, for one does not live in the foundation but in the building. Every high-rise building, such as a tall condominium building, has a strong and deep foundation, and the higher it goes, the deeper the foundation must be (e.g., the tallest building in the world is presently the Burj Khalifa in Dubai). Without this foundation, the entire building could collapse. The higher the holiness one desires, the deeper has to be the human foundation.

One particularly illuminating illustration of this two-fold structure and dynamic is found in Scripture with the four senses of Scripture (see *Catechism of the Catholic Church* nn. 115-118). Scripture has a foundation, namely, the literal or historical meaning, the meaning intended by the sacred writer, and we always begin our exegesis here, with the literal, the foundation. But, according to the Church Fathers and Medieval theologians, there are also three spiritual meanings (allegorical, moral, and anagogical), which are the meanings imbued by the Holy Spirit— hence the term, "*spiritual* senses"— and are consequently the principal meanings of a given text. Combing both levels, the Church always begins scriptural exegesis with the foundation of the literal sense or meaning of the text to avoid flights of fancy in interpretation; then she discerns the higher spiritual senses built upon this foundation, which are imbued by the Holy Spirit.

*Foundation must be Strong for a "High-Rise" Building (Holiness)*

Let us now correlate the "Two Levels" of Chapter 5 and Chapter 6 of "Christ's Human Life" (foundation) and "Divine Life" (edifice). First, in our Christian life, human components, like the duties of our state of life and the human virtues, constitute our foundation; and living divine filiation (as a son or daughter of God) in being led by the Holy Spirit, the summit of our Christian action, is the building. But it bears reiterating that the foundation is indispensable; without it the entire interior life collapses. To use the analogy of our home, we have to go from the ground level to get to the second floor. For example, an office worker who lets his prayer life slide and is slack in his duties as a father and at work, no matter how popular and gifted he is, compromises his foundation as a new Christ according to this paradigm. Likewise, a priest who lets the recitation of the Divine Office and daily prayer go, who fails in his priestly duties (e.g., not giving attention to making the sacrament of Confession readily and easily available, not replying to the telephone calls of his parishioners, seeking apostolates outside while neglecting his parish), no matter how devout he is or how popular he is with his bishop, compromises his priestly foundation.

Yet, in a house, the foundation is for the sake of the building. In the Christian life, the human foundation is the basis for something far greater: attentiveness to the presence of the Blessed Trinity within his soul and listening to the inspirations of the Holy Spirit, so as to attain the abandonment that allows the Holy Spirit to direct and possess him, to make, as it were, Christ incarnate in him. Thus, a Christian giving his primary attention to his work activities (family, profession), without due attention to the Holy Spirit, may end up depending on his human efforts, not allowing God to do the work in him. He forgets that he is a new Christ: he is not to work purely from the objective powers derived from Baptism, but also subjectively, allowing Christ to work in and through him in holiness through attentiveness to the Holy Spirit.

Summarizing what we have learned, there are then always two elements held in tension, like the "now" of the present and the "not yet" of eternity (eschatological). These two elements constitute the "both/and" structure we find in life. And this structure has a *dynamic*: the one is secondary but we must begin with it; the other is primary or dominant but comes after we establish the first. One concrete expression of this "both/and" is the pairing of "objective" and "subjective" in sacramental theology seen earlier, the distinction between validity (*ex opere operato*) and fruitfulness (*ex opere operantis*) of the sacraments: the sacramental work as the "foundation" of validity, and holiness and prayer life as the "divine edifice," union with God, that waters and makes fruitful the entire Christian life. To put exclusive focus on human effort and even ministry at the parish, the foundation of the building, would be to miss the forest for the trees.

## *2. Sanctifying the Human Foundation through a Plan of Life (Order)*

Having established the overarching "both/and" principle in the previous section, the rest of the chapter will examine specifically the foundation of the house— sanctifying the duties of one's state in life. The spiritual figure that is, perhaps, best known in the twentieth century for the sanctification of life and work is St. Josemaría Escrivá. One famous homily at the

University of Navarre captures some of the highlights of his spirituality: the presence of the Divine in everyday life (supernatural outlook); the value of work and its role in Christ's redemptive work; offering one's work in one's daily Mass; and doing one's work with perfection and order. This homily will be developed later in Chapter 8.[10]

Of the elements mentioned within Josemaría Escrivá's spirituality, this chapter is confined principally to the sanctification of the new Christ's duties through the key aspect of "order" ("structure") that directs everything else, specifically, the "Plan of Life" (section 2) and the fruits that derive from following it (section 3). Structure can represent many things: schedule, the duties of our state of life, responsibilities, plan, etc. It is almost impossible to over-emphasize the particularly vital role of order through a "plan of life" ("rule of life") in one's foundation. The greatest tragedy of neglecting a structure is that it undermines the foundation, and, by extension, the building as well— the goal of transformation into Christ and communion with the Trinity.

## A. Dispelling the Misconception that Structure Limits Creativity

Right from the start, it is important to dispel a prevailing misconception. David Allen, in *Ready for Anything: 52 Productivity Principles for Getting Things Done*, affirmed the foundational principles of his earlier work, *Getting Things Done*. He writes that people are inclined to think "that 'getting organized' is antithetical to spontaneity, intuition, and freedom," but that the opposite is the case; in fact, organization and creativity go hand-in-hand.

### Organization and Creativity: Friends or Foes?

I find it interesting how many people will think organization and creativity are mutually exclusive: 'Don't bother me about getting organized and with all those lists— I just want to be creative.' Or 'I don't need all that organization stuff— I can keep everything in my head.' Why do people think that 'getting organized' is antithetical to spontaneity, intuition, and freedom?... If you want to express yourself on canvas, and oil paints are your medium, you will organize your paints and brushes. You won't think about 'getting organized'— you'll just do it....

---

[10] Josemaría Escrivá, "Passionately Loving the World," accessed May 27, 2015, http://www.stjosemaria.org/articles/199-passionately-loving-the-world

Once you taste what it's like to operate with a clear head (I mean a *really* clear head), I doubt that you will spend much energy thinking about 'having to get organized.' You'll just do it so you can maintain the experience....

It's hard to be fully creative without structure and constraint. Try to paint without a canvas. Creativity and freedom are two sides of the same coin. I like the best of both worlds. Want freedom? Get organized. Want to be organized? Get creative.[11]

The example of the necessity for an artist to prepare brushes and oil paints before actually painting carries the point. The advantages of being organized are operating with a "clear head" and enabling creativity, for "creativity and freedom are two sides of the same coin." Applying this analogy to our house, the preparation by the artist of the paints and brushes corresponds to the foundation of the house, while the "creativity," the main task of the artist, corresponds to union with and being led by the Holy Spirit (next chapter).

## B. Perennial Wisdom Points to the Efficacy of Order in a Plan of Life

Several wise older spiritual writers have noted the importance of a schedule or some rule of life. The new Christ can learn from the wisdom of Fr. Eugene Boylan's counsels to priests. He insists upon this structure in the spiritual realm as well, on the vital necessity of some "rule of life":

... we feel bound to point out the great need that each priest has for some rule of life. If the planning of each day is left to the caprice of the moment it is likely that we shall be like fallen leaves at the mercy of every little breeze of momentary interest or passing whim, circling around in some corner, getting nowhere. Even though we be men with a strong sense of duty, determined to overcome our caprices and to live each day in accordance without ideals, yet, faced with an almost unbroken series of decisions to be made, we shall either waste all our energy in making decisions instead of carrying them out, or else we shall fail to decide and shall never succeed in devoting all our energies to any one particular task. There are so many duties crying out for attention... One cannot pray if one feels one should really be visiting the sick... It is true that it would be impossible to draw up in advance a complete plan for each

---

[11] David Allen, *Ready for Anything: 52 Productivity Principles for Getting Things Done* (New York: Penguin Books, 2003), 83-84.

day… Yet there are a number of decisions that can and should be made once and for all, and there are many things which will not be done if some regular time is not set apart for doing them.

On the other hand there is a tremendous help to be got from routine. Every man who has marched in step with his fellowmen knows how the steady swing of the group can carry a man on, far beyond the limits of his normal powers…. It is the starting and the stopping that use up power. We can easily see what a wonderful asset a regular habit of doing things can be…. Just think what it would mean in a few years if, for example, we read the Bible for even five minutes before dinner every day…. There must, then, be some rule of life; that is beyond argument.[12]

Living by whim and caprice leads to much dissipation and failure; living by a regular routine or structure facilitates progress and achievement. The greatest fruit is that its order provides the ambience that enables union with God: "A time-table arranged will facilitate not only our work but also our union with God— and this latter is the one and only principle of all supernatural fruitfulness."[13]

Dom Jean-Baptiste Chautard, in his spiritual classic, *The Soul of the Apostolate*, identifies the specific bedrock of the human foundation, the indispensable "schedule" (quoted at the beginning of this chapter): "Let the following conviction become deeply impressed upon your mind; *namely, that a soul cannot lead an interior life without the schedule we have referred to, and the firm resolution to keep it all the time*, especially where the rigorously fixed hour of rising is concerned" (emphasis added).[14] Many fail in this first of all principles, the failure to have and keep a schedule. Fr. Chautard also points out what is most important to have within the schedule, not immediately obvious, the "fixed rising time." Without a fixed rising time, the advantages of a schedule are nullified to some extent, as the schedule keeps rising and falling according to one's rising time, and might lead to abandoning the schedule altogether as one experiences failure to keep to a fixed schedule. But this structure of a schedule extends to having structure in smaller things. A transitional deacon, during his diaconate retreat, felt that God was

---

[12] Eugene Boylan, *The Spiritual Life of the Priest* (Cork: Mercier Press, 1961; orig. 1949), 130-131.

[13] Ibid., 136.

[14] Jean-Baptiste Chautard, *The Soul of the Apostolate*, 195.

engraving onto his heart the importance of keeping to a structure in his daily meditation, an insight he subsequently shared with his spiritual director.

*Some Concrete Suggestions for Making a Plan of Life*

➤ Make a <u>weekly schedule,</u> using a template that you can copy for a period (e.g., semester)— making a template saves you from rewriting the entire structure. A calendar is for listing appointments and is not a weekly schedule.

➤ Have <u>fixed times</u> for rising and retiring, meals, and prayer, as you have fixed times for starting work, taking breaks, and leaving work. Serious people do not function with loose schedules (e.g., CEOs).

➤ Have <u>fixed days</u> for regular things: grocery shopping (especially when it is less busy), laundry, meals at home, visiting elder parents or in-laws (e.g., every first Saturday of the month), seeing your dentist, having physicals, getting car tune-ups, etc.

➤ <u>Prayer time should be structured</u>: One should have a set program for prayer (e.g., meditation, Rosary, Examen, spiritual reading). For example, an hour of prayer could be comprised of a half-hour of meditation (perhaps with the Gospel of the Mass of the day), praying the Rosary and your Examen Prayer while travelling to and from work. Family Rosary is also highly recommended.

➤ <u>Avoid making your schedule look like a train schedule</u>: One can use different symbols to indicate different activities: e.g., box can indicate work or classes, one parenthesis for study times, double parentheses for events. The schedule should be simple, hourly, perhaps from about 6 am to 10 pm.

➤ <u>Weekends can be more flexible</u>: You might wish to sleep in, but it is still good to build the habit of a fixed rising (later) time for Saturday and Sunday.

➤ <u>2 Daily Sacraments</u>: A wonderful practice, if one can fit it in, is to attend daily Mass and frequent Confession (at least once a month, even weekly if one wishes to attain sanctity). The best place (but not only) to pray is before the Blessed Sacrament, to allow the "Sun's" warmth of grace fall upon you.

➤ A good supplement is a <u>daily "to-do" list</u>, which you can make each evening immediately after supper. It helps you program the next day, and you can tick off what has been accomplished as you periodically check it during the day.

## 3. The Fruits from Using a Schedule or Plan of Life

Having offered consequences of failure to maintain a plan of life, let us examine the many fruits that can be derived from being faithful to a schedule/rule of life/ plan of life. Examining these fruits provides a way of seeing constituent elements of a plan of life.

### A. Much can be Accomplished through a Schedule

Good intentions not accompanied by a schedule lend themselves to "spinning one's wheels." Examples of great figures who have accomplished much through structure abound. St. Augustine, one of the four Western Church Fathers, had a theological output that surpassed the entire literary output of all the Western Church Fathers put together, accomplishing most of this as a very busy bishop of Hippo and an influential figure in the African Church. His secret? "Safeguard order, and order will safeguard you." Within the Church, two communities known for their "systems" and their discipline, the Society of Jesus and the Opus Dei prelature, have accomplished much for the Church. The founder of the latter, St. Escrivà, writing in *The Way*, expressed the wisdom of a plan of life: "Without a plan of life you will never have order" (76); "When you bring order into your life your time will multiply, and then you will give God more glory, by working more in his service" (80); "Virtue without order? Strange virtue!" (79). Pope John Paul II, who had accomplished so much in the enormous responsibilities he carried, had as pope a regular regimen each day. One would imagine that the president of the United States must have a detailed schedule strictly administered by his executive secretary.

To use concrete examples from our day-to-day experience, we can compare what a young Missionary Sister of Charity can accomplish with her rule of life to a young woman recently converted back to the faith who only has enthusiasm to keep her going. The faithful religious sister prays about four hours a day, the newly converted young person in enthusiasm might pray that much in a good week. Or, in the seminary, one can find seminarians who day-in and day-out faithfully pray at set times twice a day before the Blessed Sacrament— their presence and fidelity leaves one with a sense of their solidity; whereas, other seminarians with a more haphazard routine of praying tend to have many resolutions but many failures in fidelity to prayer, and in the end rarely have power to influence God's people.

## B. It Allows the New Christ to Do the Will of God

A devout Christian can do many good things yet not necessarily consult the Lord to see if it is His will. She can agree to do several things that the pastor asks, but doing good things (e.g., being a lector, chairing a committee) is not necessarily doing God's will. A small booklet from the writings of St. Alphonsus de Liguori presents, in a very convincing fashion, the primary importance of identifying ourselves with God's will:

> Caesarius points out what we have been saying by offering this incident in the life of a certain monk: Externally his religious observance was the same as that of the other monks, but he had attained such sanctity that the mere touch of his garments healed the sick. Marvelling at these deeds, since his life was no more exemplary than the lives of the other monks, the superior asked him one day what was the cause of these miracles. He replied that he too was mystified and was at a loss how to account for such happenings. 'What devotions do you practice?' asked the abbot. He answered that there was little or nothing special that he did beyond making a great deal of willing only what God willed, and that God had given him the grace of abandoning his will totally to the will of God. 'Prosperity does not lift me up, nor adversity cast me down,' added the monk. 'I direct all my prayers to the end that God's will may be done fully in me and by me.' 'That raid that our enemies made against the monastery the other day, in which our stores were plundered, our granaries put to the torch and our cattle driven off — did not this misfortune cause you any resentment?' queried the abbot. 'No, Father,' came the reply. 'On the contrary, I returned thanks to God — as is my custom in such circumstances— fully persuaded that God does all things, or permits all that happens, for his glory and for our greater good; thus I am always at peace, no matter what happens.' Seeing such uniformity with the will of God, the abbot no longer wondered why the monk worked so many miracles.[15]

The monk's sanctity and power flowed from his identification with God's will.

Without obedience to God's will, the new Christ will never make significant progress to the next level (fulfilling the Holy Spirit's inspirations, that lead

---

[15] Caesarius: *Dial. distin.* 10: cap. 9, quoted in Alphonsus de Liguori, *Uniformity with God's Will* (Rockford, IL: TAN, 2008), 9-10.

to surrender). In the concrete, daily life, this might entail the following: seeking the particular vocation God gives; fulfilling the duties of our state of life; putting into practice the teachings of the Church and of Christ in Scripture; and following the counsels of our superiors. Having a plan of life will enable us to avoid following one's whim or self-will, and enable spiritual progress.

## C. It gives Order to Protect against the Danger of Activism

One of the greatest temptations of Catholics today, and of people in general, is constant rushing. We do not feel fulfilled until we are accomplishing many tasks and good works. There is a tendency to constant activity: taking our children to many sporting activities, getting involved with yoga or some fitness craze, involvement with various clubs, and attachment to globe trotting. We are constantly glued to hand held devices, especially cell phones. Robert Wiesner wrote a vivid depiction of our times:

> But our age is fraught with busyness and preoccupation, overly filled with tasks (many of them quite useless and unnecessary) and noise. We are bombarded with too much information and asked to assimilate and process events which really should be regarded as having no importance in our lives with God... To utilize an old cliché, we moderns have largely lost our ability to stop and smell the roses. We are thus impoverished, perhaps even fatally so, because our opportunities for the prayer of praise are quite radically limited.... To eliminate noise and busyness from modern life is difficult, of course. More or less constant use of the cell phone is an obstinate habit. The temptation exists to fill children's lives with endless soccer, play dates, field trips and educational opportunities, which of course severely cramp adult possibilities for silence and reflection. Most people are now quite uncomfortable with silence; quietness is another lost art in this frenetic age.[16]

Wiesner concludes with path to follow, the need for praise of God in silence:

> Yet, quiet, both inner and outer, is necessary to hear that still, soft voice which, the Prophet assures us, is the way God communicates best.

---

[16] Robert Wiesner, "The Message of the Icon: In Praise of Praise, *Inside the Vatican*, April 2019, 48.

An image comes to mind which may offer a way back to quiet and praise. A family gathers on their porch to observe a fiery sunset. Speech is forbidden; the only idea is to watch the Lord unfold His splendor in vivid golds, pinks and pastel grays. The silence can only be broken when dusk falls by a quiet prayer of praise: "Ah, Lord, You done gone did good there!"[17]

The Church and society of today find themselves invested in action but lacking in mystery and contemplation. We can become so busy in our family and work life that we do not have time for prayer, which moves God to release His graces upon our work and the world. It is order that enables us to slow down and do things in order of priority (see Stephen Covey's *7 Habits of Highly Effective People*). We can learn from strong religious communities, who have a stable rule of life that protects their spiritual life and enables them to sanctify their work. A plan of life protects from giving in to the whim of the present moment and to immediate needs.

## D. It Frees the Mind of Christ's Disciple

There is another "busyness" beyond the running around, the busyness of the mind. In one of Tom Clancy's novels, *Executive Orders*, Cathy Ryan, an ophthalmic surgeon and Professor of Surgery at the Johns Hopkins University School of Medicine, as First Lady of the United States, was always accompanied in her rounds by a Secret Service agent. When questioned by the agent about the reason for her constantly making notes, she replied: "If it's not written down, it didn't happen." An example of this is making Lenten resolutions: if we do not write them down, the chances are that, even if we remember them, we will not put them into practice. This points to the importance of writing things down, or more generally, setting things on paper or electronically. Without putting things down, especially in a schedule, we are likely to be going a mile a minute in our heads, constantly thinking about what we have to do, always "busy" in our heads and in our hearts. The moment we write down tasks to be done or resolutions to follow through, our minds and hearts tend to subside and return to peace. Our minds are too important to be used primarily as an archive, for it deprives us from living in the presence of God that fosters communion with Him.

---

[17] Ibid.

# E. Sanctifying each Hour through Contemplation Gives Spiritual Influence

Composing and being faithful to a plan of life enables the new Christ to do God's will and to do it with Him. The result is that he is now able to sanctify each hour with and in God (contemplation), which is very fruitful for the Church and the world. Beyond the first principle of fruitfulness that is doing God's will, there is a second and great truth that must be highlighted: it is not what we do so much as how we do what we do— the degree of union with God and love. This, said Pope John Paul II, was "not a paradox but a perennial truth: the fruitfulness of the apostolate is above all in prayer and in an intense and constant sacramental life. This is, in essence, the secret of holiness and of the authentic success of the saints."[18] This can be synthesized beautifully in St. Escrivá's dictum: "First, prayer; then, expiation; in the third place, very much in third place, action" (The Way, n. 82). While having a structure (e.g., through a schedule) allows us to do God's will for us, the greatest benefit might be that it now allows us to do God's will *with God*— contemplation. Having a schedule promotes recollection, what we might also call the presence of God or contemplation.

Many people find themselves busy and focused on trying to get their tasks done, to tick off that endless list of unfinished work. However, while this getting things done mode may give immediate satisfaction, it may also cause a greater loss. To employ a spatial image, getting things done at any cost is like a man gathering things in his arms horizontally on the table of human life; while living in each present moment with God, while doing exactly and only what God wants, is like digging deeply vertically, piercing through to eternity, to God. Such a person is powerful, like a child in the Father's arms, who can then move the Father's arms to help those all over the world. The secret of the saints is precisely this contemplation or union with God, and there is no comparison between the respective fruits of the two approaches. St. Faustina was told by our Lord that as she attained union with God, she would have power over Him to help, not only all of Poland, but the entire world. To overcome activism and to be contemplative, a helpful principle is to seek not to be "task-oriented" but "time-oriented." To be "time-

---

[18] Pope John Paul II, Homily at Canonization of St. Josemaría Escrivá de Balaguer, accessed on 14 August, 2015, http://w2.vatican.va/content/john-paul-ii/en/homilies/2002/documents/hf_jp-ii_hom_20021006_escriva.html.

oriented" is to sanctify tasks through sanctifying time: to follow the path of Jesus, who sought to live in the Present Moment, to fulfill the duty of the Present Moment, seeking only the Father's will and communion with the Father. Such was Jesus' life in Nazareth, and it was filled with grace.

## F. Peace of Heart and Sacrament of the Present Moment

Two other spiritual by-products of having a schedule is that first, it brings **peace of heart**, which is necessary for the action of the Holy Spirit in our hearts. Without peace of heart, we cannot hear the delicate voice of the Holy Spirit, who dwells within our hearts. And second, the schedule enables us to practice the "**Sacrament of the Present Moment**," which is vital for the spiritual life. It also protects us from following our whims and wasting time, and allows us to be goal-oriented (see Chapter 10).

## G. Sanctifying One's Work

Perhaps the greatest gift of God in the twentieth century to understand how to sanctify one's work is the charism of St. Josemaría Escrivá. It is a valuable contribution to contemporary spirituality but difficult to grasp in its foundations. The author of this book has attempted to synthesize St. Escrivá's thought in a chapter devoted to "The Lay Mission of Sanctifying the World," but within another manuscript he hopes to publish, under the tentative title, *New Evangelization: Starting Anew with Christ*.

*Synthesis*

We have seen the human foundation for listening to the inspirations of the Holy Spirit. Without the human foundation, the divine edifice can collapse. Thus it is vital to strengthen this human foundation by the use of the indispensable weekly schedule and to sanctify our human virtues and our work. Let us summarize the fruits that we have seen come from having a schedule or structure: the weekly schedule becomes a sacred Rule of Life; it accomplishes God's will and all priorities; avoids the hectic rushing and enables recollection; facilitates consecrating each hour for important needs in the world; emphasizes the sanctification of the ordinary things (the little way); enables sanctification of the hours of the day; and emphasizes the present moment.

113

This chapter discussing Christ's human foundation finds completion in two later chapters to provide specific ways to strengthen it. Chapter 9, "Human Virtues," will treat of key elements of the human foundation to become more fully like Christ in His humanity, like sanctification of work (level of "nature"). In addition, Chapter 10, "Peace of Heart & Sacrament of the Present Moment," provides the cultivation of the necessary disposition at the human level to allow the child of God to be able to listen to the inspirations of the Holy Spirit (second level of "grace"), so as to become fully like Christ the Son in His relation to the Father.

At the heart of the Christian life, it is the sacrament of the present moment that rules the day. Instead of allowing the hours of the day to drain away like water draining in a sink, through the sacrament of the present moment, the child of God, like Jesus did, lives in the arms of our Heavenly Father from hour to hour, finding eternity in each hour, preserving the water in the sink of our soul. We catch that living water, the Holy Spirit, and carry Him in communion with the Trinity in each moment without looking at the next moment, and we offer ourselves and our work for the salvation of the world.

# CHAPTER 6

## *CHRIST'S DIVINE LIFE*

### *(Led by the Holy Spirit)*

From this moment, the Evangelists show us that in all things the Soul of Christ is directed by the Holy Spirit and His activity inspired by Him. It is the Holy Spirit Who leads Him into the desert to be tempted... by the action of the same Spirit, He casts out devils from the bodies of those possessed... Finally, St. Paul tells us that in the chief work of Christ, the one in which His love for His Father and for us shines out— namely His bloody sacrifice upon the Cross for the salvation of the world— it was by the Holy Spirit Christ offered Himself...

What do all these revelations show? That in Christ, the human activity was directed by the Spirit of love. The One Who acts is Christ, the Incarnate Word.... but it is under inspiration, by the promptings of the Holy Spirit, that Christ acted. The human soul of Jesus had, through the grace of the hypostatic union, become the soul of the Word; it was filled like to none other with sanctifying grace, and lastly, it acted under the guidance of the Holy Spirit.[1] (Dom Columba Marmion)

Employing the image of a house, the "plan of life" (previous chapter) is a constitutive element of the foundation for the divine edifice, "Jesus' Divine Life," which is essentially "being led by the Holy Spirit." Blessed Columba Marmion's text above affirms that, during His entire earthly life, especially manifest during His ministry, Jesus was led by the Holy Spirit to do the Father's will. As one author indicated, it was by the Holy Spirit that Jesus was led out of Nazareth, into the desert, out of the desert, into different ministries, to Calvary, and then into Heaven. Christ is our model and paradigm, and, as "new Christs" (children of the Father), being led by the Father's Spirit constitutes our building, the purpose of the foundation. It is our path of living "filiation" (sonship, daughtership) of the Father.

---

[1] Raymund Thibault, ed., *The Trinity in our Spiritual Life: An Anthology of the Writings of Dom Columba Marmion, O.S.B.* (Westminster, Mary: The Newman Press, 1954), 221-222.

This path of being led by the Holy Spirit, being a contemplative, has profound implications for the world. For Hans Urs von Balthasar identifies two complementary components of a contemplative: intimacy or union with God, and mission. More profoundly, he teaches that there is a double moment in mysticism, as described here in relation to Mary: the solitude of being "thrust" into the very bosom of God; and then being directed back toward the community in order to build up that communion through the novelty of the interpretation of the revelation given, as seen in the life of Mary.

> The sense of being thrust up to the very bosom of God; the cataract of graces poured out, seemingly senselessly, on the unprepared servant; the solitude, both terrible and blissful, which surrounds the person thus elevated and chosen as bride; the dizzy height without anything to hold on to, remote from analogy and comparison; the utterly unique destiny of being Mother of the eternal God, and, being thus exposed to both heaven and earth, the awareness of having a sole and freely accepted responsibility for both, and for the inhabitants of both— all of this must be endured in contemplation, perhaps for only a split second which, miraculously, is not fatal. Once it was Mary who was the unique one, with no one to help her. For she was the prototypical Church. Every contemplative must go through this to some degree, once at least, if he is drawn to profess allegiance and unreserved submission to the Word of God. But he may experience this more than once, for the Bridegroom continues to bend in love over the Bride as at first. Subsequently, in a second period, the contemplative is directed toward the community. 'Behold, your kinswoman Elizabeth...'[2]

It is the path of introducing the instrument of God first to deep intimacy, and also deep surrender, that allows God to act powerfully in that person. This is the pattern or form of preparation of the great friends of God: Abraham, Elijah, St. John the Baptist, St. Paul (in the desert), and the Holy Family in the hiddenness and "silence" of Nazareth. It is also the pattern that God employs with us if He gives us a special mission— to be contemplatives in the world. It is specifically to lead us to live Christ's sonship, being led by the Holy Spirit from moment to moment in total surrender as the Father's little child.

---

[2] Hans Urs von Balthasar, *Prayer* (San Francisco: Ignatius Press, 1986; German orig. *Das betrachtende Gebet*, 1955), 96-97.

## *Introduction to the Three Stages of Faith Life*

Contemplatives in the world allow God to use them freely. They are "christs" for the world. The Church's experience is that the path to this intimacy and surrender is progressive, involving distinct steps. The Church's theology and spirituality have typically recognized three stages or steps in three dimensions for each of the following: living faith; fulfilling God's will; and accepting the cross (see table on next page). For the sake of simplicity in our spiritual life, we have to this point limited our vision to two main stages (foundation and building) for three reasons: it is simpler and more focused; the structure has two fundamental stages (e.g., ascetical and mystical Mansions of St. Teresa's Interior Castle); and the third stage is simply the culmination of the second stage.

But in this chapter, it is worthwhile to expand and see the fuller comprehensive three stages. Our paradigm of the two levels corresponds to three stages:

> Stage 1: External Observance (foundation);
>
> Stage 2: Listening to the Inspirations of the Holy Spirit (edifice);
>
> Stage 3: Total Surrender or Abandonment to God's Will.

We shall now develop all three stages, with particular emphasis on the last two.

A person can easily be content with doing just the first stage of "External Observance" (e.g., family life, work, sacramental life, formal prayer). Perhaps, one day, he begins to feel an interior call to deeper intimacy, and moves to the second stage, to listen to the inspirations of the Holy Spirit in the depths of his heart. He becomes more and more attentive to the interior voice of the Holy Spirit and His exterior "voice" in the events of life and in the call of his superiors and those in need. Then, marvelling at how the saints have opened and given themselves totally to God, he begins to give himself more fully, the third stage, abandonment to His will, so that God can do great things in and through him, so that he can make Christ live again on earth in him.

The validity of these three stages is reinforced by the presence of three stages of Christian life, each drawn from different sources, specifically of Faith (Church's understanding), Fulfilling God's Will (St. Faustina), and carrying the cross (St. Bernard of Clairvaux), and they parallel the three stages of "doing God's will" in Jacques Philippe. Let us examine these three stages to both illuminate and deepen our understanding of the three stages in Christian life.

### *Three Stages of Faith, Fulfilling God's Will, and Carrying the Cross[3]*

| 1st | 2nd | 3rd |
|---|---|---|
| Faith<br><br>*Credo Deum (esse)-* I believe that God exists. | *Credo Deo-* I believe in what God (Church) teaches. | *Credo in Deum-* I believe with an entrustment to God (gift of self). |
| *(Diary 444)*<br><br>Fulfilling God's Will<br><br>1. *First degree: "the soul carries out all the rules and statutes pertaining to* **external observance."** | 2. *Second degree: "the soul accepts inspirations and carries them out faithfully."* | 3. *Third degree: "the soul,* **abandoned to the will of God,** *allows Him to dispose of it freely, and God does with it as He pleases, and it is a docile tool in His hands."* |
| - Beginners accept God's will with patience, but conform themselves to it with difficulty, especially when it clashes with their point of view, liking, or natural inclination. | - The advanced seek the will of God as a **guide to life** and they accept it with devotion. | - The perfect find joy in it and **have no other desire but to do what pleases God.** |

---

[3] Texts are drawn from St. Faustina's *Diary*, commented upon in the work, *In Saint Faustina's School of Trust*, 14-15, 164-166.

| (*Diary* 446)<br><br>Suffering (degrees in one's conformity to God's will): | | |
|---|---|---|
| 1. "The third were neither nailed to their crosses nor holding them firmly in their hands, but were **dragging their crosses** behind them and were discontent." | 2. "The second multitude were not nailed to their crosses, but were **holding them firmly in their hands.**" | 3. "Then I saw the Lord Jesus nailed to the cross. When He had hung on it for a while, I saw a multitude of souls **crucified like Him.**" |
| St. Bernard of Clairvaux:<br><br>- "***Beginners do not indeed love suffering,*** *but rather seek to* **escape** *it. However, they choose to suffer rather than to offend God and, though groaning under the weight of the cross, they endure it with patience.*" | - "*The advanced, though* **they do not yet seek the cross, willingly carry it with a certain joy,** *knowing that each new pang of suffering represents an additional degree of glory.*" | - "*The perfect,* **led by love,** *go forth to meet the cross in order to become more like Jesus. They embrace the cross, not because it is in itself lovable, but because it offers them an* **opportunity of proving their love for Jesus.**" |

It is suggested here that these stages of growth flow together: that growth in faith will be accompanied by a corresponding growth in doing God's will and a deeper participation in Christ's cross, all culminating in the apex—surrender. Let us now examine each of these three themes individually.

First, regarding "faith," we can see a progression from believing that God exists (*Credo Deum*), to believing in what God teaches through the Church (*Credo Deo*), and, finally, to believing with an act of entrustment of one's whole being to God (*Credo in Deum*). In the first stage, we can find many people who would admit to believing in the existence of "God," even though they may not even have any formal religious attachment. An example of this is an elderly Chinese man who, having grown up in China without any formal religious affiliation or instruction, was sometimes heard to say, "God willing," or "Thanks be to God." Then, in the second stage, we would admit that there is progress in faith if a Catholic is able to accept all that the Church teaches because she speaks in Christ's name or as His Spouse, even if that Catholic does not understand the reasons, like the difficulty for some with accepting the Church's prohibition of the use of artificial contraception. There is a deeper stage that all are called to: giving oneself to God in Christ. It is a personal relationship with, and surrender to, our beloved Saviour, Jesus Christ, the ultimate faith to which we aspire.

St. Thomas Aquinas confirms our thoughts on the three stages of faith:

> St. Thomas' analysis of perfect faith or the development of this virtue distinguishes three close-knit, hierarchical stages. The first may be summarized with these words: *I believe that God exists.* Faith, however, cannot be limited only to the assent of the mind to the truths of the faith taught by the Church. The personal response to God is still missing at this stage; there is merely an intellectual approval of the truths contained in divine Revelation. Supernatural faith begins practically in the next stage, which we can summarize as: *I believe God.* Such faith consists in a personal turning to God, in seeking Him as one's final Good and End. Still, this is not that perfect faith which says *I believe in God* and is formed by supernatural love. Only then does the virtue of faith emerge integrally because there is an effort to *surrender the whole self to God.* Thus, perfect faith tends to self-surrender to God, that is, to abandonment to Him.[4]

St. Thomas clearly understood that "perfect faith tends to self-surrender to God, that is, to abandonment to Him." This fits in perfectly and corresponds to the goal of surrender in the context of fulfilling "listening to inspirations of the Holy Spirit." The stages of development to perfect faith require progressive letting go, perceiving my total helplessness, and relying more and more on God.

Second, we can also identify three progressive stages in carrying the cross. The saints have learned that the greatest spiritual progress is made under the shadow of the cross. In brief, the three stages of carrying the cross are: the outer multitude who drag their crosses after them; the more faithful ones who carry their crosses firmly in their hands; and the great friends of God who are crucified on the cross with Christ.[5]

---

[4] *In St. Faustina's School of Trust,* 14-15.
[5] We find this truth in St. Faustina's *Diary.*

People living in the later years of their life might, on looking back, perceive a certain pattern, a two-stage progression in life: an acquiring stage, that corresponds to the youth-adult growing stage; followed by a "losing" stage, the older, declining later years. The first stage consists of perfecting our humanity, developing our intelligence and common sense, our reverence to and service of our elderly parents, our human virtues like punctuality, faithfulness, responsibility, and so on. The second stage is when God causes us to lose control: by sickness, humiliation, loss of memory, a family member who is very difficult to live with, and so on. It is at this second level we live the "whoever loses his life for my sake and the gospel's will save it" (Mk 8: 35). This later stage is actually the superior stage, that of surrender and allowing God to direct us.

To recapitulate, we see that the three stages of doing God's will correspond to our stages: **1. External observances; 2. Inspirations; 3. Abandonment.** The first level of fidelity can be tied to "external observances," and the second level of docility to the Holy Spirit can be tied to obeying the Holy Spirit's "inspirations" and the completion in "abandonment."

### *1. Stage 1: External Observance*

We note quickly that Stage 1 of external observances itself has different degrees of priority. Protecting priority is essentially doing God's will. Our life can be thrown into turmoil when we get very busy or when crises break out, and it is vital to maintain priorities, that is, to do God's will.

---

"O my Jesus, you do not give a reward for the successful performance of a work, but for the good will and the labor undertaken. Therefore, I am completely at peace, even if all my undertakings and efforts should be thwarted or should come to naught. If I do all that is in my power, the rest is not my business. And therefore the greatest storms do not disturb the depths of my peace; the will of God dwells in my conscience." (*Diary* n. 952, p. 371).

"Although the path is very thorny, I do not fear to go ahead. Even if a hailstorm of persecutions covers me; even if my friends forsake me, even if all things conspire against me, and the horizon grows dark; even if a raging storm breaks out, and I feel I am quite alone and must brave it all; still, fully at peace, I will trust in Your mercy, O my God, and my hope will not be disappointed." (*Diary* n. 1195, p. 432).

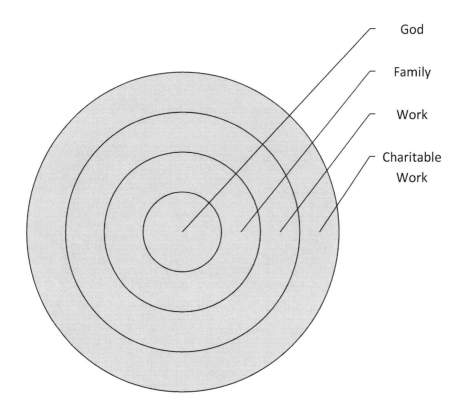

God

Family

Work

Charitable
Work

Let us present a real case. A devout Catholic doctor with a busy schedule (including attending conferences, assisting at the parish) and expecting her first child, approached her spiritual director, asking for counsel. She has guilty feelings at the thought of pulling back from parish work, feeling as if she is not doing her part in the New Evangelization. Her spiritual director drew the concentric circles above to give a visual sense of her priorities.

She found this schema very helpful when given the following explanation. The innermost circles are the most important and she must protect these at all costs. The principle is to begin to let go of activities in the outermost circle, working progressively inwards. Thus, if her husband wishes to stop participating in Sunday Mass, she will have to refuse to join him, since God comes first; if work conflicts with family, e.g., pregnancy, then the woman will take a maternity leave— the child comes first; if parish volunteer work conflicts with her professional work, then she may need to temporarily give up her duties of running the youth group. One always maintains the priority or hierarchy, and when overwhelmed, starts letting go of the outer circles first. The doctor felt quite at peace when she saw clearly what God was asking of her.

A general hierarchy of priorities that applies to everyone could look something like this:

> (i) Avoiding sin (e.g., internet temptations, missing Mass, infrequent Confession, excessive gambling, judging others, bad company);
>
> (ii) Obeying the Church and one's superiors (parents, teachers, bishops, spiritual directors);
>
> (iii) Duties of state of life: prayer, religious formation of children, work, parish and evangelization, etc.;
>
> (iv) Making a plan of life and keeping to it: Dom Chautard says that if we are to become holy, a schedule is necessary.

Here are some other examples of misplaced priority: (i) A layman who does his job unprofessionally or puts his work before his family; (ii) A seminarian who, being busy or behind in his academics, neglects brother seminarians and closets himself in his room or starts to take shortcuts in his prayer life; (iii) A devout person who does not open up to, and confide in, his spiritual director and ends up guiding himself, and seeks extreme mortifications or special devotions or plans that may not be God's will for him.

## 2. Stage 2: Listening to the Holy Spirit's Inspirations

Jacques Philippe, in *In the School of the Holy Spirit*, quotes texts from Fr. Louis Lallemant that reveal a truth that many are unaware of: all perfection consists of "taking note of the ways and movements of the Holy Spirit in our souls."

> …. All of our perfection depends on this fidelity; and *the whole spiritual life could be summed up as taking note of the ways and movements of the Holy Spirit in our souls* and strengthening our wills in the resolution to follow them, using for that purpose all the exercises of prayer, reading, the Sacraments, the practice of virtue and the accomplishing of good works.

> Some people have many beautiful practices and do a number of *external acts of virtue*; they place their efforts on material acts of virtue. That is good for beginners, *but it is much closer to perfection to follow the inner leading of the Holy Spirit and to be guided by His movements.* It is true that in this latter way of acting there is less perceptible satisfaction, but there is more inner life and more real virtue.[6] (emphasis mine)

This text points to a more fundamental truth that many are unaware of: that the Holy Spirit dwells within us and that Christian life entails a dialogue with this interior Guest. This dialogue begins with an awareness of His presence and a desire to listen to His voice. Against this reality, then, the fundamental tragedy of life and the cause of all problems is the failure to hear the voice of the Holy Spirit, who is given to us at Baptism (see St. Augustine's discovery). To use an inanimate analogy, we are like radios or receivers, meant to receive transmissions in the context of our own lives, so that others can receive the message; or like translators at the United Nations councils, who provide simultaneous translations for the Council members. If a receiver is unable to pick up transmissions or a translator is unable to hear the speaker, then both fail in their *raison d'être*, their mission. Let us insist again on this fact: the secret of Jesus' influence and power is being led by the Holy Spirit.

## A. Obstacles to listening to the Holy Spirit

What then are the difficulties that prevent us from being led by the inspirations of the Holy Spirit? A first obstacle in our Christian life is doing what is merely "good," and not what is the will of God. That which is good but not God's will is not "holy" and does not save. If the Hebrew people on the night of Passover, out of a spirit of asceticism, did not consume the lamb that was slain by each family as Yahweh commanded, their first born would have died. They would have disobeyed God and frustrated the "type" or prefiguration pattern that anticipates the consuming of the Eucharist in Holy Communion. If Jesus had decided that He could best serve mankind by going out and preaching to all nations, beginning with Samaria and bypassing Calvary, then He would have disobeyed the Father and, according to His Father's plan, would not have saved mankind.

---

[6] Louis Lallemant, quoted in Jacques Philippe, *In the School of the Holy Spirit* (New York: Scepter Publishers, 2007; French orig. *A l'École de l'Esprit Saint*, 2002), 75.

A second obstacle is to fulfill the first stage of "external observances" but never go beyond it. Fr. Philippe teaches that, while some people "place their efforts on material acts of virtue," "it is much closer to perfection to follow the inner leading of the Holy Spirit and to be guided by His movements." Here then is a great trap that we can also fall into, focusing on tasks and being led by our own will. Most Christians may find it hard to be interior. They may do formal prayers, be faithful to the Church's teaching, but not know docility to the Holy Spirit. This is staying at the level of duty, and not yet attaining "filiation," sonship or daughtership in imitation of Christ. Some may feel a certain zeal, but run around without any priority or any awareness of seeking God's will in their life. In their busyness, they may not even make time for prayer, for proper meals, not even for recreation or exercise. This hive of activity at a superficial level can feel somewhat fulfilling. Of course, what would be worse than this is not fulfilling their "external observances," their duties, in the first place.

A third obstacle, related to the second obstacle, is not going within one's heart to hear the Holy Spirit. Fr. Joseph Langford offers some helpful insights drawn from Mother Teresa of Calcutta's spirituality. He observes that people who have seen her at prayer noticed that she immediately goes to the depths of her heart. The tendency of many people at prayer is to stay at the level of their heads or the surface of their soul, and not go to the depths of their hearts.

> Mother Teresa is ever teaching what Our Lady modeled for us: that we cannot pray satisfactorily by staying on the surface of our soul. This leaves us like a paper cup on the surface of the sea, buffeted by the waves and wind of distraction. If instead we go deeper, like a diver seeking precious pearls, we will find peace and treasure. Pearls do not float on the surface. We can spend all day in the water, just as we can spend all day in prayer, and go home with nothing, unless we pierce the depths. The seat and center of our waking consciousness is normally at the "head" level…. But this is not the place of encounter with God. We need to pass to the level of the heart. The heart, in Mother Teresa's understanding of Our Lady and her interior life, represents the place of inner quiet, not feelings or sentimentality but rather inner depth, the silent place where God speaks.[7]

---

[7] Joseph Langford, *Mother Teresa: In the Shadow of Our Lady*, 57.

These words strike at the heart of the difficulty of many: "We can spend all day in the water, just as we can spend all day in prayer, and go home with nothing, unless we pierce the depths." We make little progress because we are at the surface, buffeted by the events of life, and do not descend to the depths, to our hearts, "the silent place where God speaks." Scripture speaks of the pearl of great price, which is God, and He is found, not on the surface, but in the depths of the ocean, the depths of our soul, which is our spiritual heart.

A fourth obstacle is to not find God in the events of life. Fr. Langford goes even deeper, as he describes the call of Mother Teresa to be "contemplatives in the heart of the world." Formed by Ignatian spirituality, she learned to find God, not by following *fuga mundi* spirituality (flight from the world), to escape distraction to find God. Instead, like St. Ignatius, she was able to find God in the world, even in tragic situations. This is possible from the above, from finding God in prayer: *"The fruit of prayer is faith."*[8] Fr. Langford describes a horrific accident in which a plane carrying Mother Teresa to Tanzania, on landing, veered to one side and cut up two of her religious Sisters. Surveying the carnage that her plane caused, she was heard to say under her breath, "'God's will...'— nothing more, nothing else." Only a life of contemplative prayer could produce that kind of deep faith.

> According to the second kind of spirituality represented by both St. Ignatius and Mother Teresa, we choose to find God in all things, even to the point of finding God in the worst things, in pain and in poverty, in the Cross. What seemed darkness becomes light. What seemed defeat, for Jesus in his Passion or for us in our sufferings, becomes victory.[9]

Trials can shake our faith, and it is precisely in these events that we can find God and light and victory. Summarizing this truth, he says: "Jesus told Mother Teresa that her interior life would be her only support in this difficult mission she was undertaking."[10]

A fifth obstacle that prevents us from being led by the Holy Spirit is not going to the root causes of our problems, which can be various. One cause of these difficulties can flow from attachment or holding on to something

---

[8] Ibid., 63.
[9] Ibid., 69-70.
[10] Ibid., 70.

that is not God's will (e.g., an attachment to a particular type of work, or excessive concern for one's health, recreation). When discerning God's will, our desires can emotionally affect our discernment; which is why it is important that we let go, be "indifferent," seeking only what God wants. Let us expand upon an insightful image that Jacques Philippe points to in one sentence. The Holy Spirit's passage through us can be compared to a rapidly flowing river. In spite of the volume of water and the speed through which it travels, such a river should flow with ease and relative quiet through the river bed. But once *shoals* are introduced, eddies develop and the water becomes violent, and rages and froths, and becomes dangerous to travel on.[11] Similarly, when there is "resistance" in our system that arises from some attachment, there is disturbance in our system from this resistance.

On the other hand, we can have troubles at the human and psychological level, and if we have learned to let go, we can have peace deep in our souls where God resides. One common temptation that befalls good Catholics is to be troubled by their sins or defects. A devout Catholic may be faithful in many ways, and yet have one dominant weakness (e.g., anger or unchastity) that makes him lose his peace and feel that he is failing God. Yet, God desires that we be human and little: confess with contrition, make resolutions, accept our weaknesses, and *never lose our peace*— He did not promise that we will overcome all our defects in this life. St. Francis de Sales taught that we should never be troubled by our sins and weaknesses.

## B. Examples of Listening to the Holy Spirit within the Religious Sphere

Let us consider ways to enable us to listen to the Holy Spirit. First, one of the best ways to put into practice listening to the inspirations of the Holy Spirit is by consulting the Holy Spirit in everything consequential. One such example is a new religious community that has inscribed *consulting* the Holy Spirit within the core of their charism. The community never makes a step unless it has discerned first that God wishes them to pray for a certain outcome, but they also asked God how and what to pray for.

---

[11] Jacques Philippe, *In the School of the Holy Spirit*, 53.

Another example is the response of an American diocesan exorcist to the question of what procedure or method he uses in going about treating deliverance of possible cases of infestation by evil spirits. He replied that, while keeping to the Church's general norms, his specific procedure after an initial interview is to ask at each step what the Holy Spirit wishes. He shared the insight that the situations in which he thinks he already has the answer are when he is usually wrong. Here are some concrete instances in which we may wish to consult the Holy Spirit. When a newly ordained priest needs to find a spiritual director, he could entrust the task to our Lady and have her show him whom it is that God wants to be his spiritual director. Another example of letting go is, if one is struggling with the monotony of the Ignatian 30-day Spiritual Exercises, one can try to stop counting the days and see the gift of each day, to live within the present moment— that is, allow the Holy Spirit to lead.

Second, at the end of the day, how does one know that one is following the Holy Spirit and not being led by the evil spirit? The *fruits* of such fidelity at both levels should be unmistakable: joy, peace, tranquility of spirit, gentleness, simplicity, and light. What comes from the spirit of evil brings sadness, trouble, agitation, discouragement, worry, confusion, and darkness. These marks of the good and the evil spirit are unmistakable signs in themselves. For example, when the evil spirit wishes us to pursue a course that is not God's will, he tends to move us to be impulsive, to force things, to rush and be anxious. Peace, joy, and the like are among the fruits of the Holy Spirit, the devil is incapable of producing them or consolation in general. We also make a distinction between sadness and sorrow; the latter is good, such as sorrow at one's mother's death or sorrow that leads to repentance (contrition is itself a consolation).

### 3. Stage 3: The Ultimate Goal of Self-Surrender

Jesus' path goes further: "His whole humanity was completely subordinated to the Holy Spirit; His human will completely subject to the will of God. He emptied Himself, laying down all initiative, all use of His own powers." [12]Fr. Louis Lallemant describes this third level beyond listening to the Holy Spirit: surrender or abandonment to God's will,

---

[12] Eugene Boylan, *The Spiritual Life of the Priest*, 109-110.

The goal which we should aspire to, after we have exercised the purification of our hearts for a long time, is to be *so possessed and governed by the Holy Spirit* that it is He alone who leads all of our faculties and senses and who rules our interior and external movements, and that we abandon ourselves entirely by spiritual renunciation of our preferences and our own satisfactions. Thus we will no longer live in ourselves but in Jesus Christ, through full faithful response to the operations of his divine Spirit, and by perfect subjection of all our rebelliousness to the power of his grace....

We ought to *receive each inspiration as a word of God*, which proceeds from his wisdom, his mercy, and his infinite goodness, and which can produce marvellous effects in us if we place no obstacle in its way. Let us consider what God's word has wrought: it *created* the heavens and the earth, and drew all creatures out of nothing to share in the being of God in the state of nature, because it met no resistance in that nothingness.[13] (emphasis added)

We are to be possessed by Christ through being governed by the Holy Spirit, such that it is "He alone who leads all of our faculties and senses and who rules our interior and external movements," and "we will no longer live in ourselves but in Jesus Christ." Fr. Lallemant speaks of the power of God's inspiration, "to receive each inspiration as a word of God," the word of God that has the power to create the universe out of nothing. Each inspiration of the Holy Spirit is thus a creative word spoken by God who can recreate and renew us in grace. This is the true power in the world, that works secretly in our souls, not what that we do ourselves and by ourselves.

We would be remiss in treating of surrender or abandonment and not make mention of the spirituality of St. Thérèse of Lisieux. She has been highly praised by popes, including Pope Pius X, who called her "the greatest saint of modern times," and Pope John XXIII, who said, "I have a great love for the great Teresa of Avila, but little Thérèse brings us safe to shore. We must rely on her."[14] Her doctrine is too profound for even one section of a chapter, one must therefore rely on her many expert commentators. For the specific topic of abandonment, perhaps no better can be found in English than Fr. Jean d'Elbée's *I Believe in Love*. The doctrine of St. Thérèse of Lisieux as presented by Fr. d'Elbée has influenced many, one priest calling it a "gem."

---

[13] Louis Lallemant, quoted in Jacques Philippe, *In the School of the Holy Spirit*, 75, 77.
[14] Jean d'Elbée, *I Believe in Love*, 68-70.

## A. Two Paradigms of Surrender

Let us present two outstanding twentieth-century examples of this surrender. Two great figures linked together within God's providence, both of whom radiate this simplicity of surrender, are Hans Urs von Balthasar and Adrienne von Speyr. Hans Urs von Balthasar is regarded by some as the greatest theologian of the twentieth century.[15] A decisive moment came at the age of eighteen in the summer of 1927 when he went on a thirty-day retreat for lay students in the Black Forest near Basel. It throws light on the magnificent adventure that is a call. Years later he would still remember the tree beneath which "I was struck as by lightning" and that forever seared his heart:

> Years later, he recalled his vocation came almost as lightning from a cloudless sky: "Even now, thirty years later, I could still go to that remote path in the Black Forest, not far from Basel, and find again the tree beneath which I was struck as by lightning…. And yet it was neither theology nor the priesthood which then came to my mind in a flash. It was simply this: you have nothing to choose, you have been called. You will not serve, you will be taken into service. You have no plans to make, you are just a little stone in a mosaic which has long been ready."[16]

Von Balthasar realized what God was asking: "All that I had to do was simply to leave everything behind and follow, without making any plans, without desires or particular intuitions. I had only to remain there to see how I could be useful." This experience moved von Balthasar to his depths, and would radically shape his life and his future. How did he understand this intuition? For von Balthasar, this was something of a death and a resurrection experience, bringing him into a new life in Christ. What he realized was the presence of this law of death and resurrection, "a living law that shatters us and, by shattering us, also heals us… We know God the more we are in God and not in ourselves." It was the *availability* of being

---

[15] Von Balthasar, along with his professor, Henri de Lubac, and his fellow-student, Jean Danielou, were elevated to the Cardinalate by Pope John Paul II in recognition of their contribution to theology. All three were involved in founding the patristic series, *Sources Chrétiennes*, as well as the Journal, *Communio*. Von Balthasar has written, with a prodigious output that rivals Augustine, a Trilogy, *Glory of the Lord*, *Theo-Drama*, and *Theo-Logic*, that could very well constitute a new foundation for theology.

[16] Hans Urs von Balthasar, "Pourquoi je me suis fait prêtre," in *Pourquoi je me suis fait prêtre. Témoignages recueillis*, eds. Jorge Sans Vila and Ramón Sans Vila (Belgium: Tournai, 1961), 21.

used by the Holy Spirit: "You have nothing to choose, you have been called. You will not serve, you will be taken into service. You have no plans to make…" It was this availability that we find in the hearts of Jesus and Mary; it is the underpinning of all spiritual life. It appears to constitute the bedrock of the entire theology of von Balthasar, and his great impact on theology in the twentieth century (e.g., his influence on Pope John Paul II and Pope Benedict XVI) points to the importance of this theme.

As his collaborator, Adrienne von Speyr radiates the same spirit of "receptivity" and "expropriation" that is found in the theology and writings of Hans Urs von Balthasar. The quotation below from Adrienne von Speyr, a doctor and mystic and co-founder of "The Community of St. John," depicts the surrender required by Christ of the consecrated soul, the "witness":

> But apart from these there is the little company of those who are marked out by God to give a special, qualified testimony. Their mission is not exhausted when they have fulfilled the demand, when their lives correspond to their life deposited in God, when they have radiated the grace they have received and understood returning to God as beginning anew in this world. That mission is universal and is realized to some extent in every Christian life. The witness singled out by God, on the contrary, received a distinct and personal task direct from God. Part of this mission consists, in fact, in leading the life of an exceptional witness. That means placing one's whole personal life at the service of one's existence as a witness. The witness binds himself before God to sacrifice himself whole and entire to his mission. He binds himself to do so even before hearing what his mission is. Nor will he ever get to know the content of his mission fully and completely. He will have to listen and attend to it afresh every day. The content may change suddenly from top to bottom; it may change direction at any moment and may even turn into its contrary. While carrying out his mission, its real content will be concealed from the exception, and it will certainly not be something he can view as a whole. He must always be ready for everything. There is no resting in such a mission, for it springs directly from the very source of God's life.[17]

It radiates the availability and the docility of those "consecrated" to Christ, especially the priest: "The witness binds himself before God to sacrifice

---

[17] Adrienne von Speyr, *John: The Word Becomes Flesh: Meditations on John 1-5*, vol. 1 (San Francisco: Ignatius, 1994; German orig. *Das Wort wird Fleisch*, 1949), 70-71.

himself whole and entire to his mission." He does not need to know the future at each stage, he just allows himself to be led: "He binds himself to do so even before hearing what his mission is. Nor will he ever get to know the content of his mission fully and completely. He will have to listen and attend to it afresh every day." He does not need to see the "whole," what God's project is and what his program is and where he is going, "He must always be ready for everything." This is perhaps what Adrienne von Speyr herself lived as she was called to suffer, to be a mystic, and to found a radically new community for their time: just to be available.

## B. Christ-Form—Expropriation of Self

Let us give further theological elaboration to this key concept. To what depths of Christian faith does von Balthasar link this receptivity or holy indifference? He links it to the form of Jesus Christ Himself, our only model. For von Balthasar, there is only one "form," namely, Jesus Christ. Jesus has many titles, such as "Creator" and "Saviour," but his fundamental identity is that of "Son of God." It is very instructive that on both occasions in which the Father spoke from heaven, He points to His "beloved Son," and gave us the greatest counsel on the second occasion: "Listen to Him." We have received an objective configuration to Christ at Baptism, and a priest receives further configuration at Ordination. But each needs the subjective configuration, to "listen to Him." Christ is the only Beloved of the Father, and we are pleasing to Him to the extent that He sees Christ in us and to the extent that we pray and work "in Him." He has become everything for us. In an inspired text, Pope John Paul II establishes this context of the all-embracing mystery of Christ in *Redemptor hominis*.

> Our spirit is set in one direction, the only direction for our intellect, will and heart is— towards Christ our Redeemer, towards Christ, the Redeemer of man. We wish to look towards him— because there is salvation in no one else but him, the Son of God— repeating what Peter said: "Lord, to whom shall we go? You have the words of eternal life."
>
> … we must constantly aim at him "who is the head", "through whom are all things and through whom we exist," who is both "the way, and the truth" and "the resurrection and the life", seeing whom, we see the Father, and who had to go away from us— that is, by his death on the Cross and then by his Ascension into heaven— in order that the Counsellor should come to us and should keep coming to us as the Spirit

of truth. In him are "all the treasures of wisdom and knowledge", and the Church is his Body. "By her relationship with Christ, the Church is a kind of sacrament or sign and means of intimate union with God, and of the unity of all mankind", and the source of this is he, he himself, he the Redeemer.[18]

## Mary as the Greatest Disciple

Von Balthasar highlights the greatest disciple to live this spousal relationship and incorporation to Christ— Mary. It is Mary especially who manifests this Christ-form, linked to the Church. In his doctoral thesis, Brendan Leahy (appointed bishop of Limerick in 2013) draws out some Pauline Body-Bride images in von Balthasar's role of the Church and Mary in their christological and Trinitarian background. The Church is the "Body-Bride of Christ," the Church as a community is a theological, not a sociological, affirmation (nor built upon the memory of Christ nor based on His teaching). The Church is the new community brought about by Christ's Paschal mystery and is an active sharing in the community of communities, the life of the Triune God. To keep before us the notion of the Church as coming totally from the Word made flesh, von Balthasar links two Pauline images with "Body-Bride." The first image, the "Body," highlights the Eucharistic-sacramental mediation of the Trinity. It is symbolized in the pouring of blood and water, and presents the Church as "an extension, communication, and a partaking of personality of Christ in external sacramental forms."[19] The second image, the "Bride," affirms:

> … the contra-distinct openness and response of love to Christ. It refers to that feminine element of the "supra-sexual" relationship between Christ and the Church. Through the outpouring of the Holy Spirit, the Church stands vis-à-vis Christ as a "someone," a subject, a person, a co-operating agent formed by the subjectivity and personalities of all who form the Church.[20]

Von Balthasar finds these elements personified in Mary.

---

[18] Pope John Paul II, *Redemptor hominis*, n. 7.
[19] Brendan Leahy, *The Marian Profile: In the Ecclesiology of Hans Urs von Balthasar* (New York: New City Press, 2000), 59.
[20] Ibid, 59-60.

Mary's "yes" as Mother and Bride was given in the name of humanity, reversing Eve's disobedience. Mary's location in the Mystery is to say that "the unique design God has for Mary originates within the Trinitarian dialogue of love that 'decided' upon creation and redemption."[21] God included Mary's "yes" as an indispensable part of His plan to unite all things under Christ. She was "chosen before the foundation of the world" both as the Saviour's mother and also "to correspond to the Son and be presented by Him to Himself as that 'bride' who would conclude in advance for all, and in all, the love contract between God and the world, between the eternal and the created heart."[22]

Mary as a paradigm of encountering the mystery involves expropriating herself. In her encounter with God, she does not eliminate her own history, but "fulfills and surpasses her dreams…. She delivers herself totally over to God. Totally 'expropriated,' as von Balthasar says, she plays the unique role in history God has for her…. She lives outside herself, not making her own limited plans…."[23] This mirrors the learning that von Balthasar himself mentioned earlier. He went through a period of growing emptiness, when he found that the modern attitude placed the artist ahead of his work. In a decisive moment of conversion, he felt called to simply wait and let himself be taken up by God instead of making his own plans. It was a participation in Christ's death and resurrection pattern, in which God shatters us and also heals us in doing so.[24] To be in God has the characteristics of a new event: in Jesus Christ "we are projected toward the Father whose word is always love."[25]

## C. The Effortlessness of Surrender

In this vision of replicating the Son's surrender and expropriation, the greatest wisdom is surrender. As we progress in the spiritual life, we should find that the spiritual life is *effortless*, because this summit of the spiritual life involves abandonment, which is effortless. When we overcome our own will and live by the will of the Holy Spirit, we do not have to strain; God brings everything to us. For example, a father or mother can become

---

[21] Ibid., 72.
[22] Ibid.
[23] Ibid., 47.
[24] Ibid., 48.
[25] Ibid., 49.

extremely troubled when a child gets into trouble, perhaps an inappropriate photo is put on Facebook, or the child is hanging around bad company. One can follow the human instinct of reacting angrily at the child, or one can, while trying to love the child, turn to the Lord and wait for His response with great trust. This is the path of the simplicity of a child awaiting the Father's help with great confidence: "I would not give a fig for simplicity on this side of complexity, but I would give my life for the simplicity on the other side of complexity."[26] One seminarian, in sharing his call story, summarized well what we have said of God seeking to lead with our surrender. He spoke of how he was consoled during his life by the sense of God's presence, of His accompaniment, as if God was in the passenger seat in the car with him on the journey of life and discernment of his vocation. Then one day, it seemed that God spoke to him interiorly, saying, "Now, I want to drive."

*Surrender Brings much Progress in the Dark Nights*

It appears that the more a soul surrenders, the more he participates in Christ's Passion. As we shall see in Chapter 12 on "The Stages of the Interior Life" (Carmelite), we see that the "greatest work is done in the dark night of the soul." In the dark night, there is much trial and purification. It will seem that all his work is being destroyed, that he is regressing. The greatest learning is our "helplessness," to which Mary leads us.

> The greatest work is done in the dark night of the soul: It will seem that everything that we have worked for and built up is being destroyed. When we are sick, we cannot get up as we used to and carry out our responsibilities if our heads don't cooperate and we will seem useless to others. Helplessness is the greatest disposition we can hold before God. Those devoted to Mary go through these nights more quickly: This is because Mary teaches us how to surrender to God.[27]

When we sometimes feel that God is not listening to us, we can hearken to an insight of St. Pio of Pietrelcina: that in our crises, our experience is that we are drowning in life and yet God does not seem to be answering our pleas for help. He points out a deep truth that, when we hit rock bottom, God swiftly reaches down to help us. And this is because when we hit rock

---

[26] Oliver Wendell Holmes, quoted in David Allen, *Getting Things Done*, 141.
[27] *In St. Faustina's School of Trust*, 40-42.

bottom, we realize our total poverty, and only then let go and rely on Him, as it were, reaching out to the hand that is already there, outstretched to help us.

*Experience of God's Mercy Enables Surrender*

What enables surrender is the deep, personal experience of the Father's tender mercy. It is against this horizon of love that any progress is made. A touching text in St. Faustina's *Diary* that depicts God's providence, and that inspires trust and surrender, is the following image of a little child in dire need:

> On the fourth day, doubts began to trouble me: Is not this tranquility of mine false? Then I heard these words, *"My daughter, imagine that you are the sovereign of all the world and have the power to dispose of all things according to your good pleasure. You have the power to do all the good you want, and suddenly a little child knocks on your door, all trembling and in tears and, trusting in your kindness, asks for a piece of bread lest he die of starvation. What would you do for this child? Answer Me, my daughter."* And I said, "Jesus, I would give the child all it asked and a thousand times more." And the Lord said to me, *"That is how I am treating your soul. In this retreat I am giving you, not only peace, but also such a disposition of soul that even if you wanted to experience uneasiness you could not do so. My love has taken possession of your soul, and I want you to be confirmed in it. Bring your ear close to My Heart, forget everything else, and meditate upon My wondrous mercy. My love will give you the strength and courage you need in these matters."*[28]

Love not only calls forth love in return, but love also inspires filial trust and a spirit of childlikeness. This spirit is evident in St. Faustina.

> This knowledge [of God's divine mercy], given by faith, was the wellspring of her childlike trust, complete and unwavering. On the other hand, trust was expressed in her self-surrender to God, in the fulfillment of His will, and in the relinquishment from directing her own life so that He himself might carry out His eternal designs. This disposition of Sister Faustina manifests itself in a prayer said with childlike simplicity....[29]

With the trust and simplicity of a small child, I give myself to you today, O Lord Jesus, my Master. I leave you complete freedom in

---

[28] St. Faustina, *Diary*, n. 229, 115.
[29] *In St. Faustina's School of Trust*, 28.

directing my soul. Guide me along the paths You wish. I won't question them. I will follow You trustingly.[30]

On the opposite side, Jesus revealed to Faustina that what wounds Him Who is Divine Mercy Itself is distrust of His love.

> Mankind will not have peace until it turns with trust to My mercy. Oh, how much I am hurt by a soul's distrust! Such a soul professes that I am Holy and Just, but does not believe that I am Mercy and does not trust in My Goodness. Even the devils glorify My Justice but do not believe in My Goodness. My Heart rejoices in this title of Mercy.[31]

Part of letting go is the gradual realization that holiness is the work of the Holy Spirit. There is a widespread but mistaken idea that holiness is the work of human beings: that holiness is "perfection" in the sense that it is a human work that I can achieve with courage and patience. Jesus tells us instead, "Apart from me you can do nothing" (Jn 15:5). St. Louis de Montfort teaches the truth of what a sublime work that is "grace" in incarnating a new Christ:

> Oh, what an admirable work! To change that which is dust into light, to make pure that which is unclean, holy that which is sinful, to make the creature like its Creator, man like God! Admirable work, I repeat, but difficult in itself, and impossible to mere creature; only God by His abundant and extraordinary grace, can accomplish it. Even the creation of the whole world is not so great a masterpiece as this.[32]

A most striking image of this state of surrender or abandonment to which God calls us was given by an American religious. She notes that a newborn baby in the mother's arms does *not cling* but is totally held— the baby *flops*. This is what conversion is, going back to spiritual infancy. It is no wonder that Jesus said, "unless she becomes like the children, you cannot enter the kingdom of heaven." St. Thérèse of Lisieux herself taught this direction, that holiness is not about growing bigger but about becoming smaller, about childlike abandonment in confidence. St. Thérèse saw herself as being held in the Father's arms, sitting on His lap, and this is where each

---

[30] St. Faustina, *Diary*, n. 228, 115.
[31] Ibid., n. 300, 139.
[32] St. Louis de Montfort, *Secret of Mary* (Charlotte, NC: TAN, 2010 repr. of orig., 1940), 7-8.

new Christ or child of the Father should learn to bask in unconditional love— God is not primarily a judge, but our Father.

# CHAPTER 7

## *CHURCH & MARY*

### *(Two Mothers)*

Who is She who cometh forth as the morning rising, fair as the moon, bright as the sun, terrible as an army in battle-array? (Song of Songs 6:9)

And a great portent appeared in heaven, a woman clothed with the sun, with the moon under her feet, and on her head a crown of twelve stars; she was with child and she cried out in her pangs of birth, in anguish for delivery. (Rev 12:1-2)

Having established the Trinitarian origins of the "new Christ," we now proceed in Part II to the task of "incarnating" him. For the transformation in Christ must not be simply theoretical or spiritual, but take on a concrete, incarnate pattern. When we look at the lives of the saints, we can often discern three dominant pillars or loves: the Church, Mary, and the Eucharist. For example, we find three dominant pillars in the spirituality of Padre Pio, who explicitly identifies them as "three loves." We find the same in Bishop Fulton Sheen, who had the following insight regarding our times: when the faith of the Church is strong, the Church is attacked from outside; when the faith of the Church is weak, the Church is attacked from inside (by her own children). To this, he adds that, when the faith of the Church is weak, three great realities are neglected, namely: the Eucharist, the Church, and our Lady. Following this logic, when the faith of the Church is strong, these three realities should be strong, and the Church would manifest her vitality by their strength. This is, in fact, what we find in thriving religious communities today, especially ones that attract many vocations. Similarly, in the vibrant new lay movements, we can usually find these three loves as dominant elements within their charism.

These three pillars— the Church, Mary, the Eucharist— can be identified with three figures that constitute the protagonists (main characters) of Scripture. If we look upon the Bible as one Book, and since the primary Author is the Holy Spirit (*Dei verbum*), then we find the principal protagonists of the Bible's salvation history introduced in the opening chapter (Genesis) and whose story culminates in the closing chapter (Revelation). In Genesis, Yahweh's plan to restore humanity after the sin of Adam and Eve was to send a woman and child, who would crush Satan's head (Gen 3:15: "I will put enmity between you and the woman, and between your seed and her seed; he shall bruise your head, and you shall bruise his heel"). Tradition clearly identifies the child as the Messiah to come, and scholars generally see the mother as symbolizing primarily Mary, with a secondary reference to the Church. And in Revelation 12, salvation history revolves again around a battle with Satan, again with a woman and child: "And a great portent appeared in heaven, a woman clothed with the sun... she brought forth a male child, one who is to rule all the nations with a rod of iron... Now war arose in heaven, Michael and his angels fighting against the dragon..." (Rev 12:1-7).

Commentators, such as Ignace de la Potterie, suggest that the child symbolizes the "birth" of the risen Christ, and the woman in this instance as referring primarily to the Church and secondarily to Mary. In sum, in both chapters, the child symbolizes Christ and the woman symbolizes the Church as well as Mary. These three figures thus constitute the primary actors in the drama of salvation history. In regard to Christ, His highest presence today is the Eucharist, which is precisely the principal sacrament that transforms us into Christ. And the principal agents of this transformation in the Eucharist are two mothers: the Church corporately and Mary individually. Thus, the three loves identified by Bishop Sheen and Padre Pio correspond precisely to the three incarnate protagonists of salvation history in Scripture. To become Christ and to love Christ, one has to be formed through these three figures, for our transformation must be incarnational.

In this chapter, we will examine the Church and our Lady, two mothers from whom we receive Christ and by whom we are formed. The Second Vatican Council indicates the intimate union of Christ with these two mothers: (i) the Church's unity with Christ is evident through the fundamental image of the Church as the "Sacrament" of Christ (*LG,* Ch. 1); and (ii) Mary's union with Christ by asserting that they are "indissolubly linked." And the close link between the Church and Mary is indicated by her insertion into the principal document on the Church (*LG,* Ch. 8).

# I. THE CHURCH

This section is not intended to be a treatise on the Church, a systematic ecclesiology. The Second Vatican Council was an ecclesiological Council and the twentieth century has been a century dominated by ecclesiology. Many outstanding theologians have written much on ecclesiology. The long list includes a number of impressive contributors.[1] Instead what is presented here is a brief exposition of the Church as the first of the "Three Loves," to see again in brief her essence so as to allow our hearts to be given over to her.[2]

## A. The Church as Sacrament

The Christian loves the Church because the Church is Christ's presence in the world, which is precisely what the "Sacrament" signifies and seeks to present. This image of the Church as "mystery" or "sacrament" is employed by the Council Fathers in the very first chapter of *Lumen gentium*, forming, as it were, the foundation of the other images of the Church. This image highlights the Church as mystery, as composed of two aspects, divine and human, with the divine mediated through the human or historical. A sacrament, in its basic signification, is defined as an outward sign of an inward grace. The power of this image becomes clear when one uses the significant analogy brought forward in the same chapter in *Lumen gentium* to illustrate its meaning, the analogy to the Incarnate Word, who is God-man.

The Council thus employs "sacrament" in its wider sense and applies it to two levels. First, the Incarnate Word is the "Primordial Sacrament," who reveals and brings God to man. For the Father has poured Himself totally into the Word, which Word has become incarnate and present to the world, through whom the Father's blessings are poured into the world and the world's prayers are brought to the Father. Second, as the Word of God

---

[1] Emile Mersch (*The Theology of the Mystical Body*), Rudolf Schnackenburg (*The Church in the New Testament*), Lucien Cerfaux (*The Church in the Theology of St. Paul*), Henri de Lubac (*The Splendor of the Church*), Hans Urs von Balthasar (*The Office of Peter and the Structure of the Church*), Yves Congar (*The Mystery of the Church*), Joseph Ratzinger (doctoral dissertation: *The People and the House of God in Augustine's Doctrine of the Church*), Avery Dulles (*Models of the Church*), Walter Kasper (*Theology and Church*), Francis Sullivan (*The Church We Believe In: One, Holy, Catholic and Apostolic*).

[2] Worthy of note is an article by Father Patrick Murphy entitled, "14 Reasons for Loving the Church with von Balthasar." Accessed June 15, 2013.
http://lovingthechurch.com/tag/hans-urs-von-balthasar-2/.

took upon Himself a humanity and became God-man, two natures in one divine Person, so the Incarnate Word in a second step takes upon Himself another "Body," a Mystical Body, the Church, and becomes one with it. As Augustine teaches, Christ the Head, joining Himself to His Bride and Body, the Church, becomes the *Christus Totus*, the whole Christ. Since this Whole Christ has a human dimension, then we should not wonder if it has moral weakness in its members, just as Christ's physical body was subject to physical weaknesses. As Christ is the "Primordial Sacrament," when He takes on the Church to become His "Mystical Body," the Church herself becomes a sacrament of Christ, "The Universal Sacrament of Salvation."

| (Christ) | (Church) | (Christian) |
|---|---|---|
| *"Primordial Sacrament"* → | *"Universal Sacrament of Salvation"* → | *A little sacrament* |

This means primarily that the Church does not merely continue the teachings and cause of Christ her Founder; the Church is in a real sense *the extension and presence of Christ in history and in the world*, as the Word of God was truly in the world in the physical body of Christ. It further signifies that without the Church, there is no salvation (Henri de Lubac). The union of the Christian to Christ through the Church's sacraments points to a third level, that each Christian is himself to become a "little sacrament."

## B. Mystical Identity between Christ and the Church

To develop the depths of this sacramental union of Christ with His Church, we can turn to Henri de Lubac's impressive work, *The Splendor of the Church*. This work of love of the Church is remarkable, given that it was the first fruit following his being "silenced" for ten years for suspicion of teaching heresy with his *Nouvelle Théologie* based on the teachings of the Church Fathers. It is not simply a theological work, the English title, "*The Splendor of the Church*" (its original title was "*Méditation sur l'Église*," "Meditation on the Church"), reveals his tremendous love as a son of the Church, and the reader will be well-rewarded in taking the time to read the inspiring chapter, "Ecclesia Mater."[3] There is a mystical identity between Christ and His Body; Head and members make up a single Body, one single Christ.

---

[3] In fact, his discussion of the Church as "Sacrament of Christ" anticipated the teaching of the Second Vatican Council. Henri de Lubac, "The Sacrament of Christ," *The Splendor of the Church*, trans. Michael Mason (San Francisco: Ignatius Press, repr. 2006; French orig. *Méditation sur l'Église*, 1953), Chapter VI, 202-235.

She is the tabernacle of his presence, the building of which he is both Architect and Cornerstone. She is the temple in which he teaches, and into which he draws with him the whole Divinity. She is the ship and he the pilot, she the deep ark and he the central mast, assuring the communication of all those on board with the heavens above them. She is the paradise and he its tree and well of life; she is the star and he the light which illuminates our night. (209-210)

He goes so far as to declare that the consequence of this reality is that the man "who is not a member of this Body does not receive the influx from the head, and he who does not cling to the one Bride is not loved by the Bridegroom" (210). He reinforces this mystical identity in various ways, including the quote of St. Joan of Arc, "It seems to me that it is all one, Christ and the Church, and we ought not to make any difficulty of it" (210-211). St. Augustine teaches that "in proportion that one loves the Church that one has within the Holy Spirit" (213). Her unique mission is to make Christ present to men through us: "She is to announce Him, show Him, and give Him, to all; the rest, I repeat, is a superabundance.... But she should also be in her members what she is in herself; she should be *through* us what she is *for* us. Christ should continue to be proclaimed through us, and to appear through us" (219-220).

"Practically speaking, for each one of us Christ is thus His Church" (211), and thus should not be scandalized or troubled if we are tested from within the Church. In this mystical identity:

He [Holy Spirit] spoke often before the coming of Christ, but that was solely to proclaim Christ's coming.... And he has continued to speak since Christ has returned to the Father, but only to bear Him witness, as Christ bore witness to the Father.... There is no other Spirit than this Spirit of Jesus, and the Spirit of Jesus is the Soul which animates His Body, the Church. (207-208)

Though the Church suffers many attacks and undergoes many deviations, precisely because the Church is the "Sacrament of Christ," he concludes that:

Men may be lacking in the Holy Spirit, but the Holy Spirit will never be lacking to the Church.... she will always be the sacrament of Christ, and make Him really and truly present to us. She will always reflect his glory, through the best of her children. Even when she shows signs of weariness, germination is in progress toward a new spring... the saints will spring up once more. (235)

## C. Church-Persons

What does this identity between Christ and His Church entail for the Christian? Henri de Lubac unpacks the different ramifications. He teaches us that we must become *ecclesiastics*, church-persons, with a *sentire Ecclesiae*, "thinking of the Church" (241 ff.). The Church is "full of the Trinity" (237), giving us a relationship to each one of the three Persons. This is the very realization of that communion which is so sought after. Its dimensions are vaster than the universe, all past and future and earth to heaven are present to us (Paul Claudel, 238-239). Her power is such that "Those to whom she has united are truly the soul of the world, the soul of this great human body..." (239).

The Church follows the direction of the Holy Spirit, with the inseparable threefold channels of Scripture, Tradition, and the Magisterium by which the Word reaches him. Total loyalty to the Magisterium does not keep him from an in-depth contact with Scripture or the Church's Tradition. It includes a loving knowledge of the classics of his faith, and by keeping company with those who fought for Christ, he will acquire something of the Catholic ethos (242-252). The Church-man will be obedient to the Church, especially to the vicar of Christ (270-273). He will avoid treating the Church and her legacy as museum pieces to be preserved, and realize that the Church must adapt and speak to each generation. He will recognize the splendour of his Mother and love her (273-278). He will hold himself apart from all coteries and all intrigue, seek to be "charitable rather than quarrelsome," in keeping above every faction or sectarianism, and be no friend of the itch for controversy. He will respect the legitimate diversity in the multi-form wisdom of God as found in the Church (e.g., rites).[4]

Our entire spiritual and priestly life rests upon unity with Christ's Church. To love Christ is to love His Church or as St. Cyprian says, "one cannot have God as His Father unless he has the Church as His mother." The consequence of this is that those who love Christ would have a *sentire cum*

---

[4] Ibid., "*Ecclesia Mater*," Chapter VII, 236-278.

*Ecclesia*, thinking or feeling with the Church, that is, being of one mind and heart with the Church, synthesized by Henri de Lubac's term, "ecclesiastic," "Church-man." The ecclesial dimension of our faith has also been treated in the new Encyclical, *Lumen fidei* (nn. 38-40; 47-49), quoting St. Leo the Great, "If faith is not one, it is not faith" (n. 47). Applying this vision to the priest as "another Christ," the priest also loves the Church as Christ loves His Body and Bride. Ordination then becomes analogous to a marriage, the priest, an *alter Christus*, marries Christ's Bride, the Church.

The new Christ can find a luminous example of this love of the Church in Henri de Lubac himself. John Paul II, while giving an address in Paris, publically stopped to acknowledge him:

> Pope John Paul II, who had the highest esteem for de Lubac, stopped his address during a major talk and acknowledged the presence of de Lubac saying, "I bow my head to Father Henri de Lubac." Subsequently, the Pope appointed the holy and beloved theologian a Cardinal. This book reveals who this great Churchman and theologian was, and the importance of his writings.[5]

We find another example of this Church-love in Bishop Fulton Sheen. We recall the instance in which John Paul II, visiting St. Patrick's Cathedral, embraced Bishop Sheen and said to him, "You have written and spoken well of the Lord Jesus. You are a loyal son of the Church!" Like St. Teresa of Jesus, we all wish to be the loyal sons and daughters of the Church. Among the outstanding works that can help us appreciate and love the Church, besides Henri de Lubac's *The Splendor of the Church*, possibly the finest work on the papacy, von Balthasar's *The Office of Peter and the Structure of the Church*.[6]

Robert Hugh Benson's profound insight offers a salutary caution. It is precisely those who have attained heights of friendship with Christ who are in greater danger of falling into the gulf of pride. He points out that the great *heresiarchs* or heretics who attained great heights of illumination are the

---

[5] "Henri de Lubac," Ignatius Insight, accessed September 2, 2015, http://www.ignatiusinsight.com/authors/henridelubac.asp.
[6] Tracey Rowland notes that Aidan Nichols judges this work to be "theologically the profoundest book on the papacy ever written." Aidan Nichols, *The Word has been Abroad* (Edinburgh: T & T Clark, 1998), xix, quoted in Tracey Rowland, *Ratzinger's Faith*, 21.

ones who have fallen into the greatest danger of that stage: individualism of pride.

> Of course, since every advance in spiritual life has its corresponding danger— since every step that we rise nearer to God increases the depth of the gulf into which we may fall— a soul that has reached the stage of the Illuminative way which we have called *Ordinary Contemplation*… has an enormous increase of responsibility. The supreme danger is that of *Individualism*, by which the soul that has climbed up from ordinary pride reaches the zone in which genuine spiritual pride is encountered, and, with spiritual pride, every other form of pride— such as intellectual or emotional pride— which belong to the interior state.

> … It is bound, in fact, to end in pride unless she can finish the quotation and add, "O my God, enlighten my darkness!" Every heresy and every sect that has ever rent the unity of the Body of Christ has taken its rise primarily in the illuminated soul of this or that chosen friend of Christ. Practically all the really great heresiarchs have enjoyed a high degree of interior knowledge, or they could have led none of Christ's simple friends astray. What is absolutely needed, then, if illumination is not to end in disunion and destruction, is that, coupled with this increase of interior spiritual life, there should go with it an increase of devotion and submission to the exterior voice with which God speaks in his Church: for, notoriously, nothing is so difficult to discern as the difference between the inspirations of the Holy Ghost and the aspirations or imaginations of self.[7]

With this greater privilege, "there should go with it an increase of devotion and submission to the exterior voice with which God speaks in his Church." Thus, what protects the friend of Christ are both an interior self-abasement as well as a submission to the Church. Robert Hugh Benson warns, "*Vae soli!* Woe to him that is alone!"

> *Vae soli!* Woe to him that is alone! Woe to him who having received the friendship of Christ, and its consequent illumination, believes that he enjoys in its interpretation an infallibility which he denies to Christ's outwardly commissioned vicar!…

> For the stronger the interior life and the higher the degree of illumination, the more is the strong hand of the Church needed, and the higher ought

---

[7] Robert Hugh Benson, *The Friendship with Christ: Exploring the Humanity of Jesus Christ*, 42-43.

to be the soul's appreciation of her office. It is, we are bound to remind ourselves, from the inner circle of Christ intimates, from those who know his secrets and have been taught how to find the gate of the inner garden where he walks at his ease with his own, that the Judases of history are drawn.[8]

Augustine insightfully points out that such individualism derives from belief in self, self-love and pride: "Tell us straight that you do not believe in the Gospel of Christ; for you believe what you want in the Gospel and disbelieve what you want. You believe in yourself rather than in the Gospel."[9]

## D. Incarnational Principle: Union with Christ Entails Union with Church

Here, we must affirm again the principle of the Incarnation: this union with the Son of God just described only takes place within the economy of Christ's present incarnate form. It begins with attachment to the Incarnate Word, the Son made man. John tells us that "It is written in the prophets, 'And they shall all be taught by God.' Everyone who has heard and learned from the Father comes to me" (Jn 6:45). We know that we have to go to the Father through Christ: "No one goes to the Father except through me," "I am the way, the truth, and the life." This text must mean that it is only if we are of the Father that we will go to and through His Son, but precisely as the Incarnate Word. But union with Christ also implies union with the Incarnate Word in His various manifestations: Church, in the Sacraments, especially the holy Eucharist, Scripture, His vicar and priests, our parents, the laity, and the poor. Here we see the fallacy of the statement, "I accept Christ but not the Church." Belonging to the Father comes with the belonging to the "Incarnate" Christ present in His manifold presences. Thus, the principle of the Incarnation is vital today.

This principle of the Incarnation cannot be broken. Union with Christ in His incarnate forms brings unity, dissension brings sin. Robert Hugh Benson teaches that the more we are Christ's friend, the more we love

---

[8] Ibid., 43-44.
[9] Augustine, *Against Faustus*, 17, 3.

Christ in His manifold incarnate presences.[10] The opposite of this union is division, which flows from sin. Sin causes fragmentation, as we see in the sin of Adam and Eve, that separated them from God, resulting in the three-fold division: within themselves (concupiscence), between each other, and from the universe. In contrast to sin's effects, love unites, as we see in the love of Jesus Christ on the cross that reconciles us to the Father and whose recapitulation has begun and will be completed in the eschaton. Thus, love unites and sin divides. The greater our love for the Father, the more we become one with the presences of Christ. The more the new Christ loves the Father, the more the Holy Mass becomes the heart of his day and the more he spends time before the Blessed Sacrament; the more Mother Teresa of Calcutta loved the Father, the more she saw Christ in the poor.

*Note for Priests*

Mother de la Touche counsels the priest to appreciate his privileged place and vital role within the Church. The priesthood constitutes not just any organ, but the very heart of the mystical body of Christ, the Church, without which the mystical body dies.

> And has not this Body like every living body, members and a heart. The Church is the mystical Body of Christ, the faithful are its members, the Priesthood is its heart. Yes, the Priesthood is the heart of the living Body of which Christ is the head!
>
> A body dies if the head or the heart is mortally wounded, for it is from the head and the heart that life radiates through the entire body; but it can see many of its members fall off without the source of life drying up in it. Thus, the Church can at times see with sorrow some of its members perish, without its life failing; for its head, Christ-Love, is immortal, and its heart, its holy Priesthood grafted on Jesus, the eternal Priest, cannot perish.
>
> According to the divine plan, the Priesthood, being the mystical heart of Christ and the true heart of the Church, is for the latter an organ of life as indispensable as the heart is for the human body. Without its head, Christ, without its soul, the Holy Spirit, the Church would not exist; and without its heart, without its Priesthood which warms it and gives it life, it would

---

[10] Robert Hugh Benson, *The Friendship with Christ*, 21-22. See also a more comprehensive elaboration of Christ in his manifold presences in Chapters 5-11, pp. 47-93.

be dead. It is by it that the divine movement which comes to it from its Head is communicated to all its members; that the life-giving blood of grace circulates even to its extremities; that the vital heat of love warms its members.[11]

Mother de la Touche reminds the priest that the strength and the health of the Church requires that the priest, who is a key member of its body, remain part of the hierarchy and be holy.

> But what is the holy Priesthood in itself? It is a single organ, no doubt, but nevertheless composed of a multitude of parts. The Pontiffs, the priests, all the orders of the sacred hierarchy are its parts, its molecules, if we may so express it, which, united together, form the body of the Priesthood. The Priesthood is, then, what the parts which compose it are.
>
> Now, the Priesthood is the heart of the Church, and in order to perform its operations of life, it must be robust and healthy; it must be free and ardent; its movement must be always full, always well-balanced and always continuous.[12]

## II. OUR LADY

### 1. Why Mary?

Let us now address the second of the three loves, Mary. For many, the theme of Mary immediately raises questions or doubts, and we must from the outset respond to the questions, "Why put so much emphasis on Mary?", or "Why go through Mary?" Since Vatican II has devoted much attention to the other mother, the Church, this section will devote more space to understanding the less-understood role of this mother, Mary. It would also be of great benefit for new Christ to access some of the outstanding works on Mary, especially those by St. Louis de Montfort and St. Maximilian Kolbe. Some of the recent works recommended include: H. M. Manteau-Bonamy, *Immaculate Conception and the Holy Spirit: The Marian Teachings of St. Maximilian Kolbe*; Joseph Langford, *Mother Teresa: In the Shadow of Our Lady*; Ignace de la Potterie, *Mary in the Mystery of the Covenant* (Scripture); Luigi Gambero, *Mary and the Fathers of the Church* (Church Fathers); and Henri de Lubac, *The Splendor of the Church* (Ch. 9). It may be

---

[11] Mother de la Touche, *The Sacred Heart and the Priesthood*, 189-190.
[12] Ibid., 190.

worthwhile for the priest to read Cardinal Pierre Paul Philippe's *The Virgin Mary and the Priesthood* (Alba House, 1993).

We can understand that our dear Protestant brethren, following the lead of the first Reformers, question the Catholic understanding of the role of Mary. What is of greater concern is that many Catholics do not realize her role and relationship, and some sincerely claim, seeking to protect her human dimension, that Mary "is no different from the rest of us." Obviously, Mary is no different from any of us as a human being, but that is totally untrue from the perspective of grace and holiness. Such a position would contradict the entire Tradition of the Church, and more recently, the teaching of *Lumen gentium*, the principal document of the Second Vatican Council (e.g., image of Mary as "eschatological icon"). That Mary is totally unlike us in her holiness is summarized by the well-accepted phrase of St. Bernard, "*De Maria numquam satis*," "Of Mary, one can never say enough."

Moreover, even the Anglican theologian, John Macquarrie, recognizes Mary not only as a member of the Church, but also as preeminent over the Church, a truth embedded in Pope Paul VI's declaration at Vatican II of Mary as "Mother of the Church." One senses sometimes that some fail by seeking to approach Mary primarily in an intellectual fashion, instead of approaching her as "mother" in the simplicity of their hearts. Blessed Guerric of Igny, abbot, teaches that little ones of faith have an instinctive, tender love of Mary: "Then again, is it not true that her children seem to recognize her as their mother? They manifest a kind of instinctive devotion which faith gives them as second nature, so that first and foremost in all their needs and dangers they run to call upon her name just as children turn to their mother's breast."[13]

Let us immediately disavow ourselves of a misconception by some: Mary is not the fourth person of the Blessed Trinity. The secret of Mary's greatness is paradoxical, as is the Gospel— it is found in the opposite direction. For her greatness is not found in immensity or heroic actions as we humanly understand it, but rather in her lowliness, as revealed by the words in the *Magnificat* inspired by the Holy Spirit: "for He has looked with favour on the

---

[13] Blessed Guerric of Igny, Sermon 1 on the Assumption of the Blessed Virgin Mary, OOR from "Memorial of the Blessed Virgin on Saturday, *Liturgy of the Hours*, vol. III, 1645.

lowliness of His servant."[14] The *Magnificat* prayer itself explains the new economy: the lowly will be lifted up and the proud will be cast down. Mary's greatness therefore lies in her lowliness, in the realization of her nothingness before God.

Thus is fulfilled the words of the precursor of Jesus, St. John the Baptist, "He must increase, I must decrease." She who would have been considered lowly in her culture as a woman and still a teen (compare Mary's lowliness to Zechariah's priestly state in the parallel births of John the Baptist and Jesus in the Gospel of Luke) is raised to the most exalted of heights, precisely because her emptiness allows God to fill her with His divine Self. She is great because there is nothing of Mary and everything of God in her. Mother Teresa of Calcutta recognized this fundamental condition of Mary as the secret of her efficacy:

> The Immaculate Heart of Mary refers not only to Our Lady's love and virtues, but also to her interior emptiness of self in imitation of Christ who "emptied himself" to save the human race. Our Lady's heart is the most empty of all human hearts, the most empty of self and empty of pride, and therefore the most ready to give a heart's welcome and shelter to those who are shelterless. Mother Teresa saw this as the condition both for receiving and giving God to the full.[15]

## A. Reasons for Going Through Mary

We look to establish support of Mary's mediation by looking first to the Second Vatican Council documents. Both *Lumen gentium* and *Sacrosanctum concilium* teach the vital principle that Jesus and Mary are "indissolubly linked." Though this link is not necessary in the absolute sense, it is so by God's design, and though they belong to two different levels (divine and human respectively), we have a fundamental principle established by God that must not be broken. We always maintain unity between Jesus and Mary, as we also maintain unity between Jesus and the Church. Just as we cannot say, "I love Jesus, but not the Church," we cannot say "I love Jesus but not Mary." One consequence of this principle is this: where Jesus is,

---

[14] "My soul magnifies the Lord, and my spirit rejoices in God my Savior, for he has regarded the low estate of his handmaiden. For behold, henceforth all generations will call me blessed" (Lk 1:46-48).

[15] Joseph Langford, *Mother Teresa: In the Shadow of Our Lady*, 42.

there is Mary; where Mary is, there is Jesus. We can distinguish Jesus from Mary, but we can never separate them; just as we can distinguish between Jesus and the Church, but can never separate them.

*Mandate of Christ at the Cross*

Second, the principal reason for validating Mary's mediation comes from Scripture. Christ Himself, by divine mandate, has entrusted us to Mary at the Cross: "When Jesus saw his mother, and the disciple whom he loved standing near, he said to his mother, 'Woman, behold, your son!' Then he said to the disciple, 'Behold, your mother!' And from that hour the disciple took her to his own home" (Jn 19:26-27). *Dei Verbum* of the Second Vatican Council clearly enunciates the principle that Scripture does not stand alone, but is complemented by Tradition, the second form of divine revelation, and guided by the Magisterium. The Church, assisted by Tradition and guided by the Magisterium, understands these words to mean that Jesus, by divine mandate, entrusted all humanity, represented here by John the beloved disciple, to Mary, commanding her to look after us; and by divine mandate, Jesus commanded us, in the person of John, to go to Mary and take her into our "home," that is, into our hearts and lives.

This is supported by indications within the text. John the evangelist often has a two-fold reference: addressing Mary as "woman," now the universal woman or mother; and in a generic manner refrains from using John's name, "Behold, your mother," for Johannine scholarship indicates that John represents the Church at the cross. John Paul II taught this in *Ecclesia de Eucharistia*: "To her he gave the beloved disciple and, in him, each of us: 'Behold, your Son!' To each of us he also says: 'Behold your mother!' (cf. Jn 19:26-27)."[16] The consequence is that saints like St. Bernard would synthesize this mandate in the well-known phrase: *Ad Jesum per Mariam* ("To Jesus through Mary").

*Mother of Both Head and Body*

The third support comes from Tradition in the Church Fathers. If Mary is Mother of the Head (Christ as Head of the Mystical Body), she must also be Mother of the Body. In the larger design, the Latin Fathers saw a

---

[16] *Ecclesia de Eucharistia* n. 57.

marvelous mystery revealed, with the harmony of the divine plan. The Word is born eternally from the womb of the Father, temporally from the womb of the Virgin, spiritually from the womb of the Church. More specifically, they made an analogy between the Church and Mary: as Mary gives birth at the Incarnation to Christ, the Church gives birth in Baptism to His Body.

In this new birth at Baptism, many do not realize a truth that is obscured by the Church's use of Baptism making us "adopted children" of God. Through Baptism, we are not simply "adopted" in the human sense, but truly are ontologically transformed into children of God. The reality is that Baptism, flowing from the water from the side of the Crucified Christ, causes us to enter into God's womb, as it were, as Christ taught Nicodemus, "Truly, truly, I say to you, unless one is born of water and the Spirit, he cannot enter the kingdom of God" (Jn 3:5). Jesus' sacrifice makes us truly children of the Father: God is ontologically our Father through Baptism and we now share a certain participation in the sonship of Jesus Christ.

Analogously, also at the Cross, through the labour pains of this mystical delivery, Mary gave birth to the Church, and truly became the mother of each baptized, in an order superior to the biological order, the order of grace— this is a teaching of the Church— she is not simply an "adopted" mother. As Mother in the order of grace, she is every bit our Mother as our own biological mothers; in fact, she is mother at a much superior level. As our Mother, she has followed us since our conception and loves us as a mother truly loves; but since her heart is much larger, she loves with a much greater love. This truth, which the Church knew since her beginnings, has now been enshrined by Pope Paul VI during the Second Vatican Council in declaring her to be the "Mother of the Church." As Mary gave birth to Christ, head of the Church, so she must give birth to the Body of Christ, the Church herself. Bishop Fulton Sheen explained this by saying that if Mary did not also give birth to the Church, then the Church would be a monstrosity; it would be a head (Christ) without a body (Church).

*Spouse of the Holy Spirit*

Fourth, we find in our Tradition that Mary is filled with God, and is thus the spouse of the Holy Spirit. This truth is confirmed by St. Maximilian

Kolbe in describing the Holy Spirit as "quasi-incarnate" in Mary. Like St. Thomas Aquinas who long wondered "who is God," St. Maximilian Kolbe long wondered and meditated upon the meaning of Mary's words to St. Bernadette Soubirous, "I am the Immaculate Conception." He had a divine insight shortly before his imprisonment and subsequent martyrdom at Auschwitz. He saw that the only one to whom the title, "Immaculate Conception," can apply would be the Holy Spirit himself, who is the Holy or Immaculate Conception of the love between the Father and the Son.

Thus, applying the Church's understanding of Mary as the "spouse of the Holy Spirit," he argued that, as His spouse, Mary could take the spouse's name, as a woman takes the surname of her husband. Mary so opened herself, without any obstacle in her heart, always saying "yes" to the Holy Spirit, that He inundated and possessed Mary to the degree that it was no longer Mary who is acting but the Holy Spirit Himself— He had become, as it were, "quasi-incarnate" in Mary. For theological precision, we insist that there is only one Incarnation, in which the Son of God assumed a humanity to Himself, only One person with two natures. Where the Monophysites were wrong with their theory for Jesus' divine-human makeup, this claim that God inhabited a human person would appropriately apply to Mary's constitution, thus making the Holy Spirit "quasi-incarnate." This then is indeed the secret of Mary's greatness: her emptiness and being "full of grace," full of the Holy Spirit. Kolbe goes further. Because of the above, then the intended path to God is: Mary – Holy Spirit – Christ – Father; and the grace of God flows in the reverse order: Father – Christ – Holy Spirit – Mary.[17]

*Dispenser of Grace*

The fifth support comes from certain Catholic devotees of Mary (St. Bernardine of Siena, St. Bernard of Clairvaux, St. Louis de Montfort, St. Maximilian Kolbe), as well as from some popes in informal addresses, who teach that Mary is the mediatrix or dispenser of all graces, that all graces go through her hands. René Laurentin points to Hermann of Tournai's medieval images of Mary as "the neck of the Church" and St. Bernard's

---

[17] H. M. Manteau-Bonamy, *Immaculate Conception and the Holy Spirit: The Marian Teachings of St. Maximilian Kolbe*, trans. Richard Arnandez (Illinois: Marytown Press, 1977), 61-62.

teaching that she is "between Christ and the Church."[18] While this is not a defined dogma of the Church (most of the teachings of the Church are not either), the *Catechism of the Catholic Church* has this to say:

> *This motherhood of Mary in the order of grace continues uninterruptedly* from the consent which she loyally gave at the Annunciation and which she sustained without wavering beneath the cross, until the eternal fulfillment of all the elect. *Taken up to heaven she did not lay aside this saving office but by her manifold intercession continues to bring us the gifts of eternal salvation....* Therefore the Blessed Virgin is invoked in the Church under the titles of Advocate, Helper, Benefactress, and *Mediatrix.* (n. 969, emphasis mine)

This *Catechism* text echoes the famous text of *Lumen gentium* n. 62. Pope John Paul II himself taught in *Ecclesia de Eucharistia* that all graces that come from the Eucharist go into the hands of Mary to be distributed to the Church. On the one hand, some, reflecting the position of René Laurentin, one of the Church's best-known experts on Mary (*The Question of Mary*), see this doctrine of Mary as dispenser of all graces as a disputed question. On the other hand, others believe that her mediation of graces is the Church's doctrine. J. N. D. Kelly, the patristic scholar examining the first four centuries of the Church, implies that it has become an accepted teaching today through the development of doctrine:

> Indeed, centuries had to elapse before the doctrines of Mary's exemption from original sin (in the West only) and actual sin, of her position as intercessor and mediator of graces, of her corporeal assumption into heaven and elevation there above cherubim and seraphim, could become elements in the day-to-day faith of Catholic Christians, much less be formulated as dogmas.[19]

Some question whether Mary can be allowed to distribute grace, as this is a prerogative of God. Yet, if she is indeed the spouse of the Holy Spirit and acts only through the Holy Spirit, would this be a significant support for God granting her this privilege, in the manner Jesus gave the power to the apostles to forgive sins and make present the sacrifice of Calvary

---

[18] René Laurentin, *A Short Treatise on the Virgin Mary*, trans. Charles Neumann (Washington, DC: AMI Press, 1991), 114.

[19] J. N. D. Kelly, *Early Christian Doctrines*, 5th Revd. ed. (London: A & C Black, 1993 repr.), 499.

("Whatever you bind on earth...", Mt 18:18)? At the very least, the accepted patristic title of "New Eve," as the "helper" of the "New Adam," implies great collaboration on Mary's part in the work of salvation. St. Bernard, commenting on her role of salvation in the antithesis between Adam-Eve and Christ-Mary, wrote that "We need a mediator to the Mediator..."[20] Pope John Paul II with deep insight notes that Mary's unique mediation is linked to her motherhood of the Church.[21]

*Principle of Mediation*

Sixth, we look to a principle that we find in human life and the Christian dispensation that underlies her role. This is the principle of incarnationality, which we more generally call the principle of "mediation." In this, we seek to present to our Protestant family something of the Catholic basis for veneration of Mary. It is understood that Protestants do not accept the key Catholic interpretation of Mary's mandate as given by Jesus at the cross in Jn 19:26-27 (see next paragraph). Instead, we look first to a broader principle, the general principle of mediation in human life and in the Church. For Catholics, mediation follows the pattern God Himself established in the Incarnation of His Son, which has subsequently become God's mode of dealing with humanity: incarnational, one of mediation. We must recognize first that, on the one hand, God does not need to use any instrument. The principle of incarnationality extends back to the Old Testament. Yahweh calls a specific nation, with all its weaknesses, to be a light to the nations; and within Israel, calls for a Messiah, who has a particular genealogy, that also includes a prostitute.

More fundamentally, this principle of "incarnationality" or "sacramentality" or mediation corresponds to the makeup of man. Since he is not an angel, a pure spirit, but an embodied spirit, that experiences life through the senses, then it is appropriate that God employs this method in dealing with him. And it is manifestly and abundantly obvious to anyone who has some life experience that, at the natural and human level, the principle of mediation is the foundation of all human life.

---

[20] St. Bernard of Clairvaux, *St. B. Omnia Opera*, ed. J. Leclercq & H. Rochais, V, 263, quoted in Frederick M. Jelly, *Madonna: Mary in the Catholic Tradition*, (Huntington, IN: Our Sunday Visitor, 1986), 76.
[21] Pope John Paul II, *Redemptoris Mater*, n. 38.

For example, God does not create children directly but mediately through the co-creation and collaboration of our parents, not to mention the help or "mediation" of other family members (e.g., grandparents) and teachers and priests or religious sisters, and so on. In so many ways, the basic principle is that we are not meant to "walk alone," we are strong when we walk with the aid of others, and we in turn aid others. Mediation may be the most fundamental economy by which God deals with us. In this economy, God has chosen to use the Church as mediator, along with all her sacramental forms: sacraments, ministers, as well as the communion of saints, including guardian angels. God does not actually need to use our Blessed Mother Mary, but He chooses in His wisdom that which He deems to be the wisest and best means. In His wisdom, Jesus has given us one of the greatest gifts, His own mother, the best of all mothers. The Church Fathers give concrete expression to Mary's collaboration with Christ in the title "New Eve," which title has found expression throughout the Church's history.

*Mary is God's Masterpiece and Christ's Moon*

The seventh support comes from distinguishing two levels of our relation to God and creature as well as the two levels of action of God and man. First, theology distinguishes between the *latria* (adoration), reserved to Jesus as God, and *doulia*, the veneration of Mary as an instrument or representative of God. We can in fact see Mary as the masterpiece of God, Augustine says that "God crowns His own gifts." Not only would Leonardo da Vinci not mind that his masterpiece of the Last Supper housed at the Scrovegni Chapel in Padua was praised, he would positively beam. Thus, there is no conflict between love and adoration of Jesus and veneration of Mary.

Second, the level of action of the two can be distinguished between the primary (God) and the secondary (creature), in which the secondary (creature) is subordinated to, and is a participation of, the primary action of God. An example of this is God as only Creator, and parents as "co-creators" in giving birth to their child. An image from the Church Fathers applied to the relationship between Jesus and the Church is also applied to the relationship between Jesus and Mary. Jesus is the sun, from which all divine light flows, and Mary is the moon, which receives all its light from this divine Sun and radiates that light to her children on earth during the "night" of our life. The moon, as such, is used by the sun, and points or leads to the sun.

*Two Levels of Redemption*

Theologians have employed different ways to distinguish the work of Jesus from that of Mary, especially in the context of the discussion of Mary as "co-redemptrix" or "co-mediatrix." Mark Miravalle of Steubenville University, defining Mary as "co-redemptrix," finds a key in the fact that "co" does not mean "equal to" but "with." Bruno Gherardini, while he cannot find justification for "co-redemptrix" in the texts, adds an important distinction for us. We can speak of the "co-redemption" of Mary, if we proceed from the distinction of redemption in *actu primo* (acquiring phase of the redemptive or expiatory merit) and *in actu secundo* (distributive phase). Matthias J. Scheeben affirms that Mary is redeemed and as such cooperates in redemption through the graces received from the same Christ. The prerequisites for a true mediation found in Christ are all also found in Mary. Mary is with God, insofar as she is mother of the Son of God; and is with humanity, insofar as she is a human person; and is mediatrix, insofar as she participates in the objective redemption.[22]

## 2. Role of Mary

### A. Mary as the Fulfillment of the Ark of the Covenant

As mentioned at the beginning of the chapter, we find in the Bible two primary protagonists, a woman and child: Jesus, together with Mary and the Church, constitute the primary figures in salvation history. There are a number of types (prefigurations) found in Scripture that point to Mary's significance. One of the most important Scriptural images of our Lady is that of "Ark of the Covenant." The end of Chapter 11 of the Book of Revelation speaks of the Ark of the Covenant, and this new Ark that fulfills the Old Testament Ark of the Covenant is identified in the beginning of the next chapter, Rev 12, describing a woman with great splendour, clothed with the sun and a crown of twelve stars.

---

[22] Stefano de Fiores, *Maria Madre di Gesù: Sintesi storico-salvifica*, Corso de Teologia Sistematica 6 (Bologna: Edizioni Dehoniane Bologna, 1992), provides an outstanding presentation on Mary in Italian.

As mentioned, in contemporary scholarship the majority opinion among scholars is that this woman symbolizes the Church, and some argue that she also symbolizes Mary. We see this fulfillment of Mary as the new Ark of the Covenant in Mary's visitation to her cousin Elizabeth in Luke. Luke clearly intends the parallel of the visitation with David bringing the Ark to Jerusalem (same region, both involving three months, both using the same unique word for "jumping"— by David and by John in his mother's womb) to indicate to us that Mary has become the New Ark of the Covenant. The previous Ark contained the word of God in stone (Torah) and the bread from heaven (manna); but this new "Ark" contains the Word of God in flesh and the Bread from heaven, the Bread of Life Himself. Since the Ark of the Covenant was the heart of Temple worship and the presence of God, then this fulfillment, which far surpasses the original provisional prefiguration, is where we find the ultimate presence of God on earth.[23]

## B. She is the Mould of Christ

We can begin with the specific aspects of Mary's role as mother by looking to the teaching of St. Louis de Montfort. Interpreting Tradition, he sees her principal role to be our "mould." As mentioned, as Mary formed Jesus our Head, so Mary now forms Christ's Body, the Church. This mother then is given the task of forming Christ in us. In his short work, *The Secret of Mary*, he compares the inefficiency and inequality of a sculptor sculpting a statue to using a perfect mould. Sculpting is much more arduous, takes much time, and one little mistake can ruin the entire thing. The mould, however, is faster, easier, much more secure, and most importantly, the statue is always perfect. For Mary, she who formed Jesus and was formed by Him, is the perfect mould for the God-man, and she continues to form her children into His image.

> Mary is the great mold of God, made by the Holy Ghost to form a true God-Man by the Hypostatic Union and to form also a man-God by grace. In that mold none of the features of the Godhead is wanting. Whoever is cast in it, and allows himself to be molded, receives all the features of Jesus Christ, true God....

---

[23] See de la Potterie, *Mary in the Mystery of the Covenant*, 3-35. Scott Hahn too has taught this interpretation in one of his Scripture classes at Steubenville, Scripture courses which have been recorded for distribution.

Oh what a difference between a soul which has been formed in Christ by
the ordinary ways of those who, like the sculptor, trust in their own skill
and ingenuity, and a soul thoroughly tractable, entirely detached and well-
molten, which, without trusting to its own skill, cast itself into Mary, there
to be molded by the Holy Ghost. How many stains and defects and
illusions, how much darkness and how much human nature is there in the
former; and oh how pure, how heavenly and how Christlike is the latter![24]

Those consecrated to Mary are formed into her image, the closest image to
Christ. They are taught her secret virtues, such as silence and hiddenness,
contemplation, humility, and they are able to scale the heights of perfection.
From the context of the Eucharist, Pope John Paul II teaches:

> Experiencing the memorial of Christ's death in the Eucharist also means
> continually receiving this gift. It means accepting – like John – the one
> who is given to us anew as our Mother. It also means taking on a
> commitment to be conformed to Christ, putting ourselves at the school of
> his Mother and allowing her to accompany us. Mary is present, with the
> Church and as the Mother of the Church, at each of our celebrations of
> the Eucharist.[25]

## C. Cana Points to Mary's Maternal Solicitude and Her Power of Intercession

The event of the wedding feast of Cana provides a paradigm of how Mary
takes care of us today. While Scripture gives no information on the couple
being married, it would appear likely that the couple at Cana may have been
poor, both because they did not have enough wine and because they did
not have the best of wines (at least, in comparison to Jesus' new wine).
Perhaps this is why Mary may have been keeping a close eye on the
proceedings. What matters is that it was Mary who noticed the crisis and it
was Mary who approached her Son for help, and who, despite Jesus'
response, with faith and confidence, told the stewards, "Do whatever he
tells you." Jesus' reply to Mary appears to have as background "the hour"
of Jesus, signifying that a timetable had been established by the heavenly
Father.

[24] St. Louis de Montfort, *The Secret of Mary*, 15-16.
[25] *Ecclesia de Eucharistia* n. 57.

Nevertheless, Jesus acts upon His Mother's request and, it would seem that he "adjusted" the Father's timetable to begin His first miracle. Jesus' action at Mary's request suggests that Jesus would never say "no" to His Mother. The miracle requested by Mary sets in motion certain events: Jesus begins the path to the cross, symbolized by the use of "the hour" (which John employs to refer to Christ's cross); the conversion of the Old Testament water to the wine of the New Covenant, with allusions to both the cross and the Eucharist; and this miracle led to the birth of faith in the apostles.

Today, as with the couple at Cana, Mary is aware of our difficulties and she brings them to Jesus, who so loves her that that He must accede to her every request. Henry Cardinal Newman, in his *Stations of the Cross*, gives some indication of her power of intercession before God. He depicts a touching act of Mary, in which her prayers brought help in the form of Simon the Cyrene and helped the soldiers not to be so "fierce" with Jesus:

> This came of Mary's intercession.... But she showed herself a mother by following Him with her prayers, since she could help Him in no other way. She then sent this stranger to help Him. It was she who led the soldiers to see that they might not be too fierce with Him. Sweet Mother, even do the like to us. Pray for us ever, Holy Mother of God, pray for us, whatever be our cross, as we pass along on our way. Pray for us, and we shall rise again though we have fallen. Pray for us when sorrow, anxiety, or sickness comes upon us. Pray for us when we are prostrate under the power of temptation, and send some faithful servant of thine to succour us. And in the world to come, if found worthy to expiate our sins in the fiery prison, send some good angel to give us a season of refreshment. Pray for us, Holy Mother of God.[26]

St. Louis de Montfort's understanding of Mary as "mould" has been complemented and deepened by the theology of Hans Urs von Balthasar. To understand her greatness and her role, it is best to take our attention away from her privileges (e.g., Queen of Heaven) and return to Mary's role in the life of Christ, that is to say, to her role in salvation history. Von Balthasar sees the role of Mary imitating that of the Son of God. God the Son is always the perfect Son of the Father, always the perfect "yes" to the Father. The Father's role in relation to the Son is theologically "masculine,"

---

[26] John Henry Newman, *Meditations on the Stations of the Cross* (London: Catholic Truth Society, 1999), 11-12.

the Father is pouring Himself out eternally to the Son, eternally generating the Son. The Son's role in relationship to the Father is theologically "feminine," always receiving from the Father, everything He has comes from the Father.

The Son thereby is always the perfect Son, eternally dependent and eternally giving Himself totally to the Father. As God-man, he does this by always loving the Father and doing the Father's will. Now, when God the Father was to send His Son into the world, two prerequisites on the part of the recipient vessel were essential: the Son of God, being purity itself, required a vessel that was holy or immaculate, and only Mary through the Immaculate Conception and continuing sinlessness possessed that immaculate state. Secondly, since this was a relationship of marriage— the Church was to become the Bride of Christ— He needed a partner who would give herself unconditionally to Him as a spouse, and only Mary possessed the heart to give herself totally to God. Mary fulfilled both conditions, but her "yes" (fiat) would lead her along the path of the "seven sorrows." She did this for God and for us— we will not understand the enormous debt we owe Mary until the next life.

This has tremendous consequences. First of all, within the design of God, without Mary's "yes" we would not be saved. We can extend this debt to Mary further: Mary was responsible for the first coming of the Holy Spirit in the incarnation of Christ, through her "yes" or expressed alternatively, her beauty drew God down to her; but also the debt of the coming of the Holy Spirit upon the whole Church. Since Mary's prayers are more powerful than all the prayers of the angels and saints combined (LG, Ch. 8), then it would have primarily been her prayers in the Upper Room that were responsible for the second coming of the Holy Spirit at Pentecost. In a certain sense, we owe the coming of the Holy Spirit upon us as a Church to Mary as well.

## D. The Church is Marian in Her Essence

A second consequence is that the Church is Marian in her form. That is, being a Christian does not entail having a certain devotion or veneration of Mary, or even just praying to Mary— it entails "becoming" Mary. Mary as the greatest image of Jesus, is also the symbol and model of all the baptized. Here, we must make the distinction of von Balthasar between the Petrine and Marian principles. Within the Church, there is the institutional element, especially the hierarchy, that can give the holy things (e.g., celebrate the sacraments), that is absolutely indispensable— without the graces given through the sacraments mediated by Christ's priest, the Church would be a wasteland— think of the interdict the Church imposed on Florence in the time of St. Catherine of Siena. The Marian principle represents holiness or openness to the Holy Spirit, which is the goal of spiritual life.

As part of the Petrine principle, a priest has the power to confer grace through the sacraments, but this does not make him holy— the giving of grace serves the receiving of grace; it therefore serves the Marian principle, which, as John Paul II said, is the more fundamental of the two principles. Everyone, including Peter, is called to be Marian, or as von Balthasar puts it, "the Church is called to be Marian." That is to say, the Church is Marian in her foundation. Therefore, our relationship to Mary is not merely one of simple devotion or attachment to her, but, in her, we find the "eschatological icon" (LG, Ch. 8), the model that we are called to imitate. In the context of the Second Vatican Council, one that underscores the fundamental vocation in the Church is that of the baptized and our call to holiness, it is Mary who stands as the fundamental icon of the Church.[27]

Various aspects of Mary's role surface in the Tradition through the saints. With tender attachment to her, they have universally proclaimed the great power and role of Mary. They highlight the great truth that the path to Jesus is through Mary. St. Marguerite d'Youville, the foundress of the Grey Nuns in Montréal and the first Canadian-born saint to be canonized, before she was to receive First Holy Communion, the Food of Angels, prayed these touching words to our Lady:

> Dear Mother of my God, all my contacts with your Son, Jesus, come through you. You, the Mother of Grace, the Morning Star leading to Christ; the Gate of Heaven opening all ways to Him for us— help me

---

[27] Brendan Leahy delineates three elements of Mary as model in von Balthasar: (i) Virginal openness to the mystery of God's love (totally available and detached for God's plan); (ii) Bridal response to the Word (perfect bride who incarnates Christ's life, especially His passion); (iii) Maternal christophorous existence (bearing Christ and giving Him to the world). See Brendan Leahy, *The Marian Principle*, 167-169; and Hans Urs von Balthasar, *Glory of the Lord: A Theological Aesthetics*, vol. 1, *Seeing the Form* (San Francisco: Ignatius Press, repr. 1998; *Herrlichkeit: Eine theologische Ästhetik*, I: *Schau der Gestalt*, 1961), 562. See also Ignace de la Potterie, *Mary in the Mystery of the Covenant*, xxxiv-xl, 263-264.

now. Teach me, dear Mother of God, how I should treat your Son when He comes to me. Long ago He came to you as a Child. You watched him grow, learn to walk; you listened for the new sounds He made when He was learning to speak. If He speaks to me now in Holy Communion, help me, my Mother, help me to be like you so your Son will love me too.[28]

## 3. The Fruitfulness of Consecration to Mary

### A. Concretely Living out this Consecration

St. Louis de Montfort teaches that Mary in the last age will form some of the greatest saints of the Church[29] and St. Maximilian Kolbe teaches that the world will be saved by consecration. Consecration to Mary signifies entrusting oneself and all that belongs to one to Mary; in turn, Mary takes our troubles to herself and forms us according to her image. As mentioned earlier, the general teaching of the Church, which is not a dogma, that Mary is the dispenser of all graces, indicates that all graces go into her hands first and she distributes them to us. Because of this importance of Mary, couples can consecrate their marriage to Mary and their child after Baptism before an image of Mary in the Church. Similarly, a priest can consecrate his priesthood to Mary.

Father David May, the current director of priests at Madonna House in Combermere, Ontario, in the course of giving a retreat to seminarians, enumerated some of the benefits of consecrating oneself to Mary. First, Mary brings peace to her children. During storms in our lives, we find peace if we pray the Rosary or go before an image of Mary. Second, Mary brings discernment of spirits: her children soon learn what is compatible and what is incompatible with life in Christ. Third, as Mary stood at the foot of the cross, she obtains for us the grace to be able to stand at the cross for others. And fourth, Mary's humility drives away all evil.

Another benefit of great devotion or consecration to Mary is that it appears that she will be present at the death of her faithful ones. St. John Bosco, the teacher and confessor of St. Dominic Savio, wrote that St. Dominic appeared to him after his death in a vision with a message from God. St.

---

[28] Rita McGuire, *Marguerite d'Youville: A Pioneer for our Times* (Ottawa: Novalis, 1982), 35.
[29] St. Louis de Montfort, *True Devotion to Mary with Preparation for Total Consecration* (Charlotte, NC: TAN Books, 2010), 19-20.

John Bosco asked St. Dominic what gave him the greatest consolation at the moment of death. Was it his love for the Eucharist, his prayerfulness, or other devotion? St. Dominic revealed that what gave him greatest consolation at death was the presence of Mary, to whom he had great filial love. Bishop Fulton Sheen himself said that when he dies, he hopes to hear Jesus say to him, "I have heard my Mother speak of you."

Yet another fruit is her help with the dark nights. St. John of the Cross teaches that progress in the spiritual life entails dark nights of the senses and of the spirit in order for God to reach the deep recesses in our hearts, which we cannot reach. It is like divine surgery that requires the work of the divine Surgeon. Our Lady can come to our help, for she excels in surrender or abandonment, which is the greatest wisdom of the spiritual life; it is that which allows us to surrender to His divine work in the depths of our being.

## B. Entrusting One's Spiritual Life to Mary

The saints, who manifest tremendous and deep love of Mary, found the greatest help in the spiritual life. St. Faustina entrusted her spiritual formation to Mary, to make Mary her "Instructress ":

> Mary was for Sister Faustina more than an objective model of Christian life, which she observed carefully and reflected in her own life, because She was also the Person who was actively involved in the formation of her spiritual life. This is why Sister Faustina calls Our Lady her Instructress (Diary 620) and the Mistress of the interior life, who teaches us how to live for God and souls, not only in theory but also in practice, with the example of Her own life. Hence, Sister Faustina entrusted her interior life to Mary with full confidence, asking her to guide it. *O radiant Virgin, pure as crystal, all immersed in God*— she turned to Our Lady in prayers— *I offer You my spiritual life; arrange everything that it may be pleasing to Your Son (Diary 844).*[30]

This remains understandable if we understand Mary as the spouse of the Holy Spirit, who is Himself her director, and who uses Mary as His instrument. St. Faustina drew much knowledge and made much progress also by examining Mary's life:

---

[30] M. Elżbieta Siepak and M. Nazaria Dlubak, *The Spirituality of Saint Faustina: The Road to Union with God* (Cracow: The Shrine of Divine Mercy, 2002), 93-94

As she meditated on Mary's life, Sister Faustina noticed too that living the faith perfectly, and thereby carrying out the will of God, depends on the degree of our union in love with Jesus. *O Mary*— she wrote, contemplating the mystery of Jesus' presentation in the temple— *today a terrible sword has pierced Your holy soul. Except for God, no one knows of Your suffering. Your soul does not break; it is brave, because it is with Jesus* (*Diary* 915). [31]

Mary taught her to be constantly present to Jesus in her heart.[32] She also taught St. Faustina the importance of doing God's will and of obedience.[33] She taught St. Faustina the greatest virtues: humility, purity, love of God:

As the daughter of Our Lady of Mercy, Sister Faustina was to further distinguish herself by the virtues of: humility, meekness, chastity, love of God and neighbour, compassion and mercy (*Diary* 1244). *I desire, My dearly beloved daughter*— Our Lady said some other time— *that you practice the three virtues that are dearest to Me— and most pleasing to God. The first is humility, humility, and once again humility; the second virtue, purity; the third virtue, love of God. As My daughter, you must especially radiate with these virtues.* (*Diary* 1414-15)[34]

---

[31] Ibid., 92

[32] Contemplation: "Mary taught her above all to discover God in her own soul. *The Mother of God is instructing me in the interior life of the soul with Jesus, especially in Holy Communion* (Diary 840). But not only this one time. On the occasion of preparing for Christmas, She recommended that Sister Faustina constantly adore Jesus dwelling in her soul. *My daughter, strive after silence and humility, so that Jesus, which dwells in your heart continuously, may be able to rest. Adore him in your heart; do not go out from your inmost being* (Diary 785). Sister Faustina faithfully followed Our Lady's advice and encouragement to abide with God in her own soul and there to discover His presence and His power. For this reason, she would not look for God in some far-off place, but focus her whole interior life on increasing her union with Him in her heart" (*The Spirituality of Saint Faustina*, 94-95).

[33] God's Will: "The Virgin Mary encouraged her as well to carry out the will of God faithfully. *My daughter, I strongly recommend that you faithfully fulfill all God's wishes, for that is most pleasing in His holy eyes. I very much desire that you distinguish yourself in this faithfulness in accomplishing God's will. Put the will of God before all sacrifices and holocausts* (Diary 1244). She instructed Sister Faustina to accept all God's requests like a little child without questioning them; otherwise, it would not be pleasing to God (*Diary* 529) since it would express a lack of confidence in His wisdom, omnipotence, and love. With the example of Her life into which She allowed Sister Faustina to enter, the Blessed Mother herself showed Sister Faustina what the perfect fulfillment of God's will consists in; this is to say, in carrying out externally and in interiorly harmonising one's will with the will of God (*Diary* 1437). Sister Faustina avowed sincerely that Mary taught her *how to love God interiorly and also how to carry out His holy will in all things* (*Diary* 40) without which it is impossible to please God (*Diary* 1244) nor Our Lady. Mary assured her that *most pleasing to me is that soul which faithfully carries out the will of God* (*Diary* 449)." (*The Spirituality of Saint Faustina*, 95).

[34] Ibid., 96.

The virtues of Mary are the highest or most fundamental, that which enable one to attain the highest sanctity. It is not accidental that Mother Teresa of Calcutta, who had such a familiar relationship with Mary, revered similar virtues: "Mother Teresa saw the heart of Our Lady as a model of all the virtues she held dear: poverty of spirit, humility, silence, thoughtfulness, haste in service."[35]

## C. To Live "in" Mary

We can seek to deepen our understanding of consecration to Mary through various devotees. One such example is that of Chiara Lubich, foundress of the Focolare. The movement's formal name is *Opus Mariae*, and the members in their own way seek to "live Mary." Concepción Cabrera de Armida teaches us that we must live "in Mary."

> I must live within Mary, imitating her virtues and her love for the Most Holy Trinity. The Mystical Incarnation places the soul in an intimate contact with the three Divine Persons. In them and in Mary, I shall fuse my life, not only the spiritual life, but material as well, fusing it, as well, in the offering of the Word to the Father. I shall within the same offering eat, sleep, rejoice, suffer, etc.; all of my life simplified in that constant offering, which glorifies the Holy Trinity; all of my life in union with Mary, without leaving Mary, imitating her in her love for Jesus, in her total submission to the Father, doing only that which is inspired by the Holy Spirit.[36]

Our call, therefore, is to "live within Mary" and to spend "all of my life in union with Mary, without leaving Mary." The purpose is that, within Mary, we love the most holy Trinity, "imitating her love for Jesus, for total submission to the Father, acting only under the impulse of the Holy Spirit." It is within Mary that I establish my relationship with the Blessed Trinity. As "other Christs," priests have a special place in the heart of Mary, and possess a special power of intercession before her.

---

[35] Joseph Langford, *Mother Teresa: In the Shadow of Our Lady*, 41.

[36] Concepción Cabrera de Armida, *Account of Conscience*, vol. 46, 93-94: October 27, 1925, quoted in Gustavo Garcia-Siller, *Transforming Prayer for Pilgrims* (Modesto, CA: Ediciones Cimiento, 2006), 27. But the translation given above is better, taken from the website, http://www.lovecrucified.com/spiritual_motherhood/spiritual_motherhood_conchita.html, accessed April 24, 2017.

*Synthesis*

How can we "live Mary?" The greatest advice the author has ever received was, "Whenever I have a problem, I give it to Mary and she takes care of it." It is also possibly the best advice that we priests can give to our parishioners, especially in the confessional, where they often come with troubled hearts weighed down by much anxiety. Since Mary truly is our mother and she loves us with a mother's love, and since nothing is refused her, she will not fail to help us. What this means in the concrete is that once any difficulty is entrusted to her, be it a marital difficulty, problem with children not practicing their faith, illness, conflict in the family or at work, moral weakness or sin, that problem now belongs to Mary.

Let us use an illustration. When a child become ill, he does not go to the medicine cabinet to try to heal himself, but rather he goes to his mother, who immediately takes charge of everything. Likewise, anything entrusted to Mary now becomes her problem and not ours anymore, all she asks is that we do what we can— the outcome now belongs to her. However, there is one caveat: degree of faith. If we have little faith in God through her, we will receive little; if we have great trust in her and act as if what we prayed for is on its way, then we will receive much.

Since some question the apparent "excessiveness" of the devotion to Mary, let us clarify this issue once and for all. The author would argue that one can have *improper* devotion to Mary, such as making apparitions and not the Eucharist or Church life the center of our Christian life. But he would strenuously argue that it is impossible to have "too much" devotion to Mary with this simple principle: we must love Mary to the same degree that Jesus loves His Mother. It is suggested here that we cannot possibly ever love Mary in any degree approaching the love Jesus has for His beloved Mother.

Consider what she has done for Him. Mary is the mother who opened the warmth of her heart and love to Him at Bethlehem when all its inhabitants but a few closed their hearts and houses to Him; she was the one who, with Joseph, protected Him from Herod and shielded Him from hunger and heat as they traveled through the desert to Egypt; she was the one who cared for him with incomparable love in the course of those years in Nazareth and wept in anticipation of the fulfillment of the words of

Simeon; she was the one who humanly offered her one and only Son when He underwent the sacrifice to save the world even though this experience would "crucify" her; she was the one who, if she could have done so, would have taken the place of Jesus at the cross, and who went through a certain dark night after His Ascension to heaven when she no longer had on earth the "Sun" of her heart and life. The argument that Mary is an obstacle to attachment to Christ is false, given that Jesus Himself willed this attachment to her and put her squarely in front of us as the means and path to Him. We leave the last word to St. Thérèse: "Mother, you must be the saddest of all women. All of us have you as our mother, but you do not have someone like yourself to be your mother."

# CHAPTER 8

## *HOLY EUCHARIST*

### *(Assimilation to Christ)*

The Mass is the divine act around which the life of the Church gravitates and of which she is the radiance; the center from which she receives all impulses and toward which she is continually directed; the living source from which she proceeds and the ocean to which she returns. It is the sacrifice of Redemption, at once eternal and perpetuated in time, in Heaven before God and on earth among us.

… If man had not sinned, the sacrifice would not have been one of blood…. But as injustice is rejection of infinite Love, it must be repaired by infinite Love. The infinite Love is Jesus, who offered it to his Father on the Cross and continues to offer it in the Eucharist. Unique Priest, unique Victim, immolated by a two-fold love: thanksgiving to His Father and mercy toward us….

The pages of the Gospel proclaim this eternal love of Jesus for His Father. To make the flame of love mount higher, He feeds it with sorrow. Thus, many souls hide their sacrifice, as Jesus hid His, happy to suffer and die to love God better.[1] (Jean d'Elbée)

### *Three Loves*

We have developed the thesis that the baptized is to become "Christ himself" (St. Escrivá's *alter Christus, ipse Christus*). To become a new Christ, he must have two mothers (discussed in Chapter 7) and the Eucharist, the primary means by which the Holy Spirit transforms him into the new child of the Father. As the "source and summit of the Christian life" (Vatican II), the Mass requires a much more comprehensive elaboration than can be offered in this brief introduction. The author's favourite work is a gem on the holy Mass that was used by St. Dominic Savio, St. Leonard of Port

---

[1] Jean d'Elbée, *I Believe in Love*, 221-223.

Maurice's *The Hidden Treasure.* Another inspiring work is Romano Guardini's *Meditations Before Mass,* and a practical spiritual companion to accompany the Mass is Edward G. Maristany's *Loving the Holy Mass.*[2]

We examine the Eucharist in two steps. First, we examine the background of the Mass as Calvary, which is the culmination of all history and the highest expression of God's love. Then we proceed to examine the three dimensions of the Eucharist in order: Sacrifice, Banquet, and Presence.

## THE EUCHARIST

### Background: The Paschal Sacrifice as the Culmination of Salvation History, the Fulfillment of Christ's Thirst

*(i) Christ's Sacrifice as the Culmination of Salvation History*

Christ's sacrifice on Calvary (the Paschal mystery), as culmination of salvation history, must dominate our vision. Eugenio Corsini, a specialist on the Book of the Apocalypse, affirms this dominance in John's Apocalypse: "For John, this [Lamb opening seven seals in Apocalypse] means that the whole of history is a salvation history which can be seen and properly understood only in the light of its culmination in the sacrifice of Christ."[3] Essentially, the sacrifice of Calvary is the culmination of salvation history, and the Eucharist is the perpetuation of that one sacrifice. Vatican II's *Sacrosanctum concilium,* the Constitution on the Liturgy, captures the Eucharist's centrality: "Nevertheless the liturgy is the summit toward which the activity of the Church is directed; at the same time it is the font from which all her power flows."[4] All of Christian life leads to this summit, all graces from God flow from this font.

---

[2] A well-regarded contemporary presentation in James T. O'Connor's *The Hidden Manna: A Theology of the Eucharist;* and a fine patristic-liturgical vision in Adrian Nocent's *The Liturgical Year: The Easter Season* (Vol. Three) Adrian Nocent, *The Liturgical Year: The Paschal Triduum, The Easter Season,* volume three (Collegeville, MN: The Liturgical Press, 1977. Until his recent death, Fr. Nocent, a Benedictine, taught at the Pontificio Ateneo San Anselmo, the Pontifical Liturgical Institute in Rome.

[3] Eugenio Corsini, *The Apocalypse: The Perennial Revelation of Jesus Christ,* Good News Studies 5, trans. by Francis J. Moloney (Wilmington, DE: Michael Glazier, Inc., 1983; Italian orig. *Apocalisse prima e dopo,* 1980), 121.

[4] *Sacrosanctum concilium,* n. 10. See also *Lumen gentium,* n. 11, and the *Catechism of the Catholic Church,* n. 1324.

## *(ii) The Depth of Christ's Identification with Man in Love*

If Christ's Paschal sacrifice on Calvary is the heart of history, it is not the arduous external crucifixion that is decisive, but the love within His heart. Christ's love is expressed above all by His total "identification" with those He loves: He *identifies* with man by first becoming one with him at the Incarnation; then His identification with us went to the extreme, "he loved us to the end" (see Phil 2). Hans Urs von Balthasar presents a very striking vision of what took place: because our sinfulness and egoism had caused us to shrink into ourselves, God violently racked His Son's heart on the cross from earth to heaven, so that in Him we would be incorporated and stretched to reach heaven once more:

> The measure of man had been shrunk by the sinner, and the Lord had to wrench it violently open again in the extreme suffering in the racking of his limbs on the Cross, to which corresponds a yet deeper straining apart of all the powers of his soul, he reaches the furthest dimension of that guilt of which creation has concrete knowledge: the abyss between the flaming, raging justice of God and man 'abandoned' and rejected by him. He attains this point as substitute, that is, no longer distinguishing, subjectively or objectively, between his own innocence and the guilt of others. He can, of course, be the measure of this one thing in all its degrees and modifications— the gulf between God and man, the gulf between God and the just man subject to original sin, and the gulf between God and the sinner as such— only because he is more than man, the God-man....
>
> The measure of maximum nearness and of maximum separation between God and man is given its foundation and its roots and altogether surpassed by the real nearness and the real distance between Father and Son in the Spirit on the Cross and in the Resurrection. The Son also knows what it means to live in the Father, to rest in his bosom, to love him, to serve him, and he alone can know the full significance of being abandoned by him.[5]

The depth of vicarious suffering, the taking of our place, must be seen. Jesus enters our hell, so that we would not only be saved, but also be raised to participate in His divine Sonship.

---

[5] Hans Urs von Balthasar, *Theology of History*, 68-69.

## (iii) Christ's Love Expressed in "I Thirst"

Perhaps the best way to understand the depth of Christ's love and suffering is to try to perceive the sentiments in the heart of Jesus in the words, "I thirst." Mother Teresa of Calcutta teaches that it was our Lady who led her to understand this "thirst" of Christ. We give little thought to this interior "crucifixion" of Christ— He thirsts for our love.

> *If Our Lady had not been there with me that day [vision on train to Darjeeling], I never would have known what Jesus meant when he said, 'I thirst'....*
>
> *Just think God is thirsting— and you and I come forward to satiate His Thirst. Just think of that! So the better we understand, the better we will satiate His Thirst for love of souls. Pray in a special way to Our Lady to explain this to us.*[6]

This thirst of God for our salvation extends through the long years of waiting to save us: from Adam's sin, through the Exodus, to the foreshadowing of Abraham's sacrifice of Isaac on Mount Moriah. And with His coming and drawing close to His sacrifice, Jesus' heart reveals the longing of God in poignant moments, captured by the evangelists:

> I came to cast fire upon the earth; and would that it were already kindled! I have a baptism to be baptized with; and how I am constrained until it is accomplished! (Lk 12:49-50)
>
> O Jerusalem, Jerusalem, killing the prophets and stoning those who are sent to you! How often would I have gathered your children together as a hen gathers her brood under her wings, and you would not. (Mt 23:37)

Jesus expressed with great longing the desire to undergo His Baptism, the Passion of the cross, so as to cast the fire of the Holy Spirit into our hearts, so as to incorporate us as His Mystical Body and His Bride, and to make us sons and daughters in the one Son. The recapitulation of all the universe and history ("and I, when I am lifted up from the earth, will draw all men to myself," Jn 12:32), now finds its center in Christ's sacrifice; and the reconciliation accomplished finally satisfies Christ's desire for union.

---

[6] Joseph Langford, *Mother Teresa: In the Shadow of Our Lady*, 40.

# 1. Mass as Sacrifice

The sacrifice of Calvary that has become the Eucharist has three aspects: Sacrifice, Banquet, and Presence (see John Paul II's *Ecclesia de Eucharistia*).[7] The perpetuation of Christ's sacrifice is actualized in two senses, as "re-presentation" at each Mass and as a participation in the eternal liturgy in heaven.[8]

## The Old Testament Background of the Eucharist

Since, as the Church Fathers teach us, the Old Testament prepares for or prefigures, the New Testament, the Old Testament prefigurations would offer light to the New Testament sacrifice of the Eucharist. From among various sources, one might look to Dr. Brant Pitre's *Jesus and the Jewish Roots of the Eucharist*. Dr. Pitre, whose doctoral dissertation on the New Testament and ancient Judaism gives him a unique perspective, examines pertinent texts of New Testament Scripture but through the lens of Jewish Tradition.[9]

Dr. Pitre begins his whole discussion by first asking a question of interest to us: "How is it that the early Christians, all Jewish, could so easily take to the Eucharist, especially given the injunction that the Jews could not drink blood, which represented life." The answer, he gives, is that they viewed the Eucharist in the context of a new Exodus. And the new Exodus has three

---

[7] John Paul II, *Ecclesia de Eucharistia*, n. 61.

[8] See Adrian Nocent, *The Liturgical Year*. Fr. Nocent makes ample use of the theology of Pope St. Leo the Great, so much so that in vol. 3, he cites him in the footnotes (e.g., For Vol. One, see p. 65, footnote 60; Vol. Three: p. 57, footnotes 53, 54; p. 91, footnote 94.). Volume Three on the Paschal Triduum and strongly reflects the theology of St. Leo the Great, with a specific section on the latter's theology on pages 172-176.

[9] It is worth noting that some question elements of Pitre's scholarship, yet many others support him. Nevertheless, his unique insights are worth considering, given that they make critical connections to the Jewish traditions for the many of us who lack that Old Testament background. Brant Pitre, *Jesus and the Jewish Roots of the Eucharist: Unlocking the Secrets of the Last Supper* (New York: Doubleday Religion, 2011). His scholarship, especially the literalness of his interpretations, has occasioned criticism in some quarters, including the New Testament scholar, C. Kavin Row, "Confecting Evidence: A Review of *Jesus and the Jewish Roots of the Eucharist*," *First Things* (July 2011); and John W. Martens, "Brant Pitre's book *Jesus and the Jewish Roots of the Eucharist*," *America* (March 7, 2011). Yet, his book is sold by Ignatius Press and he is supported by scholars such as Scott Hahn, Tim Gray, Carl Anderson (Knights of Columbus), Edward Sri (Augustine Institute), and Matthew Levering (see Amazon.com reviews of book). This summary is based on his CD talks: *Jesus and the Jewish Roots of the Eucharist*, CD, Brant Pitre, (Lighthouse Catholic Media).

roots of this sacrifice in the Old Testament: the Passover; the manna; and the bread of Presence. The fulfillment in Jesus thus makes the Eucharist the new Passover, the new Manna, and the new Bread of Presence (these are precisely the three elements examined thus far of sacrifice, meal, and presence). He argues that, if we make the link to the Old Testament roots, we will clearly and easily understand key aspects of the Eucharist, including that of the real presence of Christ in the Blessed Sacrament.[10] For the early Jewish Christians therefore, there was a natural fulfillment of the Old Testament elements (see Paul's Letters).

## A. Sacrifice: Representation or Perpetuation of Calvary

### *(1) Sacramental Representation of Christ's Sacrifice on Calvary*

A seminary professor, kind-hearted and well-intentioned, giving a seminar on the Eucharist, shocked the author as a seminarian by a proposal. He suggested that the word "sacrifice" had negative connotations to young people today and proposed that we remove it from Eucharistic terminology and replace it with a term that was more amenable to the young hearts. The professor's principal focus was on the meal dimension of the Eucharist. The author, though then a neophyte in theology, instinctively sensed that this would undermine the theology of and love for the Eucharist.

*The Kernel of the Difficulty*

We have a crisis in the Church: many Catholics no longer participate in Mass, and this may be due to their not perceiving the glorious reality of the Mass. Many see the Mass only as a communal prayer service, at which we receive Communion. The devout Catholic is mesmerized by the Real Presence of Christ through transubstantiation of the bread and wine, but this is not the foundation. Catholics need sublime images that attract the heart; it is hard enough to relate the Mass to an event that took place two thousand years ago, and saying that it is not true that the "historical acts of the past [Passion] are... re-presented" could leave us in limbo devotionally or mystically, with no strong moorings to keep our hearts spiritually attached to Calvary. Dom Vonier teaches that we must not get *side-tracked by good dimensions* (e.g., the real presence, the banquet, or the participation of

---

[10] Ibid., Chapter 1, 11-21.

the heavenly liturgy) *to miss out on the heart that is the renewal of the sacrifice of Calvary*:

> But the value of this book to the Catholic reader in the post-Conciliar period will not only be to give him or her an idea of how rigorous—and yet religiously exhilarating—the best Catholic theology can be. It will also be to recall them to the conviction of the Church of all ages that *the Mass is not primarily assembly or common meal, not primarily Holy Communion or anticipation of the heavenly Banquet. It is primarily the Church's sacrifice, the Christian Oblation. It is on the identity of the Holy Eucharist with Christ's glorious Passion, offered and accepted, that all the fruits of the Eucharist depend, and all the other values and aspects liturgists see in Eucharistic celebration turn.*[11] (emphasis mine)

But there is a second difficulty. Explaining how the sacrifice of Calvary and the sacrifice of the Mass are one and the same sacrifice can be interpreted as primarily a renewal of either Christ's presence or his interior oblation but not a "re-presentation" (making present) of the sacrifice of Calvary.

*Divergent Interpretations*

(i) Msgr. James T. O'Connor's *Hidden Manna*, while reiterating truths, diverges from our understanding by focusing primarily on the presence of the risen Christ who is always a Victim. Msgr. O'Connor notes that all Orthodox Traditions teach that Christ is the principal Priest and Victim at each Eucharist, and that the Mass makes us participants in His one sacrifice, drawing us into the sacrifice (drawing from *Mediator Dei*).[12] But, in his understanding, the Mass is not a repetition, which we all accept, but more surprisingly, nor even a *re-presentation* of the historical act on Calvary. It, rather, makes present Christ, who is "what he is now because of those past actions."

> When Christ becomes present at Mass, he does so not in order to repeat the sacrifice of the Cross but to draw us into it, to make us participants in his one sacrifice, priests and victim, along with himself. The Last Supper and Calvary and the Mass are all the same sacrifice, *not because the historical*

---

[11] Aidan Nichols, "Abbot Vonier and the Christian Sacrifice: Introduction to Abbot Vonier's *A Key to the Doctrine of the Eucharist*," Ignatius Insight, accessed July 15, 2015, http://www.ignatiusinsight.com/features2007/anichols_introvonier_aug07.asp
[12] Pius XII, *Mediator Dei*, quoted in James O'Connor, *The Hidden Manna*, 303.

*acts of the past are repeated or re-presented, but because of the intrinsic unity that all these actions, past and present, possess in the one Priest and Victim.* The twofold Consecration symbolically represents what is past, but makes actually present Christ who is what he is now because of those past actions. The killing and offering of the Victim has passed; the Victim who was killed and offered remains alive, but Victim still.[13] (emphasis mine)

(ii) Bishop Attila Miklósházy presents two divergent opinions. First, he shares Msgr. O'Connor's vision: "The earthly existence, death, and resurrection remain in the glorified Lord, not as acts (as such they are historical, once and for all), but as realities which affect His whole being. Christ lives always as the one who has undergone death."[14] Yet when treating of the "salvation-historical" dimension of the sacraments, he takes a different position by emphasizing that the sacrament is not just a memorial but a "re-presentation" of a past salvific event:

A sacrament is a sign of remembrance, or better, a memorial celebration, celebrating the past salvific event, the Christ-event, the mystery of Christ, especially His paschal mystery, from which all the efficacy of the sacrament derives. This happens through αναμνησις ("anamnesis"= "remembrance"), which has to be understood in the sense of the Jewish *ZIKKARON*; not merely a recalling of a past historical event, but as making the past salvific event a present reality (re-presentation, mystery-presence).[15]

(iii) Francis Fernandez, in *In Conversation with God*, highlights a key insight for us, that the interior surrender to and love of the Father is what ultimately purchased our redemption: "This internal offering of Jesus gives full meaning to all the external elements of his voluntary sacrifice — the insults, the stripping of his garments, the crucifixion. The Sacrifice of the Cross is a single sacrifice. Priest and victim are one and the same divine person..."[16] It was not Pilate or Caiaphas who offered Jesus up, but He who surrendered Himself. And for Francis Fernandez, it is this interior oblation of self-surrender and loving submission to His Father that perdures in the Mass:

---

[13] James T. O'Connor, *The Hidden Manna*, 302.
[14] Attila Miklósházy, "Sacraments in General" (lecture, Sacraments Course, Toronto School of Theology at the University of Toronto, 1971, 2015 revd edition), 18.
[15] Ibid., 7.
[16] Francis Fernandez, *In Conversation with God*, vol. 2 (New York: Scepter, 1993),184.

There is made present once again, not the sorrowful and bloody circumstances of Calvary, but the total loving submission of Our Lord to his Father's will. This internal offering of himself is identical on Calvary and in the Mass: it is Christ's oblation. It is the same Priest, the same Victim, the same oblation and submission to the Will of God the Father. The external manifestation of the Passion and Death of Jesus goes on — in the Mass, through the sacramental separation, in an unbloody manner, of the Body and Blood of Christ through means of the transubstantiation of the bread and wine.[17]

Fernandez makes it clear that the essence of the Mass is the presence of the risen Christ renewing His oblation at the Mass: "In the Mass, the priest is only the instrument of Christ, the Eternal and High priest. Christ offers himself in every Mass in the same way as he did on Calvary..."[18] While Fernandez laudably identifies the essence of Christ's sacrifice as the interior oblation, he does not go the further step of seeing the Mass as making present Christ's sacrifice of Calvary.

To restore the full understanding of the Eucharist as perpetuating or representing Calvary's sacrifice, the Old Testament and patristic theology and Tradition in the saints' teaching can give us a good beginning.

*Old Testament and Church Fathers Provide a Foundation for "Representation"*

To understand the Eucharist, we can look to see what light can be shed by the Old Testament background. We have seen in typology examples of how the entire Old Testament prefigured Christ, and especially His Sacrifice.[19] One of the clearest prefigurations to Christ's sacrifice and the Mass is the Old Testament event of the Exodus of the Israelites from Egypt. To be delivered from the angel of death in Egypt on the night of his "Passover," the Hebrew people were instructed to slaughter a lamb without blemish, sprinkle its blood on the door and lintel, and then roast and eat this lamb while standing. If we fast-forward to Jesus' arrival, when John the Baptist saw Jesus for the first time, he recognized the One whose way he was preparing and linked Him with that lamb of Egypt: "Behold, the Lamb of God, who takes away the sin of the world!" (Jn 1:29).

---

[17] Ibid., 185-186.
[18] Ibid., 186.
[19] An in-depth theological analysis of Sacrifice in the Eucharist can be found in Charles Cardinal Journet's book mentioned above, *The Mass: The Presence of the Sacrifice of the Cross.*

Now we see the parallels: Jesus was without "blemish," that is, without sin; like the lamb, He too was slaughtered but on the cross and His blood is sprinkled through the Church's sacraments; and now He too is consumed, in the Eucharistic Communion. The new element here, as John's words indicate, is the consuming of the Lamb of God and the linking of the sacrifice with the taking away of the sins of the world.[20] This is but one of a number of Old Testament texts that show how their sacrifices point to the true and efficacious sacrifice of Christ.

Let us turn to the Church Fathers through the figure of Pope St. Leo the Great, who has had a significant influence on the liturgy. For St. Leo (see his homilies), Christ's sacrifice dominates salvation history: "The passion of Christ encompasses the mystery of salvation."[21] For Pope St. Leo, as for the Church Fathers and the Church, this sacrifice has now become the Eucharist:

> Noteworthy is the fact that Leo does not distinguish between the paschal sacrifice on the Cross and the new paschal sacrifice. The paschal sacrifice on the Cross is now actualized in the Eucharistic sacrifice, so that as the baptized daily consumes this sacred sacrament, he becomes more and more what he receives. As Christ's sacrifice on the Cross accomplished once for all the new creation, so now the new paschal sacrifice continues the once for all transformation in this final age, in each today (*hodie*). What the sacraments effect specifically is configuration to Christ's Passion.[22]

And the key to St. Leo's understanding is the use of *hodie* ("today"). Adrian Nocent, the noted Benedictine liturgist, confirmed this: "When we repeatedly celebrate the sign of the Supper, we make really present in time and space the one sacrifice of Christ on Calvary..."[23]

---

[20] See Adrian Nocent's analysis of Christ as Lamb in "The Blood of the Lamb," *The Liturgical Year*, vol. Three, 74-82.
[21] Charles Anang, *The Theology of the Passion of Christ in the Sermons of Pope St. Leo the Great* (PhD diss., Rome, 1999), 256. For further development of liturgical aspects in St. Leo the Great, see Cassian Folsom, *The Liturgical Preaching of St. Leo the Great* (Excerpt of PhD diss., St. Meinrad, Indiana,1990).
[22] Ibid., 258.
[23] Adrian Nocent, *The Liturgical Year,* vol. Three, 35.

## *(2) The Eucharist in the Lives of the Saints*

We can see its power in the lives of the saints. St. Leonard of Port Maurice's *The Hidden Treasure* affirmed, as did Msgr. O'Connor, three divine figures in this sacrifice (divine priest, divine victim, divine Father to whom the sacrifice is offered), but also that it is not a mere memorial of Christ's sacrifice, and draws out more fully the ramifications.[24]

> The principal excellence of the most holy sacrifice of the Mass consists in being essentially, and in the very highest degree, identical with that which was offered on the cross of Calvary: with this sole difference, that the sacrifice on the cross was bloody, and made once for all... while the sacrifice on the altar is an unbloody sacrifice, which can be repeated an infinite number of times.... And, therefore, observe that the Mass is not a mere representation, nor a simple commemoration of the passion and death of the Redeemer, *but there is performed, in a certain true sense, the selfsame most holy act which was performed on Calvary. It may be said, with all truth, that in every Mass Our Redeemer returns mystically to die for us, without really dying, at one and the same time really alive and as it were slain— vidit Magnum stantem tamquam occisum,* 'I saw a Lamb standing as if it were slain' (Apoc. V. 6). (emphasis added)

How closely he links the Mass with Calvary is manifest in how we are to prepare to enter this mystery: "Now, tell me whether, when you enter the Church to hear Mass, you thoroughly well consider that you are going up as it were to Calvary, to be present at the death of the Redeemer."[25] In preparation, we act as if we are climbing the hill of Calvary, because, in essence, that is what is taking place.

*Padre Pio's Passion During the Mass*

A second example is to look to the Masses of St. Pio of Pietrelcina, through which he influenced many people. As a BBC commentator noted in a film years ago, "Many priests appear to celebrate Mass with great devotion. Padre Pio celebrates Mass as if his salvation depended on it."[26] Padre Pio

---

[24] St. Leonard of Port Maurice, *The Hidden Treasure: Holy Mass* (Charlotte, NC: TAN Books, 2012), 2-3.
[25] Ibid., 23.
[26] Fr. David May, "Lighting the Pauline Flame," *Madonna House*, October 22, 2008, http://www.madonnahouse.org/restoration/2008/10/lighting_the_pauline_flame.html

was fond of saying, *"C'é nella Messa tutto il Calvario"* ("There is in the Mass all of the Calvary")— it suggests that there is a sacramental and mystical identity. He also revealed to confidants that, during the Mass, he suffered Christ's Passion. Additionally, when he was asked if he were not distracted by the commotion in the congregation during his Masses, he replied that it was like that at Jesus' sacrifice on Calvary.[27]

## (3) Looking to the Catechism and Key Scholars for Clarity

While this is a controverted question best left to the liturgical experts to elaborate, we can turn to authoritative sources: *Catechism of the Catholic Church*, Thomas Aquinas, Dom Vonier and Dom Casel, and Joseph Ratzinger.

### (i) Catechism of the Catholic Church

Our first point of reference should be the *Catechism of the Catholic Church*. No one disputes the key premise that the *Catechism* states: "The sacrifice of Christ and the sacrifice of the Eucharist are one single sacrifice" (n. 1367). But the *Catechism* explicitly affirms that the Mass is a "re-presentation" of Calvary in the sense of perpetuating or "making present": "This he did [Jesus instituting the Eucharist] in order to perpetuate the sacrifice of the cross throughout the ages until he should come again," (n. 1323); "The Eucharist is thus a sacrifice because it re-presents (makes present) the sacrifice of the cross, because it is its memorial and because it applies its fruit" (n. 1366), quoting Trent, "by which the bloody sacrifice which he was to accomplish once for all on the cross would be re-presented…" (Council of Trent, DS 1740).

---

[27] See Gerardo di Flumeri, *The Mystery of the Cross in Padre Pio of Pietrelcina* and Pierino Galeone, *Padre Pio: mio padre* (Milan: San Paolo, 2005). Msgr. Galeone was a disciple of Padre Pio since he met him as a diocesan seminarian, and now continues to propagate his spirituality. One internet source reproduces a conversation about Padre Pio's suffering at Mass: "Che cosa debbo leggere nella vostra Santa Messa? Tutto il Calvario. — Padre, ditemi quanto soffrite nella Santa Messa. Tutto quello che ha sofferto Gesù nella sua Passione, inadeguatamente, lo soffro anch'io, per quanto a umana creatura è possibile." We must see in his Mass "All of Calvary," and he suffered what Jesus suffered but in a limited creaturely way. Cleonice Morcaldi, accessed July 3, 2015, http://gerardoms.blogspot.ca/search/label/Padre%20Pio.

Another magisterial text supports this teaching: "… in the Eucharist, which is, above all, the real presence of the unique and eternal sacrifice of Christ" (*Directory on the Ministry and Life of Priests*, n. 48). Thus, the *Catechism* ties the Eucharist strongly to Calvary, using phrases, like "it re-presents (makes present) the sacrifice of the cross"; it is the "real presence of the unique and eternal sacrifice of Christ." It is clear that, at the very least, we can use the language of "perpetuation" as making present the sacrifice of Calvary.

## (ii) Thomas Aquinas

For elaboration on the statements of the *Catechism*, let us now turn to a few key commentators: St. Thomas Aquinas (through Charles Cardinal Journet); Dom Odo Casel, for his new understanding of presence through "mystery" (through Louis Bouyer); Dom Anscar Vonier, for his own development of this mystery; and to Cardinal Ratzinger, known for his deep interest in the liturgy and for his understanding of the three presences.

St. Thomas Aquinas' vision converges with the understanding of the *Catechism of the Catholic Church*. Charles Cardinal Journet has examined St. Thomas Aquinas' question, "Whether Christ is sacrificed in this Sacrament" (*S.Th.* III, q. 83, a. 1). St. Thomas' key response (in the *respondeo dicendum quod*, "I answer that") is that "The Mass brings the effect of the Passion," and even more deeply, "it exercises its efficiency by a spiritual contact despite the distance of time and space, that it can touch all times in their presentiality, in their existentiality." The result is that "Where Christ's Passion is really present, Christ's sacrifice is really present."[28] What gives greater clarity is the conclusion that follows:

> In other words, the Mass brings us not only the *substantial presence* of Christ in His glorious *state*, but also the *operative presence* of His redemptive sacrificial *act*. Christ desires now, as He desired on the Cross (and until the end of the world), that the ray from His blood touch and redeem every moment of time by this contact.[29]

---

[28] Charles Journet, *The Mass: The Presence of the Sacrifice of the Cross*, 80-81. Readers unfamiliar with St. Thomas Aquinas' format might wish to be aware that he employs the following structure: three objections, a general response (with "On the contrary" and "I answer that"), and that is followed by specific responses to the three objections outlined.
[29] Ibid., 81.

Thus he argues not only for the presence of the risen Christ, that everyone accepts, but also for "the *operative presence* of His redemptive sacrificial *act*," such that "the ray from His blood cross touch and redeem every moment of time by this contact." St. Thomas highlights the re-presenting actuality by going so far as to say that "as the Mass is an image representing Christ's Passion, so that altar is representative of the cross itself..."[30]

Now, seeing that "The doctrine of St. Thomas was not entirely explicit," Cardinal Journet finds further clarification in St. Thomas Aquinas' response to the objections in the same article ("The Mass Communicates to Us the One Sacrifice of Christ"). To the first Objection (in article 1 above), regarding the unicity of the oblation and sacrifice of Christ, St. Thomas turns to a text attributed to St. Ambrose, where he uses an analogy: just as the Eucharist multiplies not Christ but many substantial presences of Christ, so the Mass multiplies many operative presences of the one sacrifice of Christ. To the second Objection, we find a key to our discussion which Cardinal Journet explains.

> ... at the Mass, the bloody sacrifice is not repeated, but *re-presented*: the altar, where the death of Christ is signified by the sacramental appearances, represents the Cross where Christ was crucified under His own appearances. We should add... that the bloody sacrifice is then *applied* to us, made present, and that the Mass multiplies not this unique sacrifice but the real presences of this unique sacrifice.[31]

As Cardinal Journet understands St. Thomas, the key is in the multiplication of "presences." The bloody sacrifice is "made present," with the result that there are "real presences of this unique sacrifice."[32] Thus, Cardinal Journet argues for both the action of the risen Christ as well as the multiplying of "the real presence of this unique sacrifice." This finally may be the key that we need to link the Mass closely with Calvary, conforming to the Council of Trent.

---

[30] Ibid.
[31] Ibid.
[32] Ibid., 82.

## (iii) Dom Anscar Vonier and Dom Odo Casel

We can turn to two key figures in contemporary liturgical reform. In the early twentieth century, Dom Anscar Vonier's theological work has raised a few questions by some. Aidan Nichols, however, offers a summary of Vonier's book, along with his positive evaluation of it. He agrees with his understanding that Calvary and Mass are the same reality but with his unusual phrasing of modes: "Calvary and the Mass are the self-same reality, in two utterly different modes."

> [For Abbot Vonier] The Holy Eucharist is first and foremost the Holy Sacrifice not because it is something different from a mere sacrament but because it is, precisely as taught by Saint Thomas, the sacrament of the Sacrifice of Christ.... The sacrifice of the Mass is the expression in sign of all that our great high priest in his once-for-all offering on the Cross underwent, did, and was. Calvary and the Mass are the self-same reality, *in two utterly different modes....*

The second paragraph confirms that the priority of the sacrificial dimension of the Eucharist: that the banquet and presence dimensions flow from the sacrificial dimension.

Dom Odo Casel of the abbey of Maria Laach did some seminal work in seeking to explain how the original salvific action by Jesus is present in the liturgical rites, which he calls "the mysteries" (*Mysteriengegenwart*, including how *anamnesis* functions). Fr. Louis Bouyer explains Dom Casel's theology. While he critiques Dom Casel's linking Christian "mysteries" with the pagan religion's mysteries, he affirms the latter's *overall legacy*, along with his influence on *Sacrosanctum concilium*:

> ... the heart of the teaching on the liturgy in the conciliar Constitution is also the heart of Dom Casel's teaching. The Constitution's constant citation of the patristic, liturgical, and earlier conciliar texts on which Casel based his interpretation, and its interpretation of these texts on the same lines as Casel show a relation of filiation that will strike all future historians.[33]

---

[33] Louis Bouyer, review in *LMD* no. 80 (1964) 242, quoted in I. H. Dalmais, "The Liturgy as Celebration of the Mystery of Salvation," in A. G. Martimort, *The Church at Prayer*, vol. I (Collegeville: Liturgical Press, 1987), 271. See confirmation of Bouyer's positive analysis of

Dom Casel argues for not just the effect of the salvific action in the liturgy, but also the redemptive work itself. That is, in the liturgy, it is the mystery of Christ's "redemptive work" that is made present again (not just its effects).

> An even more difficult and controverted question is that of the way in which the mystery of salvation is present in the liturgical mysteries. Dom Casel never stopped insisting that what is present is not simply the effect, that is the grace bestowed, *but the redemptive work itself.* He sees this reactualization as necessitated by the fact (which in his view the tradition makes undeniable) that we participate in the mystery of salvation only through a mystical and real participation in the life and death of Christ. This prior participation requires in turn that Christ live and die in the very sacramental action that makes us sharers in him.[34] (emphasis mine)

At times, he seems to veer into the reactualization (as opposed to representation) of the historical dimension, but elsewhere he repudiates this interpretation.[35]

*Synthesis*

Let us summarize our findings. The *Catechism of the Catholic Church*, St. Thomas Aquinas, Dom Anscar Vonier, Dom Odo Casel, and their respective interpreters, Cardinal Journet, Aidan Nichols, and Louis Bouyer, along with the mystical Tradition, converge on the understanding of the presence of the eternal sacrifice of Calvary at the Eucharist; and not metaphorically or symbolically, but its real presence: "*operative presence* of His redemptive sacrificial *act*" (Journet); "Mass multiplies not this unique sacrifice but the real presences of this unique sacrifice" (Journet on St. Ambrose, St. Thomas); is present in "different modes" (Aidan Nichols). Aidan Nichols gives us the insight that the real presence of the eternal sacrifice is the key to all other dimensions of the Eucharist (e.g., Communion).

---

Dom Casel's legacy in Louis Bouyer, *Liturgical Piety*, *Liturgical Studies* vol. 1 (Notre Dame, IN: Notre Dame University Press, 1964), 98; and Bouyer summarizes Dom Casel's understanding in this work, 127-128.

[34] I. H. Dalmais, in *The Church at Prayer*, vol. I, 270.

[35] T. Filthaut, *La théologie des mystères. Exposé de la controverse* (Tournai: Desclée, 1954), 26, quoted in footnote 41, in *The Church at Prayer*, vol. I, 270.

For this author, and perhaps for most Catholics, the analogy that could be most helpful is that there is a "real presence" of Calvary at Mass analogous to the "real presence" of Christ in the Blessed Sacrament— Christ is truly present in the host, and Calvary's sacrifice is truly present at Mass. As there is only one Christ but many presences in the host, so there is only one sacrifice on Calvary but many presences in each Mass. While we need to make theological distinctions, at the end of day, as Christians, we can do what St. Joan of Arc did, as quoted in the *Catechism of the Catholic Church*, where it clarified that "The Church is one with Christ": "A reply of St. Joan of Arc to her judges sums up the faith of the holy doctors and the good sense of the believer: 'About Jesus Christ and the Church, I simply know they're just one thing, and we shouldn't complicate the matter'" (CCC 795).

Any theological distinction that detaches or dissociates Calvary's sacrifice from the Mass, while these are distinct, could diminish the love of this Eucharistic sacrifice. Perhaps we can turn to the mystical dimension, a word from the inner locutions of Jesus to a monk. As this is private revelation, we can choose to accept or reject it, but what matters is the truth of the words, that "the whole of My sacrifice unfolds before their eyes":

> I want you to speak to the faithful of the Holy Mass as a true sacrifice. They have forgotten this. No one thinks any more to tell them that the action of the Eucharist renews My sacrifice upon the Cross, and that I am present upon the altar as upon the Cross, as both Priest and Victim. It is the whole of My sacrifice of love that unfolds before their eyes. You must tell them this.[36]

We must not stop at the theological elaboration without seeing above all the love in that action: "That first sin, rejection of an infinite love, could not be repaired by any but an infinite love. The Word of God became incarnate in order that love might triumph in Him and through Him"[37]; and that love calls for love.[38] It is understood that Christ's sacrifice must also be seen in light of its fulfillment in the Resurrection (see F.X. Durrwell's fine works).[39]

---

36 A Benedictine Monk, *In Sinu Jesu, When Heart Speaks to Heart: The Journal of a Priest at Prayer* (Kettering, OH: Angelico Press, 2016), 7.
37 Jean d'Elbée, *I Believe in Love*, 5.
38 Ibid., 4.
39 F. X. Durrwell, *The Resurrection: A Biblical Study* (New York: Sheed & Ward, 1970).

## B. Participation in the Heavenly Liturgy

The second aspect of "sacrifice" is that this sacrifice in a certain sense is an "eternal" sacrifice. Dom Prosper Guéranger (abbot of Solesmes Abbey for nearly forty years) wrote in *The Liturgical Year* that we participate in the heavenly liturgy.[40]

> The divine Lamb is lying on our altar! Thus we see that the Mass is the visible reality, *here and now, of the timeless eternal Mass of Heaven, described in the apocalypse.* Through it we participate in the Celestial Liturgy; through it the gates of Heaven are opened to us and the possibility of eternal life is made available to us.[41] (emphasis added)

What is being referred to here is explained in the Apocalyptic vision of St. John the Apostle in which he describes the sacrifice of the Lamb, "slain" but alive and seated on the throne, with the twenty-four ancients adoring Him, with melodies on the harp and with the burning of incense, while multitudes of angels and all creatures sing praise to the Lamb and the eternal "Amen." (Apoc. 5:6-14). There is growing recognition of the liturgical character of Apocalypse, and indications that all of salvation history is framed within the liturgy, specifically the Eucharist.

> It was argued that the major theme of the Book as a whole is that of the *worship* of God and Christ, rather than *judgment....*
>
> The Church envisioned by the Seer appears to be both earthly and heavenly, non-hierarchical, radically eschatological, and possessing earthly and heavenly, historical and supra-historical, human and divine dimensions *simultaneously....*
>
> The transformational symbolism present in the hymns enables the addressees to experience victory over the hostile forces... by providing them with a proleptic experience of standing with the angelic beings who praise God in the heavenly heights....

---

[40] Dom Prosper Guéranger, *The Liturgical Year*, St. Austin Press, 2000. One might also consider his books on the Mass, *The Holy Mass* (Baronius Press, 2006) and *The Holy Mass Explained* (Loreto Press, 2007). Dom Guéranger, abbot of Solesmes monastery and the one who brought about a renewal of Gregorian Chant, produced a monumental work of fifteen volumes, which Cardinal Manning called "a prelude to a better world and an avenue to the Vision of Peace."
[41] Ibid., Lent Volume, Chapter Five, "On Hearing Mass During The Season Of Lent."

The Apocalypse of John as 'liturgy of the Word' is thus fittingly celebrated before the Eucharist.[42]

The *Catechism of the Catholic Church* unifies the two elements of the memorial of Christ's sacrifice and the heavenly liturgy: "To the offering of Christ are united not only the members still here on earth, but also those already in the glory of heaven"; the Church "is as it were at the foot of the cross with Mary, united with the offering and intercession of Christ" (*Catechism* n. 1370). In the mystical tradition, the seventeenth century founder of the Sulpicians, Fr. Jean-Jacques Olier, insists that sacrifice must continue incessantly in heaven:

> To understand the mystery of the most holy sacrifice of the Mass and to open at one stroke the curtain that hides it from our view, we must know that this sacrifice is the sacrifice of heaven.... Others, however, who have a better knowledge of the meaning of religion and its first duty, i.e., sacrifice, will never doubt the existence of sacrifice in heaven— for even on earth the one who believes in the existence of God offers sacrifices.... No one can doubt the existence of sacrifice in heaven, which is the place of the perfect religion and the most sublime veneration of God. It is really there that sacrifice must be offered incessantly, so that religion itself is not interrupted.[43]

Jesus continues to offer Himself in sacrifice for all eternity, to which He unites all sacrifices: "As the eternal priest, Christ implies in his sacrifice all the sacrifices ever offered to God. Together with these, he offers his entire Church, dedicating it and handing it over to the Father."[44] Olier goes so far as to teach the "great care that every detail and every gesture performed during Mass must be understood in terms of sacrifice."[45]

---

[42] Anthony Robert Nusca, *Heavenly Worship, Ecclesial Worship: A 'Liturgical Approach' to the Hymns of the Apocalypse of St. John* (Ph.D. Diss., Rome: Pontificia Universitas Gregoriana, 1998), 484-486. Eugenio Corsini, at an earlier time of writing, noted that there was then already a growing perception of liturgical character of the Apocalypse, but his own focus was directed to the Paschal mystery as fulfillment of Christ's messiahship that is witnessed to by the Old Testament and of the new Jerusalem as also a present reality (see Corsini, *The Apocalypse: The Perennial Revelation of Jesus Christ*, 9, 419, & 422-423).

[43] Jean-Jacques Olier, *L'esprit des cérémonies de la messe*, ed. C. Barthe (Le Forum, Perpignan, 2004) 287, quoted in Bernhard Lang, *Sacred Games: A History of Christian Worship* (New Haven, CT: Yale University Press, 1997), 272.

[44] Ibid., 272.

[45] Ibid.

*Joseph Ratzinger Provides a Link for Uniting Representation and Heavenly Liturgy*

Cardinal Ratzinger, in his work *The Spirit of the Liturgy*, gives a theological foundation for linking all three phases of past, present, and eternal. He begins with the idea of the liturgy making the reality represented "contemporary": "In the Eucharist we are caught up and made contemporary with the Paschal mystery of Christ, in his passing of the transitory to the presence and sight of God."[46] He explains this through an analogy with the three stages of salvation history: the "shadow" (Old Testament prefigurations), "image" (Word's presence in incarnate form), and "reality" (His transfigured form in heaven). These three symbolically correspond to the three presences of Christ's sacrifice: his Paschal mystery, the liturgy, and in heaven respectively. Thus the liturgy represents the middle or "between-ness" of the time of "image," but a true presence nevertheless. Cardinal Ratzinger summarizes it thus:

> The foundation of the liturgy, its source and support, is the historical Pasch of Jesus— his Cross and Resurrection. This once-for-all event has become the ever-abiding form of the liturgy. In the first stage the eternal is embodied in what is once-for-all. The second stage is the entry of the eternal into our present moment in the liturgical action. And the third is the desire of the eternal to take hold of the worshipper's life and ultimately of all historical reality. The immediate event— the liturgy— makes sense and has a meaning for our lives only because it contains the other two dimensions. Past, present, and future interpenetrate and touch upon eternity.[47]

He seems to be concluding that the Paschal sacrifice has become eternal, and that the eternal enters history through the liturgy: "The second stage is the entry of the eternal into our present moment in the liturgical action"; and liturgy contains the other two dimensions. This brings clarity to our discussion.

---

[46] Joseph Ratzinger, *The Spirit of the Liturgy*, 57.
[47] Ibid., 60.

## 2. *Banquet*

*Eucharist as Marriage and Incorporation to Christ*

It is the Eucharist that assimilates us to Christ. "Communion" comprises the intimate union of the Lover with the beloved. The Eucharist as a perpetuation of Calvary is a work of love, much greater than of creation:

> He remained in order not to leave us alone. When a person loves, he desires the presence of the beloved.
>
> … At the banquet of love in the Cenacle, surrounded by His friends, His brothers, He worked the miracles much greater than creation: He instituted the Eucharist.
>
> He remained in order to be our food: 'For my flesh is meat indeed, and my Blood is drink indeed,' a food extraordinary in its effects. He comes into us in order to transform us into Himself. He willed more than a union, more than a fusion; He willed the unity of love: to be one with us.[48]

Christ's sacrifice now extends to providing a banquet of His body, blood, soul, and divinity. The banquet itself comprises two elements: a nuptial element (Bride) and an incorporation element (Body). First, the nuptial element flows from the marriage logic of the cross. On the cross, from the side of Christ as Second Adam comes forth the second Eve, His Spouse, the Church. As Eve, helper and spouse, was created from the side of sleeping Adam, so at the new creation and the new nuptials that is the sacrifice of Calvary, the Father now creates the new Bride of Christ, the Church, from the side of the sleeping new Adam, Jesus Christ.

Msgr. James O'Connor presents a wonderful section on the Eucharist as marriage. He points to marriage as the image of the bond between Yahweh and the Chosen People in the Old Testament, especially in the *Canticle of Canticles*. Using the Canticle's imagery, he sees this as fulfilled in the coming of Christ, God "marrying" mankind, and now extended to the Eucharistic flesh, to accomplish the marriage between Christ and His Church. Here is a marvelous text:

---

[48] Jean d'Elbée, *I Believe in Love*, 239-240.

... so, too, is it through the Eucharist that the marriage covenant between the Lord and his Bride is established. The Covenant sealed in blood between Israel and God (cf. Ex 24) was a betrothal of lovers, a love that longed for its consummation.... That search is answered when the lover, in his human Flesh, consummates the union, sealing the Covenant 'not by means of the blood of goats and calves, but by His own Blood' (cf. Heb 9:12). "This cup is the new covenant in my Blood" (Lk 22:20). This is the marriage covenant that rests on the reality of the Eucharistic Flesh that we receive. 'Let him kiss me with the kisses of his mouth— for your love is more delightful than wine.... I am my lover's and my lover is mine; he browses among the lilies' (Song 1:2; 6:3). The Eucharist accordingly becomes the prolongation of what the Word promised to Israel and begins in Mary: the process of taking Flesh to himself— Flesh for himself in Mary; Flesh to himself by uniting to his Flesh ours in Eucharistic Communion. The Eucharist is also, in this way, the literal fulfillment of the promise that, when lifted up, he would draw all things to himself (cf. Jn 12:32).[49]

The union accomplished in receiving the Eucharist is an image of the intimacy realized between Christ and His Church, and it is only a sign and reminder of the consummation to take place in heaven. Yet, already the "communion" can be compared to the "marital act" in marriage, but in a transcendent order: "As the love of husband and wife is 'singularly expressed and perfected' by the marital act, 'which signifies and fosters the mutual self-giving by which the spouses enrich each other with a joyful and grateful heart,' so Eucharistic Communion singularly expresses and perfects union with the Lord."[50]

*Eucharist as Incorporation to Christ*

This brings us to the second dimension, as in marriage, where "two become one flesh," so that Jesus and each soul are united through Holy Communion to become "one flesh" (Body of Christ). St. Augustine teaches that the goal of all salvation history is the formation of the *Christus totus*, the "whole Christ," and this is accomplished principally through the Eucharist. There is a human analogy to this process, one that Bishop Fulton Sheen employed. There is a process in nature of destruction of, and an

---

[49] James O'Connor, *The Hidden Manna*, 332-333.
[50] Ibid., 333.

assimilation to, a higher order: the plant destroys the soil as it assimilates its nutrients to itself; the cow masticates the grass as it assimilates the grass into its organism; man consumes the steak and through the Kreb's cycle assimilates or stores some of the fat and carbohydrates of the cow into his body; man now consumes the Eucharist, but it is Christ who assimilates man to Himself, since that which is of the higher order takes unto itself that which is lower. This process of nature, therefore, is analogous and contiguous to the process of divinization or transformation into Christ, which takes place primarily in the Eucharist.

### 3. *Presence*

Let us address the presence in the Eucharist in three steps: the presence of the risen Christ in the Church; the presence in the Eucharist through transubstantiation; and presence as fulfillment of Old Testament figures.

(1) *Christ's Presences in the Church*

There is a temptation to think of Him as far away in heaven, from where He reaches out to help us. Christians have difficulty conceiving of the Lord's presence after His departure at the Ascension. The Second Vatican Council has already taken steps to remind us of His manifold presence, especially in the Church and liturgical celebrations: in her ministers, Mass and Eucharistic species, sacraments, word, holy Scriptures, and when the Church gathers (*Sacrosanctum concilium* n. 7). Robert Hugh Benson's *The Friendship of Christ* develops this incarnational principle, the many presences of Christ:

> He must be known (if his relation with us is to be that which he desires) in all those activities and manifestations in which he displays himself. One who knows him therefore solely as an interior companion and guide, however dear and adorable, but does not know him in the *Blessed Sacrament*... does not know him *in his vicar, or in his priest, or in his mother*... but who does not recognize the right of the sinner to ask for mercy, or the beggar for alms, in his name... can never rise to that height of intimacy and knowledge of that ideal friend which he himself desires, and has declared to be within our power to attain.[51] (emphasis added)

---

[51] Robert Hugh Benson, *The Friendship of Christ*, 21-22.

The disciple of Christ must recognize His incarnate presence in which "He displays himself" in the world. It is a false or superficial friendship of Christ if it does not love His presences in the Eucharist, His Mystical Body, in His priests and bishops, in the sinner and the beggar. The love of Christ is true if it finds His incarnate presences in the world.

## (ii) *The Eucharist, the Greatest of Christ's Presences in the Church*

Yet no other presence of our Lord within the Church compares to that of the Eucharist, in which there is a sacramental or substantial presence. The disciple of Christ finds himself drawn to the tabernacle, in silence and adoration. Possibly no other contemporary work captures the need for adoration before the Blessed Sacrament as does *In Sinu Jesu*. Mother Louise Margaret Claret de la Touche, propagator of priestly devotion to the Sacred Heart, offers a rich connection: she links the Sacred Heart we know so well to the Eucharist. She affirms that the culmination and the practice of the love of Jesus in His Sacred Heart is expressed in the love of the Eucharist, calling them "sister devotions." She points to at least three steps in connecting the love of the heart of Jesus to the love of the Eucharist. We find the Sacred Heart of Jesus in the Eucharist; which is the apex of the love of the Sacred Heart; and, the love of the Sacred Heart leads to love and adoration of the Eucharist:

> But because we know that we shall find this Sacred Heart only in the Eucharist... we go to the Blessed Eucharist, we prostrate ourselves before the Blessed Sacrament, we adore the divine Host radiating Its influence from the monstrance, we go to the holy table with ardent avidity, we kiss lovingly the consecrated paten where the divine Host reposes each day. We surround with honour, respect and magnificence the Tabernacle where Jesus, living and loving, makes His dwelling. Oh! it is impious to say that the worship of the Sacred Heart can injure Eucharistic worship.[52]

## (iii) *Transubstantiation*

The disciple before this mystery of Christ's sacramental presence ought to have some basic understanding of how bread and wine have become Christ's body, blood, soul, and divinity. The theological term used is "transubstantiation." Transubstantiation comes from the Latin *trans*

---

[52] Mother Louise Margaret Claret de la Touche, *The Sacred Heart and the Priesthood*, 186.

("across"), signifying a change, and *substantia* ("substance"). Therefore a transformation has taken place, a "tran-substantiation" signifies a change of substance (body, blood, soul, and divinity, or more simply, the humanity and divinity of Christ) while the external "accidents" (Aristotelian theory of substance and accidents) remained unchanged. The difference between the other sacraments is that in the Eucharist Christ Himself is truly and substantially present. That host really has been *transubstantiated*, the substance itself has changed while retaining the appearance of bread, and Jesus Himself is present before us.[53]

## 4. Living the Eucharist

A huge lacuna among our Catholic laity is the lack of awareness that the sacrifice of the Mass is also to be lived out in the Mystical Body. While the priest makes present Christ's sacrifice, the people of God, by virtue of their baptismal priesthood ("offering sacrifice"), must unite to Christ's sacrifice the sacrifice of themselves, the new victims. Both St. Augustine and St. Leo the Great taught that in the Mass "we become what we eat."

*Mediator Dei* develops more specifically the victimhood called for: "they must also offer themselves as victims" (103); that the Church needs "victim souls." Johann Auer delineates aspects of the role of the Mystical Body of Christ: sharing with Christ's suffering, sharing His present adoration of the Father, and their own spiritual offering of self.[54] It is worthwhile noting that, in summarizing the developments on the Eucharist since the sixteenth century (finding eight theories), he agrees with the findings of Odo Casel and Anscar Vonier. This applies especially to the ministerial priest. The *Directory on the Ministry and Life of Priests* points to this:

> If the priest lends to Christ, Most Eternal High Priest, his intelligence, will, voice and hands so as to offer, through his very ministry, the

---

[53] "This doctrine, which has no basis in Scripture, first appeared in the early 9th century A.D., was formalized at the Council of Trent (A.D. 1545-63), and was reaffirmed at the Second Vatican Council (1962-65)." Christian Courier, "What are Transubstantiation and Consubstantiation," accessed June 6, 2015, http://www.christiancourier.com/articles/read/what_are_transubstantiation_and_consubstantiation.

[54] Johann Auer, *Dogmatic Theology 6*, 273-282. Fr. Auer has summarized the developments on the Eucharist since the sixteenth century (finding eight theories, and agreeing with the findings of Casel and Vonier).

sacramental sacrifice of redemption to the Father, he should make his own the dispositions of the Master and, like him, live those *gifts* for his brothers in the faith. He must therefore learn to unite himself intimately to the offering, placing his entire life upon the altar of sacrifice as a revealing sign of the gratuitous and anticipatory love of God.[55]

What is perhaps the most exalted form is the "victimhood of love" that St. Thérèse of the Child Jesus lived out. Where saints often speak of a victimhood to make satisfaction against sins committed against God, she lived the victimhood to make up for the love He was not receiving and to give God an outlet to pour out His love. Out of love for Jesus who is not loved, in total abandonment, she allowed Him to do what He wished in her— she had no will of her own; all was for the sake of pleasing Him— her life became a Mass, she the host (von Balthasar's expropriation).

> How are we to make this offering real, and live it practically? The most perfect victims are those who let themselves be immolated by Jesus the High Priest in perfect abandonment, letting Him choose the tests, the crosses, the trials, and also the consolations and joys. It is by all the things He chooses for them that His love burns and consumes the hearts which have given themselves to Him. Let Him be sure of your smile. To be a victim is to smile. Total abandonment— 'O Jesus, I thank You for everything'— that is enough. Jesus will immolate you in His own way. He will be the Priest of the host which you will have willed to be in His hands.[56]

The Eucharist, the sacrament of unity and love, must also build communion of the individual local churches to the Universal Church (*Lumen gentium* n. 26), to be "drawn out of their own isolation by a kind of 'ecclesial circumincession,' a living in and for one another through Eucharistic Communion."[57] James O'Connor draws out some of the implications of this transformation into what we receive. We become "christ" for the world, and are moved to serve Christ in all the poor and suffering:

---

[55] Congregation of the Clergy, *Directory on the Ministry and Life of Priests,* n. 48.
[56] Jean d'Elbée, *I Believe in Love*, 234-235.
[57] Ibid., 341.

Thus, the Eucharist ever remains the force that impels the Church's apostolate for social, political, and economic justice. The bond of solidarity established [through the Eucharist]… must unite all the Church's members to struggle against the structural and institutionalized forms of sin that oppress so many of the world's peoples. A participation in the Eucharist that fails to stimulate a 'social consciousness' is a defective participation.[58]

Let us ever briefly note a key distortion that took place after the Second Vatican Council of reducing the Eucharist to primarily a meal in the secular sense. We find a compelling argument in Cardinal Ratzinger's *Feast of Faith*. He agrees with much of the decisive work of Heinz Schürmann in linking the Last Supper of Jesus with the Church's Eucharist, but disagrees with the second of three steps in his argument ("Eucharist in connection with the apostolic community meal").[59]

*Synthesis*

The child of the Father through Baptism in the Holy Spirit, "mothered" by two Mothers, the Church and Mary, building a strong human foundation and being led by the Holy Spirit, finds in the Eucharist the greatest source of transformation or configuration into Christ, to become ever more deeply the new Christ. The Eucharist, the representation of the sacrifice of Calvary, transforms the new Christ more and more to become the crucified apostle for the world. The Mass is like our spiritual Sun, or as Padre Pio taught,

Every Holy Mass, heard with devotion, produces in our souls marvelous effects, abundant spiritual and material graces which we, ourselves, do not know. It is easier for the earth to exist without the sun than without the Holy Sacrifice of the Mass![60]

---

[58] James O'Connor, *The Hidden Manna*, 339.
[59] Joseph Ratzinger, *Feast of Faith: Approaches to a Theology of the Liturgy*, 43.
[60] Gerardo Di Flumeri, *The Mystery of the Cross in Padre Pio of Pietrelcina* (National Centre for Padre Pio, Barto, PA), 16.

# PART III:

# NEW CHRIST

# *FORMED BY THE HOLY SPIRIT*

"He has done all things well"

# CHAPTER 9

## *HUMAN VIRTUES*

*("Grace builds on nature")*

Little things are indeed little, but to be faithful in little things is a great thing. (Mother Teresa of Calcutta)

### *1. Human Virtues of Nazareth*

The template for preparation for Jesus' mission is the thirty years of formation in Nazareth. Following Christ, to use a metaphor, Christians as children of the Father are to be formed not in "Jerusalem" (e.g., Paul), but in "Nazareth" (e.g., Holy Family). Nazareth in this chapter corresponds to the "Jesus' Human Life" (Chapter 5), and specifically to the human virtues. We recall that Chapter 5 took up St. Thomas' maxim, "Grace builds upon nature," of two levels in man: the natural level of man's humanity and the supernatural level of grace, with the human "foundation" supporting the "building" of grace or holiness. Thus, if we are not humanly sound, it compromises the whole structure and we cannot attain holiness. This can be synthesized by another principle: the more human and incarnate we become, the holier we become: "It is impossible to believe in the holiness of people who lack the most basic human virtues."[1] This is confirmed by Jesus' own foundation, for Scripture tells us that "He has done all things well" (Mk 7:37). Among the recommended works on human virtues are Bishop Camus' *The Spirit of St. Francis de Sales* and Jesús Urteaga's *Saints in the World* and *The Defects of the Saints*. It should be noted that the Nazareth charism is central to the spirituality of Madonna House (Combermere, Ontario).

---

[1] Federico Suarez, *About Being a Priest*, 88-89. Chapter 3, "Training" (pp. 83-124), and to some extent, Chapter 4, "Sources of Strength" (pp. 125-169), can form a solid background for the theme of this chapter.

## A. A Conscious Decision to Follow the Path of Nazareth

We wish to present two basic paths or lifestyles for the child of God, represented by Jerusalem and Nazareth. There is a great temptation today in the busyness of the world of instant communication and trans-continental air travel to choose the path represented by the thriving metropolis of Jerusalem. In the big fast-moving city, there is a greater temptation for people to find their self-worth in how much they earn or accomplish, how many conferences they attend, how well-informed they are of world events or how many facts they have at their fingertips, and how many acts of philanthropy they are doing. It is focused more on talents and action: charismatic personality, speaking skill, culture, learnedness, sociability, astuteness, and friendships with important people. It is a foundation that is rather superficial, more focused on doing than on being— it represents here the path of "Jerusalem."

The child of God, growing towards becoming a new Christ, can be tempted to follow this path of "Jerusalem." They can feel inadequate if they can't go to Calcutta and serve the poorest of the poor, visit prisons to console those on death-row, assist those in hospices to die, or evangelize the 1.4 billion Chinese, the majority of whom are not Christians. The author was startled by the zeal of a French seminarian in the diocese of Paray-le-Monial (France), who expressed his desire to go to China and take hold of a "hose" to baptize throngs of Chinese people. This temptation to feel inadequate if one's ministry is "ordinary" comes naturally, as from the Early Church, martyrdom was considered a glorious end and the highest spirituality. In our time, some have done heroic things, like Cardinal van Thuan's imprisonment under the Communist regime in Vietnam, Fr. Walter Ciszek in the Russian prison camps in Siberia (*With God in Russia*), or John Cardinal O'Connor, with his wonderful experiences of military chaplaincy, being Cardinal Archbishop of New York and Founder of the Sisters of Life. These are exceptional people, given the privilege of doing great things for God, yet their paths do not represent the primary path of holiness.

## B. The Immense Power of the Hidden Path of Nazareth

Within the Carmelite tradition, St. Teresa of Jesus represents the privileged and exceptional path, with visions, ecstasies, and wounds of love. But there is a higher path, that of the Holy Family at Nazareth, that emphasizes silence, prayer, immolation, and it is also the Gospel (evangelical) path preached by Jesus in many ways. It was one that was lived out by the "little Theresa," St. Thérèse of the Child Jesus, who did not have the mystical experiences of her spiritual mother, St. Teresa. A book referred to earlier, Fr. Jean d'Elbée's *I Believe in Love*, unfolds the hidden path of Nazareth.

> Little Thérèse rediscovered this road of Nazareth. She approached this simplicity, but without equalling it— far from it....
>
> In our time Jesus also wants hidden saints like the "woman of Nazareth" [Mary], who distinguish themselves in nothing exteriorly, but burn interiorly. Never, moreover, have there been more saints of this kind than in our day.[2]

It is hard to discern in living in the world the power of the hidden, unknown life as exemplified by St. Thérèse. Yet it possessed such power, as expressed by her great desire to evangelize everyone from the beginning of time to the end of time from within the Carmel of Lisieux. "A single mission would not be enough for me. I would like at the same time to announce the gospel on the five continents and unto the most remote islands. I would like to be a missionary, not only for a few years, but I would like to have been one from the creation of the world until the end of time."[3] It seems that God answered her prayers: she is now co-patron of Missions, and she herself revealed the power she had hidden in Carmel: "The Creator of the Universe listens to the prayer of a very little soul to save others who are ransomed, as she is, by the price of all His Blood."[4]

## C. "Let us love our littleness"

The importance of hiddenness and silence cannot be over-emphasized. St. Thérèse keeps her distance from all that "glitters": "Let us remain very remote from all that glitters. Let us love our littleness; let us love to feel nothing. Then we shall be poor in spirit, and Jesus will come seeking us, however far away we are. He will transform us into flames of love."[5] Her language bursts in exuberance at the power of God within the *hidden soul*.

---

[2] Jean d'Elbée, *I Believe in Love*, 259.
[3] St. Thérèse of Lisieux, *Manuscrits autobiographiques*, 227, quoted in Jean d'Elbée, *I Believe in Love*, 189.
[4] St. Thérèse of Lisieux, *Letter of August 15, 1892*, quoted in Jean d'Elbée, *I Believe in Love*, 176.
[5] Jean d'Elbée, *I Believe in Love*, 126.

Led by the same Spirit, St. Josemaría Escrivá expresses similar sentiments: "You long to shine like a star, to shed your light from high in the heavens? Better to burn like a hidden torch, setting your fire to all that you touch. That's your apostolate: that's why you are on earth."[6] Elsewhere, he expresses the same desire, not to shine like a star in the firmament, but, like a "hidden torch," to set hearts afire. This is simply the hidden path of silence and immolation of Nazareth.

Fr. Jean d'Elbée lists a number of people who walked this hidden path of Nazareth: Jesus, whom the people of his hometown knew only as the carpenter, did not stand out in any way ("Isn't this the carpenter's son?"); Mary, who was likely kept on earth after Jesus' death in order to continue the silent immolation to establish the Church and give fruit to the apostles' preaching; the desert fathers watered the early Church with its sacrifices and prayers: "The desert fathers reproduced this immolation and the silence of Nazareth and thus revivified the newly born Church"[7]; St. Charles de Foucauld, who did not preach but lived a hidden path saintly example; the Little Sisters of the Poor at Rennes, when they sought miracles, bypassed the beautiful monument of the second superior general to visit the nondescript grave of St. Jeanne Jugan, the foundress expelled as superior general; St. Thérèse of Lisieux, in whom many of her religious sisters found nothing extraordinary; St. Margaret Mary Alacoque, who "immolated herself in the seclusion of the cloister, consumed with love"; St. Teresa of Jesus, who concerning her hidden cloistered sisters, cried, "What shall I do with them? Ah, I shall employ them to destroy heresy, to bring forth Doctors of the Church, to make reparation for sin, to convert souls."[8]

Fr. Jean d'Elbée makes a rather startling conclusion: God is allowing the world to run to its destruction *because he has prepared many hidden souls (Nazareth) who will become channels of His grace for the world*: "He needs truly loving souls, true hosts, truly transformed into Him by love. He needs such souls in order to save men.... Evil displays itself; good remains unknown.... These hidden souls console Him; they make reparation; they repay Him and oblige [compel] Him, I dare to say, to be merciful."[9] St.

---

[6] St. Josemaría Escrivá, *The Way* (Manila: Sinag-Tala Publishers, 1991), n. 835.
[7] Jean d'Elbée, *I Believe in Love*, 169.
[8] Ibid., 167-173.
[9] Ibid., 178-179.

Thérèse captures her path by expressing her preference for the "monotony of sacrifice" to "ecstasy."[10]

## D. The Path of the Holy Family

We are presented with two divergent paths before us; and at the very beginning of the path to follow Christ, there should be a conscious and deliberate decision to follow the road Jesus took, that of Nazareth. If Jesus, the God-man, is our model in His humanity, given that He has spent thirty of His thirty-three earthly years at Nazareth, then Nazareth must hold an important role in the lives of His disciples as well. The three greatest "saints" of the Church have all been formed in Nazareth: Jesus (as man), Mary, and Joseph. Even before Jesus fulfilled His Father's mission through His ministry and death, His thirty years in preparation were already pleasing to the Father; and it is Nazareth that prepared Him for the fulfillment of the mission entrusted by the Father.

We turn to two references by Pope Paul VI in which he presents Nazareth as a model. The first is his reference to the virtues of St. Joseph in the *Office of Readings* for his feast day. Nazareth is all about hidden fidelity, silence, littleness, simplicity, hard work. Second, in an address employed precisely in the Church's Office of Readings on the feast of the Holy Family, he reveals to us something of its great value: silence, prayer, family life, work, and the little human virtues:

> Nazareth is a kind of school where we may begin to discover what Christ's life was like and even to understand his Gospel. Here we can observe and ponder the simple appeal of the way God's Son came to be known, profound yet full of hidden meaning. And gradually we may even learn to imitate him.

> Here we can learn to realise who Christ really is. And here we can sense and take account of the conditions and circumstances that surrounded and affected his life on earth: the places, the tenor of the times, the culture, the language, religious customs, in brief, everything which Jesus used to make himself known to the world. Here everything speaks to us, everything has meaning. Here we can learn the importance of spiritual

---

[10] Quoted words are by St. Thérèse of Lisieux, Letter to Sister Agnes of Jesus: May 10, 1890, in *Letters of St. Thérèse of Lisieux*, vol. 1 (Washington, DC: ICS Publications, 1982), Letter 106, 620, quoted in Sr. Madeleine, *Within the Castle with St. Teresa*, 151.

discipline for all who wish to follow Christ and to live by the teachings of his Gospel.[11]

Thus, we see the contrast between the paths of Jerusalem and Nazareth. Jerusalem is about activism, running here and there, relying on one's great gifts, eloquence, having worldly judgment, making plans, and anticipating what plans God might have for me; Jerusalem is about flash, noise, rushing about, and self-exaltation. The little one who builds upon the model or school of Nazareth is quietly faithful, and waits on God to provide and to show him the next step; he does not lead. Nazareth is about recollection, meekness, fidelity, focus on God rather than on one's talents, agenda, or action. This suggests that all of Christ's disciples must seek to be formed in Nazareth and not in Jerusalem. God may grant glorious deeds to a few, but they represent the exception.

## E. Von Balthasar's Insights

Henri de Lubac believes that von Balthasar's spiritual diagnosis of the world is the most penetrating to be found, identifying a contemporary pathology. Von Balthasar sees much that is positive at work in the world, but in commenting upon the atheistic humanism of our contemporary world scene, suggests that we are living through a kind of "collective dark night," in a "male functionalist world," with endless activity, meetings, and talking.

> Among the features is a predominance of a 'masculine' rationalism of the *homo faber*, which has shaped a culture that sees natural things as material for manufacture. Even the human spirit is in danger of becoming material for mere self-manipulation through the various sciences. There is a loss of the wonder of being, and once devoid of philosophy and of ethics, we risk becoming victims of a pure positivism of 'making' and 'having'... Run aground, as [Karl] Barth writes, on the sandbanks of a technological rationalism, many serious questions face us about the direction we want to take in the future. Precisely because the Church's foundation is in the mystery of God's plan, the Church's consciousness and mission is closely bound with humankind's consciousness and need to rediscover mystery.[12]

---

[11] Pope Paul VI, Address, OOR on the Feast of the Holy Family, *Liturgy of the Hours*, vol. I (New York: Catholic Book Publ., 1975), 426-427.
[12] Brendan Leahy, *The Marian Profile in the Ecclesiology of Hans Urs von Balthasar*, 194 (& 165); see also 163-166, 178, 189.

This "male functionalist world" sets human effort and activity before God's action and has bypassed mystery.

*Hidden Preparation in the "Desert," the Bosom of God*

Even more profoundly, we see the path by which God typically forms great instruments in the silence and hiddenness. This sets a stark contrast between the approaches of Nazareth and Jerusalem. It is a secret preparation that also becomes a lifestyle. This path follows the pattern mentioned by von Balthasar in an earlier chapter, that there is a double moment in mysticism: the solitude of being "thrust" into the very bosom of God, before being directed back toward the community.[13] This truth is anticipated and illustrated in the lives of many Old Testament figures: Abraham being sent out into the desert; Moses prepared in the desert in his years before returning to Egypt, and also for forty days on the mountain (twice); David and his time caring for sheep, his years before becoming King in Jerusalem, and his time of fleeing from Absalom. John the Baptist is probably the one who epitomizes this pattern best, as he spent his years of preparation in the desert before preaching the imminent arrival of the Messiah.

We find this pattern continued in the New Testament. The apostles were mainly humble fishermen of Galilee and had three years of private preparation and training with Jesus. Paul at first appears to be an exception to the rule since he had been trained in Jerusalem under Gamaliel, but after his conversion, he too went into the desert of Syria for some time to prepare for his ministry. Many saints have been prepared in this way, such as St. Catherine of Siena during her hidden early years of preparation by Jesus Himself, many with apparent failures in a path of simplicity and hiddenness (versus "success" of Jerusalem), such as Saint André Bessette of Montreal, who was rejected in his first attempts to enter religious life, partly because of poor health.

### F. St. Francis de Sales' "Little Virtues"

For those of us caught up in the path of Jerusalem, reading a book like Bishop Jean Pierre Camus' *The Spirit of St. Francis de Sales* can be a revelation.

---

[13] Ibid., 174.

We happen to know much about St. Francis de Sales' virtues and personal habits through his friend, Bishop Jean Pierre Camus, who admired him so much he would watch him closely so as to mirror his virtues. And he has shared with us the basic portrait of St. Francis in his work, *The Spirit of St. Francis de Sales*, under the subsection: "Little Virtues." He noted that a unique quality of St. Francis de Sales was a preference for the "little virtues." St. Francis de Sales observed that Christians often desire the big virtues, like extreme fasting and great acts of heroism, which are the virtues shining at the top of Calvary, but overlook the greater path to everyday sanctity which are virtues at the foot of the tree of Calvary, watered by the blood of Christ— the "little virtues." The path of the big virtues can engender pride, as described by Fr. Urteaga: "Unfortunately, what do people want and look for? Novelty. The unusual. The spectacular. The sensational.... They may dazzle the heart for a while, and after everything is said and done, the soul is left empty and sad."[14] St. Francis de Sales espoused a path of true spiritual growth through the little, everyday virtues, the path of Nazareth, such as humility, meekness, gentleness, cheerfulness, and amiability.

## 2. *Virtues of Nazareth*

What does the lifestyle of Nazareth mean concretely in daily life? We will draw partly from St. Josemaría Escrivá's charism that has much to say in this area. It is worthwhile to note some overlap of our list on human virtues with his list of fundamental "key ideas" of which the following are most important: holiness coming from God alone, divine filiation, fidelity to little things, unity of life, and sanctification of work.

> ... the source of all holiness is God (and therefore we cannot attain sanctity by 'force of arms'); the reality of our divine filiation, which imbues a Christian's being and acting; the compatibility of great ideals with the struggle in the little things of each day; unity of life, the consequence of knowing we are God's children; sanctification of work, the 'hinge' for holiness in the midst of the world.[15]

---

[14] Jesús Urteaga, *Defects of the Saints* (Manila: Sinag-Tala Publishers, 1997), 252.
[15] Francis Fernández-Carvajal, *Through Wind and Waves*, 71-72.

## A. Christ Sanctified the Human

St. Josemaría Escrivá's spirituality is one that sees the glory of the human, of God in the world, of God in our midst. In a famous homily he gave at Navarre University in Spain, at a Mass that was celebrated outdoors on campus, he deviated from his prepared written homily at one point to speak from his heart. In the horizon were famous mountains, where it seemed that the sky met the earth. He said something to the effect that he could see where the earth meets the "*cielo*" (which translates as both "sky" and "heaven"), that is, where earth meets heaven (sky):

> I assure you, my sons and daughters, that when a Christian carries out with love the most insignificant everyday action, that action overflows with the transcendence of God. That is why I have told you repeatedly, and hammered away once and again on the idea that the Christian vocation consists of making heroic verse out of the prose of each day. *Heaven and earth seem to merge, my sons and daughters, on the horizon. But where they really meet is in your hearts, when you sanctify your everyday lives.*[16] (emphasis added)

He added that each part of the earth represents part of the Church, where God dwells: "We might say that the nave is the university campus; the altarpiece, the university library. Over there, the machinery for constructing new buildings; above us, the sky of Navarre...."[17] God, therefore, is not somewhere "up there" in heaven; He is present in the world and in our work, and, above all, in our hearts.

From St. Josemaría Escrivá's vision, Fr. Jesús Urteaga draws out the importance of Christ's human nature for our understanding of our humanity. The world has been changed for us because, in Christ, God has become man and lived through all our experiences. We have to see that "Everything divine which Jesus has, he realizes and manifests precisely through and by means of what he has that is human."[18] Because Jesus knew poverty at Bethlehem, it has become sacred. He knew fatigue and exhaustion, falling asleep in the boat; we too should be happy when we are

---

[16] "Homily given by Saint Josemaría Escrivá at the University of Navarre on October 8, 1967," Opus Dei, March 2, 2006, http://www.opusdei.org/en-us/article/passionately-loving-the-world-2/

[17] Ibid.

[18] Jesús Urteaga, *Saints in the World*, 111.

tired and feel the blessedness of our work. He knew physical hunger and thirst, the deepest friendship and sorrow, as with the death of Lazarus, as well as being deserted, as with the apostles. He cured illness through His hands, as He continues to do today. He spoke with the background of human life, such as farmers, children's games. He spoke with a local Galilean accent. Fr. Urteaga captures this incarnational unity well:

> Christ knew pain, and pain was made divine…. Everything human in him was virtue. In *everything* human, he is our model.
>
> What would have happened if God had not become one of us? We would never have known what to do with our human nature…. We could never have known how to behave in any of our adventures… (the adventure of pain, the adventure of fatigue, the adventure of death)…. Christ, so profoundly human, is for each and every one of us the model of human life. We must have no fear of being too human. Soul, body, feelings— all are, and *should* be, human.[19]

There is a logic that flows from the truth above: if God unites Himself to all that is human (as He now does with the sacraments— descending element), we too have to unite the human to the divine (ascending element):

> Give us, Lord, the grace to supernaturalize all those human virtues which you put in our souls when you first gave us life. We too want to unite what you united: human tasks with a divine outlook, the lowest things on earth with heaven itself, worldly things with heavenly things, life with religion.[20]

## B. Fidelity to Little Things

The Gospel principle that governs this area can be found in Jesus' words, "He who is faithful in a very little is faithful also in much; and he who is dishonest in a very little is dishonest also in much" (Luke 16:10). Since the Gospels also teach that Jesus first did and then taught ("began to do and taught," Acts 1:1), it appears that He first lived this great rule of the little things, that this was Jesus' own program or spirituality. As a result, this general rule cannot be broken without suffering tremendous consequences. We find this within the Church and also in priestly and religious life.

---

[19] Ibid., 113.
[20] Ibid.

Within the Church, for example, a priest asked by the apostolic nuncio to fill out a confidential questionnaire about a nominated candidate for the episcopacy, might experience a strong tendency to give the greatest weight to big, prominent talents, like "charisma," intelligence, being well-informed, sociability, good judgment, "balance," organization, good voice, and a charming crowd-pleaser. These acquired human talents are to be valued.

But there are two areas of greater importance: infused (divine) and acquired (human) virtues. First and clearly, higher still are the divine or infused virtues: e.g., the infused moral virtues, especially prudence and fortitude, as well as the gifts of the Holy Spirit, especially infused wisdom, counsel, and understanding. Second, rather than look for the very prominent human talents when judging a candidate, the little virtues are more hidden but quite revealing of one's character: unfailing fidelity to prayer, not seeking approval or human respect, courage and integrity to do the right thing regardless of what the media might print, not desiring promotions (Pope Francis speaks of this), love of and obedience to the Church's authority, and seeking the guidance of the Holy Spirit. In concrete situations, one can look to see if the episcopal candidate greets or acknowledges "unimportant" people, whether he listens and is not always speaking at table about himself and spouting from his font of knowledge, whether he is there at prayer in the chapel when no one is looking— all these might be better indicators of his character.

Thus, besides the infused virtues, we should dwell upon the "acquired virtues" (good habits), a topic rarely discussed in our time. We may be tempted to rely on infused virtues from the sacraments and neglect cultivating human virtues, the constant repetition of acting with good habits and against bad habits. Fr. Urteaga offers a vigorous "wake-up" call in his *Saints in the World: The Adventure of Christian Life* (of interest is the original title, "*El valor divino del humano*," "*The divine value of the human*"). He cites Dom Marmion's emphasis on the need to act against the bad inclinations and habits within us through the repetition of acts, that is, through the acquired moral virtues.[21]

---

[21] Columba Marmion, *Christ the Life of the Soul*, trans. "a Nun of Tyburn Convent" (St. Louis: B. Herder, 1925), 206, quoted in Fr. Jesús Urteaga, *Saints in the World: The Adventure of Christian Life* (Princeton, NJ: Scepter, 1997), 48.

The words of Fr. Josef Sellmair are helpful: "It is inconceivable that the…
supernatural virtues should be lively and real if the natural virtues remain
unpractised."[22] This means that the continued reception of infused virtues
from Confession and Mass are of little avail to us if the natural or acquired
virtues are not practiced. Fr. Urteaga compares the human virtues to "walls
flanking a great canal—they are the watertight bulwarks which prevent the
sides from falling in under the pressure from all around."[23] He uses
stronger language, "desertion" (like that of Judas and Demas), when we fall
off from fidelity when things get difficult: "At the first difficulty are you
going to throw down the cross which you were carrying for him who called
you? Do you not hear the voice of Christ, the sigh of God, whispering in
our ear: 'Friend, why are you here?' (Mt 26:50)."[24]

Putting the focus on strengthening the little things is not being pedantic—
such a mentality may betray immaturity, and a lack of common sense.
Looking to the little things as a way of securing a strong "foundation" for
the divine "edifice" is akin to taking pains to avoid contractors who do
shoddy work or use cheap materials (e.g., contractors in China were blamed
for the disastrous collapse of buildings following earthquakes), or taking
pains to get rid of termites so that they do not eventually undermine the
entire building. The entire spiritual life can fall and rise upon this one
principle: "He who is faithful in a very little is faithful also in much." But
these virtues are nothing other than the everyday virtues practiced by our
parents and people working in society who, day in and day out, live their
lives with great fidelity, integrity, and diligence.

If these acquired virtues are not cultivated, then problems arise. Within
priestly life, if a priest has some family of origin issue and seeks to grow in
the spiritual life, he is wise if he seeks the help of both a spiritual director
and a psychologist. With the help of a psychologist, he should be able to
return to a manageable and faithful life of ministry; the family of origin
issue should not pose problems if it is addressed. But if there are shortcuts
or compromises in human virtues, like a lack of planning, order, and
discipline, with the result that he is late for meetings, fails to return phone

---

[22] Josef Sellmair, *The Priest in the World*, trans. Brian Battershaw (Westminster, MD: the
Newman Press, 1954), 20, in Ibid.
[23] Ibid.
[24] Ibid., 84.

calls and e-mails, and gets behind in his work, including his paperwork, he might experience great stress, which only compounds the issue that he's experiencing. Such problems suggest that the priest has been too self-indulgent in some ways, not saying "no" to himself. A priest with these problems can make substantial progress over time if he sets himself in the right direction through docility in spiritual direction. But if such self-indulgence extends to lack of self-knowledge, lack of acceptance of correction, of not putting things into practice; if his preference is for much talking and expressing of opinions over lived practice, then all the spiritual direction or psychological sessions will not prevent him from running deeper and deeper into problems.

## C. Simplicity of Nazareth

Another important dimension is keeping our eyes on the "big picture" and on God's will, in a word, simplicity. As mentioned earlier, the spiritual life, with all its trials, should not be onerous, but "effortless." The great propensity in life is to be focused on the immediate world of sense (news of disasters), and become obsessed about these peripheral or secondary issues, not allowing ourselves to rise above them. This was precisely Martha's problem that Jesus sought to correct, "you are anxious and troubled about many things; one thing is needful. Mary has chosen the good portion…" The *Complete Jewish Bible* translates this as "But there is only one thing that is essential," which is congruent with the Tradition's understanding, *unum necessarium*. The "one thing that is needful" or essential is an expression of the principle of simplicity (being one, as opposed to being multiple)— and it is God's will. Thus, there is a paradox in life: on the one hand, we have to sanctify the little things ("If you are faithful in the little things"); on the other hand and more importantly, it is necessary to rise above the little things to keep our eyes on the big picture.

An event in St. Catherine of Siena's life illustrates this point. St. Catherine was inspired by God to encourage Pope Gregory XI to bring the papacy back from Avignon to Rome. The Pope had a good heart and the desire to return to Rome but was rather weak in character, afraid of the obstacles that such a move would provoke. He was troubled by a number fears, among them the opposition from the French Cardinals and the French king and fear of the reception he would receive in Rome. When things looked bleak, in a bold letter to the pope, St. Catherine strongly corrected him and urged him to be strong, and to brush aside opposition, like Christ did, with words such as "Get thee behind me, Satan."[25] When the fleet was diverted by a storm to Genoa, he sought her out there in his continued state of anxiety, and again her replies allayed his fears and strengthened him. In his amazement of her wisdom, light dawned on him and he exclaimed: "That is the source of your strength. You look at everything *sub specie aeternitatis*,"[26] through the lens or horizon of eternity.

Her big secret was the "big picture," an eschatological vision. It is infused wisdom, seen in St. Catherine of Siena, which makes us friends of God, that allows us to see with God's own eyes, as it were, *sub specie aeternitatis*. The child of God can be overwhelmed by the crises that arise, and instinctively take the path of least resistance like Pope Gregory XI. He may be tempted to lean primarily on human or acquired wisdom, to put as first priority prudence, common sense, and avoiding media attacks or legal suits, ahead of divine wisdom, the greatest of the seven gifts of the Holy Spirit. Like Pope Gregory XI, there may be times when a pastor or bishop especially may have to go beyond human prudence, and draw a line in the sand— Pope Benedict XVI has reiterated this point several times.

> Therefore the courage to contradict the prevailing mindset is particularly urgent for a Bishop today. He must be courageous.... The courage to stand firm in the truth is unavoidably demanded of those whom the Lord sends like sheep among wolves. "Those who fear the Lord will not be timid", says the Book of Sirach (34:16). The fear of God frees us from the fear of men. It liberates.[27]

Perhaps the greatest difficulty in not relying on divine wisdom is because, when overwhelmed by troubles, like Pope Gregory XI, we focus on the crisis, and the host of obstacles that come with it and allow ourselves to be pulled in many directions. Imitating St. Catherine of Siena, we must see instead that, among those many issues, there is one thing that towers above

---

[25] Louis de Wohl, *Lay Siege to Heaven: A Novel about St. Catherine of Siena* (San Francisco: Ignatius Press, 1960), 296; cf. 272-273, 282-283, 287-288.

[26] Louis de Wohl, *Lay Siege to Heaven*, 313.

[27] Pope Benedict XVI, "Bishops as modern magi: from Pope Benedict's Homily for Epiphany," *Patheos*, accessed June 25, 2015,
http://www.patheos.com/blogs/deaconsbench/2013/01/bishops-as-modern-magi-from-pope-benedicts-homily-for-epiphany/

the others, like a mountain towers over foothills— the will of God. If we focus just on the "one thing that is needful" (Martha), then all of the other peripheral issues will fall into place; it is very important to know this truth. And instead of being troubled by many issues, the matter becomes simple, and we are serenely guided by God's hand, calmly and without fuss.

A concrete episode at a seminary illustrates this point. A newly ordained transitional deacon was troubled and taken aback by a sudden rash of requests by several pastors who seemed intent on getting help for preaching at their parishes. The deacon was torn, experiencing resentment by the sense of "being used" by priests whom he regarded as friends, and yet also experiencing feelings of guilt by the prospect of having to say no. With the help of his spiritual director, he was calmly able to discern that: first, the dominant criterion is to seek God's will; second, God's will involves a primary focus on the seminary and not on the parish; third, that God's will for him in his partially busy situation did allow for three or four visits to the parish; and, finally, that, since this was God's will, he could calmly give his regrets to the pastors he could not accommodate without any qualm of conscience. The deacon recovered his peace once he established again the priority of God's will and the big picture.

Besides the inability to focus on "one thing that is necessary," a second common difficulty is to allow circumstances to overwhelm us and react with negative emotions, like worry or anger. Stephen Covey speaks of this in his book, *The 7 Habits of Highly Effective People*. His first habit, "Be Proactive," teaches us that we must not allow the troubles of life to dictate our life so that we end up "reacting" to life's situations. Instead, having the big goals or priorities before us, we can choose to "respond" according to our major goals and life principles. This was a lesson learned by Dr. Viktor Frankl, the famous psychiatrist, who had experienced the depravities of a German concentration camp.

There, he came upon a revelation. The prisoners were all treated inhumanely: some ended up falling apart, while others grew in strength from the same treatment. He came to realize then that no one could take away our dignity or freedom if we chose not to allow it, and external circumstances need not dictate our interior state or external response. Such insights gained from his experience there became the basis for his future work in psychiatry. Thus we make a critical distinction between the troubles we face and our capacity to choose to respond with calm and confidence in God.

## D. The Balance of Nazareth

That the spiritual life should be "effortless" flows from another quality— *balance*— which is an expression of simplicity. Many years ago, a survey was taken of successful CEOs (chief executive officers) of the largest companies in the United States, revealing surprising results. For such achievement-oriented people, who one might expect to be obsessed with their work, the survey results showed that most successful CEOs in fact often have a balanced life, giving sufficient time to family, recreation, and other needs. The human facts alone, such as this survey of successful CEOs, suggest that this is not the "successful" path to take. Lacking balance is like preparing for an exam without having covered one third of the material, while spending an inordinate amount of time on the other two thirds of the material. What often happens, as experience quickly teaches, is that one of the exam questions will come from the missing one third of the material, with the consequence that no matter how well the student does in the other two thirds of the material, he gets a portion of only 66.7%. Such a myopic strategy makes no sense; it lacks balance and the bigger picture.

*Note for Priests*

This temptation also plagues priests. Because of the shortage of priests in our time, there is an almost overwhelming temptation to throw ourselves into our ministry, while neglecting some aspects of our lives, perhaps unconsciously thinking that this is a necessary price for succeeding in ministry. A caring and dedicated newly installed pastor can give himself entirely to his people and their needs in an imbalanced way. He can fail to have regular meals, eat a healthy diet, get proper exercise, find time for priestly fraternity, and perhaps most of all, be very negligent in his prayer life, perhaps leaving prayer till last if he has time left over, even to the point of not praying the Divine Office. This might be admirable in diligence but not commendable in prudence. He would quickly experience a lack of peace, and sooner or later, everything would begin to fall apart around him. He may begin to question his priestly identity and the value of his priestly work, and may even leave the priesthood. As St. Charles Borromeo says, the priest should first look after the parish of his own soul (OOR for November 4).

The Church herself recognizes the need for comprehensive balance in priestly formation. For example, *Pastores dabo vobis*, the principal document of reference for formation of priests, speaks of four areas for priestly formation: human, spiritual, intellectual, and pastoral. There is need in human and priestly life for harmony of, and completeness in, all four areas. If there is not integration, that is, a lack of "unity of life," then difficulties will likely arise. It is the experience of counsellors and spiritual directors that many problems arise from neglect of one or more dimensions of human life, such as stress from a lack of recreation and interior difficulties from a lack of priestly friendships and fraternity. Above all, to give oneself totally to one's ministry and not find time for prayer and growth through spiritual and theological reading would lead to incompleteness, lack of fulfillment, and above all, a failure to sanctify our work.

## E. Silence of Nazareth

Yet the virtues of Nazareth point to another difficulty, a lack of *silence*, which has to do with the loss of contemplation. This is an aspect of our human life that has been hugely neglected and overlooked in an age of instant communication and hand-held devices, like iPhones and Blackberries, with its constant barrage of texting, tweeting (Twitter), live chatting, Facebooking, along with internet, music, photos, and movies on demand. In the lives of many saints, this insight on the treasure of inner silence and solitude appears over and over again. What is overlooked is that we are made first of all for communion with God, who dwells in the inner sanctuary of the baptized.

One Augustinian scholar remarked in a lecture that St. Augustine, given his great discovery of the importance of interiority, would have groaned at the lack of silence and contemplation today due to the omni-present handheld devices. One often finds in parishes, for example, at Mass or at Holy Hours, that there is no time for silence, and that the priest seems to think that he has to fill every moment of the Mass or Holy Hour with music or words. We now even have pre-recorded music played during the day in churches, as if silence is incompatible with adoration of our Lord before the Blessed Sacrament. Without silence and inner solitude, we cannot hear the

Holy Spirit and have communion with Him. The new Christs must learn to be thrust into the silence of the bosom of God in order to be able to have intimacy with Him (von Balthasar) and thus be able to give "God" to others. The greatest model we have is Mary, the "eschatological icon," and Mary above all teaches us the supreme need for silence, not only exterior, but also within our hearts.

## F. Listening of Nazareth

Connected to this inner silence of Nazareth is the *capacity to listen to others*. Pope John Paul II had this gift. It has been said many times that, when you meet John Paul II in person, he makes you feel as if you were the only person in the room. This gift appears in the saints and is perhaps a predisposition for sanctity. We see this in the truth that the greatest charity we can give someone is *understanding*, and this requires listening. In the forum of spiritual direction, for example, the greatest need is listening to the directee, and with our hearts as well. This capacity for listening is especially critical for the priest.

It is the conviction of Vito Giordano, an American expert who gives communication skills workshops to Fortune 500 companies, from many years of experience, that people simply do not know how to listen. When we are in conversation with another person, without realizing it, we are often thinking ahead and seeking to impose solutions. Using role playing between pairs of participants, he demonstrates how to allow the interlocutor to "empty his bucket" (pour out his concerns and troubles), and how to maintain the interior goal of "seeking to demonstrate understanding" (that the interlocutor knows he is being heard with concern). Such an approach will enable us to "peel the onion," to get to the bottom of the person's concern. He suggests that we can use the strategy of "reflecting back" the person's words, for example, by paraphrasing it, "I think you are saying this." This has the great benefit that the person feels that he is understood, and as a consequence, is now willing to listen to the speaker. It is Giordano's conviction that many of the issues and tensions in the world have to do with problems of communication.[28]

---

[28] Vito Giordano recommends Robert Bolton's book, *People Skills: How to Assert Yourself, Listen to Others, and Resolve Conflicts* (New York: Simon & Schuster Inc., 1979).

## G. Work of Nazareth: Path to Sanctification

We cannot overlook the immense importance of work in the human foundation. Since the Second Vatican Council, there has been much attention given to the theology of work, and recent Church documents have also treated the subject. Perhaps the greatest contributor to its theology and spirituality in the twentieth century is the founder of the Opus Dei, St. Josemaría Escrivá. He is said to have anticipated the Second Vatican Council in the area of sanctifying our daily work in the midst of the world, in whatever occupation we hold or wherever we are. To many, it may be a foreign concept to think of the path to holiness as going through our work, through sanctifying our daily work. In an interview with the Spanish magazine *Palabra* in 1967, St. Josemaría Escrivá succinctly explained what "sanctifying work" meant:

> The expression 'sanctifying work' involves fundamental concepts of the theology of Creation. What I have always taught over the last forty years, is that a Christian should do all honest human work, be it intellectual or manual, with the greatest perfection possible: with human perfection (professional competence) and with Christian perfection (for love of God's Will and as a service to mankind). Human work done in this manner, no matter how humble or insignificant it may seem, helps to shape the world in a Christian way. The world's divine dimension is made more visible and our human labor is thus incorporated into the marvelous work of Creation and Redemption. It is raised to the order of grace. It is sanctified and becomes God's work, operatio Dei, opus Dei.[29]

This is a profound insight: ordinary daily work that is sanctified is incorporated into God's work of Creation and Redemption and helps to sanctify the world.

The spirituality of St. Josemaría Escrivá requires much more development than can be offered here, but it is worthwhile, nevertheless, to offer a few insights from one of his spiritual sons mentioned earlier, Jesús Urteaga. Fr. Urteaga's elaboration of work in *Saints in the World* synthesizes a number of the themes mentioned earlier as aspects of Nazareth. Because his insights synthesize the teaching of Josemaría Escrivá, it would be very helpful here

---

[29] St. Josemaría Escrivá, *Conversations with Msgr. Escrivá*, no. 10, quoted in Alvaro del Portillo, *Josemaría Escrivá: Witness of Love for the Church* (Manila: Sinag-Tala Publishers), 22-23.

to draw more extensively from Fr. Urteaga to give a sense of the contours of St. Josemaría Escrivá's teaching.[30] The entire book is also about setting the reader on fire with the Holy Spirit for evangelization, using headings like "Saints, Pagan, Cowards, Pietists," "You: A Soldier of Christ," "An Age of Fire," and subsections like "The adventure of suffering" and "Time for action." In the section, "The Adventure of Work," he tells us to stop rushing about, to not be preoccupied with the work itself, but rather to find Christ right in the midst of the world and to sanctify our work.

> Listen: We live in a world in which everyone is always in a hurry; no one has time for anything. It's true for you, and it's just as true for me. Well, in this situation each of us has to make a choice: either to be overwhelmed by our work or else to sanctify it. There is no middle course. The same is true of pain: it tortures some; of other it makes saints. And it is the very same pain, the same work....

> We all have within our reach the simplest way of becoming a saint: sanctification of one's ordinary life, of its every humdrum detail. If you expect that someday you will do something big and thereby become a saint, you will never be one.[31]

Holiness is attained through the sanctification of the very work that we do. And the sanctification requires the holiness of details. Again, what matters is the "how," not the "what."

> The details, the details— that is where you will find your sanctification. All your big ideas, if they sidetrack you from the sanctification of little ordinary things, will be fatal....

> ... As a rule, time is essential for everything. And during all that time, little things. Do you not see that every big thing is made up of an immense number of little things?

> ... [Jesus in workshop with Joseph] It does not make the slightest difference what you have to do; the only thing is how you do it.[32]

---

[30] Fr. Jesús Urteaga was an Opus Dei priest, author, journalist, television host, and is one of the early members who knew St. Josemaría Escrivá well. He had doctorates in Civil Law and Dogmatic Theology, and his books have been published internationally.
[31] Jesús Urteaga, *Saints in the World*, 116.
[32] Ibid., 116-117.

The key then is to see that it is in our very work that we can become saints. People who complain that they are too busy for prayer and the spiritual life are deceived, for the sanctification lies within their work. The correct order then is to first work well, only then do we put the presence of God in it.

> Work can make you a saint! Sanctify your work, whatever it is, by doing it well. Be sure that you work well. What a ridiculous contradiction it would be to offer to God a half-finished task, a job done without care, without a willing spirit, without effort!...

> ... Learn first to do your job really well, and afterwards you will learn how to do it in the presence of God. Put plenty of human energy and ambition into your task, and later it will be easy to rectify whatever may be missing in your intention.[33]

Fr. Urteaga gives solid examples of this "professional" spirit and culture: designing churches for worship that don't look like garages or gymnasiums, publishers producing "attractive, high-quality literature," painters who know what the truth is, sculptors who refuse to mass-produce ugly statues, and movie stars who refuse to mock great Christian figures and beliefs.[34] He captures well the current temptation to give in to an overwhelming load of work and not be able to have time for the spiritual life.

> Surely you see now why I cannot let you say that while you are absorbed in that career move, that financial problem, that illness, preparing for that exam, taking care of your children, "you can't be thinking about anything else." That phrase is borderline blasphemous; at the very least, is not Christian. You will achieve sanctity precisely by means of whatever you are doing at any given moment....

> Offer your work every day. If your love is great, offer it every hour. If you wish to be a contemplative in the midst of the world, offer it to the Lord every instant of your life. Do what you should do, and whatever you do, do it well. Every night you will be tired, sometimes to the point of exhaustion. At those times just remind yourself that the lazy will never know what sanctity is.[35]

---

[33] Ibid., 117-118.
[34] Ibid., 118-119.
[35] Ibid., 120-121.

Let us reiterate: it is "borderline blasphemous" to say that your work prevents you from "thinking about anything else." To be a contemplative in the world with great love, offer your work "every hour," and "Do what you should do, and whatever you do, do it well."

In another work, *Defects of the Saints*, Fr. Urteaga, through the skillful use of a Greek mythology image, captures the two opposite and wrong approaches to work. Daedalus, a skilled architect of Athens was imprisoned for treason on an island with his son, Icarus. He conceived a plan to escape by building wings made of bird feathers, but instructed Icarus not to fly too low, for he might sink into the cold sea, or too high, and be burned by the sun. As the myth goes, Icarus was dazzled by the firmament and other heavenly things, and flew too high, so that the wax holding the straps to the wings melted, and he fell and died. The flying too low represents seeing our work as a "curse": seeing it as punishment or toil, or working lazily and unenthusiastically, being languid and negligent, just working to get by, doing the work incompletely or poorly, dragging our feet like slaves, forgetting that nine-tenths of Jesus' work was in the humble and uninteresting manual work.

It may not be unusual for a priest, due to physical ailments, heavy load, and reverses in life, to find himself flying "too low," to be dragging himself without joy or enthusiasm. At the other end of the spectrum is to fly too high, to treat work as working for oneself or as an escape: working for glory or personal gain (personal satisfaction, gloating with pride, seeking a good image or money), seeing work as meaningless merchandise or escape, clock watching (last to arrive and first to leave), being too busy for God, being indifferent to the concerns of others.[36] Fr. Urteaga concludes that work is neither a punishment nor an escape: "It is collaborating with God."[37]

We come to the key difficulty of knowing how to be able to give of ourselves. In an interview with *Zenit.org* (the website that provides news from Rome), Fr. Urteaga spoke about self-giving, saying "yes" within the charism of Opus Dei. He mentions that, along with Ignacio Echevarría, he was the last to whom the founder spoke directly about giving themselves to God.

[36] Jesús Urteaga, *Defects of the Saints*, 253-256.
[37] Ibid., 256.

I find people very soft. But at the same time there are plenty of people doing plenty of positive things. The sort of 'Yes' we're talking about is made up of daily sacrifice and self-surrender, and sometimes that demands great generosity. But it's worth while. In the evening, when you examine your conscience on what you've done that day, you can have a great sense of achievement. All those 'Yeses' add up to a lot.[38]

The generosity from saying "yes" all day is worthwhile and adds up to much at the end of day. Ultimately, to test to see if we are sanctifying work, we can turn to a well-known saying by St. Josemaría Escrivá as criterion: we must sanctify work, sanctify ourselves in our work, and sanctify others through our work.

## H. The Child of God as Gentleman/Lady

There is one aspect of human formation that is poorly emphasized, but one to which St. Francis de Sales gives priority— the Christian as gentleman/lady. To give a sense of what is required of us, it is helpful to look at the teachings of the Religious Sisters of Mercy, based in Alma, Michigan, who have a very strong formation element on etiquette and human formation in general. Three of their formation booklets heavily emphasize these elements: *The Ratio Institutionis of the Religious Sisters of Mercy* (*RI*); *Examen on Paradoxes of Growth within Consecrated Life*; and *A Handbook of Good Manners in the Spirit of Mercy*. They are usually set up in the framework of a Scripture text, a Magisterial document, texts from St. Thomas Aquinas (a patron) and their foundress, Catherine McAuley.[39] From the foundress' teachings, the Christian or consecrated person can learn much:

> ➤ If the love of God really reigns in your heart, it will quickly show itself on the exterior. (*RI* 16, under "Virtue of Gentleness")
> ➤ There are things which the poor prize more highly than gold, though they cost the donor nothing; among these are the kind word, the gentle, compassionate look, and the patient hearing of their sorrows. (*RI* 19, under "Virtue of Kindness")
> ➤ We can never be happy nor feel as we ought to feel, until we bring ourselves to the conviction that we are treated by everybody better than we deserve. (*Examen* 29, text used for all stages of formation)

---

[38] "A Lifelong Yes," St. Josemaría Escrivá, Founder of Opus Dei, December 4, 2002, http://www.josemariaescriva.info/article/a-lifelong-yes.
[39] At this juncture, the beatification process is well under way.

> Persons consecrated to God in an order which labors for the salvation of souls ought to be the most attractive people in the world, that their influence being boundless in their respective offices, they may be so many magnets to attract to Jesus Christ all with whom they come in contact. (*Examen* 6, under "Pre-entrance," text by Institute)

> Devotion to the Sacred Heart gives rest to the soul by imparting a peace and a security, a heavenly composure, which all the joys of earth can never give. It was from this Ocean of Goodness that Saint Francis de Sales drew his wonderful sweetness.

> Our charity toward our Sisters should be cordial. Now cordial means something that refreshes, and livens and invigorates. If you only love one another cordially, you have heaven already. (*Handbook of Good Manners*, 16, under "Virtue of Kindness")

This gives a little insight into the importance of human virtue. Venerable Catherine McAuley teaches that good manners and refinement are prerequisites for becoming a good Religious Sister of Mercy. St. Josemaría Escrivá constantly teaches the need of holiness for human refinement, combined with affection. Francis Fernández-Carvajal's *Through Wind and Waves* (mentioned earlier) offers additional insights by presenting something on St. Escrivá's understanding of the importance of human virtues.[40] In our times, these qualities need to be taught, especially in homes and schools. Diocesan priests in our times typically do not receive formation in being a gentleman, in having refinement of disposition. It would help if seminarians at least received some sessions on general etiquette.

### 3. Contemporary Pitfalls to Avoid

#### A. Lacking Transcendence

While we have been stressing all along in this chapter the importance of the human dimension as the "foundation" for the structure, there can be today a great temptation to become "*excessively human*," to remain exclusively at the natural level (not rising from the natural to the supernatural). This reverses the proper priority, as the foundation is for the sake of the building, namely, the divine dimension.

St. Catherine of Siena was taught how to see everything against the background of the transcendent. The Lord pointed out the necessity of living in truth:

---

[40] Francis Fernández-Carvajal, *Through Wind and Waves*, 66-71.

But I will give you a sure and certain sign about this. Know for a certainty that since I am the Truth my visions must always bear fruit in a greater knowledge of truth in the soul. The soul needs knowledge of the truth, of me and itself, so it must know me and itself; knowing me and itself, it must necessarily despise itself and honour me— which is the true function of humility.[41]

This truth is knowledge of God and knowledge of oneself before God, one's nothingness before God (self-knowledge). The truth is God's almightiness, from which point of departure, she begins to know herself. From this horizon of truth, Jesus, whom she called her "novice master," taught her the dynamic for distinguishing His visions from those of the enemy:

When my visions begin they inspire fear, but as they develop they fortify; they begin with a kind of grief but they grow sweeter and sweeter. Whereas the opposite happens in the case of visions sent by the Enemy: at first they seem to give a kind of pleasure, contentment, sweetness, but as they go on pain and nausea begin to develop in the soul of the Beholder. This is the truth, for my ways are utterly different from his ways. Undoubtedly the way of penance required by my commandments seems harsh and difficult to begin with, but the more it goes on the easier and sweeter it becomes, whereas the way of vice is pleasurable enough to begin with, but it becomes more and more bitter and painful as time goes on.[42]

God's visitations always begin with God's transcendence, a sense of His awesomeness and might; only then does he bring sweetness of his intimacy or immanence. The enemy's tactic is the reverse, it begins with pleasure: "but it becomes more and more bitter and painful as time goes on." The enemy may be employing his trap today of drawing people in the post-Vatican II period to sentimentality and a "touchy-feely" culture— it falls right into the enemy's trap. That which is of God always begins instead with a profound sense of His awesomeness— this "truth" has to be the starting point of all Christians.

---

[41] Ibid., 73.
[42] Blessed Raymond of Capua, *The Life of St. Catherine of Siena*, 72-73.

One of the symptoms of being "excessively human," of excessively depending on self and one's human gifts and pushing the divine to the background, is the neglect of exercises of popular piety or devotion. Since the Second Vatican Council, there has been much talk about "love" and "community," sometimes to the exclusion of piety: love of our Lady, devotion to the saints, and love of the Church, especially in the person of the Holy Father. Devotion or religious piety is regarded as "piousness," for simple-minded Catholics who lack the illumination of the more enlightened within the Church. Yet, when that very devotion or popular piety is perceived to be lacking in a priest, parishioners can sense something of the divine or faith missing— a schizophrenia, a lack of spiritual depth. Parishioners should sense that the priest lives against a spiritual horizon. If the priest lacks the profound self-knowledge of his utter poverty and a supernatural outlook and mortification, he will fail to make parishioners saints. Josemaría Escrivá teaches that "Our heads should indeed be touching heaven, but our feet should be firmly on the ground" (*Friends of God*, 75). André Frossard offers an example of how St. Maximilian Kolbe was able to integrate his passionate devotion to Mary so as to make it a force within his daily life.

> Of course, to the modern mind, unaccustomed to the divine, this sort of photoelectric effect of mystery on the saint is very strange in a way that it absorbs the invisible and turns it into charity. It is that we barely grant God a semblance of probability. We would hardly dream of drawing our life from the mysteries of our Faith, which are no more than abandoned wells, overflowing in solitude. The mystery, this hard mystery of the Immaculate Conception, which easily sends sacred orators ricocheting into the ether of abstractions, was for Kolbe a formidable source of energy. It fortified him; it ordered his thought; it liberated him. And his view of the world was gently noble, the view of those whom nothing troubles, nothing frightens, who know where they have come from and where they're going. At Auschwitz, he lived only for her.[43]

## B. Breaking "Unity of Life"

Thus the priest must have "unity of life." Both transcendence (divine) and immanence (human) must be found united in the child of God, but with the human subordinated to the divine. This whole area constitutes one of

---

[43] André Frossard, *Forget not Love: The Passion of Maximilian Kolbe*, 56-57.

the strongest aspects of the charism of Josemaría Escrivá, called "Unity of Life." We turn to Fr. Francis Fernández-Carvajal, who offers what might serve as commentary on St. Escrivá's vision on this unity, one that is ultimately founded on being a child of God: "Following Christ means making him the aim of all our actions in order to become identified with him."[44] It overcomes the mindset that some of our time is for God and some for study or work; it seeks instead the glory of God in all things, be it work, family, or sports. To accomplish this requires a "wide variety of ascetical practices" and the practice of frequently rectifying our fallen intentions. It means in all situations in life we are the same person, "sons and daughters of God who reflect in an attractive way that determination to follow Christ in every situation." It follows, like human love, from being in love with Christ, a love that should imbue all actions.

This has certain consequences. Quoting Augustine, it means that "In the world some days are always bad, but in God there are only good days" (*Exposition on the Psalms*, 33.2.17). It also means that it should influence our actions: to lead us to being cordial and optimistic, punctual and just at work, use time well, and take care of work. He notes, quoting another author, that it is the first time in the history of the Church that this fullness of Christian life is being asked of the ordinary Christian, of the man "in the street." He concludes by saying that great good is done to our family and society when we stay close to the Lord throughout the day, and great harm when we fail, for example, through disorder, lukewarmness, and doing tasks that deviate from God's plan.[45]

André Frossard makes the following clarification regarding this dichotomy, giving St. Maximilian Kolbe as a model of unity of life.

> Most Christians had long since cut their religion in two. Down here is the earth, with its laws, customs, and conventions that form, along with a few Christian moral principles, greatly modified by indulgence, the basis of a reasonable conception of existence. Then up there is heaven, or what is cheerfully called "The beyond," to make clear that it is not down here and that, though one thinks of it and believes in it, it is the object of perpetual deferment. This separation of heaven and earth in which each exists in its own sphere and meets the other only on feast days is a very old

---

[44] Francis Fernández-Carvajal, *Through Wind and Waves*, 90.
[45] Ibid., 90-94.

metaphysical catastrophe. It has passed by many historians unperceived, and it helps us to understand why Christianity has never succeeded in being really Christian. Kolbe did not practice this kind of dichotomy. But the unitive vision of this man who prayed even as he argued could not but seem extravagant to those who did not experience the same attraction to the divine. The "pilgrims of the absolute" are as rare as Halley's Comet, and, when they traverse our atmosphere, those who watch them rarely have any idea of following them.[46]

In this dichotomy or schizophrenia, the separation between heaven and earth, it is not fashionable to demonstrate strong attraction to the divine or to be "pilgrims of the absolute." Kolbe himself was not understood, some of his religious brothers called him "brother marmalade," perhaps also criticizing his intense devotion to our Blessed Mother.

## C. Busyness is the Tool of Satan

One of the greatest pitfalls of the modern era is to succumb to busyness, *activism*, which can serve as an escape. Over and over again, the author encounters this modern propensity to action. It is a temptation to focus on activity, motion, movement, and thereby run into lack of good order and professionalism. A priest, asked to assist the Charismatic Renewal in his diocese, noticed a tendency among some of them to think of holiness as running from one Charismatic conference or retreat to another. He counselled them to make use of these conferences, but rather to put the primary focus on sanctifying each hour, learning tools to do so (through a plan of life, the sacrament of the present moment, the Examen Prayer, etc.); and above all, to put the priority on contemplation over action. This is but one example, but the temptation is so strong that one encounters this prevailing inclination in ministry everywhere.

Without a "supernatural outlook," the priest too is in danger of spinning his wheels, with much motion but little sanctification. Busyness can take on various forms. With his heavy load, a priest can be constantly on the move, running from one task to another, from one crisis to another: not finding sufficient time to eat; not organizing himself so as to ask priests well in advance to cover for him in periods of absence or vacation; not making time for theological reading; dreading all the paperwork and administrative

---

[46] André Frossard, *Forget not Love*, 66-67.

duties, and so on. He is always on the move. Worse yet, however, his mind too is always "busy." His mind never rests, and even at prayer, he finds himself distracted, even preoccupied, with parish concerns or with tasks yet to be finished. Without contemplative prayer, which is the principal daily means by which we unite ourselves to God, and therefore the means by which we bring God into our world, then the world becomes more and more "God-less." The classic example of the power of unity of life is found in the life of St. Thérèse of Lisieux, who lived only to the age of twenty four and remained hidden in the Carmel of Lisieux, and yet has had tremendous impact on the life of the Church in our time.

## D. Lacking Organization

This aspect can be easily overlooked in our human life, seeing organization as a gift given to some and as an optional quality. If we look to nature, we find order and organization in everything. The universe has an order: in our own solar system, we find regularly spaced orbiting patterns in this sun, moon, and the earth; on this earth, we have regularly recurring sequential seasons: Fall, Winter, Spring, Summer; in our own bodies, we have spinal columns, which not only hold our body up but which also have the purpose of organizing our nervous system, such that an orthopaedic surgeon or a chiropractor can immediately tell us which vertebra's nerves are connected to which organ. Without organization, there is no order and no peace, and an incapacity to hear the Holy Spirit.

This can affect the pastoral life of a priest. After all, is he not too busy to be concerned about organization, since he was not ordained for administrative work, and since he can leave this to others more capable in this area? While we can reasonably leave many things to others, like the parish accounts to an accountant, and while we should learn to delegate and use the talents of our parishioners, to live our life in disarray is to overlook the human dimension.

*Synthesis*

As new Christs, in their desire to be holy, many fail to make signficant progress in the spiritual life because they have neglected the human foundation. It is one of the insights of the author that most problems that arise in spiritual direction are due to neglect or compromising of our human foundation. In contrast, one with strong order, fidelity to a schedule and to one's responsibilities (especially family life), perfecting one's work, and developing human virtues, forms a strong foundation to be led by the Father's Spirit.

## NOTE FOR SEMINARY USE

### *"Significant Markers of Human Maturation"*

For building a strong human foundation, it is helpful to identify significant indicators or "markers" of human maturation. One helpful article is by Sr. Marysia Weber, R.S.M., D.O., who has considerable experience in working with priests, seminarians, and religious.[47] This article, "Significant Markers of Human Maturation Applied to the Selection and Formation of Seminarians," could serve as a paper for discussion among seminary formation faculty. As the title indicates, it was written for both the selection and formation of seminarians.

Here is a brief summary. Sister Weber identifies *"Six Tasks for Human Development."* She notes that, while there are theoretical differences in various models, "all models contain similar characteristics that indicate increasing personal and interpersonal integration."[48]

1.  From Dependence to Interdependence
2.  Control and Authority
3.  Productivity and Performance
4.  Adequate/Inadequate Sense of Self
5.  Capacity/Incapacity for Healthy Friendships
6.  Spiritual Fatherhood (Generativity, Self-Sacrifice, and Service)

---

[47] Marysia Weber, "Significant Markers of Human Maturation Applied to the Selection and Formation of Seminarians," *Seminary Journal*, 35-41; "Pornography, Electronic Media and Priestly Formation," *Homiletic & Pastoral Review* (April 2008): 8-18. Sister Weber is a Religious Sister of Mercy, a psychiatrist working at their Sacred Heart Mercy Health Care Center in Alma, Michigan. Through this center, her primary work is assessing and treating seminarians, priests, and religious with difficulties. She has offered numerous formation workshops on a variety of formation issues for U.S. Bishops, seminary formators and vocation directors, and has also served as a psychological expert consultant for the Secretariat of Clergy, Consecrated Life and Vocations, USCCB. Her present work of rehabilitation has discovered that the most harmful addiction for priests and religious is internet pornography.
[48] Marysia Weber, "Significant Markers," *Seminary Journal*, 35.

Some general remarks are in order. First, the six markers indicate a certain sequence of development, such that one cannot attain a subsequent marker like generativity without developing a capacity for healthy relationships. Second, these markers imply that one is able to overcome obstacles and develop these markers, especially with the assistance of guides or spiritual directors, and in a few cases, with someone with competency in the medical field. Third, the earlier markers suggest that a strong human foundation is required, neglect of which will cause consequences, both interior, like emotional upheavals, and exterior, like the capacity for working with others. Fourth, the strong foundation is for the sake of becoming self-forgetful and self-sacrificing, that leads not only to interdependence and working with others, but also to generativity.

# CHAPTER 10

## *PEACE OF HEART &*
## *SACRAMENT OF PRESENT MOMENT*

### (*Disposition Needed to Hear the Holy Spirit*)

Nada te turbe, nada te espante, todo se pasa, Dios no se muda, la paciencia todo lo alcanza, quien a Dios tiene nada le falta sólo Dios basta.

Let nothing trouble you, let nothing frighten you, all is fleeting, God alone is unchanging, patience obtains everything, who possesses God wants for nothing, God alone suffices. (St. Teresa of Jesus, translation)[1]

That Jesus' first pronouncement after His resurrection was the gift of a divine peace of heart— the first fruit of His sacrifice on Calvary— indicates its immense importance for the spiritual life in Christ: "Peace I leave with you; my peace I give to you; not as the world gives do I give to you. Let not your hearts be troubled, neither let them be afraid" (Jn 14:27). Different texts of Jesus in the Sermon of the Mount reinforce this truth, such as, "Look at the birds of the air: they neither sow nor reap nor gather into barns, and yet your heavenly Father feeds them" (Mt 6:26). This insight arising from the Lord's heart suggests that peace of heart was the foundation within the spiritual physiognomy of Jesus Himself. Experience shows that many in the Church are not only unaware of the vital role of peace of heart to attain holiness, but that it has an accompanying "sister" in the sacrament of the present moment. The importance of the sacrament of the present moment is highlighted in different texts, "So do not worry about tomorrow, for tomorrow will bring worries of its own" (Mt 6:35). Jesus teaches us not to be troubled about the past nor fear the future but to stay in the present.

---

[1] This excerpt of a brief poem, known as her bookmark, was found in her breviary after her death, and has entered the repertoire of standard American choral literature, now used at Taizé. For translation, see "Teresa 500 Icon," The Carmelite Forum of Britain & Ireland, 2015, http://www.teresaofavila.org/teresa-500-icon.html.

## The Necessity of Peace of Heart to Listen to the Holy Spirit

Among contemporary works for fostering peace of heart, Jacques Philippe's *Searching for and Maintaining Peace: A Small Treatise on Peace of Heart*, introduced earlier, is most highly recommended.[2] Written in a very accessible manner, this little book has helped many people who were burdened and troubled in their hearts. In Part Two of the book, he covers a number of areas that commonly trouble us: fear of suffering, fear of what God might ask of me in giving myself totally to Him, discouragement from my falls, difficulty of being patient with others, and unrest because I can't see clearly what to do before a major decision.

From the very first page of his work, Fr. Philippe establishes the fundamental truth Jesus wishes to instill in us all: "Without me, you can do nothing." He writes that God would spare us many trials and tribulations of life if only we could learn that lesson for ourselves. Unfortunately, the reality is that we are not able to docilely lean on Him for everything, and so these trials become necessary to learn this lesson and enable spiritual growth. We must live our fundamental identity both as God's creatures, dependent on Him (existence, providence, etc.), and as children of God (Baptism), carried in His arms.

Having established the fundamental truth of dependence on God, or more specifically, of dependence through being led by the Holy Spirit, he identifies its prerequisite—peace of heart. As we recall from Chapter 6 of this book, Jesus being led by the Holy Spirit constitutes the building (human life is foundation), the goal of the spiritual life. This was the secret of Christ, who lived His Sonship in obedience to the Father in being led by the Father's Spirit from moment to moment. To illustrate the necessity of peace of heart for this guidance by the Holy Spirit, he employs the striking image of the reflection of the sun on a lake (the reflection of a full moon on the lake might be more helpful). On a clear and calm night, a full moon is mirrored clearly on the surface of the lake; but on a cloudy and stormy night, dissipated flashes of light flies in every direction from the agitated waves. In this analogy, the lake represents the soul and the moon represents

---

[2] Jacques Philippe, *Searching for and Maintaining Peace: A Small Treatise on Peace of Heart* (New York: St. Paul's, 2002, French orig. *Recherche la paix et poursuis la*).

the Holy Spirit. When my soul is troubled and agitated, it does not reflect the Holy Spirit; it can no longer discern the delicate voice of the Spirit.

We can see its necessity in the teaching of the Spanish lay mystic, Francisca Javiera del Valle, who reveals that she was taught by the Holy Spirit Himself. She emphatically teaches that, if we want to enter the school of the Holy Spirit, it is vital to be "the lover of quiet and repose." She develops this teaching at some length, reinforcing its indispensability.

> The Holy Spirit is the lover of quiet and repose, of that repose that the soul feels when it seeks and desires nothing but its God. When the soul is habitually in this state of repose, and desires to know nothing but the will of God in order to fulfill it at once, then it enjoys constant peace. And when this peace is there, then the Holy Spirit comes to that soul and makes, as it were, his abode there; and he governs and gives orders and commands as one who feels at home. He orders and commands, and is at once obeyed.
>
> But when we are restless and disturbed and allow this restlessness to make us lose our peace of soul, the holy and divine Spirit is greatly saddened, not because anything bad happens to him, but because it happens to us. The Holy Spirit cannot live in a soul where peace does not dwell; once we lose our peace of soul, the Holy Spirit cannot dwell within us, because the holiness of God finds it impossible to live where there is no peace.
>
> The soul without peace is, so to speak, incapable of hearing the voice of God or following his divine calling. That is why the Holy Spirit does not dwell where there is no peace, because this divine Spirit, who is always disposed to act, retreats in sadness and remains silent when he sees that the soul is not so disposed. The Holy Spirit wants to dwell in our soul for the single purpose of directing, teaching, correcting and helping us, so that with his direction, teaching, correction and help we may act always and in all things for the greater honor and glory of God. For this reason, each one of us may quite accurately and truthfully call the Holy Spirit the God who lives with us. And if peace does not always dwell in us, let us resolve today to lose everything else rather than lose the peace of our soul, which is absolutely essential if we are to have the habitual assistance of the Holy Spirit. With that assistance it is certain that we shall possess God through love in this life and possess him truly for the whole of eternity. Amen.[3]

---

[3] Javiera del Valle, *About the Holy Spirit*, 34-35.

She established in no uncertain terms that the absolutely indispensable foundation of the school of the Holy Spirit is peace of heart. Very simply the Holy Spirit does not dwell in a soul that does not have peace of heart. Without peace of heart we cannot be led by the Holy Spirit; with His assistance, "It is certain that we shall possess God through love in this life and possess Him truly for the whole of eternity." Thus, she pleads with us, "let us resolve today to lose everything else rather than lose the peace of our soul." The goal is that the Holy Spirit possess and govern our souls.

We find this truth confirmed in the life of yet another mystic, a lesson taught by the Lord Himself to Blessed Dina Bélanger. Jesus revealed to her that, in order for her to hear His voice, He had to bring her to great calm, and only then would she be able to hear His voice. The great transformation our Lord accomplished in her was the "Substitution of Christ." And in this substitution, for Jesus to act in her, she would have to let go of all worries and give them to Jesus, which would enable her to remain in a state of calm.[4] It is a lesson that all saints and mystics have learned. St. Jane Frances de Chantal teaches us to sink into the infinite ocean of God where is no past or future:

> Today, when any thoughts or worries come to mind, send them out into the ocean of God's love that surrounds you and lose them there. If any feelings come into your heart — grief, fear, even joy or longing, send those out into the ocean of God's love. Finally, send your whole self, like a drop, into God. There is no past no future, here or there. There is only the infinite ocean of God.[5]

## *1. Path to Peace of Heart*

### A. Peace of Heart through Simplicity

The way of peace, as well as of progress, is the way of simplicity. A dictionary defines "simplicity" as "the quality of being simple or uncompounded," that is, the quality of being *one*. For example, divinity is about oneness or unity: God Himself is three Persons, but in *one* God, so

---

[4] Blessed Dina Bélanger, *Autobiography*, 101.
[5] "St. Jane Frances de Chantal," Catholic Online, accessed September 1, 2015, http://www.catholic.org/saints/saint.php?saint_id=60

that Jesus can say, "The Father and I are one."[6] The whole human race is to enter the oneness of the Trinitarian unity as John describes in his Gospel.

> ... that they may all be one; even as you, Father, are in me, and I in You, that they also may be in us, so that the world may believe that You have sent me. The glory which You have given me I have given to them, that they may be one even as we are one, I in them and You in me, that they may become perfectly one, so that the world may know that You have sent me and have loved them even as You have loved me. Father, I desire that they also, whom You have given me, may be with me where I am, to behold my glory which You have given me in Your love for me before the foundation of the world. (Jn 17:21-24)

All human history proceeds in that direction through the recapitulation by Christ (Eph 1). It is love that begets unity; sin, like that of Adam and Eve, begets division.

Let us employ a real life example of the temptation to break simplicity. A pastor, with past run-ins with the diocesan chancery (administrative offices of bishop), counselled his recently ordained associate to be very leery of the bishop and the diocesan chancery, because they are not to be trusted and they might end up betraying him. He justified his position with Jesus' words, "Behold, I send you out as sheep in the midst of wolves; so be wise as serpents and innocent as doves" (Mt 10:16). Even though Jesus' words seemed to promote cultivating a protective veneer of shrewdness and even distrust (serpent), while appreciating the concern of the pastor, the young priest felt in his heart that this interpretation did not accurately represent Jesus' way.

A few years later, the young priest found the full and proper interpretation of Jesus' words from a commentary he read by St. Francis de Sales. The cunning of a serpent is like being inoculated with a vaccine, a poison introduced into our bodies so that we can build up antibodies. But we can only inject a miniscule amount of poison (vaccine), otherwise it would kill us. Similarly, the child of God and of the Church do well to have less than 1% of the cunning of the serpent, but over 99% of the innocence and docility of the dove. We can indeed experience a lack of support or loyalty within the Church because of weakness in God's instruments (e.g., a

---

[6] See also Jn 14:11: "Believe me that I am in the Father and the Father is in me."

237

chancery official, a bishop, even a Roman Congregation official), our Lord, nevertheless, desires that we foster unity and, at all cost, avoid a partisan "them against us" spirit.

The attitude of the pastor above reminds us of the argument employed by the citizens of Florence to St. Catherine of Siena in their fight with the Avignon papacy in the fourteenth century. In this rebellion, some lay Florentines were arguing that they should not have to obey the priests, as some were not living their priestly vows or promises, especially poverty and celibacy. With divine insight, she cut to the heart of the issue, recalling Jesus' own counsel to the Jewish people regarding their own lax leadership: "The scribes and the Pharisees sit on Moses' seat; so practice and observe whatever they tell you, but not what they do; for they preach, but do not practice" (Mt 23:2-3). She saw clearly that what must be primary is to see Christ's office that the priests held as His representatives, but also to pray for their conversion.

This lack of simplicity (not seeing the oneness of Christ with His office in His ministers) is a slippery slope and a temptation from the Evil One. St. Joan of Arc's proper disposition mentioned earlier regarding her response to her interrogators when they cast doubt on the Church's role applies here to simplicity as well: "It seems to me that Christ and His Church are one, and we should not complicate things."[7] Her answer was of simplicity, which does "not complicate things."

Thus, in following Jesus' teaching that highlights the "innocence of a dove" (simplicity), and combining that with Jesus' injunction, "He who hears you hears me, and he who rejects you rejects me" (Lk 10:16), we are to see the Church from a divine-human perspective: the divine dimension is the infallible and objective presence of Christ in the Church, along with the desire of Christ for unity; the human represents the weak and very fallible instruments (e.g., priests, bishops) who can fail. While maintaining obedience, we are not promoting blind allegiance to every instruction that comes from the chancery as if they were divine oracles from God, since we are dealing with areas of prudential judgment and since certain administrative officials may lack discernment.

---

[7] St. Joan of Arc, *Acts of the Trial of Joan of Arc*, quoted in the *Catechism of the Catholic Church*, n. 795.

There is another major everyday cause of anxiety, that is, an "inability to look from a higher place." A secular suggestion that mirrors this teaching comes from David Allen, whom we have mentioned earlier, for those who get stuck or in a rut. Among his "*52 Productivity Principles for Getting Things Done*," he suggests this guideline for resolving difficult situations: "For more clarity, look from a higher place."[8] In this human wisdom, he counsels us to identify our overall goal, discern the next step, and then move in that direction. Applied to the life of priests, what often distracts us is the tide of the many things that call for our immediate attention, like some mail on our desk, some emails not yet cleared from our folder, or perhaps a request for help by a friend, all of which are like little "foxes" that are harmless but tear up our garden (equanimity). These little things tempt us to focus all our attention on them, to do them first and without any order or time limits, leaving us restless as we don't accomplish our main priorities. We are called instead to hold the high priorities aloft, above all other secondary distractions, and allocate limited periods to accomplish them; we must not leave them "open-ended."

How is simplicity to be lived out each day? Ultimately, it is being a child (Jesus' teaching), more specifically, being child-like in regard to the things of God— it is being simple, being "one," as opposed to being pulled in "multiple directions." Here are some concrete examples. Simplicity is being childlike in regard to the teachings of the Bible by putting its teaching into practice within our own contexts. We can imitate the example St. Francis of Assisi and St. Anthony of Egypt, who literally put into practice the Gospel counsel, "sell everything." It is being simple in regard to ("being one" with) the Church's teachings and liturgical norms, including avoiding General Absolution, except for critical situations, and keeping to the liturgical norms of the Mass. It is being simple like Jesus, who consulted the Holy Spirit when selecting the apostles, by consulting God through my superiors (parents, teachers, supervisors) and being faithful to the duties of my state in life. It is allowing the Holy Spirit to guide me through His representative, being sincere and transparent in spiritual direction, and not guiding myself. It is being one with God by not thinking too much, so that I can stop worrying and trying to control problems, but opening myself to the Holy

---

[8] David Allen, *Ready for Anything: 52 Productivity Principles for Getting Things Done* (New York: Penguin, 2003), 43 (see chapter title).

Spirit's frequent promptings. The "oneness" of simplicity is having no gaps between my life and my words, with less talking and more action, like Jesus, of whom Scripture says, He "began to do and taught" (Acts 1:1).

Simplicity is being one with God's will and trying to accept all the events of life that He allows or sends us. Simplicity is not having two "personas," a public glad-handing persona and one's real, deeper self. Simplicity is a father being willing to correct a son who is hanging around gangs without worrying about whether he may sulk and give him the cold shoulder. In sum, simplicity is being a child. While we value the human virtues of being intelligent, sensible, and responsible, all of this must fall within the larger rubric of being a child: "Truly, I say to you, unless you turn and become like children, you will never enter the kingdom of heaven" (Mt 18:3). Simplicity is being one, and it brings peace, a good conscience, and joy.

## B. Peace of Heart through not Controlling but Surrendering

For an illustration of learning how to surrender to the Father's will by overcoming control and resistance and coming to trust, let us turn this time to two examples from a secular source: the animated movie, *Kung Fu Panda* (the characters are animals, as in Disney cartoons or George Orwell's *Animal Farm*). As Christians, we must learn to use (but not rely primarily on) tested and true wisdom outside Christianity, as all wisdom comes ultimately from God. In this movie we find examples of two different characters who are troubled and who in their own particular way are not able to let go or accept: *Po*, a giant panda, and *Shifu*, the little red panda kung fu instructor. The background to the movie is that the grand Master Oogway (a tortoise) has finally anointed the "dragon warrior," long foretold to be the one who would save his people from a great disaster. For *Shifu* and his five very talented and trained students, *The Furious Five*, the choice was unfortunate: a large and fat panda, who demonstrated great interest in kung fu but had absolutely no skills for this great task. One internet blog describes the setting for our scene:

> There is a beautiful but quiet scene in the animated movie *Kung Fu Panda* which actually expresses a piece of great wisdom. It reminds us of the art of balancing belief in our work with the illusion of our need for control.

The wise old kung fu tortoise, Master Oogway, is speaking to his disciple, Shifu, a racoon [actually a red panda] who is charged with training the unlikely Po, a giant panda, to become the next great kung fu Dragon Warrior. They are standing under the Sacred Peach Tree of Heavenly Wisdom. Shifu is at a moment of crisis of faith, unable to see the potential in his overweight, clumsy protégé.[9]

The example above concerns the instructor, Shifu, who is not able to let go of control. The scene finds him in agitation, rushing to tell Master Oogway about the escape from prison of the formidable *Tai Lung* and the looming tragedy, as well as the sheer incompetence of the panda. The key words here are: "My friend, the panda will never fulfill his destiny, nor you yours until you let go of the illusion of control."

Master Oogway points to the peach tree, with its lovely branches and its colorful, plump fruits. He picks up a peach pit, and explains to Shifu: "My friend, the panda will never fulfill his destiny, nor you yours until you let go of the illusion of control. The essence of this seed is to become a peach tree. Within this bumpy, hard-shelled pit is the potential for this entire tree, with its flower blossoms and branches filled with ripe fruit. I can plant the seed in the ground, cover it with soil, and nurture it with water and sunlight. But I cannot make the tree blossom when it suits me nor make it bear fruit before its time."

Shifu insists, "But there are things we can control: I can control when the fruit will fall, I can control where to plant the seed: that is no illusion, Master!"

Oogway replies, "Ah, yes. *But no matter what you do, that seed will grow to be a peach tree. You may wish for an apple or an orange, but you will only get a peach.*"

Shifu, anxious to produce a "winner" immediately out of his young Kung Fu Panda, says, "But a peach cannot defeat the evil Tai Lung!"

Master Oogway, while gazing into the starry night, replies, "Maybe it can, if you are willing to guide it, to nurture it, to believe in it. *You just need to believe.*"[10]

---

[9] "Kung Fu Panda wisdom," The Music Within Us Blog, accessed June 27, 2015, http://themusicwithinus.wordpress.com/2009/05/04/kung-fu-panda-wisdom/.
[10] Ibid.

Shifu's problem is that he is trying to control the situation and work things out according to his limited "human" vision (animal characters play human parts). Master Oogway's wise insight is that "You just need to believe," perhaps, believe in this greater force that chose the iron warrior and in its guiding destiny (according to their tradition). Applied to the Christian dispensation, we must fight at all cost the endemic and unconscious desire within many of us to control; and believe and allow God in His wise providence to be God and to guide history— we must allow God to "be God." And what enables us to make that leap is our belief not just in God's power, but, above all, in His love for us; a belief or trust that leads ultimately to the opposite of control, namely, to "surrender." An example of this is a woman going monthly for spiritual direction and almost every session revolves around her husband's lack of religious piety— she has an issue of control. The words inscribed at the bottom of the Divine Mercy image encapsulate the heart of Christian life: *"Jesus, I trust You."*

In concrete, everyday life, there is a helpful distinction: the distinction between "concern" and "worry." Life, as we experience it, is difficult, with many burdens and trials. But we can fall into the trap of thinking that, since a problem exists, we must immediately obsess about and be overwhelmed by it. Let us imagine a concrete scenario, in which a young man, in his love for his sister, becomes troubled when his sister's boyfriend, to whom she was engaged to be married, suddenly breaks off the six-year courtship. He is moved by fear, as his sister is no longer young and might despair of her ever finding a husband, and now experience a strong sense of discouragement, sadness, and even hopelessness. He finds himself lamenting this situation with different friends over and over again.

Such a reaction may suggest that he has moved from "concern" to "worry," taking on the burden and relying on himself. "Concern" is having the same burden but entrusting it to God through our Blessed Mother, who now takes charge of this burden (and who takes this task very seriously)— the burden is no longer his to carry but now belongs to her. She asks only that we do what we humanly can. With this abandonment to, and trust in, God, the children of God walk the path of life with great lightness and carefreeness— with the freedom of children of God. It entails learning to let go. In Fr. Jean d'Elbée's *I Believe in Love*, the author describes God as looking down upon us, and seeing us carry a heavy burden on our shoulders, says to us, "What are you doing with that heavy load on your shoulders. You are only a little child, give it to Me."[11] We are also familiar with the story of Pope John XXIII, who every night visited the Blessed Sacrament burdened with the cares of the Church, and saying to God, "God, this is your Church, you look after it. I am going to bed."

## C. Peace of Heart by Overcoming Resentment and Anger

Drawing again from the *Kung Fu Panda* movie, we also find the wisdom of peace of heart. In the first scene with *Shifu* mentioned earlier, Master Oogway stirred the mud in the pond, and asked his student if he could see to the bottom, to which the latter petulantly replied that he couldn't see if Master Oogway disturbs the pond. Master Oogway used this as a lesson: "Your mind is like this water, my friend. When it is agitated, it becomes difficult to see, but if you allow it to settle, the answer becomes clear." Very strong emotions, like that experienced by *Shifu*, disturb peace of heart, and thus prevent him from seeing clearly, and even cause havoc in our discernment.

We see a similar disturbance in discernment in the Gospel scene with Martha and Jesus. The key thing to note is that she became "upset," but we must also seek the cause of this emotional disturbance.

> Now as they went on their way, he entered a village; and a woman named Martha received him into her house. And she had a sister called Mary, who sat at the Lord's feet and listened to his teaching. But Martha was distracted with much serving; and she went to him and said, "Lord, do you not care that my sister has left me to serve alone? Tell her then to help me." But the Lord answered her, "Martha, Martha, you are anxious and troubled about many things; one thing is needful. Mary has chosen the good portion, which shall not be taken away from her." (Lk 10:38-42)

In the Gospel scene, Martha acts very much like the older sister, the responsible older sibling who looked after her younger sister and managed the family affairs. In this situation, one might reasonably expect the Lord to tell Mary to go and help Martha, since Martha was doing all the work of preparing a meal for Jesus and the family. Jesus unexpectedly corrects Martha instead: "Martha, Martha, you are anxious and troubled about many

---

[11] Jean d'Elbée, *I Believe in Love*, 86.

243

things; one thing is needful. Mary has chosen the good portion, which shall not be taken away from her" (Lk 10: 41-42). These words of Jesus should not lead us to think that Martha's tasks, and our daily work and cares, are unimportant. The key here is that Martha became *upset*, suggesting that she may not have chosen God's will and priorities first, but was likely attached to and preoccupied with secondary aspects of the household: rushing, taking charge, and getting things done— many of us have this tendency. If Martha had peace of heart, she may, on the one hand, calmly have asked Mary to lend a hand, or, more importantly, recognized the greater call of Christ's disciples to sit at the feet of the Master, learning from Him and loving Him, as the beloved disciple did at the Last Supper when he leaned on Jesus' breast. When we get "upset," not just momentary flashes but continued resentment, it may be an indication of misplaced priorities in our heart. Martha was perhaps attached to her human talents and her work, and lost the sense of priority: she "forgot" that the *Son of the Most High* was in her own house.

Besides resentment arising from attachment to secondary things, like work, and to control (Martha), there is yet another cause, often unconscious. One psychologist, with great insight from clinical experience, identifies a major source of resentment which arises from not accepting our own responsibility and blaming others:

> A person who is unconscious of himself does not live life— life just happens to him. This condition may be reflected in his speech. I once knew a woman who never said that she *did* something, but always that "it happened." This gave a most curious impression that she just drifted through life without any conscious direction, and with practically no sense of responsibility towards her own life. In her the ego has been most inadequately formed, but this did not prevent her from having very strong reactions regarding her own comfort and her expectation of what was due her. Any frustration would be met by resentment, not by an effort to do something constructive about the difficulty. This is a very important point. Resentment always means that we are not willing to do something about the situation. We prefer to assume that it is someone else's business to take care of the difficulty or that "it ought to happen to us in a better way." We do not definitely say, even to ourselves, that "Life" ought to treat us as favoured children; nonetheless, that is the implication. Resentment stems from the unconscious. It is based on an unconscious

assumption of the way things *should* be, and when this expectation is not fulfilled, the individual is unable to react directly to the actual situation, because his assumption is not conscious to him. Even if he were made aware of what his expectation was in any given situation, he would probably have to repress the knowledge, because it would be too painful and embarrassing for him to recognize how inappropriate his unconscious demand was. And so instead of facing his own childishness the individual has a mode of resentment, voiced perhaps in such terms as "People ought not to do this to me."[12]

This is a valuable insight into how false selfish expectations can be at the heart of our problems, resulting in: "Resentment always means that we are not willing to do something about the situation"; "It is based on an unconscious assumption of the way things should be." Augustine goes more deeply (Office of Readings of the Fourteenth Sunday of Ordinary Time, *Sermons* 19.2-3): we are often judgmental and critical of others because we do not look at our own sins. That is, not only do we fail to recognize our responsibilities and look to others, we also look at their sins and fail to look at our own. In doing so, we fail to follow the example of David, who after he was confronted by the prophet Nathan ("You are that man"), immediately accused himself and accepted God's punishment. Augustine emphasized how deeply David's sorrow and contrition were felt (he identifies David as Psalmist, who cries, "my sin is ever before me"), and how this allowed this great man to be restored to the full friendship and peace with Yahweh.

But men are hopeless creatures, and the less they concentrate on their own sins, the more interested they become in the sins of others.... Unable to excuse themselves, they are ready to accuse others. This was not the way that David showed us how to pray and make amends to God, when he said: *I acknowledge my transgression, and my sin is ever before me.* He did not concentrate on others' sins; he turned his thoughts upon himself. He did not merely stroke the surface, but he plunged inside and went deep down within himself. He did not spare himself, and therefore was not impudent in asking to be spared.[13]

---

[12] M. Ester Harding, *The "I" and "not I": A Study in the Development of Consciousness* (Princeton, NJ: Princeton University Press, 1965), 8-9.
[13] St. Augustine, *Sermo* 19.2.3, OOR of Fourteenth Sunday in Ordinary Time, *Liturgy of the Hours*, vol. III, 450.

Jesus calls us, the "new Davids," through "modern-day Nathans" to follow the example of David: "He did not concentrate on others' sins; he turned his thoughts upon himself. He did not merely stroke the surface, but he plunged inside and went deep down within himself. He did not spare himself…"

St. Escrivá addresses two other difficulties. First, in *Friends of God*, he points to the danger of presumptuously letting our guard down, thinking that, having made some progress in the spiritual life, we would no longer be subject to temptations; that experience of His friendship "makes us incapable of sinning" and that we would be free from Satan's attacks.

> Let us not think that because we are on this road of contemplation our passions will have calmed down once and for all. We would be mistaken if we thought that our longing to seek Christ, and the fact that we are meeting him and getting to know him and enjoy the sweetness of his love, makes us incapable of sinning. Though your own experience will tell you, let me nevertheless remind you of this truth. Satan, God's enemy and man's, does not give up nor does he rest. He maintains his siege, even when the soul is ardently in love with God. The devil knows that it's more difficult for the soul to fall then, but he also knows that, if he can manage to get it to offend its Lord even in something small, he will be able to cast over its conscience the serious temptation of despair.[14]

The second improper expectation comes from experiencing the weaknesses of our flesh and temptations, thinking that we have made so little progress and perhaps may even be regressing, allowing ourselves to fall into despair. St. Escrivá, from his experience, recommends that we find shelter in the wounds of Jesus, perhaps the most effective means of protecting ourselves:

> If you want to learn from the experience of a poor priest whose only aim is to speak of God, I will tell you that when the flesh tries to recover its lost rights or, worse still, when pride rears up and rebels, you should hurry to find shelter in the divine wounds that were opened in Christ's Body by the nails that fastened him to the Cross and by the lance that pierced his side. Go as the spirit moves you: unburden in his Wounds all your love, both human and… divine. This is what it means to seek union, to feel that

---

[14] St. Josemaría Escrivá, "Towards Holiness," *Friends of God* (Manila: Sinag-Tala Publishers, 1989; Spanish orig. *Amigos de Dios*, 1977), n. 303, 330-331.

you are a brother to Christ, sharing his blood, a child of the same Mother, for it is She who has brought us to Jesus.[15]

Possibly worse than resentment is anger. St. John Vianney has a very insightful perception of the danger of habitual anger (we are referring to the capital sin of anger, as there is a just anger)— for anger derives from the devil. Anger "is an emotion of the soul, which leads us violently to repel whatever hurts or displeases us," and makes us a slave of the devil. The following extended excerpt needs no explanation or comment.

> This emotion, my children, comes from the devil: it shows that we are in his hands; that he is the master of our heart; that he holds all the strings of it, and makes us dance as he pleases. See, a person who puts himself in a passion is like a puppet; he knows neither what he says, nor what he does; the devil guides him entirely. He strikes right and left; his hair stands up like the bristles of a hedgehog; his eyes start out of his head — he is a scorpion, a furious lion. . . . Why do we, my children, put ourselves into such a state? Is it not pitiable? It is, mind, because we do not love the good God. Our heart is given up to the demon of pride, who is angry when he thinks himself despised; to the demon of avarice, who is irritated when he suffers any loss; to the demon of luxury, who is indignant when his pleasures are interfered with.

> How unhappy we are, my children, thus to be the sport of demons? They do whatever they please with us; they suggest to us evil-speaking, calumny, hatred, vengeance: they even drive us so far as to put our neighbour to death. See, Cain killed his brother Abel out of jealousy; Saul wished to take away the life of David; Theodosius caused the massacre of the inhabitants of Thessalonica, to revenge a personal affront. . . . If we do not put our neighbour to death, we are angry with him, we curse him, we give him to the devil, we wish for his death, we wish for our own. In our fury, we blaspheme the holy Name of God, we accuse His Providence.... What fury, what impiety! And what is still more deplorable, my children, we are carried to these excesses for a trifle, for a word, for the least injustice! Where is our faith! Where is our reason? We say in excuse that it is anger that makes us swear; but one sin cannot excuse another sin. The good God equally condemns anger, and the excesses that are its consequences.... How we sadden our guardian angel! He is always

---

[15] Ibid., 331.

there at our side to send us good thoughts, and he sees us do nothing but evil. . . . If we did like St. Remigius, we should never be angry. See, this saint, being questioned by a Father of the desert how he managed to be always in an even temper, replied, "I often consider that my guardian angel is always by my side, who assists me in all my needs, who tells me what I ought to do and what I ought to say, and who writes down, after each of my actions, the way in which I have done it. [16]

St. John Vianney instead presents a moving example of the calm forbearance and patience of King Philip II that the disciple of Christ is called to live and give witness to.

Philip II, King of Spain, having passed several hours of the night in writing a long letter to the Pope, gave it to his secretary to fold up and seal. He, being half asleep, made a mistake; when he meant to put sand on the letter, he took the ink bottle and covered all the paper with ink. While he was ashamed and inconsolable, the king said, quite calmly, "No very great harm is done; there is another sheet of paper"; and he took it, and employed the rest of the night in writing a second letter, without showing the least displeasure with his secretary.[17]

Sometimes, it is very difficult to avoid resentment, as it can build up within us. Recalling the striking meekness and gentleness of Jesus on Calvary described by Cardinal Newman can be a powerful balm for our souls:

They stood around in speechless awe, wondering at Thy infinite beauty and they trembled at the infinite self abasement.[18]

When He reached the projection where His sacred feet were to be, He turned round with sweet modesty and gentleness towards the fierce rabble, stretching out His arms, as if He would embrace them.[19]

## D. Peace of Heart through Being a "Monument" to God's Mercy

A powerful temptation that can disturb the peace of many a Christian is being overwrought by one's weakness or defects. Since this is such a

---

[16] St. John Vianney, *The Little Catechism of the Curé of Ars* (Rockford, IL: Tan, 1987; orig. St. Meinrad's Abbey, 1951), 116-117.

[17] Ibid., 117-118.

[18] John Henry Newman, *Meditations on the Stations of the Cross* (London: Catholic Truth Society, 1999), Tenth Station, 24.

[19] Ibid., Eleventh Station, 26.

widespread affliction, we look to Blessed Columba Marmion's vast experience of directing souls. In one instance, faced with a nun directee who was persistently discouraged by her defects, he responded incisively with divine wisdom:

> Your last letter almost pained me, for I see that you allow the sight of your miseries— which are very *limited*— to hide the riches which are yours in Jesus Christ, and these are *infinite*. It is a great grace to see our miseries and littleness, which, in reality, are much more extensive than we imagine. But this knowledge is a real poison unless completed by *immense* faith and confidence in the "all-sufficiency" of our dear Lord's merits, riches and virtues which are all ours. *Vos estis corpus Christi et membra de membra.* You are His body and the very members of His members. The members really possess as *their own* all the dignity and merit of the person whose members they are. And this is what glorifies Jesus, namely, to have such a high appreciation of His merits and such a great conviction of *His love in giving them to us* that our misery and unworthiness do not discourage us.
>
> There are two categories of people who give little glory to Jesus Christ:
>
> 1. Those who neither see their misery nor realize their unworthiness, and consequently *don't feel their need of Jesus Christ.*
>
> 2. Those who see their misery, but have not that strong faith in the Divinity of Jesus Christ which makes them, as it were, happy to be thus weak in order that Jesus may be glorified in them. How far you are from glorifying in your infirmities.[20]

While we must be aware of our misery, it is God's infinite love that must dominate and fill our horizon and vision: "It is a great grace to see our miseries and littleness, which, in reality, are much more extensive than we imagine. But this knowledge is a real poison unless completed by immense faith and confidence in the 'all-sufficiency' of our dear Lord's merits, riches and virtues which are all ours." He calls such an obsession a "poison." Those who focus on their miseries constitute one of the two categories of people "who give little glory to Jesus Christ." He points to Paul's insight about those who do not trust in God, "How far you are from glorifying in your infirmities."

---

[20] Columba Marmion, *Union with God: Letters of Spiritual Direction by Blessed Columba Marmion* (Bethesda, MA: Zachaeus Press, 2006), 109.

In his deep union with God, Dom Marmion has received the revelation from God of His deepest truth— that He is *all mercy*, as evidenced by His economy of salvation.

> For some time past God has been making me see in a magnificent light that His Majesty's whole plan, His whole "economy" towards us is an economy of mercy. It is our miseries which, united to Christ's sufferings and infirmities, draw down all the graces He gives us….
>
> I pray for you continually that you may respond perfectly to the designs of Jesus. It is necessary to realize all your baseness before the final union, but *this baseness must be seen* in God's light. Jesus is all powerful, He can and He will sanctify us.[21]

And in God's economy of mercy, what draws down God's pleasure and grace is not our good works, but precisely our miseries which are "united to Christ's sufferings and infirmities." Thus it is vital to begin first by recognizing our "baseness." But "this baseness must be seen in God's light. Jesus is all powerful, He can and He will sanctify us." To take this to the highest level, we should desire to become "a monument of His *mercy* during all eternity," as Dom Marmion wrote to a nun:

> The holy Liturgy tells us that God manifests His Almighty power "ESPECIALLY by showing mercy and forbearance." Be for Him a monument of His *mercy* during all eternity. The deeper our misery and unworthiness the greater and more adorable His mercy. The abyss of our misery calls to the abyss of His mercy. It is a great consolation to me to see that you are walking in this way which is so sure, which leads so high and glorifies the Precious Blood of Jesus Christ and the mercy of our God. It is my way too. Help me with your prayers.[22]

Paradoxically, being a "monument of God's mercy" and her following this path gives Dom Marmion "great consolation," and he confesses that "It is my way too."

St. Jane Frances de Chantal is also in accord with situating our sinfulness within the ocean of God's mercy. Her counsel was gentle and loving, and imitating the pattern of her spiritual director, St. Francis de Sales, she gave

---

[21] Ibid., 94-95.
[22] Ibid., 98-99.

this advice to one of her spiritual daughters in her order, which teaches us how to handle our faults:

> Should you fall even fifty times a day, never on any account should that surprise or worry you. Instead, ever so gently set your heart back in the right direction and practice the opposite virtue, all the time speaking words of love and trust to our Lord after you have committed a thousand faults, as much as if you had committed only one. Once we have humbled ourselves for the faults God allows us to become aware of in ourselves, *we must forget them and go forward*.[23] (emphasis added)

Besides not being surprised at our faults and forgetting while working on them, St. Jane Frances teaches us how to lose our problems in God. The secret of happiness was not in "seeking" (e.g., happiness) but in "losing" ourselves, to "throw ourselves into God as a little drop of water into the sea, and lose ourselves indeed in the ocean of the divine goodness." She advised a man who wrote to her about all the afflictions he suffered "to lose all these things in God. These words produced such an effect in the soul, that he wrote me that he was wholly astonished, and ravished with joy."[24]

## *2. The Sacrament of the Present Moment*

### A. The Present Moment Brings God's Will

*The Heart of Holiness is Receiving God's Will in Each Present Moment*

Jean-Pierre de Caussade's *Abandonment to Divine Providence* is an inspired and brilliant road map that pinpoints the heart of holiness. The baptized as a new Christ is called to be guided above all by God's will in each present moment. The Church and saints all know that holiness entails, in the path of Jesus obeying His Father's will, seeking God's will. For example, St. Teresa of Jesus teaches that holiness does not consist of having ecstasies or mystical visitations, but in simply conforming to God's will. She also said that, if she knew that the Holy Spirit wanted something of her, she would immediately rush to do it.

---

[23] St. Jane Frances de Chantal, *Selected Letters of St. Jane Frances de Chantal*, found on the website Catholic.org. For the correspondence of spiritual direction between St. Francis de Sales and St. Jane Frances de Chantal, see *Francis de Sales, Jane de Chantal: Letters of Spiritual Direction*, in the *Classics of Western Spirituality* Series (Mahwah, NJ: Paulist Press, 1988).
[24] Ibid.

But it is Jean-Pierre de Caussade who teaches how to find it: God's will comes in each present moment in hidden "disguises." He counsels us that, as we have to see with Mary's eyes the presence of the Son of God in the baby in a poor cave and in the bloodied and battered body of Christ, so today we must see that Christ comes to us now in the poverty of humdrum events, especially in daily trials. With eyes of faith, we should see Him offering Himself to us in each present moment as He offers Himself in the Blessed Sacrament: "What a festival and never-ending feast is ours!"

> And how true it is that every painful trial, all we have to do and every impulse of the spirit, give us God exactly as he comes to us in the mystery of the Blessed sacrament. Nothing is more certain. For both reason and faith tell us that God's love is present in every creature and in every event... His love wishes to unite itself with us through all that the world contains, all that he had created, ordained and allowed.... So every moment of our lives can be a kind of communion with his love, a communion which can produce in our souls fruits similar to those we receive with the body and blood of the Son of God.... What a festival and never-ending feast is ours! God ceaselessly gives himself and is received with no pomp and circumstance, but hidden beneath all that is weak and foolish and worthless.... From these castoffs he creates miracles of love and gives himself to us as often as we believe we have found him there.[25]

Fr. de Caussade depicts two levels: at the initial level, those who live in God do all the usual exercises to draw closer to God, such as faithful prayer, adoration, Mass and Confession, spiritual direction, pilgrimages, etc.; those in whom God lives, who have already mastered living in God, have moved to the next level. While faithful to them, they are not focused on the spiritual exercises but on God's leading in each present moment, for God's presence and holy will lie in it; they are the ones who have given themselves totally to God and in whom God rules by their abandonment. These latter have untold power of influence, from them grace flows to the world:

> Those who live in God perform countless good works for his glory, but those in whom God lives are often flung into a corner like a useless bit of broken pottery. There they lie, forsaken by everyone, but yet enjoying God's very real and active love and knowing they have to do nothing but stay in his hands and be used as he wishes. Often they have no idea how

---

[25] Jean-Pierre de Caussade, *Abandonment to Divine Providence*, 48.

they will be used, but he knows. The world thinks them useless and it seems as if they are. Yet it is quite certain that by various means and through hidden channels they pour out spiritual help on people who are often quite unaware of it and of whom they themselves never think. *For those who have surrendered themselves completely to God, all they are and do has power. Their lives are sermons. They are apostles. God gives a special force to all they say and do*, even to their silence, their tranquility and their detachment, which, quite unknown to them, *profoundly influences other people.*[26]

Herein we see the power of Nazareth, for example, of our Lady's abandonment and being led from moment to moment by the Holy Spirit, as the spouse of the Holy Spirit and in whom He is "quasi-incarnate." While faithful to her duties as wife and mother, she was "simple" (one, single-hearted): her eyes were always on God and on fulfilling His will. Hans Urs von Balthasar teaches that Jesus as man gave up sovereignty of His existence and was led from moment to moment by the Father through the Holy Spirit, so that His entire human life became a witness to His Father. The abandoned soul is possessed, so to speak, by the Holy Spirit, and he becomes a mystical incarnation of Christ such that Christ lives again: "The life of each saint is the life of Jesus Christ."[27]

Our life too can be a saintly history if we know how to *meet God and His holy will* in each present moment. As the Word of God wrote divine Scripture, so now He writes a new history on hearts: each heart becomes the paper, the sufferings and actions are the ink, and the incomprehensible back of the tapestry we see now will be revealed as a divine masterpiece in heaven.

> We are now living in a time of faith. The Holy Spirit writes no more gospels except in our hearts. All we do from moment to moment is live this new gospel of the Holy Spirit. We, if we are holy, are the paper; our sufferings and our actions are the ink. The workings of the Holy Spirit are his pen, and with it he writes a living gospel; but it will never be read until that last day of glory when it leaves the printing press of this life. And what a splendid book it will be— the book the Holy Spirit is still writing! The book is on press and never a day passes when type is not set, ink applied and pages pulled.... We shall be able to read it only in heaven. [28]

---

[26] Ibid., 60.

[27] Ibid., 84.

[28] Ibid., 45.

Like the holy family at Nazareth, the abandoned soul remains hidden. The greatness of Jesus and Mary were not perceived by the townspeople of Nazareth ("Is this not the son of Joseph"). The greatness of abandoned souls often remain hidden to them, and they go through interior turmoil, often seeing others as making far greater progress. While Jesus as God knew glory, he was "destroyed" in His humanity. During the Passion, "the hearts of Jesus and Mary, in that darkest of nights, let the violence of the storm break over them."[29] The abandoned souls are not marked by great heroism, austerity, or acts of charity.

> There is nothing more distressing for a soul that wants to do only the will of God and yet cannot feel certain that it loves him.... Perfection is presented to it contrary to all its preconceived ideas, to all that it feels and to all that it has learned. It now comes to the soul in the form of all the afflictions sent by providence... This seems very far from all the sublime and extraordinary glory of holiness. A veiled and hidden God gives himself and his grace in a strange, unknown manner, for the soul feels too weak to bear its crosses, distaste for its duties, and is attracted only to very ordinary spiritual exercises. The image of sanctity which it has reproaches this soul for its own mean and despicable nature.... Yet through this loss the soul gains everything.[30]

Their whole treasure is God: "God strips them of everything except their innocence so that they have nothing but him alone."[31] This state, as with Jesus and Mary, is the highest perfection: "Nevertheless, to obey this apparent disorder is to have reached the summit of virtue, and it is one we do not reach without long years of effort. This virtue is pure, unadulterated virtue. It is, quite simply, perfection."[32] It is the perfection of a musical genius like Mozart who obey but do not allow musical rules to fetter him, and "writes without constraint and his impromptu pieces are very rightly thought to be masterpieces"; and the abandoned soul, after long practice of cooperating with grace, "gradually falls into the habit of acting always by an instinctive following of God's wishes."[33]

---

[29] Ibid., 94.

[30] Ibid., 92-93.

[31] Ibid., 89.

[32] Ibid., 105.

[33] Ibid.

*The Present Moment as a "Sacrament"*

Fr. Jean-Pierre de Caussade in *Abandonment to Divine Providence* employs a technical word to indicate the importance of the present moment— sacrament. It is helpful to present some background on the theology of the seven sacraments of the Church. In its simplest form, a sacrament is defined as "an outward sign of an inward grace." That is to say, God uses a material object (visible, tangible) by means of which he communicates his grace (invisible) to those receiving the sacrament. In Baptism, for example, God uses the "matter" of water and the "form" of the words of the priest or deacon, by which God communicates the indwelling of the blessed Trinity and its consequent sanctifying or habitual grace (remission of sins, divine filiation, and the participation in divine life), not to mention a host of infused virtues, along with the gifts and fruits of the Holy Spirit.

Fr. de Caussade teaches that there is, as it were, an "eighth" sacrament, namely, "the sacrament of the present moment." He affirms that each present moment is a "sacrament" filled with the presence of God by which He gives Himself to the world. We tend to think of present moments as a measure of time, a facet of reality that happens to us, having no particular meaning or significance; simply a result of happenstance, fate, or coincidence. In reality, nothing can happen without God allowing it.

Spiritual wisdom teaches that God has two wills: a positive will and a permissive will. In God's positive will, God sends directly what He wishes to send, and because He is Love, only good issues from Him, such as love, beauty, truth, joy, etc. In His permissive will, because of man's free will, God can allow trials to happen to us caused by the exercise of the free will of others, but through which He will bring forth great good. The supreme example of this is the Paschal sacrifice of His Son on Calvary, through which He brought salvation to the world. Thus, whether it is from His positive or His permissive will, everything comes from the hands of His Heavenly Father, and we must learn to kiss this hand that feeds us, even when He gives healing medicine that is bitter.

*Abandonment in St. Thérèse of Lisieux*

We see how profound this teaching is if we perceive that it explains the heart of St. Thérèse of Lisieux. Pope St. Pius X called her the greatest saint of modern times, and it is de Caussade's teaching that explains her secret: abandonment. If we can see that this contemplative, who lived a very short life, was able to broadcast immense graces from her hidden cell to the whole world, then one sees a path of hiddenness that is the most fruitful. This hidden path of the present comprises essentially three pillars: accepting everything God sends; doing the duty of the present moment; and heeding the inner promptings of the Holy Spirit. This is in contrast to the common path of merely seeking holy instruments (e.g., good spiritual reading, which we need) or helping out at the parish or visiting prisons, that often involve following one's own will. It does not matter that we read this or that spiritual book or do this or that apostolate; what matters is whether it is God's will. The following text of de Caussade explains how it is lived out:

> ... for most people the best way to achieve perfection is to submit to all that God wills for their particular way of life.... God speaks to every individual through what happens to them moment by moment... The events of each moment are stamped with the will of God... we find all that is necessary in the present moment.... We are bored with the small happenings around us, yet it is these trivialities— as we consider them— which would do marvels for us if only we did not despise.... If we have abandoned ourselves to God, there is only one rule for us: the duty of the present moment.[34]

There are certain features of this path of abandonment. It is captured in St. Thérèse of Lisieux's description of her being, like a ball Jesus played with, set aside in a corner and yet being totally at peace. John Beevers, who translated one edition of Jean-Pierre de Caussade's book as well as one edition of St. Thérèse's autobiography, is in full agreement that the sacrament and the duty of the present moment is the key to our entire spiritual life, and himself sees how it converges with her spirituality. She once said to a lay sister: "Your life is one that is humble and hidden, but remember that nothing is small in the eyes of God. Do all that you do with love." When asked on her deathbed what she would teach all souls who turned to her, she said that she would urge them to embark on "the way of spiritual childhood, the path of confidence and complete abandon."[35]

---

[34] Jean-Pierre de Caussade, quoted in John Beevers, Introduction, in Jean-Pierre de Caussade, *Abandonment to Divine Providence*, 20.
[35] St. Thérèse of Lisieux, quoted in Ibid., 16.

One can live this abandonment or confidence by not looking at the past or future:

> If I did not simply live from one moment to the next, it would be impossible for me to keep my patience. I can see only the present, I forget the past and I take good care not to think about the future. We get discouraged and feel despair because we brood about the past and the future. It is such a folly to pass one's time freeing, instead of resting quietly on the heart of Jesus.[36]

The sacrament of the present moment represents the heart of the spiritual life: abandonment to God's will.

## *Jean d'Elbée's* I Believe in Love

Let us draw from Fr. Jean d'Elbée's *I Believe in Love* as a commentary on the spirituality of St. Thérèse of Lisieux that eloquently and inspiringly explains abandonment. He underscores that this simple abandonment is the peak of holiness, the peak of love in the saints[37]:

> It is striking to see how the sanctity of all the saints is consummated in total abandonment. All their efforts, all their prayers, all the lights which they have received from Heaven, have led them to this.
>
> When our Lord makes some reproach to the saints, to St. Gertrude, to St. Margaret Mary, for example, it is most often their lack of abandonment which He laments.[38]

It can be summarized by what our Lord said to St. Margaret Mary Alacoque, "Let me do it": "His Sacred Heart will do everything for me if I let Him."[39] St. Thérèse of Lisieux had abandonment as her compass: "I desire neither suffering nor death, yet I love both. Now it is abandonment alone which guides me. I have no other compass"[40]; and "If He destroys my little plans, I kiss His adorable hand."[41] Our Lord asks us to do what we

---

[36] Ibid.
[37] Jean d'Elbée, *I Believe in Love*, 87.
[38] Ibid., 85.
[39] St. Margaret Mary Alacoque, Letter 133, quoted in Jean d'Elbée, *I Believe in Love*, 85.
[40] St. Thérèse of Lisieux, *Manuscrits autobiographiques*, 207, quoted in Jean d'Elbée, *I Believe in Love*, 86.
[41] Ibid., 89.

humanly can, e.g., go to the doctor when we are seriously sick, but to leave the results to Him. Fr. d'Elbée notes that many good people can be very pious and even heroic, but will not make the key immolation, that of their own will, thus fleeing from real mortification in the truest sense of the word:

> Jesus always has His victory when He has your abandonment. He needs nothing more than that for you from all eternity.... We thwart His plans by imposing our own views, our little plans, to which we hold so tightly. And, quite often, why do we do it? Through fear of a cross, fear of humiliation, thirst for enjoyment, earthly ambition, and, above all, lack of confidence.[42]

We see clearly here where Christ's victory lies, and the heart of the mystery of resistance. The key then is not to fear: "When someone asked little Thérèse to summarize her little childlike way, she answered, 'It is to be disturbed by nothing.'"[43] The one who is abandoned is like a child in the Father's arms, nestling with a great sense of security and of being loved.

*Jean d'Elbée's Suggestions for Practicing Abandonment*

With some difficulties, such as the decline of our health, we can struggle to be abandoned to God's will. Fr. d'Elbée's strategy can be summarized thus: we begin by understanding how much God loves us: to believe that we are a joy for Jesus; we recall that He remembers every little act done for Him, "engraved in His Heart"; and we are cognizant of all the joy that He receives in our giving Him our miseries with great humility and confidence.[44] Second, to encourage abandonment to God's divine will, he begins by telling us to bless God in each event because He is in it: "Remember that each event in your life brings you Jesus' will, which is Jesus Himself. It is He whom you can embrace in everything that comes to you." He does warn us that our human nature will protest: "There will be interior seething; there will be revolt of the senses; there will be moaning."[45] The peace may not be felt, but it will be the peace of Paul's "which surpasses all understanding." In a further step, he notes how tenderly the

---

[42] Ibid.
[43] St. Thérèse of Lisieux, *Novissima Verba*, 125, quoted in Jean d'Elbée, *I Believe in Love*, 91.
[44] Jean d'Elbée, *I Believe in Love*, 96-97.
[45] Ibid., 99.

Divine Surgeon acts in the intervention of lancing the pus to drain the toxins, a move we may not understand, for we do not know what is best for us:

> Moreover, the tender Master who knows the price of the Cross and the thorns, will know how to be considerate toward you. He will permit plenty of humiliations and plenty of deceptions. He will destroy many false dreams. The Divine Surgeon will put the lancet straight into the abscess, happy that you allow Him to do it. But do not be afraid — no, do not be afraid! His hand is very gentle, very skilful, moved by His Heart, which loves to the point of foolishness, and the awakening will be very beautiful…. He wants you to follow Him… even to Calvary— but also to the Resurrection, to His Heaven of Glory.[46]

Faith does not consist solely in believing in dogmas (such as Christ's presence in the Blessed Sacrament); it is also believing that *He is near us*, guiding us in everything.

Then, in a third step, Fr. d'Elbée warns of improper requests by pointing to Jesus' displeasure at St. Gertrude's request for the healing of a friend: "You trouble me, Gertrude, by asking me for the cure of your friend. I sent her this sickness as a trial. She accepts it with admirable submission to my will which gains great merit for her, and I thus prepare a more beautiful Heaven for her for all eternity."[47] This does not mean that we don't pray with all our heart for the healing of the sick, but always seeking what the Lord wills.[48] Fr. d'Elbée makes a helpful note of how God sometimes acts, pointing to the example of St. Monica. God did not grant her immediate request that Augustine not leave for Italy in order to grant her the ultimate request, that he be converted. Without going to Milan, he would never have met St. Ambrose, which would lead to his conversion. He also notes that God grants great humiliations and failures in the lives of His friends, such as St. Bernard preaching the Crusades.[49]

Regarding what God grants, it is more beautiful to leave it up to God to grant temporal things. To St. Margaret Mary Alacoque, our Lord said,

---

[46] Ibid., 99-100.
[47] Ibid., 100.
[48] Ibid., 101.
[49] Ibid., 101-103.

"Take care of my interests, and I will take care of yours."[50] Regarding those we love, we can ask what we find in the Lord's Prayer: "Lord, that they may hallow Your name, that they may do Your will, that Your kingdom may come in them and through them."[51] Our Lord is the pilot, and we, the oarsmen, have our backs to the direction we are going, allowing the Lord to guide and "see" for us.

Marvelous vistas are prepared for those who are generous in abandonment; we see only the individual links, but, one day, in Heaven, we will see the whole interconnected golden chain, and what joy we will have and how grateful God will be.[52] God asks for the heroism of the theological virtues, giving God our all so that He can do whatever He wants.

Fr. de Caussade proclaims how much he wished to be "the missionary of holy will, to teach the whole world that there is nothing so easy, so common, or so accessible to everyone as holiness."[53] All attention was focused on each new duty.[54] All spiritual life then consists simply of fulfilling the duty of the moment.

Fr. d'Elbée concludes with a method to make progress in abandonment, an examination prayer: "O Jesus, I thank You for everything." He teaches us to thank God for even humiliations or failures.[55] Abandonment is nothing other than these words of Jesus, "The one who loves me is the one who loves my will." Fr. d'Elbée has taught people of all ages and vocations this path and has found them all open to this doctrine, this way of life, "receiving it as the earth in springtime drinks the dew from heaven."[56]

## B. The Power of the Sacrament of the Present Moment

Where peace of heart is the absolutely necessary precondition for listening to the Holy Spirit, the sacrament of the present moment is the living in the moment that opens our hearts so as to receive the infilling of God's grace. If we are not in the present moment, to use an automobile analogy, we have

---

[50] Ibid., 103.
[51] Ibid., 104.
[52] Ibid., 104-105.
[53] Ibid., 110.
[54] Jean-Pierre de Caussade, *Abandonment to Divine Providence*, 1, 3, 26.
[55] Jean d'Elbée, *I Believe in Love*, 110-112.
[56] Ibid., 112.

put the cap on the car gas tank; the gas can be poured but it is not received. In one sense, all spiritual life is lived out in the sacrament of the present moment. Whatever tools or aids we use, such as peace of heart, discernment of spirits, fidelity to duties of state of life, living joyfully, all are lived out through and in the sacrament of the present moment.

*The Difficulty in Receiving the Sacrament of the Present Moment*

How do we receive the sacrament of the present moment? We do the same as we would for any of the sacraments of the Church. With the sacrament of the Eucharist, when the priest or deacon offers it, we can choose to "receive" or not accept it; we only receive Christ and His grace if we accept to receive Him. As strange as this may seem, the heart of the spiritual life is living precisely this "receiving."

In His Sermon on the Mount in the Gospels, Jesus teaches us to receive by trusting in the Father's providence, that everything is already being prepared for those who love God:

> Therefore I tell you, do not be anxious about your life, what you shall eat, nor about your body, what you shall put on…. Consider the ravens: they neither sow nor reap, they have neither storehouse nor barn, and yet God feeds them. Of how much more value are you than the birds! And which of you by being anxious can add a cubit to his span of life? If then you are not able to do as small a thing as that, why are you anxious about the rest? Consider the lilies, how they grow; they neither toil nor spin; yet I tell you, even Solomon in all his glory was not arrayed like one of these. But if God so clothes the grass which is alive in the field today and tomorrow is thrown into the oven, how much more will he clothe you, O men of little faith!... For all the nations of the world seek these things; and your Father knows that you need them.[57]

There is no such thing as an accident or a coincidence in life. Everything that happens to us is allowed by God, has been prepared for us by God. It can be compared to a mother, who with great care about what she feeds her little baby, gently and lovingly spoon-feeds her beloved child. Anyone with eyes can see that a mother is very protective of her little child and will shield him or her if she senses any danger. With eyes of faith, we can see that, in

---

[57] Lk 12:22, 23-28, 30.

His great love for us, God the Father's protective arms are wrapped around us. Through the events of each day, that is, through the "present moments" of our life, God is feeding us, and we in turn respond by receiving this food, this "sacrament of the present moment." God is present with all His bountiful graces; but only in the present moment. St. Faustina found the "seal of eternity" in each hour that contained many treasures:

> O life so dull and monotonous, how many treasures you contain! When I look at everything with the eyes of faith, no two hours are alike, and the dullness and monotony disappear. The grace which is given me in this hour will not be repeated in the next. It may be given me again, but it will not be the same grace. Time goes on, never to return again. Whatever is enclosed in it will never change; it seals with a seal for eternity. (*Diary* 62)

If we understood the sacrament of the present moment, we might choose to call it the "gift" of the present moment, because we will see how God's gifts are all given through and in the present moment.

*"Today is a Gift: That's why we call it— the Present"*

Let us turn again to the movie *Kung Fu Panda* for another of its enlightening moments. An earlier scene from *Kung Fu Panda*, perhaps even more profound than the first, has to do with the panda at a moment of great desolation, a situation that we sometimes find ourselves in. After being chosen to be the dragon warrior, the panda proves to be totally inept, failing a test with the training instruments in the gym and in his sparring individually with the "Furious Five." In this scene, Master Oogway finds "Po," the panda, by the tree of wisdom and, with wise insight, perceives the reason why the panda is stuffing himself with peaches from the tree: "I see you eat when you are upset." The panda, with deep self-pity, finally admitted that he was upset, and that it was because he found out how totally useless and unfit he was for the task, and discovered to be so by the others. He woefully concluded: "Maybe I should just quit and go back to making noodles."

Master Oogway replied with much wisdom: "Quit! Don't quit! Noodles! Don't noodles! You are too concerned with what once was and what will be. Yesterday is History, Tomorrow is a Mystery, and Today is a Gift:

That's why we call it— the Present."[58] In this play of words, in English, we express "gift" by an alternative word, "present"; so that the "present" (moment) is a gift. When troubles come, we tend to lose sight of the present moment, as well as the powerful background of God's presence. Master Oogway's response applies here: "Yesterday is History, Tomorrow is a Mystery, and Today is a Gift: That's why we call it— the Present." First, we let go of the past, which is "history," and not anticipate the future, which is "mystery"; and we live in the "present," which is a gift and is where God is found.

This very movie scene was actually once employed by an experienced spiritual director to assist a priest directee who was troubled by a situation of concern that was weighing on his heart. After the spiritual director recounted this movie scene, the priest found himself calming down, and his worry shrinking back to the "mole-hill" that it really was and not the "mountain" it appeared to be. He was able to return to peace and the sacrament of the present moment. We note how returning to the present moment helped the panda return to his peace. If we set the little events within this planet, earth, against the serene and majestic orbiting of the planets, one sees the greater picture. God, who is transcendent and therefore all-powerful, is also immanent and looks after the course of our personal lives: "Do not worry about what you are to eat and drink." We make too much of little progress or lack of progress. Before difficulties, our reaction should be, "Quit! Don't quit! Noodles! Don't noodles!"

*Duty of the Present Moment*

To live out the sacrament of the present moment, one must fulfill the "duty of the present moment." An example that illustrates its centrality comes from an event in the life of Catherine de Hueck Doherty, foundress of Madonna House, and her emphasis on the "duty of the moment." A guest who was considering a vocation at Madonna House encountered Catherine Doherty leaving her hut and inquired where she was headed. As the account goes, Catherine replied that she was going to peel potatoes, which was her "duty of the present moment," the will of God that she was to fulfill at that hour. The woman in turn explained that she "felt inspired" to

---

[58] "Kung Fu Panda Quotes," IMDb, accessed August 31, 2015, ttp://www.imdb.com/title/tt0441773/quotes.

go and pray, abandoning her work (her true "duty of the present moment"). Catherine bluntly told her something to the effect that God inspired her to tell the woman that she should take a bus and leave Madonna House.

Being "incarnate" calls us to fulfill the foundation of doing the duties of our state of life or the duty of the present moment, something that Catherine Doherty took seriously and understood well. There was no room for candidates who did not understand this fundamental element of the spiritual life— to be led by God is to do His duty of the present moment. Fulfilling the "duty of the present moment" is the way we live out the sacrament of the present moment. This is how Fr. de Caussade describes it, linking it with the all-important will of God, as given in a modern translation.

> God still speaks as He spoke to our Fathers, when there were neither spiritual directors nor set methods. Then they saw that each moment brings with it a duty to be faithfully fulfilled. That was enough for spiritual perfection. On that duty their whole attention was fixed at each successive moment like the hand of a clock that marks the hours.[59]

## C. Pitfall: Fixated on Past and Future

The most common obstacle to living the sacrament of the present moment is perhaps flight into the past or into the future. We can ask ourselves, "where" we are when we go into the past and into the future. The answer is that we are thinking too much, we are living in our "heads." It is a journey into unreality, for past and future are not realities. There is no such thing as past as a reality, for the past is only a present moment that has passed; and there is no such thing as the future as a reality, the future is simply a present moment to come. The only thing that exists is each present moment, and God is present only in reality, that is, in the present moment. Therefore, to detach ourselves from the present, and to worry about past troubles or anticipate concerns about the future, about how things will work out, is to detach ourselves from reality and deprive ourselves of the graces of God.

---

[59] Jean-Pierre de Caussade, *Abandonment to Divine Providence*, I. I, 1, quoted in a modern translation (author uses Image Books version), Fr. Brian Mullady, "A Matter of Abandonment to Divine Providence," accessed June 29, 2015, http://www.cloisteredlife.com/2011/08/reflection-on-the-contemplative-life-2/

Let us see the contrast between the periods when we are troubled and when we are peacefully in the present moment. We can be taking a walk on a beautiful day, but if we have received some bad news, we will likely be oblivious to the beauty around us; trudging heavily with drooped shoulders, walking as it were with a cloud hanging over our heads, much like the "Pig-Pen" character in the *Peanuts* comic strip (by Charles M. Shultz), always with a cloud of dirt that constantly follows him. In this state, we are "living in our minds," as the expression goes, and the troubles in our mind are weighing down our hearts.

In contrast, if we have received wonderful news, we act very differently: we can smell the freshness of the dew on the grass, hear the birds singing and the crickets chirping, feel the warmth of the sun and the coolness of the breeze hitting our cheeks, soak in the sunshine, glory in the beauty of God's creation, and our hearts expand in gratitude for creation and for all that we have received. In short, our whole organism— our senses and sense faculties, body, and hearts— is *alive*; yet when we are troubled and are predominantly "living" in our minds, we are numb and our whole organism is not truly alive. There may be a parallel here to St. Ignatius' second rule (of the fourteen rules of discernment): for all who are moving toward God, in desolation, the evil spirit attacks us through the mind, while the good spirit inspires us through imagination and other faculties.

The greatest of all benefits of this sacrament of the present moment is that it enables us to open ourselves to receive God. The insights of St. John of the Cross here are remarkable. One of the benefits of living the sacrament of the present moment is that it prevents us from falling under the tyranny of emotions with roots from the past and from paralysis from worry about the future. The past, for example, can have the following influence: "The past in particular sinks roots into the psyche, and, as time passes, accumulates influence over the mind and emotions. It feeds aggression or lust or pride."[60] He understood the great importance of unhooking ourselves from the past and the future in order to possess the present, which is the work of hope.

> The build-up of anxiety or worry which problems and crises can cause a
> person in no way helps to bring about a better situation; rather, it

---

[60] Ibid., 106.

normally makes matters worse, and harms the person herself... It is obviously never any help getting anxious... To bear it all with calm, peace, tranquility, not only opens her to many blessings; it also helps her, in these difficulties themselves, to come to a better decision and to apply a remedy that will actually do some good.[61]

A far more important benefit arising from peace of heart is the opening of oneself to God. The following is a powerful disposition of St. John of the Cross:

> John knows only two realities: the present, and eternity. Hope pulls memory off the suction pads of yesterday and tomorrow, and cups it upwards in the present. "The sacrament of the present moment", it has been called. Eternity is bearing down, like an inverted triangle, upon one point in time only: now.[62]

There really are only two realities: the present and eternity. Hope, then, frees us from the past and future and "cups it upwards in the present," towards eternity. John of the Cross sees Mary as a perfect example of living the present moment. The text is profound and speaks for itself. "She moved freely, refusing to let herself be paralyzed by past or future. In her mountain climb, she renounced the need for pre-planned handholds, opting instead to surrender to the guidance, the hand of Another. Her hope set her free to be possessed in each present moment by 'the Holy Spirit.'"[63]

In other words, worrying results in the memory being turned downwards (concave). Instead of being preoccupied in getting many things done horizontally, one digs vertically into the present moment, to push through to eternity, to be turned upwards (convex). Living in the present moment makes this possible: "Eternity is bearing down, like an inverted triangle, upon one point in time only: now."[64] The abandoned soul does not allow the hours of the day to drain away like water draining in a sink, but lives in the arms of our Heavenly Father from hour to hour, finding eternity in each hour, preserving the water that is the Holy Spirit in the sink of our soul for the salvation of the world.

---

[61] St. John of the Cross, *Ascent of Mount Carmel*, Book 3, 6.3, quoted in Iain Matthew, *Impact of God*, 106-107.
[62] Iain Matthew, *Impact of God*, 107.
[63] Ibid.
[64] Ibid.

# CHAPTER 11

## *JOY*

### (*Presence of the Holy Spirit*)

> Cheerfulness is a sign of a generous and mortified person who forgetting all things, even herself, tries to please God in all she does for souls. Cheerfulness is often a cloak which hides a life of sacrifice, continual union with God, fervor, and generosity. A person who has this gift of cheerfulness very often reaches a great height of perfection. For God loves a cheerful giver and He takes close to His heart the religious He loves.[1] (Mother Teresa of Calcutta)

The child of the Father, as he assimilates the interior sentiments of Christ, seeks in particular to develop a deep joy. For joy constitutes a major disposition in Jesus' personality, though it may be harder to discern than some of His other attributes. For it is one of the fruits of the Holy Spirit, who overshadowed Him twice (at His conception and Baptism). At the Last Supper, John points to Jesus' joy, that is to become our destiny: "These things I have spoken to you, that my joy may be in you, and that your joy may be full" (Jn 15:11). Scripture also connects joy to Jesus' sacrifice, "who for the joy that was set before Him endured the cross, despising the shame…" (Heb 12:2). It is difficult to define joy. We commonly associate joy with cheerfulness, as a purely human consolation we experience when all is going well. Joy here, however, signifies a divine fullness of the Holy Spirit and is a sign of His presence, and that goes beyond peace of heart. And this joy is present both in times of happiness and in times of trial, as the apostles experienced: "Then they left the presence of the council, rejoicing that they were counted worthy to suffer dishonor for the name" (Acts 5:41). The text of Mother Teresa above highlights key aspects of a joyful soul: the generous and mortified soul seeks souls for Christ, its joy is a cloak for a life of sacrifice and union with God, often reaches heights of perfection, and pleases God. It indicates a certain self-forgetfulness that

---

[1] Mother Teresa of Calcutta, Explanation of the Original Constitutions, quoted in Brian Kolodiejchuk, *Mother Teresa: Come Be My Light: The Private Writings of the "Saint of Calcutta"*, 33.

rises above self-interest, and that keeps our eyes on God, with an assurance that we are loved and protected. It seeks to spread the sweet fragrance of the Holy Spirit and possesses the quality of drawing people to God. Joy is a requisite disposition for all new Christs. Through this fruit of the Holy Spirit, they are more easily led interiorly by the Holy Spirit and, at the same time, are protected from easy assault by the evil spirit.

This chapter will take the unusual step in portraying dimensions of joy in the life is a religious Sister, as she is a great inspiration of joy— Mother Teresa of Calcutta.[2] She has been chosen because she was a giant of the twentieth century who touched many people and presents a model for all. This chapter introduces Mother Teresa as a paradigm of joy, and then presents six joys of Mother Teresa through identification with different elements of our faith, drawing from other sources to elaborate each element. One possible resource for this theme of joy for priests is Cardinal Ratzinger's *Ministers of Joy: Scriptural Meditations on Priestly Spirituality*, a compilation of homilies. He covers many reasons for priestly joy, with some overlap of this chapter's content.

## 1. Paradigm of Joy: Mother Teresa of Calcutta

Mother Teresa of Calcutta established three fundamental pillars or virtues to be practiced by her spiritual daughters. Each year, in preparation for the renewal of their vows on their "Foundation Day" ("The Queenship of Mary," August 22), on the three consecutive days leading up to this feast day, conferences are given on the three pillars of "loving trust," "total surrender," and "joy". Given that joy constitutes one of the three pillars of her charism and that she constantly inculcated love of joy and cheerfulness in her religious daughters (she did not want to see long faces), let us look to her life and her charism to see if we can find in her a paradigm of joy, specifically from a recent work by one of her key collaborators, Fr. Brian Kolodiejchuk, M.C., *Mother Teresa: Come Be My Light*.[3]

---

[2] Joseph Ratzinger, *Ministers of Joy: Scriptural Meditations on Priestly Spirituality*. We note another work by Ratzinger on joy, Pope Benedict XVI, *The Joy of Knowing Christ: Meditations on the Gospels* (Ijamsville, MA: Word Among Us Press, 2009).

[3] Brian Kolodiejchuk, *Mother Teresa: Come Be My Light*. He is a founding member of the Missionary of Charity Fathers, the postulator of the Cause of Beatification and Canonization of Mother Teresa, and director of the Mother Teresa Center.

When the process of canonization of Mother Teresa was opened and all her documents examined, facts previously undisclosed came out into the open. What was revealed was that Mother Teresa left the Loreto Congregation to go into the streets of Calcutta at the request of Jesus Himself through mystical revelations. On the train to Darjeeling, Mother Teresa first heard the call for this new mission, followed by a series of other mystical interventions by Jesus. Jesus expressed His great love of the poor in India and how "he wished to go into the holes" of their poor lives. To this end, He desired that she establish a congregation of nuns, and they would live out His command, "Come, be my light," among these poor ones. He wanted to reach out to touch them, but because of His present transfigured form, He wished to do so through their humanity— "carry me with you into them":

> 1947. "My little one, come, come, carry me into the holes of the poor. Come, be My light. I cannot go alone. They don't know Me so they don't want me. You come, go amongst them, carry Me with you into them. How I long to enter their holes, their dark, unhappy homes. Come, be their victim. In your immolation, in your love for Me, they will see Me, know Me, want Me. Offer more sacrifices, smile more tenderly, pray more fervently and all the difficulties will disappear."[4]

## 2. Six Joys in Mother Teresa's Identification with Christ

### A. Joy from Being One with the Father's Will

The child of God through Baptism seeks, like Jesus, to please the Father. Though she was unaware of it at the beginning, God the Father had a great plan for Mother Teresa. It entailed her leaving her family and her native Albania, going to Ireland for formation, and thereafter to India. There, as a Loreto religious, she received a further call: to found a new congregation of Sisters to care for the "poorest of the poor." The great turning point in her life may have been the crisis that arose from her reluctance and balking before this formidable task. She understood clearly what saying "yes" would entail, knowing the hardships that lay before her in the streets of Calcutta. Yet, after Jesus' appeal of love, she obeyed His direct call, and later would summarize her spirituality as always saying "yes" to Jesus: "A hearty 'yes' to

---

[4] Ibid., 98. The many distracting "dashes" in the original quotation have been replaced by commas for the sake of the reader.

Jesus and a big smile for everyone." This saying can be a motto for all new Christs.

We can develop further one dramatic instance of her conforming to the Father's will when on a visit to her Sisters in Tanzania (Chapter 6), the plane swerved off the runway into the waiting crowd and cut down two of her Sisters with the propeller. With the heavy burden of knowing that it was the plane that carried her that caused this carnage: "Mother Teresa knew that she was indirectly responsible, yet despite her immense pain, despite her being heartsick at the inadvertent tragedy and burdened by the pain all around her, as she left the plane and surveyed the agonizing scene, she simply whispered, *'God's will.'*"[5]

We can get a better picture of this conformity to the Father's will by also looking at the lives of saintly people. Saints, in conforming to God's will, as a rule, go through great crosses, as they are called to bear the burdens of others, to "carry" others like spiritual parents. Many saints have experienced tremendous adversity especially toward the end of their lives, understanding this to be the culmination of their own sacrifice and the destruction of the seed that gives rise to the Resurrection: St. John of the Cross in the attacks and slander he endured at the end of his life; St. Augustine seeing the Barbarians laying siege to his city as he was dying; St. Catherine of Siena being tempted near the end of her life in seeing all her work as arising out of pride and self-will, as the Pope she helped bring to Rome himself turned against her; St. Alphonsus Liguori being expelled from the congregation he founded; St. Jeanne Jugan, foundress of the Little Sisters of the Poor, forced out of leadership and sent to beg on the street until her retirement; St. Maximilian Kolbe seeing all his work destroyed and his life taken away.[6]

But it appears that God may also be calling, not just individuals, but also certain groups to shoulder heavy burdens, a victimhood, which requires great faith to perceive and generosity to accept. An inspiring example of such conformity to God's will was by a Japanese doctor. He suffered the loss of his wife in the Nagasaki bombing, and yet saw it as a sacrifice,

---

[5] Joseph Langford, *Mother Teresa's Secret Fire: The Encounter That Changed Her Life, and How It Can Transform Your Own* (Huntington, IN: Our Sunday Visitor, 2008), 177.

[6] See Maria Winowska, *The Death Camp Proved Him Real: The Life of Father Maximilian Kolbe, Franciscan*.

requested primarily of the Catholics: "Was not Nagasaki the chosen victim, the lamb without blemish, slain as a whole burnt offering on an altar of sacrifice, atoning for the sins of all the nations during World War II?"

> I have heard that the atom bomb... was destined for another city. Heavy clouds rendered that target impossible, and the American crew headed for the secondary target, Nagasaki. Then a mechanical problem arose, and the bomb was dropped further north than planned and burst right above the cathedral... It was not the American crew, I believe, who chose our suburb. God's Providence chose Urakami and carried the bomb right above our homes. Is there not a profound relationship between the annihilation of Nagasaki and the end of the war? Was not Nagasaki the chosen victim, the lamb without blemish, slain as a whole burnt offering on an altar of sacrifice, atoning for the sins of all the nations during World War II? We are inheritors of Adam's sin... of Cain's sin. He killed his brother. Yes, we have forgotten we are God's children. We have turned to idols and forgotten love. Hating one another, killing one another, joyfully killing one another! At last the evil and horrific conflict came to an end, but mere repentance was not enough for peace.... We had to offer a stupendous sacrifice.... Cities had been leveled. But even that was not enough... Only this hansai [holocaust] on His altar... so that many millions of lives might be saved.

> How noble, how splendid, was that holocaust of midnight August 9, when flames soared up from the cathedral, dispelling darkness and bringing the light of peace [the emperor is said to have given his agreement in Tokyo for peace at the exact time the Urakami cathedral burst into flames]. In the very depths of our grief, we were able to gaze up to something beautiful, pure, and sublime. Happy are those who weep; they shall be comforted. We must walk the way of reparation... ridiculed, whipped, punished for our crimes, sweaty and bloody. But we can turn our minds to Jesus carrying his Cross up the hill to Calvary.... The Lord has given; the Lord has taken away. Blessed be the name of the Lord. Let us be thankful that Nagasaki was chosen for the whole burnt sacrifice! Let us be thankful that through this sacrifice, peace was granted to the world and religious freedom to Japan.[7]

This Japanese doctor was transformed by the grace from Calvary to bear his own Calvary and to cry out with joy: "In the very depths of our grief, we

---

[7] Dr. Takashi Nagai, *A Song for Nagasaki, Inside the Vatican*, Letter #37, 2010.

were able to gaze up to something beautiful, pure, and sublime," to express thanksgiving, because "peace was granted to the world and religious freedom to Japan."

The children of the Father can benefit from looking to the teachings of St. Faustina Kowalska to understand how someone like Mother Teresa was able to follow Jesus unreservedly. Her *Diary* is very insightful, as it contains many of Christ's instructions given, as it were, in a personal "spiritual direction." The key is that the Divine Mercy motto, "Jesus, I trust in you," is not trust in God generally, but trust in God's *divine mercy and love*. It is specifically the revelation of God's divine mercy that informed St. Faustina's faith and gave her a supernatural outlook on life and the gift of *abandonment*. The consequence was that, in a spirit of faith, St. Faustina perceived in each moment the unique treasures of divine grace and that we have already here on earth the beginning of eternal life in the human soul. She wanted to evaluate all events in life, especially difficult moments, and neighbours, *in the spirit of faith, to see them as God sees them*. One biographer writes:

> The spirit of faith gradually led St. Faustina to a total surrender of her whole self to God. This total gift of self and of her autonomy arose from the conviction of the merciful love of the Heavenly Father, in whose protective arms we may peacefully place ourselves....
>
> ... Accepting everything from Him, she drew closer to Him through everything.... The desire to accept everything from the fatherly hand of God led Sister Faustina to complete abandonment in every circumstance in life.[8]

This abandonment to God and His will engendered in St. Faustina's heart is clearly manifested on various occasions:

> I accept everything that comes my way as given me by the loving will of God, who sincerely desires my happiness. And so I will accept with submission and gratitude everything that God sends me. (*Diary* 1549, 549)
>
> My most sweet Master.... I will put Your gifts to the best use of which my soul is capable. Living faith will support me. Whatever the form might

---

[8] *In St. Faustina's School of Trust*, 24-25.

be, under which You will send me Your grace, I will accept it as coming directly from You, without considering the vessel in which You send it. (*Diary* 1759, 624-625)

Even if I were to hear the most terrifying things about God's justice, I would not fear Him at all, because I have come to know Him well. God is love.... I have placed my trust in God and fear nothing. I have given myself over to His holy will; let Him do with me as He wishes, and I will still love Him. (*Diary* 589, 248)

A deliberate decision to close oneself to God's will, resulting in being "out of synch" with God's will, is what spiritual writers might call *resistance*, specifically, resistance to the Holy Spirit. Resistance has many forms: disobeying an instruction of a parent/teacher/superior/bishop; disobeying an injunction of the Church; not accepting a cross or a moral weakness; and trying to control the outcome of an event. When we resist God in some area, we become weighed down interiorly, even frustrated and resentful. The moment we are able to let go of our resistance, like Mother Teresa did before Jesus' request to go to the streets of Calcutta, we will immediately sense a transformation within us, and grace and peace seem to flood into our souls once more.

## B. Joy in her Personal Love for Jesus

Since her early childhood, Mother Teresa had a tender spousal love of Christ: "She discloses that Jesus was the first and only one to captivate her heart"; "From childhood the Heart of Jesus has been my first love"; "From the age of 5 ½ years, when first I received Him, the love for souls has been within. It grew with the years." A further stage of her love— by saying yes—her vow at thirty-six:

In the years following her final profession, Mother Teresa's passionate love for Jesus continued to prompt her to seek new and hidden ways of expressing her love. The most striking of these was an exceptional private vow she made in April 1942: "I made a vow to God, binding under [pain of] mortal sin, to give to God anything that He may ask, 'Not to refuse Him anything.'" God had been kindling in her an ever-greater intensity of love that moved her to make this magnanimous offering. Only later did she explain the reason for it: "I wanted to give God something very beautiful" and "without reserve." This vow, truly a folly of love, expressed

Mother Teresa's desire to "drink the chalice to the last drop" as she resolved to say "Yes" to God in all circumstances.[9]

When Mother Teresa balked initially at Jesus' call, Jesus appealed specifically to this love. Before her very natural fear, our Lord appeals to her spousal love for Him.

> *"Are you afraid now to take one more step for Your Spouse, for me, for souls? Is your generosity grown cold? Am I a second to you? You did not die for souls. That is why you don't care what happens to them. Your heart was never drowned in sorrow as was my Mother's. We both gave our all for souls, and you?... No, your vocation is to love and suffer and save souls and by taking the step you will fulfill My Heart's desire for you."*[10]

This personal love for Jesus entailed possessing the same love of the Sacred Heart of Jesus for the poor East Indians.

> *"I want Indian nuns, Missionaries of Charity, who would be my fire of love amongst the very poor, the sick, the dying, the little children. The poor I want you to bring them to me, and the Sisters that would offer their lives as victims of My love would bring these souls to Me. You are, I know, the most incapable person, weak and sinful, but just because you are that, I want to use you for My glory. Will thou refuse.... Little one, give Me souls. Give Me the souls of the poor little street children. How it hurts, if you only knew, to see these poor children soiled with sin. I long for the purity of their love. If you would only answer My call and bring Me these souls. Draw them away from the hands of the evil one. If you only knew how many little ones fall into sin every day."*[11]

*Taking upon ourselves the sufferings of Mother Church*

Before this inspiring example of Mother Teresa, the children of the Father might ask what obstacle to growth they might find in themselves. Blessed Columba Marmion, from his vast experience of spiritual direction, points this out well in a letter written to a spiritual directee.

> We become so to speak one with Him, *when we take upon us, with Him, all the sorrows, the sighings, the sufferings of Holy Church and intercede in the name of all, full of confidence in His Infinite merits.* When we act thus habitually, we go out of ourselves, we forget our own little sorrows and annoyances and we

---

[9] Brian Kolodiejchuk, *Mother Teresa: Come Be My Light*, 28-29.
[10] Ibid., 96-97.
[11] Ibid., 49.

think much more about God and souls. In return, God thinks of us and fills us with His grace: "Give and it shall be given to you: good measure and pressed down and shaken together and running over shall they give into your bosom."

My dear child, I am speaking to you in this way because the more I see of religious, both men and women, the more I am convinced that the great cause of their troubles is that most of them think too much of themselves, and too little of Jesus and souls. If they could once and for all go out of themselves and consecrate their whole life to Jesus and souls, their hearts would become wide as the ocean; they themselves would fly upon the path of perfection: "I have run the way of Thy commandments when Thou didst enlarge my heart."[12] (emphasis added)

It is in this that the author highlights the greatest obstacle of the spiritual life. Christ is the shepherd who left the 99 in heaven to seek the lost sheep. His entire life was one of self-forgetfulness as he took upon Himself the burden and sins of all humanity. For the new Christ, the greatest tragedy is self-absorption or self-interest in one form or another. For example, we often tend to be obsessed by our spiritual progress or lack thereof, our physical ailments, present crises; the list goes on. We have within ourselves an innate propensity to revert back to self over and over again, the way a magnetic compass points to the earth's magnetic poles. If we want to make progress in the spiritual life, we have to go out of ourselves: "seek first the kingdom of God and the rest will be given to you"— the two great commandments of love of God and of neighbour must dominate our horizon. Dom Marmion points out the vital law of spiritual life: we "go out of ourselves, we forget our own little sorrows and annoyances and we think much more about God and souls"; and then "In return, God thinks of us and fills us with His grace."

There are two basic approaches in seeking to grow in holiness: the more common way of growing through virtue and spirituality (e.g., working on moral weakness, seeking greater fidelity to prayer and devotions, perhaps daily Mass and frequent Confession, etc.); and the less common path of seeking to love Jesus and to seek the salvation and welfare of His flock as the main horizon, while striving to grow in individual virtues. The first way tends to lead to turning to self, the second way is the way of the saints.

---

[12] Columba Marmion, *Union with God*, 130-131.

Here are two examples of Dom Marmion's teaching being lived out. There was the case of an Augustinian priest who, while celebrating Mass at a parish had a mild heart attack, and was taken by ambulance to the hospital. Some three months later, on meeting for the first time since his heart attack, a young visiting diocesan priest enquired solicitously about his condition, after which he concluded: "Father Henry, I guess you have to take it easier now and be careful with your heart." This remarkable older priest responded in a wise and paternal manner: "I have learnt one thing: I take care of Jesus and He takes care of me."

One supposes that he was indeed being prudent, taking the necessary medicine and following his doctor's instructions. But in doing so, he was not allowing himself to be caught by secondary aspects, like health, and kept his primary attention on Jesus' children in the world; like Dom Marmion taught, in doing this, Jesus would look after his health. A newly ordained diocesan priest made this very pact with Jesus: he would look after Jesus' flock; Jesus would look after his family. This meant practically that, from that moment on, the priest would put their cares into Jesus' hands, not even praying for them, and expecting Jesus to grant much grace to them. Jesus did indeed surprise him; among the blessings was the entry into the Church of his parents a year before his father died. In contrast to this was the action of a newly ordained priest who asked to be moved to a parish close to his widowed mother on two consecutive occasions within the first years of his priesthood. An older parish priest said it was not a good sign for a young priest, who indeed soon after left the priesthood.

## C. Joy from Being One with Jesus as His Presence ("Come, be my Light")

Jesus asked Mother Teresa to live the call, "Come, be my light." To do this, she had to unite herself to Christ in holiness and become Christ's "other self" in the world. To live "Come, be my light" entailed allowing Jesus' radiance to shine through her; it would involve a transformation into Christ. But how is this possible if Jesus alone is the Light? Scripture teaches us in the Gospel of John that Jesus, and only Jesus, is the Word of God Himself, and thus the light of the world: "In him was life, and the life was the light of men" (Jn 1:4); "I am the light of the world; he who follows me will not walk in darkness, but will have the light of life" (Jn 8:12).

How then can Jesus ask Mother Teresa, "Come, be my light," if only Jesus is the light of the world? Jesus' teaching clearly indicates in the Gospels that we are to be His light: "You are the light of the world. A city set on a hill cannot be hid. Nor do men light a lamp and put it under a bushel, but on a stand, and it gives light to all in the house. Let your light so shine before men, that they may see your good works and give glory to your Father who is in heaven" (Mt 5:14-16). Jesus Himself is sending Christians to the world as His light, and therefore, she too can be a light to the world.

How this is possible is found in a critical distinction. To be Jesus' light, Mother Teresa must allow Jesus to be the "light": she is to be a "lamp" that carries the light or allows the light to shine in her. As a lamp carrying Jesus the light, while He asked her to "Come, be my light," to take Him into the holes of the poor, it was not she who was to touch them but He through her. She was to carry Jesus to them, a critical distinction.

> Jesus had promised her that *he himself would be the one to touch the poor through her*. In imitation of Mary, she was called to a life of such union with her Lord as to "be his" on souls. For this, holiness and oneness with Christ would become her all-consuming goal— so to allow Jesus to live his own life in her among the poor. This required a deep interior life, the diligent practice of prayer, and the total surrender and sacrifice of self— precisely that it might be "he and not she" doing the work. This union was constantly nourished by Jesus' special presence in the Eucharist, received in Communion and adored in silent prayer. From there she went out, carrying him and caring for him at the Calvary of his mystical body.[13] (emphasis mine)

The secret to being Christ's light, therefore, is not ministry itself, the going out, but holiness of life, union with Jesus, through a deep interior life— total surrender of self, communion with Jesus through the Eucharist— so that she can carry Jesus to the mystical body. Her power lay in simply being the "pure instrument" of Christ and nothing else— this is holiness.

This union with Christ is for the sake of "identification," to become Christ's other self. We see this journey lived out in the saints we have

---

[13] Joseph Langford, *Mother Teresa: The Light of Love*, Catholic Education Resource Center, accessed September 4, 2015, http://www.catholiceducation.org/en/faith-and-character/faith-and-character/mother-teresa-of-calcutta-the-light-of-love.html.

examined, a journey elaborated upon by authors like St. Teresa of Jesus, St. John of the Cross, Concepción Cabrera de Armida, and St. John Eudes. It mirrors what we have seen in Blessed Dina Bélanger's "Substitution of Christ." As described earlier in this book, David Perrin notes that St. John of the Cross understands that this transformation into God is the goal of the spiritual life, becoming the "new man" of Paul (the "new self," as Perrin describes it).[14] Thus, God Himself as Love enters the world once again through the "new self" (we have used "new Christ") This is what took place in Mother Teresa, as she became Christ's light for India, and for the world.

The transformation of union is an identification with Jesus. Concepción Cabrera de Armida (Conchita), teaches us what dispositions are needed in our hearts to become one with Jesus: "The Lord wants me to take a closer look at Him, to make Him the only target of all my aspirations... to live all His life... without wanting anything more than Him... Without speaking, nor thinking nor feeling, with a union of wills, like Him... in Him... for Him... and through Him."[15] This is what it means to become Christ, to do everything with Him and for Him. St. John Eudes teaches this same truth, one that is very Pauline:

> He belongs to you, but more than that, he longs to be in you, living and ruling in you, as the head lives and rules in the body. He desires that whatever is in him may live and rule in you: his breath in your breath, his heart in your heart, all the faculties of his soul in the faculties of your soul.... you ought to be in him as the members are in the head. All that is in you must be incorporated into him. You must receive life from him and be ruled by him.... Let him be the only source of your movements, of the actions and the strength of your life....

> Finally, you are one with Jesus as the body is one with the head. You must, then, have one breath with him, one soul, one life, one will, one mind, one heart. And he must be your breath, heart, love, life, your all. These great gifts in the follower of Christ originate from baptism.... Through the holy Eucharist they are brought to perfection.[16]

---

[14] David B. Perrin, *For Love of the World*, 94-95.
[15] Concepción Cabrera de Armida, *Account of Conscience*, Vol. 22, 378 (May 27, 1906), quoted in Gustavo Garcia-Siller, *Transforming Prayer for Pilgrims*, 29.
[16] St. John Eudes, *Treatise on the Admirable Heart of Jesus* 1.5, OOR on Memorial of St. John Eudes, August 19, *The Liturgy of the Hours*, vol. IV, 1331-133a2.

Here finally we find a more detailed depiction of the program for a child of God the Father to develop so as to become a new Christ (note the similarity to Blessed Dina Bélanger's "Substitution of Christ" and the importance of the Eucharist). It is important to note here, and elsewhere in the Church's teaching and Tradition, that the language used is not merely symbolic. Rather, it describes a reality that is divine, and therefore full of mystery, and to be taken not so much literally but with awe and a childlike openness to new revelation and a new journey in God. The text of St. John Eudes can serve as a rule of life for the religious and priests as well.

## D. Joy in Quenching Jesus' Thirst for Souls by Identification with the Cross

Jesus preaches that those who mourn are blessed, *"Blessed are those who mourn."* The fourth element of faith we find in Mother Teresa is her identification with the poor in India in their poverty and darkness:

> She was called to share in a distinct way in the mystery of the Cross, to become one with Christ in His Passion and one with the poor she served. Through this sharing she was led to a deep awareness of the "painful thirst" in the Heart of Jesus for the poorest of the poor.

> The darkness she experienced and described in her letters, in which the strength and beauty of her soul shines forth, was a terrible and unrelenting torment. In the lives of the saints, it is almost without parallel; only the experience of St. Paul of the Cross is comparable in length.[17]

The key to this is the desire to share in Christ's painful "thirst," a spirituality of quenching Christ's thirst on the cross, so central that, in each chapel of all Missionary of Charity houses in the world, the words of Jesus are found below the crucifix, "I thirst."

*Dark Night: Identification with the Poor*

Mother Teresa had to "identify" with Christ's poor in material poverty and spiritual darkness. Once she began her new mission in the streets of Calcutta, she began to experience a heavy and burdensome darkness within her soul, that reminds us of the dark night of the spirit described by St.

---

[17] Brian Kolodiejchuk, *Come Be My Light*, 335.

John of the Cross. In this state of alienation and darkness, she felt no fervour, and did not sense God's pleasure but rather His apparent abandonment of her. She struggled greatly to understand and accept this darkness. After ten years of enduring this burden, Fr. Joseph Neuner, her new spiritual director, was able to shed light by explaining that this darkness was a part of her mission. She wrote in her letters to Fr. Joseph Neuner that she felt like an "ice box" interiorly, devoid of any feelings of God's presence, living in interior darkness, as if God had abandoned her.

Through Fr. Neuner, she came to see that it was Christ's darkness and pain that she was sharing and it was for the sake of her people. The Son of God, to help us, did not simply bless us from heaven but descends from heaven to "identify" with us, to become one with us and our troubles, taking them upon Himself— this is the way of divine love. This was also the way of Mother Teresa. Mother Teresa had to carry India as her "child," and bring her to God. This requires identification, becoming "one" with India, in both India's material poverty and India's lack of Christ's light. Thus Mother Teresa's life had to be marked by both material poverty and spiritual darkness. She lived with this interior darkness for fifty or so years, until just before her death.

She also came to know the power of this suffering for the work of her Sisters. The people they served were in darkness and at the cross: "The same great crowd—they were covered in darkness. Yet I could see them. Our Lord on the Cross. Our Lady at a little distance from the Cross— and myself as a little child in front of her."[18] In the following revealing text, the Sisters would be given to see that, as Jesus identified with us in our darkness, they too would have to identify, to be one, with the darkness of the people they served:

> My dear children— without our suffering, our work would just be social work, very good and helpful, but it would not be the work of Jesus Christ, not part of the redemption.— Jesus wanted to help us by sharing our life, our loneliness, our agony and death. All that He has taken upon Himself, and has carried it in the darkest night. Only by being one with us He has redeemed us. We are allowed to do the same: all the desolation of the poor people, not only their material poverty, but their spiritual destitution

---

[18] Ibid., 99.

must be redeemed, and we must have our share in it.— Pray thus when you find it hard— "I wish to live in this world which is so far from God, which has turned so much from the light of Jesus, to help them—to take upon me something of their suffering."—Yes, my dear children—let us share the sufferings— of our poor—for only by being one with them— we can redeem them, that is, bringing God into their lives and bringing them to God.[19]

This became a joy for Mother Teresa. She marvelled at God's love for the poor in India, and she longed to identify with Christ in His passion for India.[20] Here is the apex of the spiritual life that mirrors Christ's passion.

*Link between Joy and Suffering in "Com-passion"*

Nonetheless, suffering is a great mystery that confounds most people. It is important, therefore, to understand that this is Gospel teaching and the pattern established by Christ Himself, one that all His "friends" are familiar with. To examine this Christian wisdom further, let us turn to Pope Benedict XVI's commentary on "Blessed are the poor in spirit." In his outstanding scholarly yet accessible scriptural work, *Jesus of Nazareth*, Pope Benedict XVI speaks of the link between joy and suffering for Jesus' sake and for the sake of His people. In the commentary on the Beatitude, "Blessed are those who mourn," he speaks of how "blessed" are those who mourn in "*compassio*," in "suffering with" (*cum-passio*) others.

> Tradition has yielded another image of mourning that brings salvation: Mary standing under the Cross with her sister, the wife of Clopas, with Mary Magdalene, and with John (Jn 19: 25ff). Once again, as in the vision of Ezekiel, we encounter here the small band of people who remain true in a world full of cruelty and cynicism or else with fearful conformity. *They cannot avert the disaster, but by "suffering with" the one condemned (by their com-passion in the etymological sense) they place themselves on his side, and by their "loving with" they are on the side of God, who is love.* This "com-passion" reminds us of the magnificent saying in St. Bernard of Clairvaux's commentary on the Song of Songs (sermon 26, n. 5): "Impassibilis est Deus, sed non impassibilis"— God cannot suffer, but can "suffer *with*." At the foot of

---

[19] Ibid., 220.
[20] For deeper insight into Mother Teresa's darkness, see Carol Zaleski, "The Dark Night of Mother Teresa," *First Things* (May 2003). Carol Zaleski is a professor of religion at Smith College in Northampton, Massachusetts.

Jesus' Cross we understand better than anywhere else what it means to say "blessed are those who mourn, for they shall be comforted." Those who do not harden their hearts to the pain and need of others, who do not give evil entry to their souls, but suffer under its power and so acknowledge the truth of God— *they are the ones who open the windows of the world to let the light in.* It is to those who mourn in this sense that great consolations are promised. The second Beatitude is thus intimately connected with the eighth: "Blessed are those who are persecuted for righteousness' sake, for theirs is the kingdom of heaven" (Mt 5:10).[21] (emphasis mine)

Thus, for Pope Benedict XVI, suffering with others and suffering our own crosses open us to great consolations and "open the windows of the world to let the light in." This insight may have arisen from the experiences of his own suffering in Nazi Germany and in being attacked in his office as Prefect of the Sacred Congregation of the Doctrine of Faith. Further on, commenting on "Blessed are you when they persecute you," he continues with the idea that joy and reward accompany the identification with Christ:

The Beatitude concerning the persecuted contains, in the words that conclude the whole passage, a variant indicating something new: Jesus promises joy, exaltation, and a great reward to those who for his sake are reviled, and persecuted, and have all manner of evil uttered falsely against them (cf. Mt 5:11). The "I" of Jesus himself, fidelity to his person, becomes the criterion of righteousness and salvation.[22]

This constitutes an overturning of the world's standard— which would never associate suffering with joy— a new wisdom.

The truth of this teaching was highlighted by St. Escrivá, when he looked back upon the hammer blows he had received in earlier years:

When God sent me those blows back in 1931, I didn't understand them... Then all at once, in the midst of such great bitterness, came the words: "You are my son (Ps 2:7), you are Christ." And I could only stammer: "*Abba, Pater! Abba, Pater! Abba! Abba! Abba!*" Now I see it with new light, like a new discovery, just as one sees, after years have passed, the hand of

---

[21] Pope Benedict XVI, *Jesus of Nazareth: From the Baptism in the Jordan to the Transfiguration* (New York: Doubleday, 2007), 87.
[22] Ibid., 90.

God, of divine Wisdom, of the All-Powerful. You've led me, Lord, to understand that to find the Cross is to find happiness, joy. And I see the reason with greater clarity than ever: to find the Cross is to identify oneself with Christ, to be Christ, and therefore to be a son of God.[23]

St. Escrivá in those early years, as his biographies would later reveal, endured much privation, calumny, and suspicion. The revelation of God as Father and our divine filiation allowed him to accept the cross in identification with Christ in this striking statement: "You've led me, Lord, to understand that to find the Cross is to find happiness, joy"; to identify himself with, and even to become, Christ for the world.

The Christian wisdom built on Christ's Beatitude, "Blessed are those who mourn," does not signify repression of human good or happiness. Christian wisdom goes further than limited superficial pleasure: it experiences a synthesis between happiness and renunciation. All that God has made is "good," and the Christian recognizes the goodness of creation, as the Book of Genesis teaches us. Man is made for joy, but *he renounces good gifts for an even greater gift and happiness.* One author, Fr. Segundo Galilea, describes this synthesis clearly and succinctly.[24]

---

[23] John F. Coverdale, *Uncommon Faith: The Early Years of Opus Dei* (Princeton, NJ: Scepter, 2002), Ch. 6.

[24] Segundo Galilea, *Temptation and Discernment* (Washington, DC: ICS Publns., 1996), 77-80: "Christian mystics and many believers have discovered the rather elusive synthesis of happiness and renunciation. Happiness is perhaps the most essential thing of the human being's vocation, *we were made for joy, and God wills it for us, not only in heaven, but also here on earth* within the limitations of our human condition and always in a way that does not endanger our eternal happiness. Yet God also calls for many forms of renunciation, of self-denial, and He commands us to take up our cross each day (see Lk 14:27, 35). Poverty, austerity, and mortification are values of the Christian way. But the synthesis can only be understood from the *experience of faith.* To begin with, one can only be happy if one has a good conscience, and sometimes renunciation and mortification of what gives pleasure is necessary to avoid sin, immorality, vices, or imperfections of an interior freedom still subject to servitude. Any slavery is dehumanizing, and what is dehumanizing does not give pleasure. But beyond this avoiding sin, there is also the Christian understanding of giving up legitimate pleasures. It does not preclude the very healthy Christian understanding towards the goodness and gift of life and the happiness and joys God offers, involving a love of creation and a grateful recognition that all is a gift from God. What we are speaking of here, seen in the experience of the saints, is an undertaking of austerity, denial of self, and mortification for a *Greater Happiness.*" (emphasis mine)

The saint or spiritual person finds here and now greater happiness in poverty than in riches, in austerity than in legitimate well-being, in foregoing a pleasure rather than in enjoying it.

… To be Christian all renunciation proceeds from a great love for the poor and crucified Jesus. It is the love to give oneself and be identified with Jesus that causes this happiness to be greater than the pleasure foregone, not renunciation or mortification for its sake.

The joyful experience of *giving something to God out of pure love, imitating very poorly the completely gratuitous gift of love God makes to us, is inexplicable for those who have not begun to fall in love with Jesus crucified….*

Christian renunciation is not inhuman. It situates us at the heights of humanism, whose essential premise tells us that *we find human happiness in love, encountering greater happiness in greater love.* The love with which we make the renunciation or mortification, growth in love for God, and the happiness it gives us are the most important criteria for discerning its legitimacy and appropriateness.[25] (emphasis mine)

Fr. Galilea calls Christian renunciation the "heights of humanism," which entails giving out of pure love and being identified with our beloved Crucified Christ. *Love is the key* to the cross.

Crosses include misunderstandings, persecutions, false accusations, suffering judgments, etc., as we see in the life of Mother Teresa.

At this point in life, Mother Teresa even drew spiritual joy from her interior trail: Here was "the joy of having nothing," of "absolute poverty," of the "poverty of the Cross" to which she had been aspiring from the beginning.

… Mother Teresa was pleased to see her followers share in her "joy of suffering for God's poor." As her prolonged spiritual aridity continued, she willingly accepted being deprived of consolations while helping her sisters to "feast" on them. God was using her as a channel to pour His love on His children.[26]

---

[25] Ibid., 79.
[26] Brian Kolodiejchuk, *Come Be My Light*, 228.

St. Faustina supports this vision, as she writes in a similar vein:[27]

> I have come to see that if the will of the Heavenly Father was fulfilled in
> this way in His well-beloved Son, it will be fulfilled in us in exactly the
> same way: by suffering, persecution, abuse, disgrace. It is through all this
> that my soul becomes like unto Jesus. And the greater the sufferings, the
> more I see that I am becoming like Jesus. This is the surest way. If some
> other way were better, Jesus would have shown it to me. Sufferings in no
> way take away my peace. On the other hand, although I enjoy profound
> peace, that peace does not lessen my experience of suffering. Although
> my face is often bowed to the ground, and my tears flow profusely, at the
> same time my soul is filled with profound peace and happiness.... (*Diary*
> 1394, 497)

This is an outstanding depiction of the link between cross and identification
with Christ. If examined, it can be discerned in our experience of everyday
life that, when trials come, and we learn to bear it, in time we shall see great
fruits and graces given.

In the trials of life, one is tempted with discouragement and even despair.
Perhaps we can give the last word in this section to Julian of Norwich's
famous reassurance from Christ that "all shall be well."

> It seemed to me if sin had not existed, we would all have been pure and
> like our Lord, as he made us. Thus, in my folly, before this time, I often
> wondered why, by the great foreseeing wisdom of God, the beginning of
> sin had not been prevented, for then, I thought, all would have been well.
> This stirring definitely ought to have been given up; nevertheless, I
> mourned and sorrowed on its account without reason or discretion. But
> Jesus, who in this vision informed me of all I needed to know, answered
> in these words, saying, "Sin is necessary but all shall be well, and all shall
> be well, and all manner of things shall be well."[28]

---

[27] Other texts emphasize the point further:
"This day is so special for me; even though I encountered so many sufferings, my
soul is overflowing with great joy." (*Diary* 916, 356).
"Oh, how misleading are appearances, and how unjust the judgments. Oh, how
often virtue suffers only because it remains silent. To be sincere with those who
are incessantly stinging us demands much self-denial. One bleeds, but there are no
visible wounds. O Jesus, it is only on the last day that many of these things will be
made known. What joy - none of our efforts will be lost!" (*Diary* 236, 117).

[28] Julian of Norwich, *Showing of Love*, ed. Julia B. Holloway (The Liturgical Press), Ch.27.

## E. Joy in Being One with the Eucharistic Jesus

To understand Blessed Teresa of Calcutta, we have to understand the power of the Mass in her life. It begins with a "deeply contemplative stance," to be "professionals in prayer," for love of Jesus.

> It was a deeply contemplative stance. Her sisters were to be "professionals in prayer" who sought to serve Christ by serving his poor. And they were not simply social workers. "It is the presence of Christ which guides us," she explained. To a man who once saw her cleaning the wounds of a leper and said, "I wouldn't do that for a million dollars," Mother Teresa replied, "Neither would I. But I would gladly do it for Christ."[29]

These sentences give us some idea of the sacrifice her work entailed. Yet what was it that gave her strength to do this? She herself reveals her secret to us. In an interview with journalist from *TIME* magazine, when asked, "Why have you been so successful?", she pointed to the Mass and Adoration: "Jesus made Himself the bread of life to give us life. That's where we begin the day, with Mass. And we end the day with Adoration of the Blessed Sacrament. I don't think that I could do this work for even one week if I didn't have four hours of prayer every day."[30] In fact, in the very first section of the Constitutions of her community is inscribed the injunction that her Sisters are to participate at Mass, and only then proceed to serve the poor. We can add that she also tells the journalist that another motivation was to see Christ in the poor.

Those serving Christ in carrying the burdens of His people should never be discouraged because they are all-powerful by uniting themselves with Christ's sacrifice on Calvary. We find something of this in Fr. Teilhard de Chardin, as he describes the desire to be transformed into Christ, which is accomplished by the Eucharist ("fiery bread"). In his most popular essay, "Mass of the world," as he stands on the soil of China, he makes all the world his altar and at the Offertory of the Mass, offers all the labours and sufferings of the world. This is also found in his book, *Hymn of the Universe.*

---

[29] James Martin, "My Life with Mother Teresa," accessed July 2, 2015,
http://www.jameslau88.com/my_life_with_mother_teresa_by_james_martin.htm.
[30] Edward T. Desmond, "Interview with Mother Teresa," The National Catholic Register, accessed July 2, 2015, http://www.servelec.net/mothertheresa.htm.

First of all I shall stretch out my hand unhesitatingly towards the fiery bread which you set before me…. This bread, in which you have planted the seed of all that is to develop in the future, I recognize as containing the source and the secret of that destiny you have chosen for me. To take it is, I know, to surrender myself to forces which will tear me away painfully from myself in order to drive me into danger, into laborious undertakings, into a constant renewal of ideas, into an austere detachment where my affections are concerned. To eat it is to acquire a taste and an affinity for that which in everything is above everything — a taste and an affinity which will henceforward make impossible for me all the joys by which my life has been warmed. Lord Jesus, I am willing to be possessed by you, to be bound to your body and led by its inexpressible power towards those solitary heights which by myself I should never dare to climb.[31]

As with Teilhard de Chardin, the Eucharist allows the new Christ to be possessed by Christ, to be stretched, "to surrender myself to forces which will tear me away painfully from myself in order to drive me into danger, into laborious undertakings…." In the previous section, we had discussed the joys of identification with Christ's cross for the world, now we find the source of that strength, the "perpetuation" or "re-presentation" of Calvary in the Mass.

## Note for Priests

Because the priest carries a special burden in serving God's people, let us add a note to console him in joy. Cardinal Ratzinger, in a profound meditation on Psalm 16 (in the fifth verse that was recited when he received tonsure), makes a link between God as the priest's inheritance, linking it with the cross, and ending with the culmination of the Eucharist as the priest's great inheritance on earth. He begins by contrasting the 11 tribes of Israel, whose relationship with Yahweh is built upon a secular inheritance of land. But the unique tribe of Levites, who lack this concrete expression of attachment to God through ownership of the Promised Land, instead has God: "The Lord is the portion of my inheritance and of my cup: it is

---

[31] Pierre Teilhard de Chardin, *Hymn of the Universe* (London: Collins, 1965), 28-29.

thou that wilt restore my inheritance to me.'[32] The fruit is "Directly and uniquely he [Levite] is thrown into dependence on Yahweh alone and immediately, as we are told in Psalm 22 (verse 11)."[33]

This spiritualizing of the Law points towards the New Testament and Christ and truly roots God as the new "land" and the "inheritance" of the New Testament priest.

> What is important for us about this psalm is therefore on the one hand that it is a priestly prayer and on the other that here we can perceive the Old Testament's inward self-transcendence in the direction of Christ, the Old Covenant's approach to the New, and thus the unity of the history of our salvation. To live not from possessions but from worship means for this person praying to live in God's presence, to establish one's existence in inward approach to him…. Yahweh has thus become the "land" of the person…. "I keep the Lord always before me" (v. 8). The psalmist accordingly lives in the presence of God; he places himself continually before his face…. "because he is at my right hand." To go with God, to know he is at one's side, to be in his company, to look on him and let oneself be looked on by him…. To be a priest thus means to come to him, in his abode, and thus to learn to see: to abide in his abode.[34]

The path or cup will involve suffering, being "counselled" or "educated" by God, but the priest will come to see it as joy.

> "The Lord counsels me": my life now becomes a word from him. In this way this becomes true: "Thou dost show me the path of life" (Ps 16:11). Life ceases to be a dark riddle. We see how it goes. Living opens up, and in the middle of all tribulation of "being educated" it becomes joy. "Thy statues have been my songs," says Psalm 119 (verse 54), and here in Psalm 16 we find nothing different: "Therefore my heart is glad and my soul rejoices" (v. 9); "in thy presence there is fullness of joy, in thy right hand are pleasures for evermore" (v. 11).[35]

Finally, in interpreting the Lord as my "cup," he finds its fulfillment of the priest's inheritance in the Eucharist itself: "priestly life in the presence of God becomes actual as life in the eucharistic mystery."

[32] Joseph Ratzinger, *Ministers of Joy*, 111-112.
[33] Ibid., 113.
[34] Ibid., 114-115.
[35] Ibid., 117.

288

… Psalm 16 talks of the Lord as "my cup" (v. 5)…. The priest of the New Covenant praying this psalm can find expressed in this in a particular way that cup through which the Lord has most profoundly become our land: the eucharistic cup in which he distributes himself to us as our life. In this way the priestly life in the presence of God becomes actual as life in the eucharistic mystery. At the profoundest level the eucharist is the land that has become our portion and lot and of which we can say: "The lines have fallen for me in the pleasant places; yea, I have a goodly heritage."[36]

The result is that "At the profoundest level the eucharist is the land that has become our portion and lot." This is another aspect for priests to be "Ministers of Joy," the title of the compilation of homilies in this book.

## F. Joy from Being One with Our Lady

We find a particular vision of Mary's role in the experience of Mother Teresa of Calcutta. It is described in a beautiful work by one of her closest collaborators, who also co-founded the Missionaries of Charity Fathers, Fr. Joseph Langford, *Mother Teresa: In the Shadow of Our Lady*. Sharing Mother Teresa's mystical relationship with Mary sets Mary in an even greater connection; between Mother Teresa and the poor, and between the poor and the Crucified Jesus.

> Our Lady becomes a bridge both between Mother Teresa and the poor who cried out to her, and between the poor and the crucified Jesus who thirsted for them, who yearned to love and be loved by them.
>
> Our Lady says of the poor, *"They are mine."* Mother Teresa shared in our Lady's grace of motherhood toward the neediest of her children. She spent her life enclosed in our Lady's *"most pure heart,"* even as we see her *"enclosed"* by our Lady's arms in the third part of her vision:
>
> *With great love and trust stand with Our Lady near the Cross. What a gift of God….*[37]

Our Lady, as an extension of Jesus, claims the poor as her own: "They are mine." And by sharing our Lady's motherhood, in standing at the foot of

---

[36] Ibid., 119.
[37] Fr. Joseph Langford, *Mother Teresa: In the Shadow of Our Lady*, 22-23.

the "Calvaries" in the world, Mother Teresa was enclosed in our Lady's "most pure heart" and by her arms— what a tender vision. He adds a particular point for those of us who feel fear and lack of strength to carry out our work of evangelization. He explains that Mother Teresa sees that John has run away at the Garden of Gethsemane like the rest of the apostles, but it was in meeting our Lady that he found strength to stand at the cross.

> In her [Mary] he found a love, a strength, and a serenity that surpassed his own, and a heart to open his own to the words he alone among the Twelve would hear. Our Lady brought John to faithfulness, and to witness the thirst of her Son. This is what she did for Mother Teresa. This is what she offers to do for every disciple.
>
> …. Without an intimate relationship with Our Lady, the command to pick up our cross daily and follow the Lord will prove too difficult and demanding.[38]

For us, we must have the three elements that make up our mission: the poor (materially and spiritually), the crucified Christ who stands with the poor, and our Lady; we now in turn seek to satiate Christ's, "I thirst." We wish to imitate Mother Teresa in following this path: "So the cycle of grace is completed. Surrounded by the poor, Mother Teresa stands with our Lady before Jesus crucified."[39]

In treating of consecration to Mary, Fr. Joseph Langford makes a beautiful analogy between the path of St. Juan Diego and Mother Teresa of Calcutta, setting St. Juan Diego's as a paradigm for Mother Teresa. He notes that Mary asks Juan Diego to bring the roses to her so that she could arrange them in his *tilma* (cloak worn by native Americans) before he presented it to the bishop. Likewise, our Lady arranges Mother Teresa's life and work. The tremendous trust that our Lady asks of him, of Mother Teresa, and of us inspires a great joy.

> Mother Teresa allowed our Lady to prepare and arrange all within and around her, and she entrusted her entire future to her care. This is why, though she faced trials and problems of every kind, Mother Teresa never

---

[38] Ibid., 24.
[39] Ibid., 25.

worried. All was left to our Lady, the one who had said so tenderly to Juan Diego:

"Listen and keep in your heart, my littlest one: there is nothing for you to fear, let nothing afflict you. Let not your face or your heart be worried. Do not fear this sickness or any other illness. Let nothing worry or afflict you. Am I not here, I who am your mother? Are you not in my shadow, under my protection? Am I not the fountain of your joy? Are you not in the folds of my mantle, in my crossed arms? Is there anything else you need? Don't let anything afflict you or perturb you."[40]

We too who serve Christ hear with joy the same words: "Am I not here, I who am your mother? Am I not the fountain of your joy? Are you not in the folds of my mantle, in my crossed arms?" Mother Teresa wrote these words to someone facing disappointment and hardship: "Don't be afraid. Put your hand in our Lady's hand and walk with her."[41]

*Conclusion*

Though Mother Teresa of Calcutta is a woman and religious, her six "joys" can serve as a template or inspiration for all baptized and also religious and priests. They mirror what we are called to be in our life as sons and daughters of God and also in the lives of consecrated souls like Mother Teresa. The key to joy is not what we commonly expect, "receiving gifts" from Jesus or "acquiring" virtue or talents. It is rather Mother Teresa's "losing herself" and experiencing loss in her life through six joys: in uniting oneself with the Father's will; in personal love for Jesus; in becoming His presence in the world; in quenching Jesus' thirst by identification with the crucified Christ for the sake of souls; in being one with the Eucharistic Jesus; and in being one with our Lady. "He who finds his life will lose it, and he who loses his life for my sake will find it" (Mt 10:39).

---

40 Ibid., 37.
41 Brian Kolodiejchuk, *Come Be My Light*, 290.

# CHAPTER 12

## *SPIRITUALITY OF COMMUNION*

### *(Crown of the Holy Spirit)*

God in His deepest mystery is not a solitude, but a family, since He has in Himself fatherhood, sonship, and the essence of the family, which is love. (Pope John Paul II)[1]

In his Apostolic Letter *Novo millennio ineunte* (January 6, 2001), Pope John Paul II gave the Church a "blueprint" for action in the Third Millennium: "To make the Church *the home and the school of communion*: that is the great challenge facing us in the millennium which is now beginning, if we wish to be faithful to God's plan and respond to the world's deepest yearnings."[2] In other words, the principal goal within this blueprint for the Third Millennium is to cultivate "a spirituality of communion." We find this goal mentioned also in his document, *Mane nobiscum Domine*,[3] and quoted by the Pontifical Council for Social Communications, *Ethics in Internet* (n. 5)— this is the program of the Church. The spirituality of communion converges with the heart of the New Testament, as we find, for example, in John's Gospel in Jesus' discourse on love at the Last Supper, the culmination of His teachings. There, the theme of love dominates within a Trinitarian background: "As the Father has loved me, so have I loved you; abide in my love.... This is my commandment, that you love one another as I have loved you. Greater love has no man than this, that a man lay down his life for his friends" (Jn 15:9, 12-13).

---

[1] Pope John Paul II, Homily at Mass on his apostolic journey, Puebla de Los Angeles (Mexico), Palafox Major Seminary, Sunday, 28 January 1979 (or see *Puebla: A Pilgrimage of Faith*, Boston: Daughters of St. Paul, 1979, 1986). Pope John Paul II has made this a central theme in his talks, like ad Limina visits of bishops (e.g., *Ad Limina* Address to the Bishops from Michigan and Ohio, "Fostering and Strengthening the Spirituality of Communion" (May 6, 2004), in *Origins* vol. 4, no. 1 (May 20, 2004) 13-14, and addressing some 100 bishop friends of the Focolare Movement March 13, 2003 at Castel Gandolfo, near Rome, attending a Congress on the "Spirituality of Communion: Ecclesial Unity and Universal Fraternity."
[2] Pope John Paul II, *Novo millennio ineunte*, n. 43. We can also look to *Tertio Millennio Adveniente* for more insights.
[3] Pope John Paul II, *Mane nobiscum Domine*, n. 21: "It [Eucharist] is a *fraternal* communion, cultivated by a 'spirituality of communion' which fosters reciprocal openness, affection, understanding and forgiveness."

This book began with the Trinitarian relations (Father, Son, Holy Spirit) and now comes full circle to find its completion in Trinitarian communion. Discerning the principal vocation of the Church, Trinitarian communion, is vital. Only if we clearly see that this Trinitarian communion— that is like a furnace of love—is all about relations among the Father, Son, and Holy Spirit, can we make a spirituality of communion the goal of our Christian life. Without a clear objective, we the members of the Church can easily go astray in the course of our particular vocations. This follows from the principle taught by St. Thomas Aquinas: "A small error at the outset can lead to great errors in the final conclusions."[4] That is, a small error at the beginning deviates further from the truth the further one follows that trajectory. This is our highest vocation, being part of the Trinitarian family (child of the Father, spouse of Christ and a new Christ, temple of the Holy Spirit) as made clear by the document on religious life, *Fraternal Life in Communion*:

> In creating man and woman in his own image and likeness, God created them for communion. God the Creator, who revealed himself as Love, as Trinity, as communion, called them to enter into an intimate relationship with himself and into interpersonal communion, in the universal fraternity of all men and women.
>
> This is our highest vocation: to enter into communion with God and with our brothers and sisters.[5]

## 1. The Holy Spirit's Immense Work of Unity in the Contemporary Period

### A. Two Thousand Years Course

The path or goal of "communion" (*communio* in Latin, *koinonia* in Greek) is actually a recovery of the central image of the Early Church, especially among the Eastern Church Fathers. Within the theology of the Eastern Church, this powerful image forms the basis for the entire framework of our faith: the link to the Trinity; the link between the universal Church and

---

[4] Thomas Aquinas, *On Being and Essence* [*De Ente et Essentia*], trans. Armand Mauer (Toronto: PIMS, 1968), Prologue, 28. The more literal translation is: "A slight initial error eventually grows to vast proportions, according to the Philosopher."
[5] Congregation for Institutes of Consecrated Life and Societies of Apostolic Life, *Fraternal Life in Communion*, n. 9.

the local churches; and the link to Baptism, and especially to the Eucharist. Fr. Johan Roten, analyzing the historical development of the Church, has identified three distinct ages: (i) Personalist Communion ecclesiology (from the Early Church to the Middle Ages); (ii) Institutional ecclesiology (from the Middle Ages to 1960); and (iii) recovery of Communio ecclesiology (in recent times).[6] It appears that today, the Holy Spirit is leading us to a recovery of "communion" that was present in the Early Church, but in a renewed way.

But upon deeper examination, we discern that this theme was already at the heart of the Old Testament. One such discovery was made by the Scripture scholar Scott Hahn, a convert to Catholicism, who proposed in his doctoral thesis the idea that Yahweh's "covenant" with man constituted the heart of Scripture. He concludes from his investigation that the Old Testament "covenant" signified "making family" with God, or, as it were, God gathering His family together— thus we are talking about communion. In his thesis, Hahn finds the progressive development of six covenants (Adam, Abraham, Noah, Moses, David, Jesus), each becoming progressively more universal, culminating in the universal and definitive covenant of Jesus Christ, which finds Christ bound to His Bride, the Church. So important was this insight of this vision of "covenant" as making family that he initially held that covenant as the fundamental key to all Scripture. He relates that he subsequently came to see the deeper truth: while covenant is fundamental, it is the Paschal mystery that constitutes the heart of Scripture.[7]

## B. Work of the Holy Spirit

More closely to our times, we can see an immense trajectory towards communion in the Church and world. This trajectory within Christianity began with the initial movement toward unity in the ecumenical initiatives in the late 19th century among Protestant missionaries. Subsequently, much

---

[6] Johan Roten, "Three Periods of the Church's History" (lecture, Ecclesiology course, Marian Library/International Marian Research Institute, summer 2001). Johan Roten is the President of the Marian Library/International Marian Research Institute at the University of Dayton, Ohio, and a professor with a background in social studies and social philosophy, as well as theology (von Balthasar).
[7] Scott Hahn, *Kinship by Covenant: A Biblical Theological Analysis of Covenant Types and Texts in the Old and New Testaments* (Ph.D. Dissertation, Marquette University, Ann Arbor: UMI, 1995).

later, there has been a gradual upswell and movement within the Catholic Church, beginning with figures like Yves Congar, which culminated at the Second Vatican Council, where ecumenism constituted a major theme for the Council Fathers. Since then, the Popes have repeatedly emphasized the vital importance of this work. Not only has there been a movement towards unity among the Catholic Church and the Christian denominations, like *ARCIC* (dialogue between the Catholic Church and the Anglican Communion), or the dialogue between the Catholic Church and the Lutheran Federation (which led to the historic "Roman Catholic-Lutheran Joint Declaration on the Doctrine of Justification" on October 31, 1999), but there have also been movements toward unity in the inter-faith domain: in the relations between Christian denominations and non-Christian religions, such as with Judaism, Islam, Buddhism, to mention a few of the mainstream non-Christian religions. All of this converges within an era and context in which, given the great progress in technology, especially in communication and travel, the world itself has become more and more of a global village (communion). We now have the United Nations, economic blocs like the European Union and NAFTA, and even unions for collective security, like NATO.

## C. Trajectory within the Roman Catholic Church

Our present turn to communion (seen especially in the twentieth century) in the Roman Catholic Church is both a recovery of and a modified version of the early Church *koinonia*. Scholars point to a more recent turn toward communion underlying the Second Vatican Council: in the completion of the unfinished work of the First Vatican Council with its emphasis on papal primacy, complementing the primacy of the Pope with collegiality; and in the Church as "People of God," and the emphasis on the mission of the laity. While Vatican II did not explicitly treat "communion," it is, according to Cardinal Ratzinger, certainly the foundation of the images or "models" of the Church at the Council, which came to be recognized and developed at the 1985 Extraordinary Synod of Bishops. The 1985 Synod clearly identifies communion as the fundamental image of the Church, and that it was implicitly present in the Second Vatican Council documents. Alois Grillmeier recognized *communio* (communion) as a pervasive theme in *Lumen gentium*, the most important of its documents:

The Church is the unity of communion in the Holy Eucharist, in the Holy Spirit, in the visible (hierarchical) administration, and in the various ministries. She is the animated [*beseelt*= "ensouled"] unity of the body in the diversity of the members and ministries. Not only the charismatic gifts, but the hierarchical order, too, is a self-communication of the Spirit. He thus becomes incarnate in the Church and forms a mystical person, so to speak, out of many persons.[8]

All elements of the Church constitute a unity, and the Holy Spirit Himself "becomes incarnate in the Church and forms a mystical person." Walter Cardinal Kasper noted that, in talking about *communio*, we are talking primarily about structure, but the very reality that derives from the Trinity: "The word *communio* refers to the actual 'thing' (*res*)."[9]

The movement towards communion is especially evident in the new lay movements, that Pope John Paul II has called "signs of the new springtime." They include charisms that have unity as the heart of their charism, including the Focolare, Comunità di Sant'Egidio, Taizé;[10] and many others, like the Neo-Catechumenal way, who have it as a prominent pillar. In regard to religious life, we have noted that communion is highlighted in the relatively recent Vatican document on religious life, "Fraternal Life in Communion," which is a worthwhile reference for any religious community for meditation over a year, as did the Discalced

---

[8] Alois Grillmeier, "Geist, Grundeinstellung und Eigenart der Konstitution 'Licht der Völker' [*Lumen gentium*]," in Baraúna, I:161, quoted in Maximilian Heinrich Heim, *Joseph Ratzinger*, 62. Fr. Grillmeier is a highly regarded scholar, became known especially at the Second Vatican Council, and was made Cardinal by Pope John Paul II in 1994 in recognition of his theological contributions.

[9] Walter Kasper, *Die bleibende Bedeutung des Zweiten Vatikanischen Konzils*, ed. Fr. Köniz (Düsseldorf: Patmos, 1986), 66, quoted in Maximilian Heinrich Heim, *Joseph Ratzinger*, 62.

[10] *Comunità di Sant'Egidio* is a public lay association of over 50,000 members in over 70 countries. It began with a young man, Andrea Riccardi, who gathered together some high school students, to listen to and put into practice the Gospel. They list 5 elements in their charism: prayer, communicating the Gospel, solidarity with the poor, ecumenism, and dialogue. The liturgies of *Comunità di Sant'Egidio* in Rome are based in Santa Maria in Trastevere, and they are not only known for their work with the poor, but also for going to areas of conflict to help reconcile warring parties, as they did in ex-Yugoslavia. Taizé is a unique ecumenical monastic community in Burgundy (not too far from Lyons), begun with Brother Roger, who left Switzerland to go to his mother's country, France, and began helping those going through ordeals in the Second World War. He was forced to return to Switzerland where the community began, but later was able to return to his original site. At present, it comprises over 100 monks, some in disadvantaged countries. Over 100,000 young people, including many from Eastern Europe, are drawn there every year for prayer, Bible study, sharing, and communal work.

Carmelite Order in 2008-2009.[11] The document opens with a title, which is also the subtitle of the whole document, *"Congregavit nos in unum Christi amor"* ("The love of Christ has gathered us into one").

Such an immense and universal movement towards unity in recent times suggests more than the work of human goodwill— it indicates the activity and workings of the Holy Spirit Himself, the Spirit of unity and love. This conclusion agrees with the teachings of the Second Vatican Council documents and the assessment of recent popes. Pope John Paul II and Pope Benedict XVI, in particular, have recognized the hand of the Holy Spirit, who has provided us with the Second Vatican Council to prepare us for the Third Millennium, so as to engage in a new evangelization and a renewal of the work for unity. If this is true, then, the Holy Spirit who sent out the apostles and the first Christians to evangelize the world (see *Acts of the Apostles*), is now sending today's apostles in the Church out to a new, *duc in altum*, to re-evangelize and re-unify the world.

## 2. Background for a Spirituality of Communion

To give some theological background on the spirituality of communion, we look to writings and discourses of Marc Cardinal Ouellet and Joseph Cardinal Ratzinger.

### Commentary by Marc Cardinal Ouellet

The former Archbishop of Québec City, now the Cardinal Prefect of the Congregation for Bishops, Marc Ouellet, offers a good introduction for two reasons. First, Cardinal Ouellet wrote a commentary on Pope John Paul II's spirituality of communion in his article, "Witnesses of Love," that provides us with the main constituent elements. Second, he has a strong background in the theology of von Balthasar and von Speyr, who, with their scriptural and patristic foundation, have a vision centered on a spirituality of communion— von Balthasar was a founder of the *Communio* Journal.

---

[11] Congregation for Institutes of Consecrated Life and Societies of Apostolic Life, "Fraternal Life in Community," accessed July 7, 2015, http://www.vatican.va/roman_curia/congregations/ccscrlife/documents/rc_con_ccscrlife_doc_02021994_fraternal-life-in-community_en.html. (The Discalced Carmelite Women Religious were given the mandate to study this document for 2008-2009).

## A. "Witnesses of Love": Reflections on *Novo Millennio Ineunte*

Cardinal Ouellet wrote a reflection on John Paul II's Apostolic Letter *Novo millennio ineunte* (n. 5).[12] The title, "Witnesses of Love: Reflections on the Holy Father's Apostolic Letter *Novo millennio ineunte*," indicates the heart of his message. He begins with a profound quotation from the Pope: "God in His deepest mystery is not a solitude, but a family, since He has in Himself fatherhood, sonship, and the essence of the family, which is love." The section titles of the article represent the constituent pillars of a spirituality of communion: (i) Trinitarian origin; (ii) resulting ecclesial communion; (iii) love as prior (to both contemplation and action); (iv) receptivity as a condition for communion; (v) the priority of "person"; (vi) the Eucharist accomplishes communion; and (vii) the call to become witnesses of love (the title of Ouellet's article). These titles can provide the fundamental framework for a program of communion in the Church.

Cardinal Ouellet began with a Trinitarian background, with the Triune God seeking a relationship with humanity, that is, to extend the Trinitarian communion to personal beings created in His image. Against this background of communion with the Trinity, all created personal beings find their proper setting or place. The Church is thereby not so much an institution, but a school of communion, that prepares us for communion with the Trinity, now and in eternity. This Trinitarian communion must be seen as love being poured forth into the world, calling forth a response on our part, to "receive" that love— all Christian life, therefore, consists of "receptivity." This receptivity is at the heart of the relationship between Jesus Christ as Son of His Father, and also forms the heart of the relationship between Mary and God. Mary is the model of receptivity; the Church and all humanity is called to imitate Mary's receptivity.

In this Trinitarian outpouring and the call to receptivity to attain communion, the human person takes precedence over all tasks, ministry, and aspects of the Church. A spirituality of communion brings, for example, a renewed vision of the Church: the perception of the bishop presiding over a bureaucracy (Chancery) changes to one of spiritual father

---

[12] Marc Cardinal Ouellet, "Witnesses of Love: Reflections on the Holy Father's Apostolic Letter *Novo millennio ineunte* - 5, *L'Osservatore Romano*, Weekly Edition in English, 29 August 2001, 7.

or shepherd of his flock; the Eucharist, often viewed in terms of Christ's Real Presence, is now seen as communion with Christ the Bridegroom; Catholics, inclined to see themselves as called to follow doctrinal teachings and fulfill moral precepts, see themselves as witnesses of love, incarnated in practice in small communities. We see, then, that a spirituality of communion changes the entire program as well as the approach within the Church. According to von Balthasar, we have to get away from the current theologically "male functionalist" obsession with "doing" and move to the theologically feminine aspect of "receiving." How this is translated into concrete elements will now be addressed.

## B. Trinitarian Communion in the Context of "Sacrifice" Flowing from the Eucharist (Cardinal Ouellet's Retreat, 2005)

Cardinal Ouellet gave a fuller elaboration on the spirituality of communion in a Recollection given to seminarians in Lent 2005.[13] Here is a synopsis of his talks, which presents the mystical background to develop what was given in the previous article. It is here that we see more clearly the influence of von Balthasar and von Speyr in the emphasis on the Eucharist as a key to understanding God's plan of communion.

Cardinal Ouellet begins with Christ in the Trinitarian background. Starting with the need to emphasize the reality of sin once more, he spoke of Christ as the only-Begotten of the Father; no mere human being could take responsibility for all sins. Redemption is a Trinitarian event, for Christ as Son of God is able to bring us back to the realm of the kingdom through His loving obedience. His act is also the act of love for the Father ("The world must know that I love the Father")— this is His unique motivation above all of His other motivations. He is the Lord: He who allowed Himself to be led by the Spirit is now able to breathe the Spirit forth from His flesh, the Spirit is His Holy Spirit; that is the power of the risen Lord. And His body will also be the Body of the Church, which will be linked to the Eucharistic body of Christ.

---

[13] Marc Cardinal Ouellet, "Spirituality of Communion" (Annual Retreat conferences, St. Augustine's Seminary, Toronto, April 2005). Permission was granted by fax by Cardinal Ouellet on September 14, 2015 to publish these personal notes summarized by the author of the Cardinal's conferences.

From the human side, sacrifice is painful because of our sin and our culture of the "I" or "ego"; unlike the Trinitarian communion, which is selfless love, gift of self. The Father holds nothing for Himself, He generated Himself; and the life of the Father is the Son and the life of the Son is the Father, and both meet in the Holy Spirit. Both meet in communion, and Christ brought this to us, to tell us something about God in shedding His blood, and to help us connect to the true meaning of being: being relational or being given. Sacrifice means "*sacer facit*," making sacred; to consecrate for divine things. We are consecrated when we are baptized, and we do not belong to ourselves but to Christ, which is to be called to be a self-gift, Trinitarian life, which is given to us through the sacraments.

So priests are called to reflect the image of God dynamically, through holiness and unity, following Christ, to renounce marriage and to be a good shepherd. Cardinal Ouellet offered contemporary examples of living this sacrifice: Edith Stein ("Let us go and die for our [Jewish] people"); Mother Teresa of Calcutta (her dark nights began with her ministry in the streets of Calcutta), who insisted on having a good priest to make sure the Eucharistic body was the same as the body of the poor; Pope John Paul II, in his slow, living martyrdom with his illnesses while continuing his pontificate.

Going further, Cardinal Ouellet teaches that Christ's sacrifice has become the Eucharist, and all Scripture points to this sacrifice, as seen in the example of the conversion of Scott Hahn, a Scripture scholar who was converted to Catholicism through covertly attending the Eucharist. The Eucharist is the open heart of our Lord. It was at the cross that, from the wounded heart of Christ, flowed blood and water. We are brought right into the Trinity in the Eucharist. This Eucharist is a Trinitarian event, our being invited and included in the self-offering of the Son to the Father, and the opening of our hearts to receive the ultimate gift, the Holy Spirit. The Sunday Mass, the meeting with the risen Lord Sunday after Sunday, calls us to be an *ecclesia* (gathering, Church) around God. He calls us to be a sacrament of Trinitarian love in the world.

## Mary, Woman of Communion

Cardinal Ouellet now links Mary to this vision. All of what we have presented is seen clearly in the life of Mary, and is now accomplished in the Church through her help. In her abandonment, she becomes the "other self" of Christ. She was brought beyond family ties to the moment of the cross, where she stood at the foot of the cross, where she welcomed the Word, not only His life but also His death; she welcomed even His cry of abandonment. In her, the Church believed: from Nazareth, to the cross, and to Pentecost.

The Gospel does not tell us that Mary had apparitions or prophecies, she knew from within— she did not need external manifestations. So in the power of the Spirit, she was prepared and accompanied and expanded for the Word. She became the bride of the Lamb that was slain, for which she was prepared mysteriously within. So Mary's mission was expanded and became co-extensive with Christ's mission, and accompanies the Word wherever He goes today: in the Church's proclamation and liturgy. This faith is expanded in our own hearts, we share in Mary's faith. For Mary's faith is more fundamental for unity of the Church than Peter's ministry. Her faith, in the Holy Spirit, brings the interior unity of the Church, while Peter looks after the external unity of the Church; but the two are inseparable.

From John 25, we have "Behold your mother... and from that moment, the disciple took her into his own home." Mary within the home of John nurtures him, nourishing the apostolic ministry as *"Regina apostolorum"* ("Queen of the apostles"). We rely on her if we want to give life to others. For the priest if he wants to have a living faith and not be a functionary of rituals, he needs to keep Mary in his "home." All the baptized need to be aware that the Church is not just an organization. It comprises many persons; yet there is one person (Mary) who, through the power of the Holy Spirit, is present to all persons. So let us take her into our home as John did.

Mary was there for the real offering (Calvary), and she was there spiritually with the same soul, sentiments, and spirit as Christ's, and with immaculate faith. So we owe to Mary our being part of the Church, being part of the self-sacrifice of Christ; she believed *"in actu primo redemptionis,"* from the first moment of redemption. She was pre-redeemed to be interiorly or spiritually part of the mystery, so that she could be an active participant from the very first moment. Thus we know that the sacrifice of Christ is the sacrifice of the Church. Mary's presence at the foot of the cross is full of meaning: when Christ was speaking in His agony to her with the title, "Woman," He is giving her a mission, an expansion, "you must now take this poor sinner in place of me"; to which, St. Bernard comments, "What a sacrifice to take a sinner in the place of Christ."

Cardinal Ouellet links our being taken up into Christ's self-gift (now become the Eucharist) in our self-gift, that is, involving our personal sacrifice. There are people who went to die for the redemption of the world, like St. Maximilian Kolbe, who gave his own life for the father of a family. He was anticipating this moment, was waiting for it. He was offering himself also for the ten others who would need a shepherd in dying in prison. To the surprise of the camp, as they went to their death, these condemned men sang and recited psalms. The guards could not stand St. Maximilian's gaze because they could not stand his gaze of mercy. He died by lethal injection on the very feast of the Assumption.

These are witnesses of absolute love. Pope John Paul II said that today's culture of death, especially abortion, is sustained by Parliament. He reminded us that there are other tragedies besides abortion. John Paul II always spoke the truth, because he too was with the Word. At the end of the Recollection, Cardinal Ouellet counselled the seminarians to speak the Word of God, to be friends of the Bridegroom, and to stay with Him through Mary, to become holy priests.

In summary, the spirituality of communion is based upon, and flows from, the Trinitarian communion of self-gift. In this renewed vision, the human person (as with the Trinitarian Persons) takes priority over work and ministry, for it is love (as God's essence is love) that constitutes the heart of the Church; and this is accomplished through the Eucharist (the sacrament of love) with the help of Mary, so that we too become witnesses of love. Coming from the Second Millennium in which the "institutional" dimension of the Church dominated, the Holy Spirit is leading us anew to the heart of the Church— the personal dimension of Trinitarian love lived in a spirituality of communion.

### 3. Living the "Spirituality of Communion"

The "spirituality of communion" is the living out of the very Trinitarian communion, lived out in the Church in its openness, tenderness, affection, love, and mercy in many forms.

## A. Communion in the Thought and Lives of Recent Popes

### (1) Pope John Paul II

Since Pope John Paul II called for a "spirituality of communion," how does he understand it being lived out in the Church? *Novo millennio ineunte* captures this to some degree. We finally see what John Paul II himself had in mind when he called for a spirituality of communion. The spirituality of communion must become "the guiding principle of education." It precedes making practical plans and is not primarily about action to be undertaken.[14] It is a disposition of openness in our brothers and sisters, recognizing the light of the Trinity shining on their faces.

> A spirituality of communion indicates above all the heart's contemplation of the mystery of the Trinity dwelling in us, and whose light we must also be able to see shining on the face of the brothers and sisters around us. A spirituality of communion also means an ability to think of our brothers and sisters in faith within the profound unity of the Mystical Body, and therefore as "those who are a part of me." This makes us able to share their joys and sufferings, to sense their desires and attend to their needs, to offer them deep and genuine friendship. A spirituality of communion implies also the ability to see what is positive in others, to welcome it and prize it as a gift from God: not only as a gift for the brother or sister who has received it directly, but also as a "gift for me." A spirituality of communion means, finally, to know how to "make room" for our brothers and sisters, bearing "each other's burdens" (*Gal* 6:2) and resisting the selfish temptations which constantly beset us and provoke competition, careerism, distrust and jealousy. Let us have no illusions: unless we follow this spiritual path, external structures of communion will serve very little purpose. They would become mechanisms without a soul, 'masks' of communion rather than its means of expression and growth.[15]

In sum, it indicates above all "the heart's contemplation of the mystery of the Trinity dwelling in us," our unity and fraternity within the Mystical

---

[14] "But what does this mean in practice? Here too, our thoughts could run immediately to the action to be undertaken, but that would not be the right impulse to follow. Before making practical plans, we need *to promote a spirituality of communion,* making it the guiding principle of education wherever individuals and Christians are formed, wherever ministers of the altar, consecrated persons, and pastoral workers are trained, wherever families and communities are being built up" (Pope John Paul II, *Novo millennio ineunte,* n. 43).
[15] Ibid.

Body, to "see what is positive in others, to welcome it and prize it as a gift from God," to see others "as part of me, and "to know how to 'make room' for our brothers and sisters, bearing 'each other's burdens.'" Without this "communion" disposition, the Church structures "become mechanisms without a soul." This disposition or spirituality of communion was the experience of many who met Pope John Paul II. When Elena Bonner, the wife of Andrei Sakharov, the brilliant Soviet physicist turned human rights campaigner, met Pope John Paul II privately (he made time in his packed schedule for her more than once as he did for Irina Alberti), though a very tough woman, she came out of the meeting crying, and said to Irina Alberti, "He is the most remarkable man I've ever met. He is all light. He is a source of light..."[16]

George Weigel, with great insightfulness, points out how this spirituality of communion is lived out in the life and approach of John Paul II. He describes how many on the side of restoration criticize John Paul II, finding him a good "priest" and "prophet," but failing as "king." This charge was especially directed at him for not taking strong action on certain bishops dissenting from the Church's teaching. Weigel points to the keen insight of John Paul II into the dignity of each human person, and his method was "not to impose but propose." This is a critical point in understanding John Paul II.

> He has a very deep respect for persons. He is patient, waiting with some situations until the moment comes when nobody feels offended. People mistake his respect for person as weakness. It isn't. He also respects competence. When he gives a responsibility to an office, a congregation, or an individual, he lets them do it. This doesn't mean he is weak. He trusts his collaborators, and he is not a worrier. He is neither afraid of making a decision nor does he force a decision if the situation is not mature.[17]

Weigel points out to critics who claimed that Pope John Paul II was not focused on an administrative papacy but an "evangelical" one, one that mirrored the Gospel example of Christ, that in the end would bring about

---

[16] Interview with Irina Alberti, April 13 & 16, 1998, quoted in George Weigel, *Witness to Hope: The Biography of Pope John Paul II* (New York: HarperCollins Publishers, 1999), 570.
[17] Interview with Jozef Cardinal Tomko, November 14, 1996, in George Weigel, *Witness to Hope*, 857.

much greater good: "The Pope's relative lack of attention to managing his bureaucracy— at least as measured by the practice of his predecessor, Paul VI— has created the time and space in which to conduct an evangelical papacy of great intellectual creativity and public impact."[18]

Many fruits flowed from Pope John Paul II's spirituality: a reaching out to non-Catholic Christians and non-Christians; drawing many young people, inspiring many vocations— witness the huge and diverse crowds, including heads of state, present at his funeral, and the massive international turnout for his beatification. In his dealings with young people, after he listened to them intently, he would still, while offering suggestions, tell them, "You have to decide, you have to decide." His way was the way of receptivity and listening, of a father's solicitude, but allowing each person to find his way and be led by the Holy Spirit in his heart. In addition, he supplemented that approach with his prayers and his "blood." He knew that it is not words that convict, but blood, the cross, that convicts hearts.

It is possible that Pope John Paul II's own spirituality of communion developed out of his involvement as a priest with youth. He himself pointed to the one who taught him this path when he told Jan Pietraszko, a priest and bishop, at a dinner, "Bishop Jan, I learn theology from you," and in the telegram he sent on the occasion of the bishop's death, "You showed me the way to young people."[19] In an interview with Professor Stanislaw Grygiel, this long-time friend of Pope John Paul II explained Pietraszko's pastoral method: "There was no particular conceptual method. All he did was to be among us young people in church and outside. He prayed, lunched, meditated and had fun with us. We saw in him a fascinating way to be in the world. Drawn by him, we looked for the spring from which, on his knees, he drank pure water."[20]

Professor Grygiel distinguished between those with just learning from Pietraszko and Wojtyla, who "showed us how culture implies cultivating the land on which man grows and matures 'to rise again.'" For "there is nothing more dangerous for society than learned men without culture. Unless

---

[18] Ibid., 855.
[19] Wlodimierz Redzioch, "Imparò a conoscere le persone vivendo con Loro," *L'Osservatore Romano* (October 18, 2008), reproduced as "Nothing is more Dangerous than Learned Men without Culture," *Inside the Vatican* (April 2010): 52.
[20] Ibid.

culture helps man rise again, it is not culture." Grygiel explained that their friendship with the young grew into an "everlasting friendship," and with their children and grandchildren, and how available they were: "There were no barriers between friends. Wojtyla and Pietraszko were always on hand and available. We could go to them whenever we wanted. We could knock on their door even at night. Sheep never ask their shepherd for an audience, they just follow him night and day."[21] Grygiel offers some words of wisdom in the care of the young that can be of help to priests in their work as shepherds, that pastoral care is about "living together." "Pastoral care is not a theory, but something which involves living together. Theories are just to be memorized. Pastoral care demands wisdom that originates from people living for one another. Wojtyla knew this very well."[22] Pope John Paul II's great influence on youth (e.g. World Youth Days) may stem from his "communion" as a priest with youth.

## (2) Pope Benedict XVI

The person of Joseph Cardinal Ratzinger, now Pope Emeritus Benedict XVI, reflects all charity and communion. He is known around the neighbourhood he lives in beside the Vatican for his friendliness to the shop owners and stray cats. Incidents that reflect this charity abound: in not accepting a Vatican apartment on his appointment in Rome as Prefect of the Sacred Congregation for the Doctrine of the Faith to allow an aging Cardinal to remain in the papal apartment given him; spontaneously agreeing to preside at a wedding of a Canadian engaged couple who attended his private Mass at St. Peter's Basilica; his kindness to theologians who have crossed the line in matters of faith; and his meekness in the face of all the barrage of criticism as "Panzer-Cardinal" or the Pope's "Rottweiler" as Prefect of the Sacred Congregation for the Doctrine of the Faith. It is not surprising then that his first Encyclical as Pope was on charity: *Deus caritas est*. However, in his book, *The Meaning of Christian Brotherhood*, he takes this aspect of communion as "brotherhood" to the extreme: we, the "elect" (baptized) must become the "reject," so that the reject (unbaptized) can become the elect. In this book, he speaks of three levels of brotherhood, the first two, by creation and through membership within the chosen People, have failed in maintaining the unity of the family

---

[21] Ibid.
[22] Ibid., 53.

of God. Only the final brotherhood and family accomplished by Jesus on the cross can unite us to the Father in the divine family and to one another.

In the Old Testament, there were always the elect and reject combination: Cain-Abel, Isaac-Esau, and Jacob-Ishmael. The same duality continues today in the elect of those who have faith and are baptized and the unbaptized (reprobate). But, unlike Cain, we must not accept our election and ignore our brother. We have to seek him out at three levels: missionary outreach; agape love in example and help; but above all, when he does not listen, like Jesus, we are to become the reprobate so as to allow others to become the elect.

> Just as Christ, the chosen one, became in a sacred exchange the one rejected for us in order to confer on us his election, this exchange relationship recurs constantly in salvation history following him....

> ... she [Church] must always remember that she is only one of two sons, one brother beside another, and that her mission is not to condemn the wayward brother, but to save him. [23]

We are called in each age to continue this vicarious relationship, and we should not be troubled if we are few.

> The disciples of Jesus are few, but as Jesus himself was one 'for the many', so it will always be their mission to be not against but 'for the many'. When all other ways fail, there will always remain the royal way of vicarious suffering by the side of the Lord. It is in her defeat that the Church constantly achieves her highest victory and stands nearest to Christ. It is when she is called to suffer for others that she achieves her highest mission: the exchange of fate with the wayward brother and thus his secret restoration to full sonship and full brotherhood.[24]

Cardinal Ratzinger's approach goes counter to our immediate inclination to lament or criticize the ills of our time by taking them upon ourselves through vicarious suffering.

---

[23] Joseph Ratzinger, *The Meaning of Christian Brotherhood* (San Francisco: Ignatius Press, 1966; German orig. *Die christliche Brüderlichkeit*, 1960), 79-80. See Gen 17:18-21 and also Gal 4.
[24] Ibid., 84.

## (3) Pope Francis

A few years into his pontificate, the heart of mercy of Pope Francis towards all those who suffer is common knowledge. His years of ministry as priest and bishop in Argentina offer many examples of "communion" with the poor, marginalized, persecuted, and all who suffer, especially in the slums (*villas miserias*, "villas of misery"). Perhaps less known is his openness towards other religions, including his dialogues with Rabbi Abraham Skorka.

Pope Francis, in collaboration with Rabbi Skorka, has published a book of their remarkable dialogues, which dialogues themselves constitute a concrete illustration of the spirituality of communion. His introduction to the book points us to a path. There he considers whether Argentineans really want dialogue. He perceives that Argentineans do want dialogue but succumb to attitudes that hinder it: "domination, not knowing how to listen, annoyance in our speech, preconceived judgments and so many others." From having his own experience of living out this communion, he shares some practical instructions that assist us to live this out ourselves:

> Dialogue is born from a respectful attitude toward the other person, from a conviction that the other person has something good to say. It supposes that we can make room in our heart for their point of view, their opinion and their proposals. Dialogue entails a warm reception and not a preemptive condemnation. To dialogue, one must know how to lower the defenses, to open the doors of one's home and to offer warmth.[25]

These counsels are remarkable in their openness to, and respect for, the other and his or her opinions. They clearly arise from his own practice of this "open" heart. In one of his dialogues, he notes that the origin of all dialogue and of this "*path*" of dialogue begins with a dialogue with God. And this dialogue has two searches: an interior search for God within our hearts, but also allowing ourselves to be found by Him.

> I would say that one encounters God walking, moving, seeking Him and allowing oneself to be sought by Him. They are two paths that meet. On

---

[25] Jorge Mario Bergoglio-Abraham Skorka, *On Heaven and Earth: Pope Francis on Faith, Family, and the Church in the Twenty-First Century* (New York: Image Books, 2013; Spanish orig. *Sobre el cielo y la tierra*, 2010), xiv.

one hand, there is our path that seeks Him, driven by that instinct that flows from the heart; and after, when we have encountered each other, we realize that He was the one who was searching for us from the start.[26]

Then he makes a rather startling insight. This dialogue with God and with others must begin within the heart, it involves meeting oneself first, it involves interiority or "recollection": "What every person must be told is to look inside himself. Distraction is an interior fracture. It will never lead the person to encounter himself for it impedes him from looking into the mirror of his heart. Collecting oneself is the beginning. That is where dialogue begins."[27]

## B. Insights on Communion from a New Ecclesial Movement: Focolare

If the new lay movements are special gifts of the Holy Spirit for our time, and are also at once a response to the needs of our time, then it is helpful to look to their lead. To understand where the Holy Spirit is leading us, we look at one of the most prominent movements, the *Focolare* (Italian for "hearth"), whose canonical title is *Opus Mariae* ("Work of Mary") and whose external charism is that of unity. They have profound insights to offer in this area.

It should be noted that the interior heart of their charism is the consoling of the abandoned Christ on Calvary, "My God, my God, why have you abandoned me?" Chiara Lubich, the late foundress of *Focolare*, teaches that God is calling us to a collective rather than an individual sanctity, and that, when we love each other, we make God present. This lay movement began with the experience of Chiara and a few companions during the bombing of her home town of Trent, where she felt called to live literally the words of the Gospel concerning love.

> As we spent long hours in the air-raid shelters, the entire Gospel, every word of the Gospel, attracted us, and we put it into practice. Yet we were particularly struck by the passages that spoke explicitly of love: 'Love your neighbor' (Mt 5:43); 'Love your enemies' (Mt 5:44); 'For the whole law is fulfilled in one statement, namely, "You shall love your neighbor as

---

[26] Ibid., 2.
[27] Ibid., 3.

yourself"" (Gal 5:14). These were extraordinarily powerful words, unique in their capacity to bring about a radical change of life. And this is what happened to us.[28]

But this love was rooted in the Trinitarian communion, and found external expression in the abandonment of Christ on the cross.

> How had Jesus loved us? We perceived the answer when the light of the charism focused our attention on the cry of Jesus on the cross, 'My God, my God, why have you forsaken me?' (Mt 27:46). This was the meaning of 'as I have loved you'; this was the measure of his love. And this was the measure of the mutual love required of us—a measure without measure—to give everything, not to keep anything for ourselves, to be ready, yes, to lay down our life but also our spiritual and material possessions as well.

> In his cry Jesus had truly given everything; even his very sense of union with the Father had dimmed. In his feeling disunited from the Father, Jesus became for all the source and path of unity with God and for people with one another. In his abandonment Jesus emptied himself out of love, made himself nothing, so as to give us the most luminous explanation of the meaning of love: to empty oneself, to 'not be,' to disappear, so as to be love in action. This is the truest, fullest, most authentic love.[29]

Chiara Lubich felt drawn to this self-emptying that enabled her to be filled with total love. She sees this spirituality of unity as needed, not only to transform the Church and the world, including families, parishes and religious communities, and ecumenical dialogue, but to be extended into the world: "The Council teaches that the new commandment of love is 'the fundamental law' not only 'of human perfection,' but also 'of the transformation of the world.' The Movement has experienced this in various fields: politics, economics, culture, art, healthcare, education, media and so on."[30] One of the unique forms that she has instituted is the "Economy of Union," where little cities of economic sharing and mutual

---

[28] Chiara Lubich, "The Spirituality of Unity and Trinitarian Life," *New Humanity Review* 9 (2004): 2 (*livingcitymagazine.com*). "This is the acceptance speech given at the conferral of an honorary doctorate in theology by the University of Trnava, Slovakia, on June 23, 2003."

[29] Ibid.
[30] Ibid., 4.

love are lived. It was launched in 1991 in Sao Paolo, Brazil, with the aim of living the experience of the first Christian community in Jerusalem, that shared everything and where no one lacked anything.[31]

We can find a theological elaboration of Chiara's vision in the theology of Hans Urs von Balthasar. The latter himself had spoken of something similar to Chiara Lubich's "Economy of Union": the importance in the renewal of the Church by forming "islands of humanity."[32] Brendan Leahy introduces this idea in his work, *The Marian Profile*, describing von Balthasar's proposal for "Islands of Humanity."[33] For von Balthasar, "love alone is credible" (the title of one of his works), and our social, political, and economic orders with their globalization and struggle for social justice need to rediscover and be regulated by the "law" of Christian love.

In pointing to the lack of culture in general wrought by the entire pseudo-human bureaucratic machine, how are we to construct a new civilization? What he suggests are concrete forms of gospel life and mutual love, islands of humanity, through which Christians would contribute to the rebuilding of a cultural humanism, luminous points of the re-discovery of ultimate meaning, centered on Christ. These islands of humanity are those points where the living presence of Jesus among His disciples bear witness to God, analogous to Christ's presence among us sacramentally (so also outside the sacraments): for where two or three are gathered in his name, He is in their midst (Mt 18:20). It involves a leavening of the world from inside, an "inculturation." The Church must pursue her task that alternates between two impossible poles, "preaching to the world purely from without, and transforming it from within."[34] "The Community of St. John," the secular institute of priests and laypeople, both men and women, living in the world that von Balthasar and Adrienne von Speyr established, sought to live this vision.

---

[31] Ibid., 5.

[32] See Hans Urs von Balthasar, *Test Everything: Hold Fast to what is Good* (San Francisco: Ignatius Press, 1989), 50 ff.

[33] See Brendan Leahy, *The Marian Profile*, 195-198.

[34] Hans Urs von Balthasar, *Theo-drama: Theological Dramatic Theory, IV: The Action* (San Francisco: Ignatius Press, 1994), 465, quoted in Brendan Leahy, *The Marian Profile*, 196.

## C. Communion in the Lives of the Saints

When we examine the saints, we find that this spirituality of communion constitutes their heart. St. John Bosco and St. Angela Merici offer two examples of saints who learned to carry their young charges in their hearts. They impart touching and affectionate words to their spiritual sons and daughters in regard to youth in the religious congregations they established. The boys of the "Oratory" knew how much they were loved by Don Bosco: "My dear boys, I love you with all my heart and it is enough that you are young that I can love you so much"; "You will find writers more talented by far and more learned than I, but with difficulty, will you ever find anyone who loves you in Jesus Christ more than I and who wants your true happiness."[35] St. John Bosco had these words for his spiritual sons, citing the example of Jesus Himself:

> I have always labored lovingly for them, and carried out my priestly duties with zeal. And the whole Salesian society has done this with me. My sons, in my long experience very often I had to be convinced of this great truth. It is easier to become angry than to restrain oneself, and to threaten a boy than to persuade him. Yes, indeed, it is more fitting to be persistent in punishing our own impatience and pride than to correct the boys. We must be firm but kind, and be patient with them…. This was the method that Jesus used with the apostles. He put up with their ignorance and roughness and even their infidelity. He treated sinners with a kindness and affection that caused some to be shocked, others to be scandalized, and still others to hope for God's mercy. And so he bade us to be gentle and humble of heart….
>
> There must be no hostility in our minds, no contempt in our eyes, no insult on our lips. We must use mercy for the present and have hope for the future, as is fitting for true fathers who are eager for real correction and improvement. In serious matters it is better to beg God humbly than to send forth a flood of words that will only offend the listeners and have no effect on those who are guilty.[36]

---

[35] "Don Bosco," *Cagliero*, accessed July 9, 2015, http://www.cagliero.org.au/index.php?option=com_content&view=article&id=72&Itemid=503

[36] St. John Bosco, *Epistolario*, Torino 1959, 4, 201-201, OOR, Feast day of John Bosco (January 31), in *The Liturgy of the Hours*, vol. 3, 1338-1339.

St. Angela Merici shared similar affectionate wisdom with her spiritual daughters, to win them by maternal affection: "Charity wins souls and draws them to virtue."

> As our Savior says: '*A good tree is not able to produce bad fruit.*' He says: A good tree, that is, a good heart as well as a soul on fire with charity, can do nothing but good and holy works. For this reason Saint Augustine said: '*Love, and do what you will,*' namely, possess love and charity and then do what you will. It is as if he had said: Charity is not able to sin…. Mothers of children, even if they have a thousand, carry each and every one fixed in their hearts, and because of the strength of their love they do not forget any of them. In fact, it seems that the more children they have the more their love and care for each one is increased…. Be sincerely kind to every one according to the words of our Lord: '*Learn of me, for I am meek and humble of heart.*' Thus you are imitating God, of whom it is said: '*He has disposed all things pleasantly.*'"[37]

The spirituality of communion appears in Mother Teresa of Calcutta, who came to see how vital kindness and community were through her experience as a religious: "Let no one ever come to you without leaving better and happier. Be the living expression of God's kindness: kindness in your face, kindness in your eyes, kindness in your smile"[38]; "We cannot do great things on this earth, only small things with great love." A particularly striking text is one in which she says that, if we are to err, we must err on the side of kindness: "I prefer you make mistakes in kindness."

> Be kind to each other. I prefer you make mistakes in kindness than you work miracles in unkindness. Be kind in words. See what the kindness of Our Lady brought to her, see how she spoke. She could have easily told St. Joseph of the Angel's message yet she never uttered a word. And then God Himself interfered. She kept all these [things] in her heart. Would that we could keep all our words in her heart. So much suffering, so much misunderstanding, for what? Just one word, one look, one quick action, and darkness fills the heart of your Sister. Ask Our Lady during this novena to fill your heart with sweetness.[39]

---

[37] St. Angela Merici, *The Spiritual Testament*, OOR, Feast day of Angela Merici (January 27), in *The Liturgy of the Hours*, vol. 3, 1332-1333.

[38] http://thinkexist.com/quotes/mother_teresa.

[39] Brian Kolodiejchuk, *Come Be My Light*, 196.

We also find this charity of communion incarnated in the life of St. Faustina. In a very heart-warming incident found in her *Diary*, St. Faustina relates words of Jesus, who was Himself impressed by her charity. Among the people she cared for was a destitute young man. Jesus later appeared to her and revealed that the young man was Himself, and that He Himself, having heard from those who approached her door as gatekeeper and had tasted the warmth and sweetness of her tender mercy, had come to experience it first-hand.

It is very difficult to overestimate the importance of kindness in the spiritual life. A priest studying in Rome learned what kindness wrought in the life of an African priest. He encountered a Kenyan priest working in one of the Vatican Congregations in Rome who shared his story, one that emphasized the importance of kindness. In Kenya, this priest's father had gone to the local Catholic school and begged for entrance for his son who was not Catholic. The principal, a religious, went out of his way to allow this boy in and without having to pay tuition, all with great kindness. It was this kindness that led this Kenyan boy to become Catholic and to eventually follow a call to the priesthood.

## D. Conditions for Fostering Communion

### (1) *Fraternal Solicitude— Everything Goes Through Our "Neighbour"*

A spirituality of communion presupposes the clear awareness that our entire relationship with God goes through our neighbour. In our daily life, there is that inevitable tendency to focus on work: getting things done, obsessing over our responsibilities, and forgetting the great truth that it is people who come first. In the life of St. Catherine of Siena, we see lived out the great truth of charity Christians are to live. After a few years of being formed by Jesus Himself, St. Catherine was then being sent out to the world.

When she pleaded to the Lord that they continue their private encounters, He taught her this great truth: "Love of me and love of one's neighbor is one and the same thing" and "You cannot do anything for me but you can serve and help your neighbor."[40] It was the Gospel teaching, "Love God whom you cannot see in the one you can see." This is more clearly drawn out in her only work, *The Dialogue.*

> I would have you know that every virtue of yours and every vice is put into action by means of your neighbors.... ... If you do not love me you do not love your neighbors, nor will you help those you do not love. But it is yourself you harm most, because you deprive yourself of grace....
>
> In the same way, every evil is done by means of your neighbor for you cannot love them if you do not love me. This lack of love for me and for your neighbors is the source of all evils, for if you are not doing good, you are necessarily doing evil.... I count whatever you do to them as done to me.... More particular are the services done to those nearest you, under your very eyes. Here you owe each other help in word and teaching, and good example, indeed in every need of which you are aware...
>
> It is indeed true, then, that every sin committed against me is done by means of your neighbors. I have told you how every sin is done by means of your neighbors, because it deprives them of your loving charity, and it is charity that gives life to all virtues. So that selfish love which deprives your neighbors of your charity and affection is the principle and foundation of all evil.
>
> ...The service you cannot render me you must do for your neighbors. Thus it will be evident that you have me within your soul by grace, when with tender loving desire you are looking out for my honor and the salvation of your neighbors by bearing fruit for them in many holy prayers.[41]

Within this love is the spirituality of communion to which we are called that has many expressions. Jesus told his disciples to go out two by two, and some communities live this literally, like the Neo-Catechumenal Way. We are inspired by the warm friendship between St. Basil and St. Gregory Nazianzen. One can come up with creative ways to support one another: for example, Dom Columba Marmion's early days as a seminarian when he made a pact with two others to pray for each other.

---

[40] Louis de Wohl, *Lay Siege to Heaven: A Novel about St. Catherine of Siena* (San Francisco: Ignatius Press, 1960), 77.

[41] St. Catherine of Siena, *The Dialogue, Classics of Western Spirituality* Series, trans. S. Noffke (New York: Paulist Press, 1980), 33-37.

## (2) *Universal Solicitude*

Regarding love of God through our neighbour, there is a temptation to be inward-looking in the Church, and so to be less concerned about the plight of the larger Church that suffers from so many evils. In an interview with the *National Catholic Reporter*, Cardinal John Onaiyekan of Nigeria noted that the concerns of the Church in the First World are not necessarily the concerns of his people in Africa, whether it is the "Vatileaks" or the reform of the Roman curia: "… I'm more interested in how we're able to project the message of Jesus to our people. Not only Catholics, but everybody… those are the issues I'm looking at."[42] From his deep insights of living in a third-world country, Cardinal Tagle of Manila captures something of the global destruction of communion. He asks why communion has not been achieved in spite of all the exchange of words:

> When financial wizards talk about ways of manipulating the economy for their own profit, you do not call that communion; that is corruption! When politicians talk to people about grand promises without intending to fulfil them, you do not call that communion; that is cheating! When the powerful "negotiate" among themselves while neglecting the weak, you do not call that communion; that is oppression! When so-called enterprising persons deal with each other on how women and children could be profitable merchandise, you do not call that communion; that is slavery! When communion consists in Jesus who is the Word of Life then the common good becomes central. And that is pleasing to God's eyes.[43]

The true disciple of communion has a universal outlook, moving away from our mundane, trivial everyday concerns to the foundational needs of Christ in our brothers and sisters and the new evangelization.

## (3) *Beyond Justice to Love*

One great obstacle to communion is the primary focus on justice, for our mercy must transcend justice. Pope Benedict XVI's new document, *Caritas in veritate*, teaches that justice, while necessary, find its culmination in love:

---

[42] John Cardinal Onaiyekan, Interview with the *National Catholic Reporter*, quoted in Matthew E. Bunson, *Pope Francis*, 70.
[43] Archbishop Luis Antonio Tagle, Address at 50th Eucharistic Congress 2012 in Dublin, quoted in Matthew E. Bunson, *Pope Francis*, 74.

First of all, justice. *Ubi societas, ibi ius*: every society draws up its own system of justice. *Charity goes beyond justice*, because to love is to give, to offer what is "mine" to the other; but it never lacks justice, which prompts us to give the other what is "his", what is due to him by reason of his being or his acting. I cannot "give" what is mine to the other, without first giving him what pertains to him in justice. If we love others with charity, then first of all we are just towards them. Not only is justice not extraneous to charity, not only is it not an alternative or parallel path to charity: justice is inseparable from charity, and intrinsic to it. Justice is the primary way of charity or, in Paul VI's words, "the minimum measure" of it, an integral part of the love "in deed and in truth" (1 Jn 3:18), to which Saint John exhorts us. On the one hand, charity demands justice: recognition and respect for the legitimate rights of individuals and peoples. It strives to build the *earthly city* according to law and justice. On the other hand, charity transcends justice and completes it in the logic of giving and forgiving. The *earthly city* is promoted not merely by relationships of rights and duties, but to an even greater and more fundamental extent by relationships of gratuitousness, mercy and communion. Charity always manifests God's love in human relationships as well, it gives theological and salvific value to all commitment for justice in the world.[44]

Beyond justice, the context of God's appeal to us is of love, flowing from the Trinitarian love: "Charity always manifests God's love in human relationships as well."

The two paths, justice and love beyond justice, are exemplified in St. Josemaría Escrivá's depiction of two types of shepherds.

There are two kinds of shepherd. The shepherd who stays behind the sheep and leads them by loosing the dog on them, throwing rocks at those who stray, shouting at those which straggle behind. And there is the shepherd who goes in front, opening up a path and removing obstacles, encouraging the flock with his whistles.[45]

A priest in his homilies can end up berating parishioners, whom he feels, are not living up to the Church's teachings on Sunday Mass or morality.

---

[44] Pope Benedict XVI, *Caritas in veritate* n. 6.
[45] Josemaría Escrivá, AGP [General Archives of the Prelature], P01, V-66, 14, quoted by the Prelate of Opus Dei, Priestly Ordination of Deacons of the Prelature, Basilica of St. Michael in Madrid, Spain, (September 6, 1999).

This is the shepherd who stands behind his sheep and curses them and throws stones at them. Then, there is the other type of shepherd, with the heart of the Heavenly Father, who goes to the front and leads by example, and, overcoming self-pity, gently draws the sheep behind him with great warmth and compassion.[46] The latter shepherd, standing at the front, will encounter the wolves first and must be willing to lay down his life for his sheep— this is the path of expiation. One seminary faculty member, put in charge of discipline, became increasingly frustrated at the failings of a few seminarians. One perspicacious layman with special gifts of discernment reminded him that, while discipline was necessary, he must first and above all be a father (not a disciplinarian)— the seminary must not be principally an institution (rules, discipline), but a family.

---

[46] John Paul II, Homily at an ordination, August 9, 1985, quoted by the Prelate of Opus Dei, Priestly Ordination of Deacons of the Prelature, Basilica of St. Michael in Madrid, Spain (September 6, 1999).

# CONCLUSION

In today's world, many Christians can become troubled by their sins and failings, and can doubt whether God can truly love them in this apparent state of prostration. Even more, we can struggle to find God's presence, to unconsciously view God as very distant, in the heavens, and wonder if He truly cares, if He is truly concerned about our day-to-day personal, family, or work concerns. In our daily human struggles, it can feel as if God is not answering our pleas for help, and thus we must adopt a "grin and bear it," an "offer it up" stoic approach to life's trials. The answer lies within Baptism; but what we are taught is some vague teaching of being incorporated to the Church, a short catechesis of the rites of Baptism, and a generic sense of being a child of God. Yet it is primarily the deep experience in our hearts of what it means to be a child of God that can make sense out of life's troubles and give joy and meaning; but it must be linked directly to Christ's sonship to bring out its profound depths. It is, more deeply, to experience the same love that the Father has for the Son.

This book has sought to recover the heart of the Christian identity as a child of God through Baptism, to enable us to be ravished by this love. On the cross, Jesus did not just redeem us from our sins, the obstacle that separates us from God, He also prolonged His agony to obtain for us a share of His sonship, an ineffable, sublime gift of staggering proportions. This means that each baptized has, through a second and spiritual birth in God's "womb," ontologically become a child of God the Father (not a legal adoption), such that each can truly call Him *Abba*. All this is accomplished by the Holy Spirit being poured into our hearts to become temples of the Holy Spirit, who simultaneously incorporates each baptized into Christ, as it were, in a mystical incarnation, to truly become a new Christ. The destiny is therefore that each of us becomes more and more conformed to His Son, Jesus Christ, to become "another Christ, Christ Himself," so that in heaven there will be one Christ, the "Whole Christ" of Augustine. In Baptism, we receive the Holy Spirit and faith. If we transpose the following text on faith as seeing and living the truth of being God's children, then it may give us great joy:

If we never ceased to live the life of faith [as children of God], our intercourse with God would never be interrupted and we should talk with him face to face.... God in his glory will give us this union in heaven; here on earth we can enjoy it by faith. The only difference is the way it is given to us.

It is faith which interprets God for us.... Faith transforms the earth into paradise. By it our hearts are raised with the joy of our nearness to heaven. Every moment reveals God to us. Faith is our light in this life. Faith tears aside the veil so that we can see the everlasting truth [of God's love as Father].[1]

This new identity of the baptized as a child of the Father should become our greatest joy (as it was for St. Marguerite d'Youville and St. Josemaría Escrivá). It is this filiation that explains why we have received so much: the universe as a dwelling, guardian angels, the Church as Mother, the sacraments, Scripture, Tradition, etc. We can only dream of what it will be like to fully taste and experience this filiation and the Trinitarian relations in heaven. There, we will not just be in some happy place, but will be participating in the very Trinitarian relations and processions; we will become a part of the Family that is the Trinity. In this life, our goal (normally referred to as "holiness") is to become more fully configured to Christ as new Christs. As new Christs, we should hear deeply in our hearts the words of the Father to Christ, "You are my Son, the Beloved."

---

[1] Jean-Pierre de Caussade, *Abandonment to Divine Providence*, 37.

Made in the USA
Monee, IL
03 March 2020

22647684R00199